A Nation of Extremes
The Pioneers in Twentieth-century Ireland

A Nation of Extremes
The Pioneers in
Twentieth-century Ireland

DIARMAID FERRITER

IRISH ACADEMIC PRESS
DUBLIN • PORTLAND, OR

First published in 1999 by
IRISH ACADEMIC PRESS
44, Northumberland Road, Dublin 4, Ireland
and in the United States of America by
IRISH ACADEMIC PRESS
c/o ISBS, 5804 NE Hassalo Street,
Portland, OR 97213 3644

Website: http://www.iap.ie

© The Pioneer Total Abstinence Association of the Sacred Heart 1999

British Library Cataloguing in Publication Data
Ferriter, Diarmaid
A nation of extremes: pioneers in twentieth century Ireland
1. Ireland – Social conditions   2. Ireland – Social life and customs
3. Ireland – History
I. Title
941.7
ISBN 0–7165–2623–9

**A catalogue record for this title is available
from the Library of Congress**

Typeset in 10.5 pt on 12.5 pt Palatino
by Carrigboy Typesetting Services, County Cork
Printed by Creative Print and Design, Ebbw Vale, Wales

For my parents, with love and respect

Contents

Abbreviations

CA	Capuchin Archives
CTAF	Catholic Total Abstinence Federation
CTAU	Catholic Total Abstinence Union of America
DJ	Department of Justice Files, NAI
DT	Department of Taoiseach Files, NAI
FMU	Father Mathew Union
ICAA	Irish Countrywomen's Association Archives
IER	*Irish Ecclesiastical Record*
ILC	Intoxicating Liquor Commission
JIESH	Journal of Irish Economic and Social History
JSSISI	Journal of the Social and Statistical Inquiry Society of Ireland
LVA	Licensed Vintners' Association
LVAA	Licensed Vintners' Association Archives, Anglesea Road, Dublin
Pioneer	*Pioneer Magazine*
PTAA	Pioneer Total Abstinence Association
PAA	Pioneer Association Archives, Sherrard Street, Dublin
PC IC	Pioneer Column in the *Irish Catholic*
NAI	National Archives of Ireland, Bishop Street, Dublin
NLI	National Library of Ireland
SOCA	Sisters of Charity Archives, Sandymount, Dublin

Acknowledgements

The preparation of this book was made possible with the assistance of a number of different people. The Pioneer Association deserve much credit for making the enlightened and brave decision to allow unlimited access to their archives. Fr Bernard McGuckian and Fr Micheál Mac Gréil have been patient, encouraging and helpful over the last two years, and without their broad-mindedness this study would not have appeared. I am also grateful to the staff of the Pioneer Association in Sherrard Street and Fr Dan Dargan for their unfailing assistance. The staff of the Licensed Vintners Association, Fr Benedict of the Capuchin Archives, Sr Marie Bernadette of the Sisters of Charity Archives and Peter Walsh of the Guinness Museum also gave invaluable help, as did the staffs of the National Library, the National Archives and the library in University College Dublin. As always, Mary Daly has been inspirational and generous, as has Margaret Mac Curtain, and I am eternally grateful to both for sharing their wisdom. I am also indebted to Deirdre Mac Mahon for sharing her unique insight, Tim O'Neill for his advice and understanding, and my other colleagues in the history department at UCD; Tom Bartlett, Michael Laffan, Ronan Fanning, James McGuire, Susannah Riordan, Brendan MacSuibhne, Georg Grote, Jackie and Catherine. Maeve Bradley was instrumental in preserving my sanity and in keeping things in perspective, as were the post-graduate tutors in the history department. Thanks also to my parents, Nollaig and Vera, for their constant emotional support, inveterate liberalism, and for instilling in me a recognition of the dangers of flying on one wing, to Cian for his love and empathy in sharing all the highs and the lows, to Triona for providing sanctuary, and Muireann for the laughter. I have been privileged to enjoy the warmth of Carmel, Karen and Ronan Furlong and the memory of Donal. As well as providing a truly memorable summer, Martin and Ann-Marie were incredibly supportive at all times and I will always be grateful to Greg for his tolerance, humanity and loyalty. Thanks also to Stephen, Mark, Peter, John, Adrienne, Lisa, Michelle, Sheila, Rose, Aisling, William, Lindsey, Sean, Pat, Paul Murphy, Dolores Rouse, Philip Harvey and especially to Kevin Maher, Paul Rouse and Catriona Crowe for shared levity, stimulating friendship, constructive confrontation and support. Finally, to Irish Academic Press, Eleanor McNicholas and Linda Longmore for all their patience, enthusiasm and editorial assistance.

Introduction

The drinking of alcohol is an integral part of Irish social life and is accepted as such by most people . . . Historically, the Irish have often been described as having a legendary and unenviable reputation for drinking. There is evidence that the description of the Irish as a particularly alcohol-prone race is a myth. Indeed it is doubtful whether Ireland ever occupied a prominent role with regard to alcohol use or misuse.
National Alcohol Policy, Department of Health, 1996

It is not a myth . . . Drinking in Ireland is not simply a convivial pastime, it is a ritualistic alternative to real life, a spiritual placebo, a fumble for eternity, a longing for heaven, a thirst for return to the embrace of the Almighty. People drink more because they like living less than they think they ought to, and the more overwhelming the evidence of the irrefutability of life's attractiveness grates with their own experience, the more the nagging unhappiness makes alcohol the only way of filling in that shortfall, which is in essence an absence of beliefs . . . In the end there is nothing but pain.
John Waters, *An Intelligent Person's Guide to Modern Ireland*, 1997

The centenary of the Pioneer Total Abstinence Association of the Sacred Heart has offered an opportunity to appraise the Association, as well as the debates about the role of drink and temperance in the social, religious and cultural development of twentieth-century Ireland. The willingness of the Pioneers to confront their history is indicative of a recent tendency on the part of certain voluntary organisations to invite historians to analyse their records with a view to a scholarly assessment of their content. In view of the undeveloped historiography of the social and cultural history of this century, this openness is particularly welcome. Given that the Association is, and always has been, a Catholic spiritual organisation that was established during an era of intense religious and cultural nationalism, a researcher might understandably baulk before vast amounts of bland documents

1

dealing with theological and scriptural aspects of temperance, and yet more records characterised by brash Catholic triumphalism. This however simplifies the context in which the Association operated.

The Pioneer Association was founded in the Presbytery of the Saint Francis Xavier Church in Gardiner Street, Dublin, in December 1898. It was the brainchild of a Jesuit priest, Fr James Cullen, a man extra· ordinarily demonstrative in terms of personal piety. Disgusted by the vast expenditure on drink and the material and moral shortcomings this engendered, he sought to harness an elite group of Catholic social activists to publicly (by wearing a pin) challenge the interchangeability of the terms 'drink' and 'Irish'. Privately, by taking a life-long pledge, they declared their devotion to the Sacred Heart of Jesus. Given that temperance had traditionally been associated with Protestantism, it was significant that Cullen tapped into a new climate of discipline within Irish Catholicism. He aligned his piety with the wider theme of an Irish cultural revival and in turn specifically claimed abstinence and temperance as legitimate, if not imperative, Catholic concerns. Cullen and his successors in the 1930s and 1940s were unapologetically extreme in their approach. Cullen had learnt two lessons from the famed, if short-lived, temperance crusade of the Capuchin, Fr Mathew, in the 1830s and 1840s. First, though Irish Catholics could be receptive to a well-orchestrated crusade against drink abuse based on religious and social motives, it was pointless to pledge to groups *en masse* in a carnival-like atmosphere. Second, that it was necessary to back the Pioneer movement with a tight structure, administrative efficiency and absolute strictness. The movement was to be based on the parish unit, under the watchful eye of a spiritual director, with overall control exercised by a central council in Dublin.

Alongside this new temperance mindset, however, a pervasive heavy drinking culture lingered in twentieth-century Ireland leading to an ambiguity about Irish attitudes to drink. The Pioneer Association in the first half of the century certainly seemed a success in terms of membership figures and increasing devotion to the Sacred Heart. But despite occasional mass displays of outward devotion, the piety seems to have remained fundamentally internal and undemonstrative, making little inroads in terms of challenging the wider drink culture. A narrow institutional history could not elucidate this ambiguity. The history of the Pioneers and Irish society is better served by the investigation of a wide range of archival sources. The very breadth of the subject, covering socio-economic and religious themes as well as cultural and political developments, demands this. In many ways, this book is the story of a nation of extremes.

As well as material from the Pioneer archive, the temperance issue is examined from many other vantage points, particularly those with a vested interest in drink. Most of this documentation has not appeared in print before, and in using it this study seeks to make a fresh and provocative contribution to the social and cultural historiography of modern Ireland.

CHAPTER ONE

Origins

The question of moderate drinkers is a more vexed and difficult one. Some teetotallers would go to the length of imposing strict abstinence upon all others. Yet, surely such devotion somewhat oversteps the limit of prudence, even when it does not smack of arrogance and officiousness. Nevertheless, we must all acknowledge that the drunken class is recruited from the ranks of the moderate drinkers.

Rev J.J. Vaughan, *Drunkenness versus Teetotalism*, 1889

It is well to remember that the Christian religion condemns Intemperance, commands temperance and commends Total Abstinence.

Rev Hugh O'Neill, 1893

The above citations give some indication of the attempts by clerical figures to map out the social and religious parameters of the temperance issue in late nineteenth-century Ireland. It was appropriate that by the 1890s they had been forced to publicly tease out the intricacies of the drink issue, as the nineteenth century, not just in Ireland, but across the world, had witnessed a variety of temperance movements and associated debates which covered all aspects of social, cultural, political, religious and economic life. At the very end of the decade, on 27 December 1898, a prominent Irish Jesuit, James Cullen, was to decide on his interpretation of the temperance question, resulting in the formation of the Pioneer Total Abstinence Association of the Sacred Heart. That it was a rigid interpretation cannot be denied, and this was precisely his intention. Undoubtedly, he had been influenced by the contemporary debates on the morality or indeed Christianity of total abstinence, but had come to the conclusion that an absolutist approach was a necessary corollary to the ambiguity and differences of opinion which accompanied the temperance debate. He would also have been conscious of the long-term impact of the crusade of the Capuchin friar, Theobald Mathew, in the 1830s, which although involving the administration of the pledge to vast numbers, had left virtually nothing in the way of an organisational framework. It was an appropriate time, he had surmised, for a new departure – a calculated drive to be strict and selective rather than a desire for an all-embracing crusade.

It was quite appropriate that at a time when the nationalist consciousness had been revived, both politically and culturally, the drink question would be tackled by those who were products of what Emmet Larkin termed the 'Devotional Revolution' – the tightening of Catholic Church structures, practice and discipline in Ireland.[1] The temperance question, it was felt, could be wedded to the wider cultural and spiritual ethos of Irish Catholicism, and in turn increase the potency and competence of the Irish national character. The alarming recognition that the terms 'drink' and 'Irish' were becoming interchangeable in a caricature which, it seemed, involved the dimunition and downgrading of Irish claims to be independent, was an added spur to increased activity in this sphere.

Historically, Ireland was not short of observers, both domestic and foreign, on the curious and pervasive Irish relationship with alcohol. In the early seventeenth century, Fynes Moryson, a British visitor, wrote of the curious mixture of over-indulgence and crudity which seemed to be associated with Irish drinking habits, practices which seemed to traverse class and gender boundaries:

> The Irish aquavitae, vulgarly called usquebagh . . . refresh the weake stomacke with moderate heate and a good relish . . . both men and women use excesse therein . . . not to speake of the wives of the Irish Lords or to refere to it the due place, who often drink till they be drunken, or at least till they voide urine in full assemblies of men. I cannot (though unwilling) but note the Irish women more specifically with this fault which I have observed in no other part to be a womans vice, but only in Bohemia.[2]

At the end of the seventeenth century, the association of drink with sporting endeavours was remarked upon by another English visitor, John Dunton, when he wrote of hurling matches in which parishes or baronies would challenge one another, the teams consisting of up to twenty a side: 'The prize is generally a barrel or two of ale, which is brought into the field and drunk off by the victors on the spot, though the vanquished are not without a share of it too.'[3] At the beginning of the nineteenth century, a similar observer, Robert Bell, wrote of entertainments such as dancing, athletics and wrestling in which the natives indulged after Mass on a Sunday: 'Good humour and contentment always prevailed at these meetings, as long as they drank no whiskey, but whenever that fiery spirit was introduced, intoxication and quarrels were the inevitable consequences.'[4] Even if there was a tendency towards racial bias, these observations give an indication of the extent to which alcohol could permeate Irish life – wakes and funerals were another obvious example. Whether these were human as opposed to specifically Irish weaknesses was a question which would provide for interesting deliberation and indeed rancour. It was an issue legislators had spasmodically turned their attention to, as when in 1784 the Irish parliament removed all taxes previously imposed on beer in an attempt to encourage consumption of this less potent beverage rather than spirits and so reduce drunkenness. However, the fact that between 1811 and 1813 over 19,000 illicit spirit stills were confiscated would suggest a thriving underground market in an attempt to avoid excise and transport costs.[5] It was perhaps this ability to mix ingenuity and an utter disregard for the law with the slovenliness that was the product of drinking the fruits of this lawbreaking, which coloured certain English attitudes towards Ireland – a contradictory stereotype, noted by R.F. Foster, which depicted the Irish both as quick-witted and ingenious but also lazy and intellectually inferior.[6]

The 'crusade' of Fr Mathew as it emerged in the late 1830s was a complex phenomenon, though it was dealing with a very definable and specific abuse. The gross exaggeration of the number of pledges he administered continued right in to the twentieth century. In the Dublin archives of the Capuchins, a letter written in 1912 from the Provincial to Rome, recalling Mathew's glorious deeds, insists he administered the pledge to over 12 million people.[7] The hagiographical treatment of the movement was perhaps to be expected in the late nineteenth and early twentieth century. Colm Kerrigan's book, *Father Mathew and the Irish Temperance Movement 1838–1849*, published in 1987, succeeded in redressing the balance, charting the transition from 'moderation' to 'teetotal' in mid-1830s temperance societies, a departure which was accompanied by increased working-class involvement. This move was perhaps deemed necessary by the belief, as reflected in a resolution passed at the first annual meeting of the Hibernian Temperance Society, established in Dublin in 1830, that 'the unhappy propensity of our countrymen to the use of ardent spirits is one of the chief causes of pauperism, disease and crime prevalent in Ireland.'[8] This preoccupation with the social consequences of excessive imbibing was reflected in the wording of the pledge administered by Fr Mathew: 'I promise with the divine assistance, as long as I continue a member of the teetotal temperance society, to abstain from all intoxicating drinks, except for medicinal or sacramental purposes, and to prevent as much as possible by advice and example, drunkenness in others.'[9]

The Fr Mathew episode highlighted the relative ease with which a temperance crusade could be transformed into a temporary mass movement, but it also exposed a multitude of difficulties, as evidenced by Kerrigan – the disinterest, for example, of the Catholic Bishop of Cork, Dr Murphy, mirroring a troubling indifference on the part of the 'official' establishment to temperance, the hostility of Protestant newspapers who believed that Catholic abstinence was predicated on a manipulation of Catholic superstition rather than rational argument, confusion over the role of the clergy in such a movement, its link with nationalist politics and the failure to establish a national structure to provide durable foundations for the future of the movement.[10] These themes were to remain relevant to debates concerning the direction of the temperance movement in Ireland and elsewhere. Kerrigan's figure of 700,000 pledge recipients is also an indication that the Fr Mathew phenomenon penetrated less deeply than was believed, or contrived at by future hagiographers.[11]

Equally challenging dilemmas faced other temperance movements. In England, for example, there was little social stigma attached to excessive drinking in the eighteenth century, but during the nineteenth century the temperance movement flexed its muscles, albeit in various guises. In the 1830s it was dominated by the middle class, but by the 1840s there was more of a working-class ethos. By the 1870s there was increased emphasis on gospel temperance, and by the 1890s temperance had emerged as a political issue, most notably in various demands for legislation to curb excessive drinking. There was a message in these shifts of emphasis which was to prove useful to the future organisers of the Pioneers. The historian Shiman wrote: 'The temperance societies that survived the century – with life if not with vigour – were those that were sufficiently firm in their temperance principles to be flexible enough to absorb the ever-changing modes of popular culture and to utilise them within the temperance context.'[12] Many religious figures of both Catholic and Protestant beliefs simply did not believe that it was the responsibility of the Church to deal with problems posed by the flock's drinking habits, and in England the Catholic church was prone to condemning those temperance societies for whom temperance was 'converted into a fantastic form of deism'. Notwithstanding this, the Rev J. Sisk in Chelsea in 1838 formed a Catholic temperance society to organise Irish Catholics in England.[13]

The first prohibition law in the western world was passed by the legislature of Maine in America in 1851, and can be seen to have elevated the whole temperance question on to a higher plane in that it tended to force advocates to be more specific in their aims and demands. The idea of political as opposed to moral persuasion was to become an increasingly divisive issue in the temperance world. On a religious level, this had been reflected in 1829 when Dr John Edgar, a Presbyterian minister from Belfast, who had been convinced of the value of abstinence by the work being done by the New England states of America, warned that while temperance was undoubtedly virtuous, coercion was not, concluding that 'to command to abstain is anti-christian'.[14] During the following decade in England there was a clear division between 'moderationists' and 'teetotallers'. The historian of British temperance during this period, Harrison, viewed the teetotal missionaries as attempting to uphold rural standards of conduct in an urban environment, but social factors aside, he was convinced that 'the religious beliefs of teetotal leaders were more important for giving them their immense energy than for channelling it in any particular direction.'[15]

This was a question of crucial importance – that of direction. In America, it was the very multitude of directions which complicated the temperance reform agenda. In Boston in 1835, where there was a population of 10,000 Irish Catholics presided over by a bishop and four priests, an Irish temperance society was founded. Their resolutions indicated a desire not to be pigeon-holed, either religiously or politically: 'Resolved that it will be a leading trait in the character and conduct of the members of the Irish Temperance Society not to recognise each other as Protestants or Catholics, nor as Whigs or as democrats, but as temperance men and temperance men only'.[16] However, later in the century the Irish-American temperance lobby found themselves at odds over the nature of their agenda – whether it was to be religious or political or both. In an address to the Catholic Total Abstinence Union of America in the 1880s, Rev Cotter, a Presbyterian, made reference to the Irish land agitation and insisted that impoverished Irish tenants were drinking to excess because 'English laws have driven them out of their homes', an indignity compounded by the exploitation of them by unscrupulous license-holders. He, in turn, was cautioned by Archbishop Ireland who admonished his hyperbole and warned him to remain within the bounds of theological accuracy, asserting that liquor selling in itself was not a violation of natural or divine law. In his pastorals, Archbishop Ireland preferred to concentrate on castigating Sunday trading, focusing on the personal responsibility of drinkers to the sanctity of their home and family life.[17]

Despite these insistences, by the end of the nineteenth century, Fr Cleary, the president of the CTAU was still convinced that a principled Catholic could not, in conscience, run a saloon.[18] Many individual temperance reformers found their own views changing as the social and religious parameters of the temperance debate expanded. Mrs Williard, the president of the Women's Catholic Temperance Union from 1875 to 1898, began her career as a moral persuader but became much more of a political agitator in her latter years in charge of the Association.[19] The reality was that there was no unanimity amongst temperance groups about the necessity for legal, political and moral change. They had equal difficulty in defining 'moderation'. The United Kingdom Alliance group which came to prominence in Britain at this time had first mooted the idea of 'Local Option', where the residents of a particular area could decide themselves by popular vote whether or not they wanted drinking facilities in the vicinity. They also specifically highlighted the need for Sunday closing. Given that the temperance men of the 1870s tended to be economically and socially comfortable, there was a strong class bias inherent in their emphasis – the moral improvements that they envisaged going hand-in-hand with a decrease in drinking, such as thrift, discipline and cleanliness.[20] The same applied to America, particularly after the Civil War, where social conditions became a subject deemed worthy of debate, with temperance being viewed as another plank on which to build a more prosperous society, spurred on by the second Plenary Council of Baltimore in 1866. By the 1880s, temperance workers in America were characterised as a 'jolly looking set of gentlemen, the majority of whom are hard smokers and hard working business men.'[21]

In Ireland by the middle of the nineteenth century the attribution of excessive drinking to an external agent (the British), and the identification of Ireland's political liberation with a disappearance of this drinking was a convenient weapon in the hands of a politician like Daniel O'Connell. In this guise, according to Elizabeth Malcolm, the temperance platform was another weapon in the renewed struggle with Britain, despite the fact that during the O'Connell era the Irish temperance movement was sectional in its composition and conservative in its views.[22] Despite the obvious religious connection, in the sense that O'Connell's association with Catholic emancipation was intrinsic to his ability to mobilise, he demonstrated a conveniently pragmatic, and perhaps inconsistent, attitude to the drink question, in that he tended to laud the heroics of Fr Mathew, but equally because brewers and distillers were essential to the Irish economy, tended to downplay the extent of the Irish drink problem and personally imbibed, supposedly for medicinal reasons. The extent to which the playing of the temperance card was in any way advantageous in the political arena was to remain a vexed question, right through to the twentieth century. Thomas Davis certainly displayed an interest, believing that the moral elevation of the Irish race had to be inextricably linked to its political progress, decrying the tragedy of the Irish drowning their acknowledged subjection in drink. He wrote of the Irish man's 'natural excuse for making it [the subjection] greater in order to achieve liberty and luxury for an hour by the magic of intoxication.'[23] Those who came to dominate the political and religious landscape of later nineteenth-century Ireland however, tended to show little interest, as evidenced by the indifference of those such as Parnell and Cardinal Paul Cullen. Nonetheless, there were individual bishops such as Leahy and Croke of Cashel and Bishop Furlong of Ferns, who displayed greater interest, and Archbishop Walsh of Dublin found the centenary of the birth of Fr Mathew a convenient occasion to instigate the establishment of temperance societies in Leinster.[24]

The historian is invariably left with an impression of ambiguity and equanimity however, regarding the degree to which these societies could do meaningful long-term work, which was compounded by the fact that temperance was not historically seen as a particularly Catholic virtue. Often, much depended on the personality of the bishop or the particular nature of the abuse in his diocese. John MacEvilly, Bishop of Galway from 1851 to 1881 and Archbishop of Tuam from 1881 to 1902 was particularly forceful about drink abuse and has been described by his biographer as 'a constant and consistent advocate of temperance.'[25] He was a keen advocate of the Sunday Closing movement launched in England and in 1867 wrote to one of its organisers, Dr Spratt, supporting closure of pubs between 6pm on Saturday and 6am on Monday. In this letter he also displayed an awareness of the important social role of the pub, adding that it would be wise to orchestrate alternative diversions for working-class people on a Sunday 'so as to make their withdrawal from the public houses less felt.'[26] Obviously not content that movements such as these were effective, he decided in 1874, in a letter read in all diocesan churches, to make it a reserved sin for Catholics to sell alcohol on a Sunday, and that those who disobeyed were 'those few who are amenable to no moral law or religious restraint'. In 1877 he established his own Galway Temperance Society.[27] It is tempting to see MacEvilly at this stage as an exception. Few bishops would go to the extreme of singling out drink abuses as occasions of sin meriting reservation. Yet what was also notable was the impression created that those who indulged were the few who made a caricature of the majority viable, and that these were pitiful creatures beyond redemption at any level.

In this context it is worth examining one of the most intriguing aspects of social history in nineteenth-century Dublin. This was the

Donnybrook Fair, an annual festival which in time became inevitably associated with wanton drink abuse and general debauchery. The campaign against this perceived blot on the Dublin landscape involved an alliance of both church and civil authorities, in an attempt to swallow it in religious revival, temperance crusading and vigilant policing; to, as historian Fergus D'arcy put it 'civilise and moralise the masses, to imbue them with the mores of the ascending middle class and to prise them from their traditional attachment to rough sports and physical assertiveness.'[28] Those involved represented a curious though durable coalition of evangelical Protestants and militant Catholics. The new Catholic curate for the parish in 1853, Rev Patrick J. Nowlan, combined forces with anti-slavery and temperance activist, James Houghton, and Dr John Spratt, prominent in the temperance movement and a campaigner against animal cruelty. They also received rhetorical support from Cardinal Cullen in challenging the ascendancy of what he termed 'this moral plague spot'. The civic side to the drive towards purity involved depriving the traditional hosts of their drink license, and though it was a long-drawn-out dilution of the fair's potency, with legal loopholes and stubborn indignation contriving to provide a steadfast resistance, it was a campaign which ultimately succeeded in curbing the excesses. D'arcy saw the building in 1866 of a new parish church devoted to the Sacred Heart and overlooking the old fair green as suitably symbolic and 'an expiatory monument for the vices and wickedness of Donnybrook Fair'.[29]

While the Donnybrook Fair episode was perhaps illustrative of the ability of a contemporary coalition of forces to oust a clearly definable, though in overall terms relatively minor, drink problem, it provides little evidence that on a national scale, Irish temperance reformers had a blue-print for a long-term assault on intemperance. While undoubtedly the second half of the nineteenth century was a period of consolidation for the Irish Catholic Church, temperance was not yet deemed worthy of a pivotal place in the hierarchy of priorities. The archives of the Irish College in Rome for this period point to progress being made in the practice of religion, with numerous requests to enrol people in various religious societies and permission for faculties to administer sacraments. Likewise parish missions were increasing in popularity by the mid century, fuelled, it would seem, by the development of devotion to the Sacred Heart which had first been encouraged in Cork by Bishop Moylan (1757–1815), and in Dublin by a prominent Jesuit, Fr Mulcaile, at the close of the eighteenth century. On March 10, 1873 every Catholic parish in the country was consecrated to the Sacred Heart.[30] In the last quarter of the nineteenth century, the increased centralisation of the Irish

Catholic Church, engineered by Cardinal Cullen, was concomitant to an increased emphasis on discipline, as evidenced by a decree of the synod of Maynooth in 1875 which demanded that parish priests put an end to 'unchristian wakes', an injunction which was frequently reiterated.[31] By the end of the century, Ireland was left with a Catholic religious practice including the development of Marian devotion and a huge increase in the number of sodalities and vocations, underpinned by the increasing availability of cheap and regular religious publications.

Perhaps it can be argued that these were the tools which needed to be in place before an effective temperance drive could be launched. Keenan, a historian of nineteenth-century Irish Catholicism has also illustrated that for much of the century changes in social policy tended to be instigated by the laity or the junior clergy, lacking decisive leadership from the Hierarchy. He went on to stress that for much of this era temperance was an anomaly in the Irish Catholic Church because it did not flow from traditional Catholic theology which suggested moderation rather than abstinence. Secondly, the organisation of the movement, when present, was not tied into the diocesan-parochial structure and thirdly, unlike joining confraternities or the priesthood, the manner of membership involved no careful selection, probation or standards of moral conduct.[32] Keenan also makes the observation that the bias towards temperance education and training when it eventually became pronounced 'came about through the ordinary pastoral ministry at all levels, not through a revivalist style movement'.[33] These seem pertinent assessments and invite an exploration of the means by which the temperance position, so localised and shrouded in doubt for much of the century, came to have a more clear-cut prominence and higher profile by the last decade of the century. Once again, it involved a coalition of different interest groups.

Much of the evidence is almost entirely observational and unsupported by the availability of hard statistics. The development of the nineteenth-century economy meant that at times there was more cash available in the rural economy. Because of the conspicuousness appertaining to their distinguished office, and the extent to which their income was dependent on their parishes, priests themselves could be viewed as an indicator of the extent of excessive drinking. Keenan remarked that 'their besetting sin was drink. The evidence available is not statistical but merely the common reports of observers'.[34] Other analysts have pointed to the patriarchy of the small-farmer class of the nineteenth century who reinforced certain strictures on the eating of food, this dietary abstinence being substituted by drinking. The logic appears to be that because of a guilt and uncertainty associated with food, and the lack of stricture against drinking, people when feeling weak drank rather than ate, unlike, for example, Jewish customs, which would have insisted on drink as well as food abstinence. An American sociologist, Robert Bales has also argued that as a whole, the Irish clergy were tolerant about drinking, as evidenced by their mute reaction to the carousing and faction fights occasionally linked to the celebration of saint's and feast days and the endurance of pilgrimages. Likewise, the 'Meitheal' custom which operated in many rural districts where farm families co-operated in distributing the burdens of farm labour often involved payment in drink rather than money.

There was also a frequent citation of drink as a medicinal remedy, particularly in the guise of a preventative and palliative measure against cold and damp, so much so that several witnesses before the British House of Commons Inquiry into Drunkenness in 1834 had questioned 'Whether in such a moist climate as Ireland, whisky is at all necessary to health'.[35] Alcohol was also seen, for example, as a necessary treatment for measles if combined with a concoction of boiled nettles. A perusal of the items listed under 'alcohol' in the Irish Folklore Commission provide many other examples of medicinal and superstitious uses of alcohol, uses which were slow to be ousted from the rural domain. The cheapness of drink in a society with little prospect of economic and social betterment increased the tendency towards excessive drinking. 'In short', wrote Bales, 'It is hard to think of a medicinal use of alcohol which has not been current, at one time or another, in the Irish culture.'[36] Obviously there were also political and economic aspects to the drink question at this stage, in the sense that it could form the basis for a certain solidarity between groups comprising the social system. The notion that the temperance movement could provide a political and economic context was evidenced in the American temperance movement, where it could involve consolidating a particular class's 'new status', or help to defend class positions threatened by economic and social change. Temperance for example, became an important part of middle-class American identity in the nineteenth century, reflecting a prioritisation of self-mastery, thrift and superior moral conduct.[37] In this sense the American temperance movement had very important consequences for the Irish experience.

Given the huge emigration to America after the Great Famine it was perhaps inevitable that Irish-Americans would become involved in issues of class and status, and the barriers to them. Kerby Miller points out that the aspirations and achievements of these emigrants could be ravaged by an alcoholism 'born of debilitating self-doubt', and that many of the Irish working class based in cities like Boston, New York, Chicago and Philadelphia where much of the populace was housed in slum conditions where mental illness thrived, transplanted an idyllic small village Irish outlook, turning to drink for solace 'in bar rooms awash with broken dreams of lost childhood homes'.[38] Despite this sentimental depiction of the drunken Irish dilemma, it was not the only side to the emigrant experience. Another historian of this period, Light, points out that by the last quarter of the nineteenth century, buttressed by the acquisition of property and the culmination of savings, a significant proportion of the Irish working class began adopting 'a stable, prudent and thoroughly respectable life-style', which sought to undermine the drunken stereotype. In a city like Philadelphia, where beneficial temperance savings and building societies were run on an ethnic basis, an institution like the Irish Catholic Benevolent Union, with 10,000 members by the 1880s, could contribute to a certain bourgeois respectability among the Irish-American Catholics.[39] Developing this point, David Doyle noted that while there was never any particular impetus to create a 'Catholic politics' in the United States, drunkards could be seen as a barrier separating those who managed to improve their social and economic status from the minority (especially newly arrived emigrants), and those who did not. While political temperance was identified with anti-Catholicism, 'even as Catholics they were taking on something of the colouration of mainline American Protestantism; overt moralism, public activism, voluntarism, lay initiative, individualised rather than communal piety'.[40]

The association of the Irish in America with drink was also enhanced by the opening of liquor saloons by those with Irish connections in cities such as Boston during the middle of the nineteenth century. Latter day American sociologists became intent on surveying the sociological aspects of the Irish-American drink culture by tracing its roots back to Ireland. Bill Stivers estimated that the lack of industrialisation in Ireland underpinned an Irish rural variant of bourgeois morality which encouraged heavy drinking. He also drew connections between drinking and a commitment to one's occupational code, both as a facilitator of group integration and an affirmation of male identity. But he was also keen to stress a fluid caricature which was not wholly negative:

> 'My contention is that early in the nineteenth century a negative identity of drunkard was foisted upon the Irish by a cultural stereotype and related institutional practices. But, later in the nineteenth century Irish-American culture and the stereotype of the Irishman in American culture converged around a more positive image of the Irish drunk – the

'happy drunk' – a stage caricature Irishman. What had been a negative identity – drunkard – was transformed into a positive group identity.'[41]

Seemingly, long-term assimilation, whilst not obliterating the association of 'Irish' with 'drink' had at least served to expand the caricature. Pious patriots would find little solace in Stiver's attempt to trace the transference to America of Irish drinking habits. Writing as a foreign observer he seemed determined to challenge sacred cows in his attempt to locate the root of the Irish drinking psyche, but much of his work is predicated on sociological theory rather than historical evidence. He saw male drinking in the late nineteenth century as essential for the maintenance of a new family system, the Irish male group growing in importance in direct proportion to the emergence of the new single inheritance farm economy, the low marriage rate, and the advanced age of those marrying. In short, he saw the pub as a symbol representing those destined to stay on the land, and he located in these Irish drinking customs, a rite of separation (having the status of bachelor), a rite of transition (being accepted into an already established bachelor group), and a rite of incorporation (entrance into the public house and the taking of the first drink). In summary, excessive drinking was cultural remission or 'a release from sexual puritanism.'[42] He also went on to suggest that unlike in other countries, temperance in Ireland could make no inroad into cultural definitions of masculinity and that teetotallers, because of their detachment from the bachelor group, would be viewed with suspicion as 'potential chastity breakers'. Given the minuteness of his analysis and perhaps anticipating his conclusion it was ironic that Stivers prefaced his thesis with the warning that 'To the non-Irish world perhaps no behaviour is more associated with the Irish than drinking. It is therefore with great trepidation that one undertakes an analysis of Irish drinking.'[43] His conclusion was certainly not trepidatious and could perhaps be deemed somewhat exaggerated, but the themes he saw as emerging in the nineteenth century certainly were representative of the challenges faced by Irish temperance reformers. Even if they were not acknowledged as such in contemporary rhetoric, they were enduring themes and provided the social backdrop to many rural areas polluted by drinking and mental illness, which was why, along with chastisement of the drunkard by reformers, they would invariably qualify this by lamenting the lack of alternative social outlets. However, in terms of the emigration of the drink problem, the fundamental point made by Stivers was that while in Ireland drinking was a sign of male identity, in America it came to be a symbol of Irish identity.[44]

Likewise, given the large numbers emigrating to Britain during the nineteenth century, there was a focus on the impact drink made on the Irish communities. Roger Swift has written of the degree of demoralisation of Irish emigrants in the early and mid-Victorian period 'when they figured so largely in the official parliamentary and social reportage of the day', but traced a shift by the end of the nineteenth century with the creation of a more enduring religious and political community.[45] Once again, as in America, assimilation did not necessarily mean a curtailment of the drink problem, but rather the ability of a pub-dominated Irish Catholic neighbourhood to stand alongside a relatively stable immigrant church. The impression garnered is that whilst many desired serious reform by the late nineteenth century of these communities – the missionary Jesuits at the Saint Francis Xavier church in Liverpool, for example, were determined during this period to gather up Irish Catholic street urchins, feed them breakfast and march them off to mass – drinking among the Irish in Britain was still frequently associated with riotous behaviour, and one is left with an impression of temperance exponents totally unsure how to handle reform, and perhaps too tolerant. Historian Raphael Samuels wrote that priestly interventions were frequently and urgently renewed in the aftermath of debauchery but they seemed to have carried 'no expectation of permanent moral reform'.[46] Charles Booth, the Victorian social campaigner, described these beleaguered clerics as 'Lenient judges of the frailties that are not sins and of the disorder that is not crime'.[47]

The challenge to be addressed was how these themes and their manifestations were to be tackled in Ireland, given the ambiguity if not hostility shown towards temperance, and the ingrained tolerance shown towards alcohol abuse. The sheer proliferation of Irish social concerns in the late nineteenth century ensured that intemperance was in no sense in a solitary league. Amongst the Catholic Hierarchy in their canon of denunciations, intemperance had to take its place alongside such issues as rogue landlords, packed juries, poor housing and working conditions. Again it is possible to single out individual bishops for their endorsement of a temperate lifestyle, but it is not accurate to write of a unified or co-ordinated campaign. The Northern dioceses seemed to witness most of the hierarchical activity in this sphere. In 1878 Daniel McGettigan of Armagh bemoaned the widespread practice of drinking at wakes. The Bishop of Clogher decided to take things a step further and established the Abstinence League of St Patrick, having originally founded a temperance society in Monaghan in 1885.[48] However those intent on a more aggressive approach were repeatedly seen to be wading into dangerous water. In April 1887 Michael Logue,

Bishop of Raphoe wrote to a confidant: 'I am trying to establish temperance societies in several of the parishes . . . In one parish the whole congregation, amounting to almost 3000 people took the pledge from periods of from one to five years' and he expressed his intention of seeking blessings and indulgences for those pledged.[49] However within a few weeks he was named Coadjutor Archbishop of Armagh. Bernard Canning continues the story, underlining the confusions associated with this undeveloped Catholic temperance activity: 'He continued his visitation of Raphoe and made the hawking of Poteen among the people a kind of reserved case in two or three parishes where it was doing mischief. He was later to have doubts about the validity of his actions in that period of interregnum, and sought Kirby's [Tobias Kirby, Rector of the Irish College in Rome] advice, and if necessary, action to remedy any irregularity he may have caused.'[50]

Seemingly, the answer to much of this ambiguity and lack of coherent focus was to aim for a more specific agenda, involving a greater coalition of temperance forces. Part of this scrutiny involved dispelling the perceived lazy assumption that individual total abstinence was a sufficient sacrifice. Through the pages of the *Irish Ecclesiastical Record*, the historian can attempt to glean the efforts to widen the parameters of the religious/drink debate. In 1868 the journal drew attention to a new association, entitled The Association of Prayer for the conversion of those addicted to intemperance.[51] According to those involved, for total abstainers to avoid drink was the fulfillment of the command to avoid 'proximate occasions of sin', but this was not deemed enough in itself. It was now time, according to the author, to begin to associate abstinence with the ability to help those in less fortunate circumstances, lest the accusation of smug self-fulfillment be allowed to prosper. The author wrote that total abstainers had:

> . . . a tendency to erect themselves into a mutual admiration society . . . the result is that they are apt sometimes to become just a little self-sufficient and to assume an air of superiority which gives to their golden-headed statue, with its breast and arms of silver, a decidedly clayey foundation, threatening future humiliations and general unstableness.[52]

Hyperbole and the pompous semantics which could characterise some nineteenth century clerical writing aside, it was an important point, and can also be seen as a questioning of the value, if any, inherent in pledging people *en masse*, towards undefined ends. In the same year, the spokesperson for this Association of Prayer emphasised the need for the importance of a spiritual hue: 'According to Catholic principles, the whole matter lies in a nutshell. Not one of those organisations will be productive of real and lasting good unless it be made fruitful by the dew of heavenly grace'. The fundamental aim was to preserve the spiritual purity of those contemplating tampering with drink and to convert those who were addicted in order to save them from a spiritual abyss. There was in the view of the author, a Catholic spiritual onus on the strong to intervene to save the weak, and in an acknowledgement of the pervasiveness of the threat, he concluded 'few indeed can say that they have no friend in danger'.[53]

If there was a social dimension to this spiritual quest, it was directed specifically at those occasions where Christians undermined religious celebrations or contrived to seek pleasure in the Christian commemoration of pain. Thus, a few years later in Dublin, the *Monitor*, which was the organ of The Association of Prayer in honour of the Sacred Thirst and Agony of Jesus to repress intemperance, made a point of prefacing its arguments by quoting St John and Matthew on the plight of the crucifixion of Jesus: 'Afterwards, Jesus said I thirst, and they gave him vinegar mingled with gall.' It was appropriate that they were emphasising this message to the 330 parishes they claimed were affiliated to their association, given that they were intent on launching a 'holy truce of the infant Jesus' which had originally been suggested by the Rev F. Richardson for the feast of St Patrick in 1868. This involved a commitment not to enter public houses on Christmas Eve or St Stephen's day 'to hinder Christmas from being a demon's holiday'.[54] The above associations, aimed at both spiritual sanctification and the identification of specific abuses, were significant in the context of the 1875 pastoral letter of the Irish Hierarchy, issued from the National Synod, in which they sought to extrapolate from drink abuse a heightened national consciousness and to associate excess drinking with prolonging and abetting the evil foisted on the Irish by external forces: 'Drunkenness has wrecked more homes once happy than ever fell beneath the crowbar in the worst days of eviction.'[55]

However, to organise a more concentrated temperance campaign, it was necessary to back the abstinence case with wider and varied opinion. The traditional reliance on the medicinal use of alcohol has been referred to, another practice which seemed to invite the dispelling of myths, and the creation of alternatives. As early as 1830 the Hibernian Temperance Society had relied on sophisticated tracts which reconciled the anti-spirits movement with medical opinion amongst the upper classes who sought to justify their social position by demonstrating superior morality.[56] In America the publication by Dr Benjamin Rush of his 'Enquiry into the effects of spirituous liquors on the human body and mind' in 1784 had opened the debate on the physical and mental effects of alcohol and perhaps gave a certain impetus to those establishing the initial temperance societies in the larger American cities. In an address to the Dublin Statistical Society in 1849 on the connection between intemperance and crime, James Houghton stressed the need for statistical data and plain fact to bolster the moderationists' and abstainers' case, insisting that drink destroyed the desire to acquire knowledge, hence the ignorance of criminals.[57] Nine years later, perhaps with the benefit of more advanced medical knowledge, Houghton saw fit to deliver a paper entitled 'Some facts which suggest that the desire for alcoholic stimulants is not only transmitted by hereditary descent, but it is also felt with increasing strength from generation to generation and this strongly tends to deteriorate the Human Race'. During this Darwinian address he referred throughout to alcohol as 'the poison' and attested that even moderate drinking was dangerous ('the drunken man is harmless') and could lead to sterility and under-developed children.[58] By the third quarter of the century these ideas were growing in momentum and tended to be accompanied by calls for legislative reform.

In 1875, David Ross, another to contribute to the proceedings of the Statistical Society suggested 'practical checks on excessive drinking and habitual drunkenness'. He had been strongly influenced by a medical declaration concerning the ill-effects of alcoholic drink which had been published in some London newspapers at the end of 1871, and signed by 266 physicians and surgeons, who were also demanding restrictive legislation.[59] Ross believed that any impending law change had to tackle not just drunkenness but the whole concept of recla-mation and reformation of character, if only because the mass of the community did not see it as a crime in any sense. He certainly believed in institutionalising drunkards, but only if this was placed alongside a programme of rehabilitation. His address was a curious mixture of Victorian class Darwinism sprinkled with a dash of liberalism – 'the only curative treatment of habitual drunkards must be with their own consent'. Similarly, he believed that while right-minded people should as a matter of course be total abstainers, legislating for abstinence would be an unpalatable interference with civil liberties. He also sought to define drunkards: 'They are persons not incapacitated by nature as are idiots and lunatics, but reasonable persons who are gifted with reasoning powers beyond the common, and at the worst are only incapacitated by persistent indulgence in an evil habit.'[60]

On a religious level nineteenth-century rhetoric as to the Christianity of total abstinence was more likely to flourish within the ranks of Presbyterianism and Quakerism than Catholicism. In the 1860s, a Presbyterian minister from Belfast, the Rev Harkness, engaged in a public debate with the Rev Woodward, Dean of Down, who had disputed the contention that the practice of total abstinence was in accordance with the example of Christ, because he had used wine at Cana. He saw it as duplicitous for abstainers to attempt to present themselves as strict inheritors or interpreters of Christ's teaching. Harkness regarded this as an indulgent cop-out and contended that abstinence was not about scripture but context and the need to give example to the weaker. He informed his audience that Jesus did not marry, eat ham or wear European clothes, but this did not mean that those who believed in his church followed suit. The simple question faced by those who had the capacity to drink or abstain was to consider in which way they could do the most good – 'We abstain, whenever thereby we can do good – good to ourselves and others.'[61] Harkness was in reality extending the logic previously used by John Edgar, Professor of Divinity in Belfast, who along with G.W. Carr had been a prime mover in establishing the New Ross Temperance Society in 1829. In his reflections on spiritual temperance, Edgar had written: 'God gave good appetites but man perverted them . . . if our country were in the same state of temperance as Judea in the time of Christ, we would not object to the customary use of fermented liquor.'[62]

Another significant aspect of temperance developments in nineteenth-century Ireland and elsewhere was the importance assigned to the role of women in helping either to develop or retard an abstaining ethos in society. Despite their subjection in society as a whole, there was a fixation with the power of women of all denominations and classes, a preoccupation which was to last until well into the twentieth century, so much so that originally Fr Cullen's Pioneer movement was exclusively for female members. As early as 1784, an anonymous Swiftian-type tract had appeared in Dublin entitled 'An epistle to the fair maidens on the subject of drinking'. Women, it was asserted, determined the manners of a country, therefore female intoxication was more dangerous and destructive to the order of society than the excess experienced by men. Immediately, the idea of female responsibility in this regard is introduced: 'If they are chaste, prudent and industrious; the men are brave, virtuous and preserve their freedom; but where the women are giddy, lewd, idle or kept in absolute subjection; the men are consequently vicious, effeminate and slaves.'[63] A century later, F.W. Farrar, the Dean of Canterbury, also focused on the most pitiful of drunks – 'Women that nigh turn motherhood to shame, womanliness to loathing.'[64] Fr Mathew tended to view women more in the context of martyrdom, when he addressed them in Dublin's Marlborough Street in 1840:

He was (he said) placed under some difficulty in addressing so large a number of females because he knew not in what language to address them. He was well aware what it was which brought them there – namely to take the total abstinence pledge, but he knew also that very little necessity existed for doing so as regards themselves and that, therefore, they only did so for the purpose of showing good example to their children, their friends and neighbours.[65]

Others had little difficulty with addressing women in more forthright terms, albeit often in the abstract. Women, it seems, were in the curious position of being alcohol's most powerful abuser and its most hapless victim. This paradox in the construction of female piety was something which also shone through in the temperance literature of evangelical Ulster in the nineteenth century. It was believed that women had the power to be effective moral persuaders in the temperance debate, but they were also presented simultaneously as physically and morally weak – 'their purity, innocence and virtue – their chief weapons in the war against 'the demon drink' were fragile creations indeed'.[66] The realm of scientific and medical opinion was to remain the preserve of men, but the impact of drink on the different sexes was paramount in this literature: 'This theme is brought home time and again in temperance literature; men can have "narrow escapes" and return to the straight and narrow, but it is next to impossible for "fallen women" to be redeemed.'[67]

Recent research seems to indicate that the more dated accounts of temperance in nineteenth-century Ireland have underestimated the role played by women in the organisational and intellectual evolution of the subject. Maria Luddy, for example, has criticised Elizabeth Malcolm for underestimating the role of women. She points out that not only did women establish their own temperance societies, but that this in turn spurred them on to engage in other philanthropic work, such as the establishment of inebriate homes and preventative institutions for the benefit of 'fallen' girls and women.[68] She points to women like Jane Carlile and the establishment of the Ladies' Temperance Union in Belfast in 1862. Carlile stressed the importance of women inculcating temperance habits in children believing that 'on them chiefly, the rising generation are depending for the formation of their religious principles and habits.'[69] Another such woman was Isabella Tod who founded the Womens' Temperance Association in Belfast in 1874. By 1894, all branches of the WTA had merged into the Irish Womens' Temperance Union with the motto 'United to Win Ireland'. Temperance was linked with the demand for improved sanitary and health conditions. In keeping with the tradition of the separation between Protestants and Catholics due to the social and religious divisions of the nineteenth century there were more Protestants and Presbyterians than Catholics at the first annual conference of the IWTU. There was a political dimension to their activism also, and Tod was later to use women's' involvement in temperance work as an argument for the granting of female suffrage.[70] In the female Catholic sphere, the work was largely left to nuns who seem to have had an extraordinary ability to champion vast charitable endeavours in a very subtle fashion, and many organised sodalities which included the spiritual and practical aim of sobriety. By the mid-nineteenth century 81 per cent of all convents worked exclusively or overwhelmingly with the poor, and Catriona Clear in surveying their work as mould-breakers and path-finders in the field of education and social work, cites their great adaptability in the face of changing social conditions.[71] This was an achievement which was certainly not lost on Fr James Cullen when he sought suitable mentors for his new temperance initiative.

At least by the last decade of the nineteenth century, some of the issues to be faced by the temperance advocates were becoming more crystallised, and were certainly dictating a much wider social political and religious agenda, to the extent that of the situation in America, Gusfield could write: 'It is the breadth of the temperance movement in the late nineteenth century which is so impressive. Almost every progressive, radical or conservative movement had some alliance with it.' He sees this scope as being exemplified by a character such as Frances Williard of the Women's Christian Temperance Union, who incorporated in her programme for action not just temperance but Populism, Fabianism and Christian Socialism.[72] In other countries its potential for propaganda was evident. In Wales, for example, temperance at various stages throughout the century could be linked with the use of the Welsh language, religious nonconformity and political nationalism.[73] An emphasis on thrift and 'impulse renunciation' pointed towards Victorian respectability, and this could be coupled with a religious revival designed to dilute the customs of drinking, gambling, adultery, cruel sports and Sabbath breaking. In Wales, according to the historian of this period, W. R. Lambert, there was a switch away from moderation towards total abstinence because an anti-spirit pledge in a country dominated by beer was somewhat trite, and certainly superfluous.[74] On a political level, the temperance question in Wales could be broadly divided between the nonconformist Liberal temperance advocates and the Anglican Conservative Party, highlighting the efficacy of Welsh non-conformity as an agent of social control. In 1894,

T.E. Ellis, a Welsh Liberal MP, defined temperance as 'religion influencing social life'.[75] Perhaps inevitably, by the last decade of the nineteenth century the politicisation of the temperance agenda led to a greater polarisation in attitudes to drink. In relation to England, Lilian Shiman noted that by this stage temperance missionaries were either completely hostile to drunkards or utterly disinterested in their plight: 'The anti-drink agitators of the 1880s and 1890s deliberately fostered by many of the extreme teetotallers who wanted a clear-cut issue, led to an increasing polarisation in the attitudes of the country's population on the issue of drink; one was either for drink or against it, but not in between.'[76] This was an aspect which Lambert also documented in Wales, when he wrote that in the lively oratory of the non-conformist abstainers, 'everyone who was not a friend was an enemy.'[77]

The temperance debate in Ireland had not yet become polarised to this extent, and this was more than likely attributable to a preoccupation with the impact of the Great Famine and maybe a sense of disillusionment after the Fr Mathew impetus had faded. Nevertheless, the advocates were becoming more explicit about what they wanted. An important illustration of this was a lecture given on the temperance question in 1893 by the Rev Hugh O'Neill, a professor at St. Colman's College, Newry. The occasion was the re-opening of the Fr Mathew Total Abstinence Hall and Reading Room at Rostrevor. That it had taken so long to re-open the hall was indicative of the decline in the appeal of the Mathew ideals, but, nearly sixty years on, the orator was armed with fresh insight and statistics of a medical, religious and political nature. O'Neill was interested in the physiological cause of 'this dipsomania', and surmised in a musing that was to be heard frequently, that 'it may arise from climatic influences; it may be the result of the nervous feverish life which is the accompaniment of the higher civilisation of this latter part of the nineteenth century.'[78] He also referred directly to the economic cost of drunkenness and quoted the figures presented by the Irish Association for the Prevention of Intemperance, an interdenominational temperance lobbying group which had been established in 1868, which illustrated that drink expenditure in the United Kingdom in 1892 had been £140,866,262. The Irish drink bill alone for 1891–2 had been an astounding £13,014,771, and this was accompanied by 100,528 arrests for drunkenness in Ireland. He appealed to nationalist sentiments by asserting that 'The amount spent on drink in Ireland in ten years would leave every farmer in the country the owner in fee simple of his holding, if it were applied to that purpose.'[79] On a religious note, he rejected as a Manichean aberration the idea that drink in itself was evil and summed this up in the phrase 'the Christian religion condemns intemperance, commands temperance and commends total abstinence', though he was quick to point out that 'a temperance movement based solely on philanthropic or broadly Christian principles, though not a bad thing in itself, will never reform the people.'[80]

Interestingly, in the context of the hagiography which was associated with Fr Mathew, he spoke of the 'comparative failure' of Fr Mathew's movement because it had not resulted in any significant change in the social customs of the people and no reforming legislation. He suggested that in order to effect change in obliterating drink abuse prevalent at such events as wakes and social gatherings, not only must 'the fallen be reclaimed', but success depended on a temperance crusade predicated on quality rather than quantity – 'not on the number of its adherents but on their devotion to its principles.'[81] He went on to dispute the contention that alcohol was of medicinal value, asserting that stimulants were futile as an adjunct to diet, in the same way as opium in Egypt or India. Dealing with the role of the state, O'Neill spoke of the need to reduce the number of drink licenses, the abolition of mixed-trading, forcing public houses into providing non-alcoholic refreshments and to penalise those selling drink to minors. He categorically dismissed the cliché that it was impossible to make people sober by an Act of Parliament on the grounds that it was perverse logic to argue that no legislation could be passed to promote the cause of morality and honesty: 'Yet no-one is so absurd as to say that the law should leave absolute freedom to every indecent exhibition or publication or that it should permit fraud and refuse to endorse contracts.'[82]

It was an erudite address, and O'Neill demonstrated a sophistication in being able to weave the various points of the temperance debate into a cogent fabric, without sounding extreme, which was perhaps helped by his acknowledgement of the fundamental flaws in previous temperance endeavours. Rather than sounding bleak, there was an optimistic message throughout, and this was seen as necessary if temperance was to become a new departure. Others, more intent on focusing on specifics, used the remainder of the decade to carve out particular agendas, no doubt helped by the technological advances which had led to a more widespread distribution of the printed word. Clerical commentators were apt to use the pages of the *Irish Ecclesiastical Record* to digress on the various aspects of the debate. In 1892 the Rev John Nolan, writing on the physical effects of alcohol intake reiterated that it could not be used as a food, because it failed to give heat to the body, nor aided digestion, informing his readers that the first narcotic symptom produced in the system by alcohol was incipient paralysis, the effect on womens' brains being 'particularly horrific'.[83] The following year, elaborating on 'The Irish drink disease', Daniel O'Brien called for a more rounded education on the subject as 'A temperance movement mainly affects one generation' and was indelibly linked to the dullness and bleakness of Irish life.[84] Thomas Dunne, writing on the causes of and remedies for Irish intemperance, blamed land-lordism, a love of sociability and hereditary factors and bemoaned the stereotype which left him cringing at the tale of a Chicago teacher in conversation with young pupils: 'Tell me what you know about Ireland', 'Please Sir, the people there all wear green and live on whiskey.'[85]

By the end of the century, the Social and Statistical Inquiry Society of Ireland, having been forerunners in analysing the physical effects of excess drinking, turned their attention to the role of the state. In 1897 a correspondent suggested a need to distinguish between private and public morality, which, interwoven with the laws of economics, 'pursue their course regardless of preacher or moralist'.[86] The issue of the taking and administering of the pledge was also tackled, in order to distinguish between its impact and usefulness in theory and in practice. Given the confusion surrounding both, M. Geoghan argued that there was a need for both total abstinence and temperance associations to work alongside each other, suggesting that to extend the temperance pledge allowance only at such times as Christmas 'from 6p to 9p a day' would limit debauchery. He also urged imbibers to confine alcohol intake to mealtimes, but suggested women should totally abstain because of their formative roles as mothers, and the fact that they did not have large financial allowances. Interestingly, this particular observer evidenced more temptation to drink in rural districts because of the frequent association of drinking with fairs, markets and hurling matches, concluding that 'It is friendship itself which is turned into an agent of intemperance.'[87]

The Jesuit, James Halpin, focused on the issue of educational responsibility and the necessity of inculcating temperance habits from an early age 'to make it a shame as well as a sin', suggesting that a relevant educational curriculum would include temperance instruction for boys, and thrift, hygiene and cookery for girls, alluding to the annual report of the Irish Association for the Prevention of Intemperance which drew attention to a promise by the National Board of Education to issue temperance manuals to assist in this work. He looked to the positive influence of temperance work in schools in America and Canada and remarked ironically that in the Western world there was a pre-eminence of animal protection groups over child protection groups.[88]

James Hallinan, in a pamphlet based on a fictional conversation between two friends, preferred to focus on the abuse of drink at wakes and its implication for the way Ireland honoured its deceased, claiming in 1899 that 'We have still amongst us, up and down through the land, ways and customs which, to my mind are semi-barbarian, unCatholic and utterly unworthy of this Catholic country.' Exonerating the Irish populace somewhat from blame due to an ignorance of their religion, fuelled by the Penal Laws of the eighteenth century, he accepted that this was the root cause of bodies being laid out in the home rather than in the church. The subtext of his argument was that the peasantry should cling to their conservatism but not to their vulgarisms, including the 'mawkish ignorant sentimentality' evidenced in attitudes to the dead, the distribution of drink at funerals, and the idea that a poor person's respect for the dead, and indeed living, was measured by the profusion with which the hospitality was dispensed, so utterly unlike the pious and dignified Catholic peasants he had witnessed in the highlands of Bavaria. He recommended that the abusers be deprived of a priest and a corpse Mass.[89] Assuming the role of powerful preacher and moraliser, in the same year the indomitable Archbishop Ireland delivered a thundering two-hour address to the Irish Sunday Closing and Early Saturday Closing campaign at the request of 'a committee of influential citizens of Cork'. He invoked the memory of Fr Mathew, and from his pastoral experience, cited drink as the emigrants' greatest stumbling block. In the words of A.M. Sullivan, an Irish Nationalist MP, he equated 'Ireland sober' with 'Ireland free'; castigated the estimated number of Irish public houses (19,000), focusing specifically on Cork, where, with 576 pubs, there was one for every 126 citizens. Insisting that the breweries were too powerful, and that temperance advocates had both science and public-opinion on their side, he called for 'A modern Holy War' against excessive drinking.[90]

Abuse directed at brewers and licensed vintners by temperance advocates, at least publicly, tended at this stage to be veiled rather than explicit, which was a reflection both of their economic social and political influence, and perhaps of the belief that excessive drinking was not primarily their fault. As far back as 1817, a Licensed Vintners' Association had been established to vigorously safeguard vested interests. As an industry, the brewers and distillers had experienced mixed fortunes. In the mid-eighteenth century Irish brewers found themselves in difficulty, largely due to the English Industrial Revolution which had the effect of lowering the costs of English brewers exporting from English ports to Ireland. Along with industries such as glass-making and grain-milling, Irish brewers found that the only feasible recovery was to operate on a much larger scale.[91] This involved a substantially smaller number of malt houses with twice the output – as witnessed by the fact that in 1785 there had been 2,216 malt houses, but by 1835 there were a mere 388 producing double the previous amount. The distilling industry found itself in difficulty by the mid-nineteenth century, adversely affected to an extent by the Fr Mathew crusade, but also hampered by the raising of export duties after 1863. By the mid-1860s there were only twenty-two distilleries in operation. Three of the Dublin distilleries amalgamated in 1899 accompanied by a doubling in exports. Economic historian Louis Cullen points out that the number of breweries declined from 247 in 1837 to 41 by 1901, and that Dublin brewers, especially Guinness, accounted for 96 per cent of exports at the end of the nineteenth century.[92] By the First World War, Guinness, with a capital of £5 million employed only 2,000 people, which was considerably less than in the mid-nineteenth century, and even though by 1914 the production of whiskey had returned to the levels of the 1830s, prosperity tended to mean few large distilleries and low employment, and, as Cormac O'Gráda has noted 'Nor could distilling ever provide the employment of which industrial revolutions are made.'[93] It would be trite to assume that all brewers and distillers saw it in their interests to preside over a drinking culture predicated on excess. Indeed, it is quite likely that the Guinness firm, owned as it was by temperate, thrifty and industrious Protestants, would have approved of moderation, and the large-scale public advertising which was to become associated with the drink was very much a product of the mid-twentieth century.

It was evident to most temperance reformers by the end of the century that it was more appropriate to push for changes in the licensing laws and their administration, a theme which gained momentum at the beginning of the twentieth century. The fact that the licensing laws governing Ireland were distributed over twenty-five Acts of Parliament only seemed to reinforce a liberal interpretation of their provisions, if not ignorance of their content. This added a further layer to the temperance case and was perhaps the primary reason for the House of Lords' 1898 Commission on Intoxicating Liquor, which in common with other such commissions was good at highlighting and specifying abuse and wrong-doing, but rather weak on proposing solutions. Nonetheless, this Commission did expose much of the malpractice in relation to the operation of the licensing laws, the deplorable condition and excess number of public houses and the vigorous canvassing of Justices and packing of Benches when the granting of licenses was being decided.[94]

The message throughout the century was that there was much for Irish reformers to learn from abroad, but much of the evidence of external experience tends to reflect the approach of newly industrialised societies who had a more clearly defined social and political status than Ireland. The temperance advocates in these countries invariably articulated their message in terms of adding a layer of respectability to an already relatively culturally sophisticated society. In this sense the Irish situation was different. Certainly, there was an emphasis on the necessity of not repeating the same mistakes – of stressing total abstinence as a life-long commitment as opposed to a middle-aged damage-limitation exercise. Thus, as Elizabeth Malcolm points out, by the 1890s 'The Catholic temperance movement, unlike its predecessors did not expect to convert the existing generation (except the most ardent Catholics) to abstinence: it looked rather to successive generations brought up without the taste of alcohol.'[95] That it was to be blended with simultaneous movements for regeneration and Irish cultural revival, such as the Gaelic Athletic Association and the Gaelic League, and in the political domain as an additional badge of patriotism, was also a reflection of the idea of using tradition with an eye to the future. Reflecting on the distaste expressed by such political figures as Bulmer Hobson and Patrick Pearse for excessive drinking – indeed in some cases any drinking – Malcolm continues: 'Thus was temperance in Ireland transformed from a largely conservative and Protestant doctrine into one preached by Catholic nationalists, often with markedly revolutionary overtones.'[96] While this is an exaggerated assertion – rhetoric had still to be supplanted in the temperance sphere by co-ordinated action – it does reflect the fusion of varieties of Irish temperance thought which knitted in the 1890s, and it was appropriate that this was the decade which reflected an increased power and dominance by the Catholic church.

Many historians and political scientists have reflected on the mentality underlying this power which was being reflected in the rhetoric being used by proponents of spiritual purity and ideological nationhood through abstinence. Thus, one could read in the *Irish Ecclesiastical Record*: 'The great victory which Ireland is on the point of winning, politically and nationally is being won by those means – wise learning, close application to business in all its details, unfaltering perseverance. Are we to doubt that she will gain a great victory, morally, over intemperance by those means also?'[97] If this seems hopelessly far-fetched, it does point to the differences between the ethos and prognosis for the future of temperance in Ireland at this critical juncture in comparison to developments in other countries. In England during the nineteenth century, temperance did not have the same rural and conservative populace on the verge of land-ownership as did Ireland, and had to compete with such developments as Chartism and the rise of the Labour movement. Shiman wrote: 'Temperance did not decline because it failed to reach its goals; it withered away because its frame of reference and its values were no longer valid in English life in the twentieth century.'[98] The reverse was the case in Ireland. Likewise, reflecting on the fate of Welsh temperance, Lambert surmised that with the onset of the 1890s, the issue lost both its religious potency and 'its distinct identity in the face of the advance of the twentieth century Welfare State',[99] again a set of criteria which did not apply to Ireland until a much later stage. Similarly, given its preoccupation with defining the bounds of cultural and political nationalism at this stage, Ireland was not yet subjected to the same polarisation which began to emerge in the temperance movement in America in the last decades of the nineteenth century – issues such as 'human freedom' and the extent of civil and religious liberties which struck discord in the ranks of the Catholic Total Abstinence Union.[100]

Given Ireland's small size and the fact that cultural debate was being steered in a common direction by both priest and politician, temperance, while it could not entirely dictate social and cultural prerogatives, certainly found a sizeable niche in a new regenerative era. Perhaps this is why elements within Irish Catholicism, firstly on a broad cultural level, secondly in a more narrowly spiritual way and thirdly in a semi-populist manner, sought to more aggressively champion the temperance ground, capitalising on a growing self-confidence – the culmination of what Desmond Fennell saw as a Victorian and Rome-dominated mindset.[101] Tom Garvin also alluded to this and viewed the Catholic Church in the late nineteenth century as a crucial carrier of a tradition of nostalgia which could fittingly associate with modernity. This culture and a new obsession with the moral fibre which was shared by such publications as the Nationalist newspaper, D.P. Moran's *The Leader*, satirised the Irish drink interest:

> It was expressed most typically in the form of denunciations of the real and fancied ill-effects of alcohol. Prohibitionism tends to prosper when a rural society is challenged by industrialisation and Ireland was no exception, even though the industrialisation to which the Irish were reacting was situated mainly outside Ireland. There was a strong prohibitionist undercurrent in the Gaelic League and Sinn Fein. Catholic Bishops deplored the evils of drink ceaselessly during the last decade of the nineteenth century. Irish Catholicism is the only branch of the International Catholic Church to have a strong, almost evangelical tradition of total abstinence originally imported from America.[102]

It is tempting to glean from this sweeping analysis that a temperance movement in Ireland was an organisational and cultural *fait accompli* at this point. It was nothing of the sort, and this points to the danger of allowing rhetoric or 'undercurrents' to suddenly assume the status of definitive cultural definers. On a concentrated level, the temperance battle in Ireland was in its infancy. It needed to be compounded by a spiritual regeneration within Irish Catholicism, particularly to offset the age-old belief that abstinence was the preserve of a Protestant or dissenting tradition of religious practice. Catholic piety, particularly devotion to the Sacred Heart as initiated by St Margaret Mary Alacoque, the seventeenth-century French Visitation nun and mystic, was to be deepened and aligned to the concept of sacrifice. It was a particularly pessimistic form of Catholicism, and such popular publications as the *Irish Messenger of the Sacred Heart*, with a huge readership, and a simple emphasis on piety, reflected, in the words of McRedmond, 'the God of stern judgement rather than the God of Mercy'.[103] The encouragement of frequent communion and sacraments was perhaps a method of counteracting the puritanical strands evident in nineteenth-century Catholicism. It is important to remember that these practices were imports, but the degree of intensity with which they were pursued by the leaders of Irish Catholicism served to enhance the myth that such practices as devotion of the Nine First Fridays and Marian devotion (following the 1879 apparition at Knock in County Mayo) were particularly Irish products, and not mediated through Ireland by the Gallic atmosphere of Northern Europe, especially France. This was a feature noted by Desmond Fennell in his reflections on the changing nature of Irish Catholicism: 'So far had the myth-making gone at home that a wide range of popular devotions, which had originated in the Latin countries of Europe in modern time and established themselves in Ireland in the last couple of centuries were widely regarded as peculiar to Irish Catholicism.'[104]

As well as harnessing theoretical intellectual energy and justifications in the spiritual arena, it was also crucial to endow the temperance thrust with an element of populism, particularly to make it accessible to younger generations. This was reflected in the production of propaganda and anecdotal temperance manuals which were apt to depict moral responsibility in a direct way, frequently using lyrics to illustrate why a temperate lifestyle was essential to the maintenance of a decent, respectable and, of course, Catholic home. Thus, in a collection of temperance songs and poems published in 1896, one could sing of 'The Reformed Wife':

FIRST VERSE

Dear Mary when we married here, some twenty years ago,
Our hearts were high and hopeful
Though our scanty funds were low,
But yet by toil and industry we filled our little shop,
And life ran smooth and pleasant, till my Mary took her drop

FOURTH VERSE

The children are neglected and our shop is poor and bare,
Our parlour once so pretty, scarce a table has or chair,
Our Nell is so neglected that her head is like a mop,
There is no-one now to care her, since her mother took her
drop.

This particularly poignant collection included such other gems as 'Bacchus dethroned', 'The sober lemonade' and the more thundering 'Make war on the demon drink'.[105]

Given the various trends in Irish temperance thinking which had by the 1890s crystallised into a compelling, if still not entirely coherent force for the expression of patriotism and strict Catholic spirituality, it was perhaps fitting that the Pioneer Total Abstinence Association of the Sacred Heart emerged in the dying days of 1898. It should be stressed that the Pioneers as an organisation was very much shaped by one priest's interpretation of the various temperance arguments and challenges. In this respect, Fr James Cullen was interested initially in quality rather than quantity and in recruiting only women. It should also be emphasised that Cullen's work for temperance was only one aspect of his vast spiritual and practical programme for contemporary Catholics. The historian has been greatly assisted by a biography of Cullen published by the Jesuit Fr Lambert McKenna in 1924.[106] McKenna based his work on the private diaries of Cullen which have since been lost, which makes his study even more valuable. A native of Wexford, Cullen was at a relatively advanced age before deciding to join the Jesuit novitiate. It was fitting that the temperance crusade emerged under the auspices of this order given the tradition within the Jesuits of an active apostolate where members of the Society were given a degree of freedom in pursuing individual agendas. The tight discipline and structures which originated with the founder of the Society, Ignatius of Loyola, and the huge expansion in activity and status they had witnessed since 1814 when the Jesuit Order was restored worldwide are also worth noting. By 1829 the Irish Jesuit community had been raised to the rank of vice-province. By 1860

Milltown Park in Dublin was opened as a novitiate, and after the establishment of a foreign mission in Australia in 1865, the rank of province was attained. 1873 witnessed the publication of the influential periodical the *Irish Monthly*, and the 1880s saw the opening the Philosophate, and later Theolgate at Milltown Park, the entrusting of University College in Stephen's Green to the college and, in 1888, the First publication of the *Irish Messenger*.[107]

Cullen was born in Wexford in 1841 and worked in the 1860s as a curate in his home county, where he frequently encountered social problems of which he believed the root cause was excessive drinking. It was under the auspices of Dr Furlong, Bishop of Ferns, and a staunch opponent of the abuse of drink at fairs and wakes and on Sundays that Cullen first began to experiment in the administration of pledges. It was a loose practice which he came to doubt as a permanent solution to the problem of intemperance. Attempting to contextualise this reluctance, McKenna wrote:

> The pledge then was considered a violent and abnormal expedient to be used merely in the case of those whose will was so weak that the last drop of liquor drove them to excess. It was consequently a stigma of weakness, even an acknowledgement of a sinful past and an inability to exercise normal self-control . . . but Fr Cullen saw clearly that the pledge was not enough. It got its strength only from religion and therefore, the whole religious life of the men must be made more vigorous and sensitive.[108]

In this religious context, it was in devotion to the Sacred Heart that Cullen saw a more vigorous and sensitive medium through which to advocate abstention, and his pursuit of this was further fuelled by his appointment as director for Ireland of the Apostleship of Prayer in 1887. This was followed in 1889, when, in preaching a temperance sermon at St Peter's church in Belfast, he refused to conclude it with the customary administering of a general pledge. Recalling this critical episode in the preface of the first minute book of the Pioneer Association, Cullen justified it on the grounds that the Fr Mathew pledge had been 'so easily assimilated and so lightly regarded', and that it was necessary to consolidate a more selective and lasting pledge based on a 'Heroic Offering' involving total abstinence. He also believed it needed to be accompanied by 'a more detailed and perfect organisation'.[109] The devotion to the Sacred Heart had been promoted by the pre-suppression Society in Waterford, and according to McRedmond, the historian of the Irish Jesuits, it alleviated the Puritanical tendencies which had infiltrated nineteenth-century Catholicism:

> The Sacred Heart, which symbolised Christ's infinite love, stood between the fearful soul and a God who was very remote and very stern. It is scarcely surprising, then, that Fr Cullen, who must have felt within himself the need for a hopeful emphasis of this kind, should have become the outstanding promoter of the Sacred Heart devotion.[110]

In subsequent musings, both in public and private, Cullen created the impression that he was very conscious of his standing as a sponsor of new methods – of pioneering a change in the approach to temperance and the accompanying pledge, hence the name Pioneers. When writing in the *Irish Ecclesiastical Record* in 1892 as director of the Apostleship of Prayer, he targeted drink as one of the great 'we will not say errors, but misfortunes of our country and our race', and that under the auspices of the publication of the *Irish Messenger*, after religion, temperance was to be the 'foremost subject of recommendation to its readers'.[111] In subsequent years he was also to point out that a figure like Dr Furlong of Ferns, in his attempt to transfer public fairs and markets from holidays to weekdays had been 'unaided by civil law' which not only strengthened the argument for a spiritual crusade but also suggested that Cullen had forthright views on the role of civil law also. He later alluded to the practical and social side of the temperance question when he referred to the attempts by Fr Rossiter the former Superior to the Missions in Enniscorthy, to establish an 'Anti-treating league' in seeking to tackle the 'rounds system' in Irish public houses, seen by reformers as the bane of Irish social life.[112]

That he wanted his new departure initially confined to women was indicative of Cullen's belief in their spiritual and social superiority in terms of sacrifice, and the fact that, more often than not they bore the brunt of over-indulgence in drink. Later he insisted that despite all the countervailing arguments, he was fully convinced of the 'Mysterious power and privilege of women' in this regard.[113] In spiritual terms, this elevation of the female was connected to his personal devotion to the Blessed Virgin Mary, and Cullen was in the habit of reciting three Hail Marys every day in honour of the Immaculate Conception, something he encouraged in others. McKenna records this intense devotion in Cullen's private words: 'I devotedly love her. She fills my whole life. I feel her sweet presence as a golden haze of warm and love around me.'[114] In broader spiritual terms, Cullen also drew inspiration from the scriptures.

Prayer, self-denial and a charitable disposition were for him the hallmarks of genuine religion, because, as elucidated in the readings of 1 Corinthian 12, all were members of the mystical body of Christ with a consequent responsibility to help one another: 'Now Christ's body is yourselves, each of you with a part to play in the whole' (Verse 27). The idea of inviting people who had no personal problem with the use of alcohol to voluntarily make a life-time sacrifice was thus presented as part of a genuinely charitable disposition. What was particularly distinctive about the inspiration of the Pioneers was the focus on Sacred Heart devotion as represented by the wearing of a pin displaying the Sacred Heart image. Once again, there was a tridium of benefits to this devotion, to which Cullen could adapt his abstinence programme. The idea was that sinners would find in the Sacred Heart mercy and forgiveness, those with a mild faith would become fervent, and the already truly devoted could be elevated to near perfection. Thus, it was believed Heaven could be persuaded 'By the gentle violence of Total Abstinence, the conversion of excessive drinkers'.[115]

It is essential to grasp the spiritual context underpinning Cullen's crusade which he insisted was the most important facet of temperance work, and was repeatedly, indeed on occasions obsessively, emphasised as the fundamental aim, despite the numerous challenges posed by the culture of Irish alcohol intake. The idea was that no matter what changed externally, the spiritual basis would be a reassuring, sanctifying and permanent comfort. But it is also important to draw attention to the contemporary social environment. The Dublin in which he founded the Pioneers in 1898 was a city marked by poverty and uncertainty. The population had expanded from 265,316 in 1831 to 381,442 in 1901. Death rates per thousand of the population were high – 25.01 in the decade 1851 to 1860, and 29.65 in the 1890s.[116] Historian Mary Daly has pointed out that it was difficult to assess exactly the extent to which drink contributed to poverty – in 1894, the Society for Saint Vincent de Paul claimed that of the 114 families visited that year in Dublin city, 20 'would not have required relief but for the intemperance of the head of the family'. However given the middle-class social background of its membership, the extent to which the truly destitute were visited is open to question.[117] Given that there was no significant decline in the city's death rate until the early twentieth century there is no doubt that, religious values aside, Cullen, based in Gardiner Street in the inner city, and believing in the teaching of St Thomas (that there should be common use, if not ownership, of all wealth), was heavily influenced by his social conscience. For the time being, however, Cullen was intent on placing all the dimensions of the drink question into a tight framework, to be overseen by a disciplined army, under his direction, and his frequent use of military terminology in referring to his new association was an indication of what was to come. McKenna quotes him as writing: 'I feel I never could be satisfied with the spiritual help I now enjoy. I need more rules.'[118] Rules, and how to enforce them, were to be the major preoccupation of the Pioneer Association in its initial years.

NOTES

1   Emmet Larkin, *The Roman Catholic Church and the Creation of the Modern Irish State, 1878–86* (Dublin 1975)
2   Andrew Hadfield and John McVeigh (eds.), *Strangers to that Land: British perceptions of Ireland from the Reformation to the Famine* (Ulster Editions and Monographs, 1994), p. 55
3   ibid.
4   ibid.
5   Mary E. Daly, *A Social and Economic History of Ireland since 1800* (Dublin 1981) pp. 73–4
6   R. F. Foster, *Paddy and Mr Punch: Connections in Irish and British history* (London 1993) p. 193
7   Capuchin Archives Box B10 (7), Fr Thomas to General Curia in Rome, May 7, 1912
8   Cited in Colm Kerrigan, *Father Mathew and the Irish Temperance Movement 1838–1949* (Cork 1992) pp. 25–6
9   ibid., p. 65
10 ibid.
11 ibid., p. 80
12 Lilian Shiman, *The Crusade against Drink in Victorian England* (New York 1988) p. 3
13 ibid., p. 60
14 John Dunne, *The Pioneers* (Dublin 1981) p. 14
15 Brian Harrison, *Drink and the Victorians* (London 1971) p. 170
16 Joan Bland, *The Story of the Catholic Total Abstinence Union of America* (Washington 1951)
17 ibid., p. 109
18 ibid.
19 ibid.
20 Shiman, *Crusade*, p. 109
21 Bland, *The Story*, p. 127
22 Elizabeth Malcolm, 'Temperance and Irish Nationalism' in F.S.L. Lyons (ed.), *Ireland under the Union: Varieties of Tension* (Oxford 1980) pp. 70–75
23 ibid.
24 ibid.
25 Liam Bane, *The Bishop in Politics: The life and career of John MacEvilly* (Westport 1993) p. 79
26 ibid.
27 ibid.
28 Fergus D'arcy, 'The decline and fall of Donnybrook Fair: Moral reform and social control in nineteenth-century Dublin', *Saothar*, vol. 13, 1988
29 ibid.
30 Peter O'Dwyer, *Towards a History of Irish Spirituality* (Dublin 1995) p. 226
31 ibid.
32 Desmond Keenan,*The Catholic Church in Nineteenth-Century Ireland: A sociological study* (Dublin 1983) p. 152
33 ibid.
34 ibid., p. 241
35 Robert E. Bales, 'Attitudes towards drinking in Irish culture' in David Pittman and Charles Snyder (eds.) *Society, Culture and Drinking patterns* (London 1962) p. 159
36 ibid., p. 179. See also Irish Folklore Commission Collection, University College Dublin
37 Joseph Gusfield, 'Status Conflicts and the changing ideologies of the American temperance movement' in Pittman and Snyder (eds.), *Society and Culture*, p. 102
38 Kerby Miller, 'Assimilation and alienation: Irish emigrants' responses to industrial America' in P.J. Drudy (ed.), *The Irish in America: Emigration, assimilation and impact* (Irish Studies 4, Cambridge 1985)

39   Dale Light, 'The role of Irish-American Organisations in assimilation and community formation' in P.J. Drudy (ed.) *Irish in America*
40   David Doyle, 'Catholicism, politics and Irish America since 1890' in Drudy (ed.), *Irish in America*
41   Richard Stivers, *A Hair of the Dog: Irish drinking and American stereotype* (New York 1976) pp. 13–14
42   ibid., p. 90
43   ibid., p. 75
44   ibid.
45   Roger Swift and Sheridan Gilley, *The Irish in Britain 1815–1939* (London 1989)
46   Raphael Samuel, 'The Roman Catholic Church and the Irish poor' in Roger Swift and Sheridan Gilley (eds.), *The Irish in the Victorian City* (London 1985) pp. 267–301
47   ibid.
48   Bernard Canning, *Bishops of Ireland 1870–1987* (Dublin 1987)
49   ibid.
50   ibid.
51   *Irish Ecclesiastical Record*, vol. 5, 1868–9
52   ibid.
53   ibid.
54   *The Monitor* ,vol. 2, Dublin 1872
55   Hugh O'Neill, *The Temperance Question in Belfast* (Belfast 1893)
56   Harrison, *Drink and Victorians*, p. 103
57   James Houghton 'The connection between intemperance and crime' *Journal of the Social and Statistical Inquiry Society of Ireland*, 1849
58   James Houghton, 'Some facts which suggest the idea that the desire for alcoholic stimulants is not only transmitted by hereditary descent', *JSSISI*, vol. 2, 1858
59   David Ross 'Suggested. practical checks on excessive drinking' *JSSISI*, vol. 6, 1875
60   ibid.
61   I. N. Harkness, *A Vindication of Our Blessed Lord* (Belfast n.d.)
62   John Edgar, *Scriptural Temperance, a Discourse* (Belfast n.d.)
63   Anon., *An Epistle to the Fair Maidens on the Subject of Drinking* (Dublin 1784)
64   F. W. Farrar, *Temperance Address* (London 1899)
65   Anon., *An Accurate Report of the Very Rev T. Mathew in Dublin in the Cause of Temperance'* (Dublin 1840)
66   Andrea Brozyna, ' "The cursed cup hath cast her down", Constructions of female piety in Ulster evangelical temperance literature 1863–1914' in Janice Holmes and Diane Urquhart (eds.), *Coming into the Light: The work, politics and religion of women in Ulster 1840–1940* (Belfast 1994)
67   ibid.
68   Maria Luddy, *Women and Philanthropy in Nineteenth-Century Ireland* (Belfast, 1995) pp. 202–8
69   ibid.
70   ibid.
71   Catriona Clear, *Nuns in Nineteenth-Century Ireland* (Dublin 1987)
72   Gusfield, 'Changing status'
73   W. R. Lambert, *Drink and Society in Victorian Wales* (University of Wales Press, 1983), p. vii
74   ibid.
75   ibid.
76   Lilian Shiman, *The Crusade*, p. 196
77   Lambert, *Drink and Society*
78   Hugh O'Neill, *The Temperance Question* (Belfast 1893)
79   ibid.
80   ibid.
81   ibid.
82   ibid.
83   John Nolan, 'The physical effects of alcohol intake' *IER*, 1892
84   D. O'Brien, 'The Irish drink disease' *IER*, 1893
85   T. Dunne, 'The causes and remedy of Irish Intemperance' *IER*, 1893

86   Anon., 'The struggle between the State and the drink', *JSSISI*, vol. 10, 1897
87   M. Geoghan, *IER*, vol. 11, 1890
88   James Halpin, 'Temperance and the schools', *IER*, vol. 12, 1892
89   James Hallinan, *Our Duties to the Dead and how We Discharge Them* (Dublin 1899)
90   John Ireland, *A Message to Ireland* (Dublin 1899)
91   Louis Cullen, *An Economic History of Ireland since 1660* (London 1987) pp. 90–92
92   ibid., p. 145
93   Cormac O'Grada, *Ireland: A new economic history 1780–1939* (Oxford 1994) p. 297
94   Malachy Magee, *1000 years of Irish Whiskey* (Dublin 1980)
95   Elizabeth Malcolm, 'Temperance and Irish Nationalism'
96   ibid.
97   M. Geoghan, 'The pledge in practice' *IER*, vol. 11, 1890
98   Shiman, *The Crusade*, p. 242
99   W.R. Lambert, *Wales*, p. 165
100 Joan Bland, *Hibernian Crusade*, p. 166
101 Desmond Fennell, *The Changing Face of Catholic Ireland* (New York 1968)
102 Tom Garvin, *Nationalist Revolutionaries in Ireland 1858–1928* (London 1987) pp. 67–8
103 Louis Mc Redmond, *To the Greater Glory: A history of the Irish Jesuits* (Dublin 1991)
104 Fennell, *Changing Face* p. 208
105 John Casey, *Temperance Songs and Lyrics* (Dublin 1896)
106 Lambert McKenna, *Life and work of Fr James Aloysius Cullen* (London 1924)
107 Pioneer Association Archives, *Irish Province News*, January 1961, centenary supplement
108 McKenna, *Fr James Cullen*
109 PAA, Fr Cullen's Introduction in the Minute Book of the Saint Francis Xavier Pioneer
     Council
110 McRedmond, *To the Greater Glory*, pp. 276–9
111 James Cullen, 'The apostleship of prayer' in *IER*, 1892
112 PAA, Transcript of Cullen's Address to Cork Rally, 1911
113 ibid.
114 McKenna, *Fr James Cullen*, p. 160
115 Bernard McGuckian, *Pioneering for 80 years* (Dublin 1978)
116 Mary E. Daly, *Dublin, the Deposed Capital: A social and economic history 1860–1914* (Cork
     1984), p. 240
117 ibid., pp. 81–3
118 McKenna, *Fr James Cullen*, p. 79

CHAPTER TWO

Foundations

Religion was the central core of daily existence. Even the most
barren tenement rooms always had the ubiquitous oil lamp with
red shade burning in front of a statue of the Sacred Heart . . .
Religion was especially important to women who depended on it
for refuge and solitude. It has been said, with much truth, that men
had their local pub while women had their parish church.
Kevin Kearns, *Dublin Tenement Life*

Fr Cullen met the fate of all reformers . . . It is not easy to combine
with this extremism the prudence and diplomatic finesse which are
needed as anaesthetics for the surgery of reform.
P.J. Gannon SJ, *Life of Fr Cullen*

Having developed his own attitude to abstinence and outlined the
benefits which would accrue to those who made this special spiritual
sacrifice, Cullen became intent on following it through with a degree
of ruthless efficiency. It was an intensity which mirrored his own inner
spiritual life and routine. Cullen suffered few fools, disliked ambiguity
and above all stressed the need for uniformity. Always in great haste,
given the variety of his organisational commitments, he frequently
sent postcards rather than letters, some of which have survived. One
of these, sent six weeks before the inauguration of the Pioneer
Association, witnesses him urging the recipient to ensure temperance
catechisms were paid for (Cullen had written a catechism in 1892), noting
'the great cause of failure in Fr Mathew's work, his debt'.[1] Sixteen years
later he wrote to a fellow Jesuit, Fr Flinn, who was to succeed him as
Central Director of the Pioneers, urging him to 'do what you can and
God will do the rest'.[2] Taken together, the two directives characterise
the utter determination to keep temporal affairs in order so that spiritual matters would in turn be treated sympathetically. In addition,
Cullen was keen to imbue his work with populist credentials when
appealing to a broader audience, particularly after the establishment in

1912 of a weekly 'Pioneer Column' in the *Irish Catholic* newspaper, which was to become one of the longest running regulars in Irish newspaper history. It was a recognition by Cullen of the need to have a regular forum to write about temperance issues in a direct and non-theoretical manner. But whilst using all-encompassing arguments and rhetoric, the control and actual running of the Association was confined to a select few.

It was this idea of exclusivity which prompted Cullen to invite four prominent Dublin ladies to the presbytery of the Saint Francis Xavier church in Gardiner Street on December 28, 1898. Cullen recalled the reasons in his introduction of the first minute book of the SFX Pioneer council, in which he loosely traced the evolution of the Association. The idea was that men would follow the purity of a female example: 'As may be gathered from the composition of the first meeting, it was principally intended for the women and girls of Ireland', they being the 'most energetic and devoted apostles of temperance', mothers being drink's most 'guiltless victims' who had traditionally looked on helpless as their children were doomed by drunken fathers to 'ignorance, dirt and misery of every kind, moral and physical'.[3] The four women were Mrs Anne Egan, Miss Lizzie Power, Mrs Mary Bury and Mrs A.M. Sullivan. Anne Egan, who lived in Rutland Square where the family hotel was situated, had been born in Roscrea and educated at the Loreto convent in Bray. She was later to serve as a Poor Law Guardian in the old North Dublin Union. She had been connected with temperance activity in late nineteenth-century Dublin as a member of the Philanthropic Reform Association. She died in 1922 at the age of 70, and one of her sons, John Egan, was to become a Jesuit priest based in Australia.[4] Miss Lizzie Power was resident in the Loreto convent in North Great George's Street. A prominent member of various sodalities, she was an aunt to a Jesuit Fr Patrick Power, whom she raised after his parents' death. An extract appeared in the annals of the Holy Childhood Sodality in 1920, after she had been killed by a motor-car outside the Saint Francis Xavier church in Gardiner street, and was an indication of her zealous religious devotion. Referring to her 'loss to the cause of poor pagan children' and her anti-proselytising activities, it continued:

> You could hardly name a charity in Dublin – most Catholic and chari-
> table of cities – to which Miss Power did not lend a hand, while all the
> time her most devoted, untiring services were given to the work of the
> Holy Childhood, ever her labour of love and predilection, as it had been
> before for her sister Mary whom, on the latter's early death in April
> 1898, she succeeded as Honorary Secretary and member of our Central
> Council of the Irish branch of the Association. Thus from the Summer of
> 1898 to December 1919 Miss Power devoted her time, her gifts, her pen,

her influence, her prayers to the immeasurable fruitful apostolate of the Holy Childhood for the temporal and external welfare of the myriad perishing, unbaptised innocents of heathen lands.[5]

Mrs Mary Bury did not provoke such stirring obituaries. A resident of Mountjoy Square, she was the widow of William Bury who had been a Town Commissioner in Queen's Street. Another deeply pious woman, her son, James Bury, became a Jesuit, and her sister was a Mercy Order nun based in Clonakilty, County Cork. Sr Columba, another nun in the order was later to recall that 'All the sisters who met her thought her a very saintly woman and a perfect Lady.'[6] Two of her daughters were educated in Gumley House, Isleworth in London which would seem to indicate a degree of wealth. She died in 1926.

Regarding the fourth woman, Mrs A.M. Sullivan, Cullen was later to recall that 'She was the leader of our tiny little band' and frequently made a point of mentioning her impeccable nationalist credentials. She was born in New Orleans in Louisiana in 1844 where her Irish father was the owner of cotton plantations. At the age of seventeen, with her mother, Frances, she came to Ireland as part of a 'Grand Tour' of Europe. Here, she met and fell in love with A.M. Sullivan, editor of the *Nation* newspaper and future nationalist MP, and the pair eloped and married. After his death, even though she was left with nine children, she took up the temperance cause of which her husband, so proud to have known Fr Mathew, had been an advocate. Her charitable disposition was also reflected by the fact that in 1887, with Mrs Bury, she founded the Sacred Heart Orphanage in Drumcondra.[7]

It seems the women's' credentials were impeccable, combining deep personal piety, a regard for the poor and marginalised, and strong connections with the Jesuit order. But little information exists about them – that they were the first cell of a movement which was to grow so vastly in twentieth-century Ireland indicates the extent to which reforming women can be denied their proper place in Irish history, where it becomes convenient to refer to them as 'four dedicated ladies' and then move quickly on.[8] The broadness of their religious and charitable endeavours also points to the proliferation of sodalities and reform associations in late nineteenth- and early twentieth-century Dublin, and the extent to which temperance advocacy was frequently combined with a variety of other spiritual and charitable endeavours.

Cullen undoubtedly held the contemporary view that a woman drinking to excess was an act so heinous that it put the tragedy of intemperance onto an even higher plane. A contemporary Jesuit, Fr Tim Halpin, writing in 1907 summed up the view that 'It is in the case of the woman surely that the shame and disgrace attaching to drunkenness assume their worst form', believing that a better knowledge of cooking on the part of women would 'solve half the drink problem'.[9] Likewise, another Jesuit, Fr P.J. Gannon, in his record of the life of Cullen, recorded that 'She who otherwise would be an angel of mercy and comfort spreading happiness around, is now an incarnated demon dealing destruction and despair'.[10] Cullen preferred to focus on the angelic traits and the redemptive power of female sacrifice and spirituality, but his determination to keep the Pioneers a female haven was short-lived. He personally recorded the story of how he brought the men on board. In February 1899 as part of a temperance mission in the church of St Peter and Paul in Cork, he preached on the need for temperance work, appealing for volunteers for his new Association. Afterwards, a number of young men approached him in the sacristy requesting to join, but Cullen insisted that he wasn't prepared to start 'a battalion of male Pioneers for the men and boys of Ireland' until after he had returned from a year's mission to South Africa. He recorded, however, that the men persuaded him to inaugurate a male centre immediately in case he would never return. The message Cullen left before he embarked on his mission was 'go slowly, very slowly, but always surely'. By the time he returned from South Africa a year later, the Sisters of Charity of North William Street, to whom he had entrusted the administrative running of the Association had enrolled over 1,200 members.[11]

Cullen effectively kept the Association under tight control. Under his central directorate, branches were formed with members banded together in groups of thirty-three, in honour of the thirty-three years of the life of Jesus. Each band included a promoter to enlist new members and ensure that the special Pioneer pin or emblem which was to be publicly worn became an acceptable, if not common, feature of Irish Catholic practice. In his own words, they were required 'to stimulate the zeal and fill in gaps as they occurred by death or departure and to keep constantly before these members the all important necessity of always wearing the Sacred Heart pin, pendant or brooch.'[12] Each branch was to be affiliated to the Central Council in the SFX Church in Gardiner Street, and would have, along with a Spiritual Director (preferably a local priest), a president, secretary, treasurer and four or more councillors: 'These officers should meet at a given time and place, and investigate the antecedents of applicants and admit, reject or postpone them as should seem advisable to them. They should ever bear in mind that only those of previous temperate lives should be admitted to membership.'[13] The required probationary period, before full membership was allowed, was two years.

In 1904, Cullen decided to inaugurate a juvenile branch of the Association to introduce the pledge concept to upcoming generations, with a particular aim to counteract, again in his own words, 'the erroneous and misleading' nature of accepted beliefs regarding the value and supposed necessity of alcohol 'as a beverage or medicine'.[14] This was the continuation of a concern he had originally aired in his first *Temperance Catechism*, published in 1892, where he urged those committing themselves to a pledge to stand firm in the face of ridicule and sneering banter. This *Temperance Catechism* contained the written approbation of nineteen Catholic Bishops. The Bishop of Limerick, Dr Collins, used the pages to express the belief that temperance had to maintain itself with 'intellectual conviction', while Archbishop Walsh of Dublin congratulated Cullen on his non-confrontational approach, 'as aggression so often forms a prominent feature in the writings of would-be reformers.'[15] It was perhaps convenient for Walsh to write along these lines, given that his interest in temperance work was at best superficial.[16]

Cullen aggressively pursued the aim of operating the infant Pioneer Association on strict lines. Foremost was the need to emphasise that all alcoholic drinks were prohibited to members, except when adminis- tered by a doctor. It was interesting that in his own reflections, the reason he felt the need to be so exact and explicit about the all-embracing scope of the prohibition was 'owing to multiplied queries as to the nature of beverages' – the list he recorded included all spirits, beer, porter, ale, brandy, wines, champagne, claret, ginger wine, cordials, ciders and sherry. For any half-hearted abstainer intent on embracing a loop-hole made possible by an advancement in manufacturing, he qualified his list by adding that 'if in the future any other alcoholic stimulants be manufactured, it will likewise be included in the prohibition.'[17]

Thoroughness, both in forming and enforcing the rules was to be the hall-mark. In his explanatory leaflets which appeared at the begin- ning of the century to buttress his authority and dispel any ambiguity concerning the nature of the Association, Cullen explained in exact terms why the new members were called Pioneers: 'The members of the Association are styled Pioneers, because they help to lead the way in the vanguard of temperance reform by word, example and prayer – because they resolve to brace and overcome any difficulty that impedes their undertaking – and lastly, because they are determined by God's grace to persevere in their resolution unto death.'[18]

As well as setting out the structure of the Association – a central directorate, a central working council, branch working councils and promoters, Pioneers, Probationers and Juveniles – he also detailed the requirements of each meeting. They had to consist of the reading of minutes and correspondence, the recitation of instructions for working councils, the treasurer's report, consideration of applicants, any temperance business which had locally or nationally emerged, and prayers to conclude, of which the 'Heroic Offering' was the most important. It was strictly emphasised that Pioneer branches were not religious sodalities and could not be permitted to organise as such, particularly with regard to obligatory meetings and subscriptions. The Association was to be funded from the proceeds of the sale of the Pioneer pin.[19] In this, Cullen's strictures differed from the approach of other more scattered Catholic temperance organisations which emerged spasmodically in the early twentieth century. Thus the members of the St Brigid's Total Abstinence Sodality for women, established in Dundalk in 1899, had to pay a shilling on joining and thereafter a subscription of one penny per week. The money in this case operated as an investment in assurance: 'In case of her death, her relatives shall be entitled to the sum of 20 shillings', or if a member got married, or even more edifying, entered a convent, she would be entitled to 30 shillings.[20] There was no question of Cullen allowing the Pioneers to be used for such material purposes and he was insistent on the need to avoid aggrandisement and to counter any charges of opulence with the provision that 'to ensure perfect equality amongst the members it was decided from the beginning that our emblems should not be manufactured in any precious metal (gold or silver etc.).' Any of what he termed the 'trifling profits', which accrued from the sale of pins, managed by the Sisters of Charity in North William Street, would be donated to the maintenance of their orphanage.[21]

Cullen's rhetoric concerning equality, and his determination to run a highly disciplined Association in accordance with his view that much of nineteenth-century temperance work had been undermined by the absence of structure and rules, did not preclude a focus on other aspects of moral and religious improvement. While prioritising spiritual salvation, he constantly placed the theme of temperance and abstinence in the wider context of the need to improve the social environment of the deprived, whether or not the poverty was the result of excessive drinking. Unlike many of his religious peers, he did not indulge in the sanctification of deprivation, so prevalent in early twentieth-century Dublin. Thus the early explanatory leaflets urged members to promote cleanliness, neatness and thrift in their homes, and 'Where practicable and possible, refreshment rooms where tea, coffee, milk, mineral waters and substantial meals may be easily and cheaply procured by all Total Abstainers.'[22] While the issue of domestic improvement and purity was placed firmly in the female sphere, Cullen also had specific directives for the male promoters: 'Promoters should endeavour to procure healthy amusement for young men and boys whether in Brigade meetings, night schools, etc. during the winter – or in outdoor games, during other Seasons of the year – as everyone knows that boys in towns cannot with difficulty be induced to stay after meals in their small and only too often wretched, squalid homes.'[23]

Cullen's most gushing rhetorical flourishes were still aimed directly at Irish women, concentrating on both their duties and their rewards. This can be seen in the following extract from one of the earlier Pioneer Annual General Meetings which were held at this time in the Rotunda hospital. In November 1904, Cullen claimed that huge progress was being made, with an estimated membership of 38,000, and that only the previous day, an order for five pounds worth of Pioneer pins had been placed. He thanked the student priests for their commitment and support (he had established a branch at Maynooth in 1901), and he also singled out the Gaelic League as a body which was contributing enormously, directly and indirectly, to the advancement of the Association. But the main focus of his attention was the women 'Who commenced this pioneer work and whose generous enthusiastic efforts have mainly lifted it to its present pinnacle of success, and their reward will be that they will enjoy the pleasure and privilege of witnessing their fathers, their brothers, their sons, their husbands and their friends marching under the banner of the Sacred Heart.'[24]

Nonetheless, words were rarely sufficient and he continually sought to translate rhetorical aspirations into organised action which would include the role of women. With another Jesuit, Fr James Fotrell, he organised a yearly pledge branch for women under the auspices of the SFX Church, bringing women into a guild to visit the poor in their own homes. Characteristically, the aim was to cover a wide brief under strict guidelines. The minute book records that 'Fr Cullen referred briefly to the amoralisation amongst the poor all over the country caused by the drink evil' and that it was 'such a fruitful source of proselytism amongst the poor, especially in the city.'[25] With his usual vigour he propounded the need for an active female lay apostolate centred around home visits 'with a special view to their social and moral improvement, to aim particularly in promoting temperance, cleanliness and thrift'. This was also necessary, it was believed, to secure the attendance of women and girls at yearly pledge Association meetings, to induce them to join sodalities, to keep registers of their attendance, to pursue absentees, to get children to Mass on Sundays and to 'secure attendance of all school children at school by means of classified register'.[26] Under the control of Cullen, the lot of the female Catholic moral guardian was to be a busy one.

There was a political agenda also, though Cullen studiously avoided this when publicly writing or speaking on the Pioneers in the initial years. His aim for the social, religious and moral improvement of the Irish was undoubtedly underpinned by his personal patriotism, and he proudly referred to having been born in the same county (Wexford) which was an important battleground for the men of the 1798 rising. He was to be spared the tragedy and division of the Irish Civil War, dying the day after the Anglo-Irish Treaty was signed, but Lambert McKenna noted from a perusal of his diaries that, particularly at the time of the 1916 Easter Rising, 'His mind and heart were much occupied with the Irish struggle.'[27] This preoccupation was coloured by his hatred of British imperialism, and he believed that part of this imperialism had involved subjecting and subduing the colonised through encouraging them to drink to excess. In a hand-written manuscript, dated five months before his death, Cullen reflected on the historical impact of this imperialism in the context of the drink question. He wrote of the British Government crushing the Irish with taxation 'to pay for the support of an alien and detested religion', and of merciless evictions caused by 'vicious' Land Laws, and an avoidable famine which saw 'tens of thousands left to die of starvation . . . by the roadside in sight of their burning cabins or in wild sorrow and hatred, crowded together in ships . . . to seek a life forbidden them at home.'[28] Specifically on the subject of drink, he reflected on an imperialist mentality which thought 'It would be better that the race drank itself out of existence as did some savage tribes of South Africa who drank themselves out of existence by the aid of a British mission'. He also referred acerbically to Arthur Balfour's tenure as Chief Secretary in the late nineteenth century. Cullen recalled that when approached with demands for increased funding for education, Balfour suggested that the Irish generate more revenue through increased consumption of drink. Cullen's analysis of this anecdote was suitably dramatic: 'In a word, Ireland was a drink doomed country, possibly destined to ignominious extinction by the vice of self-indulgence in drink, but meanwhile invited to increase drink revenue and so enable England to give the required subsidy.'[29]

Whatever Cullen's private thoughts, he did not translate this kind of rhetoric into political rabble-rousing on Pioneer platforms. Although continually appealing to patriotic instincts, he was adamant that party politics should not enter into Pioneer discourse. He sought rather to appeal to nationalist sentiments by using military semantics on numerous occasions. The Pioneers were an army, a battalion marching to the battlefield of the drink question. Thus at a rally in the Mansion House in Dublin in 1903 he referred to members of the Association as 'well disciplined troops', and in the explanatory leaflets, he excoriated a lack of zeal on the part of some, particularly those who had mislaid, or refused to display, their Sacred Heart pins: 'They remind one of good for nothing soldiers, who, in the face of the enemy, have forgotten to bring their guns or ammunition to the field of battle.'[30] This was to be an oft-repeated admonishment. Cullen could not contemplate the half-hearted or sceptical assuming any position of authority in the spiritual and social battle against drink. In his own reflections on the evolution of the Association he referred to his desire to 'have no loose bricks in the solid wall of Pioneer masonry', and his belief that 'One genuine Pioneer is worth a hundred weary wobblers.'[31] At the 1904 Annual Meeting in the Rotunda, he also castigated those who were apt to approach the pledge sacrifice ambiguously – the cowards who, in a society in which so much of social activity was centred around drinking, hid their emblems, or wore them part-time: 'They slyly conceal it in their watch-pocket if it be a pendant, they hide it in the folds of their scarf if it be a pin, and if it be a brooch, they muffle it up in their shawls or locate it at the back or side of their necks.'[32] As usual, Cullen's devotion to detail of the smallest kind was manifest. His policy of ridiculing those deemed to be suspect was perfectly consistent with his idea of exclusivity and strictness. That the theme of 'less than absolute devotion' was one he repeatedly returned to was not just a reflection of his obsession with rules. It was also a reminder that there was, and would continue to be an element of nervousness and reticence about publicly displaying piety, given that there were inevitably many who would undoubtedly resent what was, in effect, a silent sermon. But with the Association gathering momentum, Cullen felt in a position to be robust about obligations. It was also felt necessary at this stage to appoint a central directorate of Jesuits sympathetic to the aims and methods of the Association. Cullen, as spiritual director was joined by Fr James Fotrell, Fr Thomas Murphy and Fr William Doyle. The Association received an added boost in 1905, having been enriched with Papal Indulgences.

Obviously, there were many other factors and issues which impinged on the whole direction and stance of the Total Abstinence movement, to which Cullen, and indeed Irish society at large, turned attention. These included temperance as a wider cultural phenomenon and its relationship with Irish identity, concern with licensing issues and the state's approach to drink traffic and control, liaising with other interest groups and temperance advocates, and the theological aspects of the pledge itself. That temperance had entered the wider lexicon of Irish cultural progress was reflected in the Gaelic Athletic Association annual of 1907–08. In writing on the 'Ideal Gael', it could refer to 'a matchless athlete, sober, pure in mind speech and deed, self-possessed, self-reliant, self-respecting, loving his religion and his country with a deep and restless love, earnest in thought and effective in action.'[33] The historian, William Mandle, however, poured cold water on this myth of purity, and his criticisms seemed to indicate that for the likes of Cullen, there was a mountain to climb. He wrote: 'It might be thought the artificial glow cast upon Gaelic games bears little relation to the realities of squabble and drunkenness, fights and injury, that attended so many fixtures and indeed official meetings.'[34] Temperance advocates and sponsors of domestic sport were not the only groups who sought to dispel the seemingly interchangeability of drink and Irish identity. Abroad, emigrants were also capable of taking umbrage at what they saw as crude and demeaning racial stereotyping. Stivers, in his examination of Irish-American drink habits, records that at an American performance of the play *The Fatal Wedding* in 1904, 'An Irishman from the audience rushed to the stage to protest at 'an insult to Irish womanhood' – a scene with a drunken Irish servant girl'.[35]

At home, many other commentators along with Cullen advocated abstinence from alcohol or moderate intake for a multitude of reasons. Across all sections of the Irish community the pub had assumed a status which was pivotal , in sickness and in health, in poverty and in wealth. Kevin Kearns in his study of Dublin tenement life, recalls that in communities such as these (close to Cullen's Gardiner Street Headquarters), drunkards were more often treated with sympathy than with condemnation, and he suggests, exaggeratedly, that many tenement dwellers were addicted to drink from birth due to the constant smell from the Guinness Brewery in the Liberties. The pint, often called the 'liquid food', could occasionally be administered to babies in the belief that it could cure worms. 'Red Biddy' wine, potent and cheap, could be resorted to in the downtrodden's quest for inebriation. A tenement dweller, John Gallagher, recalled that whilst the pub was primarily a form of escapism, it had a wider practical function: 'It was a man's world and a lot of deals were done in public houses and a lot of jobs were got in public houses.'[36]

Contemporary foreign observers and sociologists, like the French travel writer, Paul-Dubois, sought to be detached in their assessment of the Irish drink culture, but tended to still play the race card. He drew attention to a town like Tralee in Kerry, with 117 pubs for 9,367 inhabitants, where the social power of the publican (or 'King Bung' as they were sometimes called) could be enormous. Paul-Dubois came to some ambivalent conclusions asserting that 'alcoholism, though a less serious evil than is commonly stated is nevertheless more serious than is sometimes believed', but he finished by insisting: 'Not to mention the moral ruin resulting from alcoholism, we come to the physical harm worked on a race constitutionally and organically weakened by intense poverty and poor-living and consequently less able to stand stimulants than the Anglo-Saxons.'[37]

The various customs mentioned in the previous chapter as intrinsic to the nature of drink abuse in Ireland had not been ousted by the early twentieth century. 'Treating', or the buying of rounds, was still the most common form of social drinking. What was the attitude of Cullen to a practice like this and to the publicans who prospered on its fruits? It was difficult, in orchestrating a Catholic temperance campaign, to make membership contingent, not only on a pledge, but on the prohibition of participation in social customs associated with drinking, particularly as it was a professed aim not to be seen as fanatical, nor to suggest that drink in itself was evil. It was a balancing act Cullen never quite mastered, which, given the vociferousness of his approach, was perhaps understandable. Lambert McKenna suggested that he was prone to 'over-explicitness in denouncing vice, especially drunkenness', and that while Cullen was utterly convinced that his own way was best 'this very narrowness of outlook caused an intense concentration of purpose and was in great measure the secret of his success, but at the same time fraught with certain dangers.'[38] This could also cause consternation and resentment within the ranks of his own Society. Cullen undoubtedly had the backing of many fellow Jesuits, and there was a strong tradition of Jesuits being permitted to embark on personal initiatives at their chosen pace and with the approval of their superiors. But McKenna also draws attention to the fact that there were other Jesuits who did not approve of him using the *Irish Messenger* publication to advance what was very much a personalised crusade.[39]

There were other barriers to overcome, not only the deep roots of drink in the Irish psyche but also the fact that while reformers of Cullen's kind may have had relatively good relations with the Hierarchy, the latter as a body tended to be ambivalent on the subject of temperance, particularly given the importance of the liquor trade in the Irish commercial system. The drink trade also had a tradition of philanthropy. This served to make politicians wary of nailing their colours to the temperance mast, as was evidenced in relation to the budget of 1909 when Lloyd George, with a loathing of the drink trade, sought to increase tax on spirits and introduce new valuation procedures for public houses, with the aim of introducing new rates which would eventually lead to the non-renewal of licences for many Irish public houses. Politically, at this stage, the publican was in a very strong position despite the changes being mooted. Andrew Sheppard, in a thesis on the subject wrote: 'The Conservatives, being the party of the drink trade in Britain were not likely to introduce anti-drink legislation; the Liberals, in deference to the Irish Parliamentary Party were usually prepared to make concessions on, or exclude them altogether from, the operation of restrictive laws.'[40] The budget of 1909, particularly the intention to increase taxes on Irish whiskey tended to unite nationalist publicans (and indeed some Unionist distillers), rather than focus attention on the merits of temperance, or perhaps, as Sheppard suggests, it was not in the interests of reformers to introduce the temperance card at this juncture, where it would quickly assume the label of 'anti-National': 'Catholic temperance Spokesmen for the most part maintained a diplomatic silence. In their rare pronouncements on the subject they usually contrived a face-saving ambivalence.' Even the Irish Catholic, later to be used by Cullen to promote the Pioneer Association in a weekly column, was critical of the Irish Parliamentary Party for not doing enough to protect publicans.[41] The problem for the temperance lobby in instances such as these was that opposition to measures tended to be framed in national terms rather than as specific issues relative to the licensed trade. Thus the temperance delegation who met with Lloyd George, urging him to follow through his proposal, failed in their bid to ensure the introduction of what Dr Healy, Archbishop of Tuam had called 'this shameful tax'.[42]

In short, nationalist politicians were not apt to digress on the social implications of excess drinking, it of course being considered subordinate to the problem of securing political dominion status. Madeleine Humphreys, in a thesis on this issue after independence, believed that 'it is difficult to quantify a tangible or sustained contribution the Cultural National movement made to the advance of temperance.'[43] While this statement is too sweeping to withstand scrutiny and the new archival material available on the subject, it does point to the reasons why in the eyes of Cullen it was fine, indeed necessary, for the temperance outlook to be wedded to that of a Catholic and nationalist hue. It was important that the spiritual and social aspects be prioritised above and beyond the explicitly political. To be successful, temperance was seen as having to involve a coalition of many forces, including the political, but at the beginning of the century there was little scope for political agitation in this sphere, a situation which was not to change until the onslaught of the First World War.

When Fr Cullen's original *Catechism* was published in 1892, Dr McAlister, the Bishop of Down and Connor, had wondered 'is it not strange that it should be necessary to write a book to persuade Catholics to refrain from drunkenness.'[44] It was a pertinent question, given that for Catholics, the deliberate act of drunkenness was considered a sin, and it points to the battle that Catholic temperance workers almost continually had to wage between theory and practice. It is doubtful if the majority of Irish Catholics in the early twentieth century saw drunkenness (especially if it was occasional) as casting doubt on their Catholic credentials. Indeed, the immortal words of Jack Boyle in Sean O'Casey's *Juno and the Paycock* were probably more representative: ' I don't believe he was ever drunk in his life – sure he's not like a Christian at all.'[45] Likewise, in relation to the more academic side of the temperance argument, it was doubtful if there were many people 'outside those interested in the temperance movement who will plod through thirty pages of a continuous temperance argument: scrappy reading is the order of the day.'[46] It was, however, necessary to grapple with the whole concept of pledge-taking – was it a promise or a vow, and was it a sin to break it, be it venial or mortal? Or was it a private contract between the individual and God? J. C. MacErlain, reflecting in 1907 on the legacy of Fr Mathew, was convinced that 'more and more of the fact that the success of the temperance movement is always assured in proportion as its principles and doctrines are correctly and fearlessly placed before a discriminating and reflective public'.[47] Aside from those versed in pledge-taking during temperance sermons, this particular 'public' was merely academic wishful thinking, and the elucidation of theory rarely went beyond the specialists.

Concerning the theological aspects of the pledge, Cullen's view was set out specifically in the Handbook of the Maynooth branch of the Pioneer Association. 'The pledge of the association is not a vow. It is the solemn expression of a sincere and serious purpose to follow out a line of conduct that is in itself not of precept, but of counsel.'[48] Lambert McKenna, not in the role of biographer, but as a theologian reflecting in the pages of the *Irish Ecclesiastical Record*, gave an idea of the distance between academic shepherd and flock, and the arrogance which was associated with actively inviting the confusion between theory and practice. He believed that the pledge could be seen either as a resolution imposing no new obligation in conscience, or as a strict promise of fidelity and, as such, binding only under pain of venial sin, and, as no number of venial sins could equal a mortal sin, the breaking of the pledge could not be seen as a mortal sin. But McKenna, referring to the plain Catholics of Ireland who took these pledges, felt that in the interests of success and perseverance it was better for them to believe that they were committing a sin by breaking the pledge. He justified this by referring to the common practice of Catholics in the confessional, confessing to the breaking of the pledge: 'But strange to say he will frequently confess breaking the pledge and not say a word about the drunkenness which was the consequence of breaking it.'[49] This was probably the case – Irish Catholics were perfectly capable of making their own brand of distinction between theory and practice and between intent and mistake. But it did highlight the practical difficulties involved in administering and monitoring a personal pledge. Over ten years later, again in the pages of the *Irish Ecclesiastical Record*, there was evidence of the dilemma which could arise for those attempting to monitor drink abuse. Appearing on a page devoted to answering queries concerning the practice of religion and observance of Canon Law, this query was to do with the practice of drinking at wakes, an abuse which Cullen and others abhorred and is worth quoting in full, as it encapsulates the distinction between practice and theory, and the ramifications of absolute attention to theory:

> 'Question: At midnight during a 'wake' in a country house, a priest visits the wake and finds the man of the house, whose wife is dead, slightly under the influence of drink. No-one else in the house shows any sign of drink, no drink is found in the house or on the premises, though inquired and searched for. The Maynooth statutes (p. 149, N. 514), completely reprobate 'the custom, calamitous and ruinous to Christian people of supplying intoxicating drink in the house of the deceased or near the place of burial', and the bishops are exhorted to 'inflict grave punishment on those who transgress in this respect'. Would the punishment be sufficient if the priest were to absent himself from the funeral and refuse to collect the offerings?

> Answer: There is no doubt that the punishment would be sufficient: equally, no doubt, we believe that it would be unjust and exorbitant. There are two fundamental conditions, among others, that ought to be observed in inflicting ecclesiastical punishments; one, that there should be no penalty unless an offence against the law has been committed; the other that, so far as possible, the innocent should not be punished with the guilty. Neither condition would be fulfilled in the case. To judge from the account given, there was no offence against the statute. There is no evidence that drink was supplied in the wakehouse: even the 'man of the house' may have got it elsewhere. And it is well to remember that every man is to be regarded as innocent till proven guilty. Then as regards the innocent victims. The deceased herself was the first. Even the most hardened sceptic will admit that, whatever be said about others, she, at all events was guilty of no offence against the statute.'[50]

Of course, turning a blind eye would have rendered all these column inches unnecessary, but in the realm of temperance, there was a message in episodes such as these, principally the need to keep temperance thinking as clear-cut as possible. It has been suggested earlier that for Cullen it was a difficult balancing act, and became even more so the wider the temperance net became. What, for example, was to be the Pioneer's attitude to others drinking, or could they facilitate others drinking? Cullen's successor, Fr Flinn, recalled the following when he pressed Cullen as to whether 'treating' or the buying of rounds was a violation of the Pioneer pledge.

> Fr Cullen, who was extremely slow to answer the question, said it is not against the rule but it is against the spirit. He added that the greatest failure in temperance work in Ireland was the anti-treating pledge – it was killed by the clever word of a publican: 'So you know this mean man's pledge'. If I made anti-treating a rule of the Pioneer Total Abstinence Association, I would bring down the whole Association on that rule.[51]

It is crucial to grasp the significance of this anecdote which again was indicative of Cullen's desire to avoid the short-comings of previous temperance movements, but it also indicated the implications of having too many rules, open to too many interpretations. One strict rule and one strict method of organisation was, as he saw it, the only way to overcome this danger of a multitude of interpretations, or indeed the belief that pledge-taking imparted to the individual the right to tear down public houses. Strict, simple and spiritual was his solution.

This trinity of aspirations was inevitably widened, particularly given the increased attention which drink and the administration of the licensing laws was receiving in the first decade of the twentieth century. It was agreed across a broad spectrum that the licensing laws, and indeed the flouting of them necessitated serious consideration and reform, and temperance reformers could use them as a stick with which to beat the vintners. In 1906, Andrew Reed, a barrister and former Inspector General of the Royal Irish Constabulary, convened a conference to discuss Irish licensing and temperance reform, citing himself as 'a perfectly independent person standing between the temperance reformers and the body of licensed liquor traders'.[52] That he had to preface his departure with a claim to hold the middle ground was an implicit acknowledgement of the likely division a call for legal changes would cause, particularly given the complicated administration of the licensing laws which were distributed over twenty-five Acts of Parliament. It was interesting that in calling for a political campaign led by the Catholic bishop of Raphoe, Dr O'Donnell, and the

Protestant bishop of Clogher, Dr Darcy, Reed was insistent that the clergy were the legitimate leaders of such an initiative because the licensing issues particularly affected the areas of religion and morality.[53]

The proposals are worth reflecting on, as they encapsulate many of the issues which dominated the licensing debate for the next forty years. It was proposed that, as an antidote to the physical and moral degeneration of many Irish pubs, a rating qualification of £25 should be required for all towns with a population of 10,000 and over; that licensing authorities should be able to impose a temperance bar on licensed premises; that complete Sunday closing should be extended to the five exempted cities (The 1906 Sale of Intoxicating Liquor (Ireland) Act had legislated for early Saturday closing and complete Sunday closing in Ireland except for the 'bona fide' cities of Dublin, Belfast, Cork, Limerick and Waterford, though the hours they were permitted to open were reduced from five to three.) In this context it was felt appropriate to quote T.W. Russell on the results of a plebiscite among the population of Dublin in 1882, which it was said, had revealed that 76,867 people were in favour of Sunday closing and 13,702 against. The conference also proposed that pubs should be required to close at 9 pm on Saturdays and 10 pm on other days; that there should be the public 'outing' of those who sought to sell drink to habitual drunkards, and that there be a modification of the 1901 Act which had deemed publicans liable to prosecution only if they knowingly sold alcohol to someone under fourteen years of age. This, it was attested was being abused 'so that his assistants in his absence, can sell or deliver liquor to children with impunity.'[54] Many of the proposed changes were felt to be long overdue – in 1902, Balfour had looked for greater caution in the signing of certificates for the renewal of licences and the granting of occasional licences, as well as calling for more control to be exercised over the quality of the liquor sold at fairs and races. In the same year, resolutions passed by County and City magistrates had called for a stricter enforcement of Sunday licensing laws and expressed regret that the power granted to Justices was so seldom exercised.[55]

In a letter to the Reed conference of 1906, Cardinal Logue had suggested that it was useless to restrict the number of licensed premises if spirit grocers' licences continued to be granted, drawing attention to the issue of mixed-trading. This was another major preoccupation of the temperance reformers, particularly as it was believed that it facilitated women drinking socially. Dr McMoidie, the moderator of the Presbyterian General Assembly, added a note of caution when he wrote: 'I have often thought it might be well to assume in all temperance work that publicans have some conscience, instead of indulging in tirades against them.'[56] Dr Michael Fogarty, Catholic bishop of Killaloe, preferred to draw attention to illicit middle-class drinking – 'the species of drunkard who never appears in the police court, his family being more or less respectable, but who is known to be a misery to himself and oftentimes a ruin to his family.' Michael Davitt, the land agitator, writing to the same conference insisted that changing laws was not the solution, but rather the provision of amusements and cheap popular employments to entertain the youth as was being done in cities like Stockholm and St Petersburg.[57]

There was an ambiguous conclusion to this conference, with a vague commitment to the establishment of a standing committee which would meet again. It had certainly succeeded in exposing the areas to be tackled by the temperance reform movement, and the variety in emphasis and diversity of opinion on a preventive culture in relation to drink. Though Cullen was not an active participant, the issues raised were frequently tackled by him, particularly after the inauguration of his Pioneer Column in the *Irish Catholic*. What was clear was that there was to be a secular and non-spiritual agenda to which Pioneers, implicitly and explicitly, would be invited to turn their attention. Another issue of licensing reform which was frequently aired in the early part of the century, and continually endorsed by Cullen was the Gothenburg system of Local Option, a system in which the management of the drink traffic of specific localities was invested in a non-profit limited liability company, with any surplus going to the public treasury. Cullen, in his *Catechism*, had insisted that it reduced the local taxes on ratepayers.[58]

Regarding the number of pubs in Ireland, there was no-one at the start of the century prepared to suggest that Ireland had too few. Given the mixing of trades it was difficult to pinpoint exactly how many licences were being operated, but it was certainly in the region of 17,000. In an article for the *Journal of the Social and Statistical Inquiry Society of Ireland* in 1902, William Lawson, stressing the need for licensing and public house reform, pointed to a representative rural town like Thurles, where of the 77 public-houses, 38 were operating under a £10 valuation. Lawson believed the licensing system was taking advantage of the weakness of 'the careless, the unsuccessful, the incompetent, the lazy and the criminal', deplored the squalid conditions in which they drank and articulated middle-class disgust at women who 'have no sense of shame in entering a grocery and having a drink while waiting for the goods.'[59] Lawson, like others, had undoubtedly been influenced by the House of Lords Commission on the subject which had reported in 1898. Lawson admitted that some justices were attempting to discourage the granting of new licences, but he highlighted evidence given to the Commission concerning the fluid, if not farcical state of licensing affairs.

By 1908 it was estimated that there were nearly 23,000 licensed retail outlets in the country of which 17,273 were public houses (or 'on licences').[60] Figures of this proportion encouraged activists to provide alternative entertainments and social outlets, rather than tackling head on the proliferation of alcohol outlets. In 1908, Cullen bought a former wooden exhibition pavilion and arranged its re-erection in Upper Sherard Street, financed by public subscription. He named it the Saint Francis Xavier Hall. In his own words, he did this 'in view of applying a keenly and long felt need of legitimate recreation and moral development for the members of the Pioneer Association and of the Catholic people of a neighbourhood generally.'[61] In this hall, which had a capacity of 1,200, concerts and dramatic performances were organised, and attached to the main building was a suite of rooms 'intended only for young men who are members of the Pioneer Association', comprising a newsroom, with all the daily papers, a large billiard room, and a council room for meetings and dealing with applications for membership.[62] It should be noted that Cullen was by no means the first to do something practical about the need for a viable alternative to the pub, but he differed in his strictness, and by making the recreational atmosphere very much ancillary to the rules of the Pioneer Association. A more relaxed approach and differing priorities were in evidence at the St Joseph's Temperance Hall in Longford, with its reading, billiard and smoking rooms and gymnasium. Here, the promoters, under the patronage of the Bishop of Ardagh and Clonmacnoise, were informed that if they fell into intemperate habits, they would initially be let off with a warning, but when it came to recreation 'members are strictly forbidden to lie on the billiard tables. Players should call for the rest when required.'[63] Cullen would have rolled his eyes towards heaven in despair.

While the language of unity and co-operation was frequently used by temperance advocates, including Cullen, in the context of increasing the number of abstainers in Irish society, to a large extent the Pioneers tended to operate in practice as a self-contained unit, particularly in relation to the way they were organised, and with regard to the strictness of their pledge. However, they were accompanied in their quest by a number of other groups. Two in particular are worth examining, in order to give an idea of the breadth of the temperance debate in Ireland at this time as well as its limitations, and also to illustrate different priorities, especially Cullen's strict, almost absolutist, approach.

Rather than the Jesuits, the Capuchin order was entrusted by the Hierarchy in 1905 with the job of preaching a temperance mission in an attempt to inculcate sober habits in the masses. The Hierarchy had kept their request simple but all-embracing – 'That the Capuchin Fathers be asked to set apart a certain number of their body for the preaching of a temperance crusade in the country.'[64] The Hierarchy, in the wake of increased concern about drink abuse, and particularly the continued association of drink with many Catholic occasions and practices, doubtless chose the Capuchins for this task because of the temperance crusade of their celebrated nineteenth-century Provincial, Fr Mathew. The order itself had taken the original initiative in October 1901, when in a memorandum in response to increased drinking they suggested the establishment of a Fr Mathew Total Abstinence Association, with the expressed desire that the Association be 'Catholic and non-political', and that a secondary aim of temperance work would be 'to inculcate habits of thrift, to encourage Irish industries, and to advance general welfare'.[65] A booklet outlining the objects, means and constitution of the Association, was standard temperance material of its day. To qualify for the life badge, putative members had to be at least fourteen years of age, and must have been abstainers for at least twelve months; it being believed 'an association of converted drunkards is an impossible society; membership of such a society would brand the character of the individuals and bring shame and confusion to their families and friends'. The two chief centres were located in Dublin and Cork, and meetings consisted of the prayers of the association, a decade of the rosary and a sermon. The pledge consisted of the following: 'For the greater glory of God and the salvation of souls, in honour of the sacred thirst and agony of Jesus and the sorrowful heart of Mary, I promise to abstain from all intoxicating drinks and thus to discourage their use in others'. There was also a juvenile branch, children enrolling as early as the time of their First Holy Communion. This group was called the Young Irish Crusaders League, once again giving this movement the military gloss which reformers like Cullen preferred. Indulgences were duly granted to the Association by Pope Pius X in response to the petition of the Master General of the order, Fr Pacifus of Se Jano.[66] Members were also encouraged to make good use of the Association's publication, the Fr Mathew Record, 'because it is the only Catholic journal in Ireland devoted to the cause of temperance, because it is printed on Irish paper with Irish ink and bears the Irish trademark.'[67] If this was not enough to affirm the Association's impeccable patriotic credentials, it was also decided to instill temperance through rallying songs, which give a particular flavour of the ethos of this period:

> We hear the cries of Ireland, we see her darkened homes
> We see a blot upon her frame, in every glass that foams
> We see the children hunger pale, no joy in all their days
> No guiding light to lead them on along the upward ways!

There was an alternative version for the children of the Young Irish Crusaders:

> With hearts that ne'er shall falter, at Ireland's call we come
> to drive the demon drink away from every Irish home,
> We come – the Young Crusaders – to walk where saints have trod,
> To toil today for happy homes for Ireland and for God.[68]

The upbeat military sentiments, however, masked the enormous difficulties, physical and otherwise, inherent in preaching a nation-wide mission and in keeping a uniform procedure, and illustrate why Fr Cullen chose an alternative method. In Sligo in 1906, the Capuchin Provincial, Fr Paul, explained the position of the order in the light of the bishops' request. It was claimed that three principles were to be prioritised in elucidating this mission – the need to save the present generation, to protect the rising generation and to reclaim deserters. In short, this seemed to indicate a desire to make the whole of Ireland sober, something which Cullen, with his elitist approach, had little interest in attempting, even rhetorically. The Provincial was also pre-occupied with what he saw as the traits of the Irish people with regard to temperance: 'Our people are easily led for good or for evil . . . They can fight opposition very well, but they cannot stand sneers or jibes or nicknames, unless they have a priest at their back or a high motive to inspire them.'[69] While this may have displayed a sensitive insight into the practical difficulties of lay Catholics taking pledges, the reaction to it was illustrative of the way in which temperance crusades became compromised. The Provincial admitted: 'We consider that in preaching the crusade, we cannot decline to meet the wishes of some prelates who in certain circumstances are satisfied with a modified pledge and may ask us to administer it.'[70] Once again, this was at odds with the one steadfast rule which was the hallmark of Cullen's movement. With regard to the actual preaching of the sermons, shortage of directors was a problem for a mission that sought to span the whole country. In 1907 the Provincial wrote to the General Superior detailing the work which had been done by twelve Capuchin Friars involved in the mission. He claimed that during the previous year the sermon had been preached in twenty-three of the twenty-eight dioceses, covering 117 parishes, with the pledge administered to 200,000 people. He referred to it as 'eminently successful', and he saw fit to qualify his judgements on the progress of the mission with the need to stress that the English and Scottish people drank more 'but owing to the warmth of our celtic nature and the generosity of our people, alcoholic drinks have more injurious effects upon them – physically, socially and economically, than upon a race of more stolid character and more abundant resources.'[71]

The reality behind this rhetoric tells a different story, and the details have survived in the records of the Capuchin order giving a graphic indication of the practical problems faced by those who were entrusted with sponsoring mass conversion without having effective back-up or a long-term programme. Capuchin temperance missionaries were required to spend a week on the mission. The temperance sermon was preached not later than the Wednesday, and referred to each succeeding night. The pledge was given on the night of the temperance sermon and on Friday and Sunday. It was insisted by the Provincial that the life-long pledge was 'to be always given and the people are to be earnestly exhorted to take it.'[72] But some of the reports which survive from the missions conducted in 1906 draw attention to the difficulties. In Ballyforan in October, there were a variety of pledges to choose from – 1,193 took the full pledge, one quarter took only the anti-treating pledge, and eighty-three heads of families took a pledge not to give intoxicating drink at wakes or funerals. However, the local parish priest had no interest in temperance, and thus no temperance organisation evolved from this mission.[73] In Athleague, the parish priest personally took the pledge, and the missionary Capuchin recorded the following: 'No organisation, but about 1,100 took the pledge, and owing to the frequent maledictions which the worthy PP calls down upon backsliding blackguards and scabby sheep, are likely to keep it.'[74]

Other reports indicate a failure to note the numbers of those who took the pledge, priests practically bribing parishioners to participate, and others insisting that a mission once a year for a week was simply not enough to effect lasting change. The Capuchins were stoic. In November, Achill proved to be a nightmare, as reflected in this wry entry: 'Ochone, ochone, the memory of it is enough to make one laugh or weep. The people are moral, but absolutely indifferent, if not worse.'[75] There was a streak of pragmatism, turning to disillusionment, running through many of the reports – thus for Ballygat, the report read: 'Had moderate success – about 1,600 took the pledge. Had over 3,500 communicants. No organisation and little possibility of it, for the men leave every year for England. Had six priests helping us. No enthusiasm of any kind, and people are stolid, rough and thriftless. Goodbye to Galway if the rest is like this parish.'[76]

It was hardly a ringing endorsement of the mission, which in practice was ill-conceived, ambiguous and one which prioritised quantity over quality – the exact opposite to what Cullen believed was the essence of an elite programme for long-term improvement. What was significant was the way in which the Capuchins were still basking in the legacy of Fr Mathew without being aware, or admitting to, the inherent weakness of his movement, which had been lack of organisational back-up. They were more concerned with image and figures than substance, and rhetoric and generalisations rather than specifics. From September 1906 to April 1914, their record of badges distributed was as follows: Life badges, 499,088; temporary pledges, 492,323; children's' badges, 47,738, making a total – convenient in propaganda terms – of over one million.[77] The capacity for self-delusion regarding the figures on paper was manifest, and was particularly in evidence in a report sent by Fr Thomas of Kilkenny, the Irish Provincial, to the General Curia in Rome in response to queries as to the progress of the mission in 1912. He prefaced his report with a section on the curse of drink in Ireland's history and the fact that Ireland was 'a victim and not a culprit, and that no other country could put forth such an excuse for indulgence in alcohol.' He then went on to make the outrageous claim that Fr Mathew, in working his social and religious miracle had administered the pledge to 12 million people.[78]

He outlined how, after the 1905 invitation from the Hierarchy, in some dioceses, especially in large cities like Belfast and Limerick, the mission had lasted a month, in others a fortnight and in most a week. Between 1905 and 1912, there had been 312 weeks of missions. He quoted a figure of 70 per cent of adults in most parishes taking the pledge, with an average of 800 in each parish, and all together, administering the pledge to 1,141,191 people. He quoted praise for the missions as it had appeared in print from the hierarchy, Provincial Press, Judges and magistrates and clergy, County Councils and Civic officers. He again sought to make a direct connection between this work and the labours of Fr Mathew:

'Surely his mantle has visibly fallen upon them, from North to South, from East to West, they have traversed the Island, everywhere calling back to life with the enthusiasm which marked their illustrious

brother's campaign and everywhere dissipating the errors and pre-
judices which for so long had clouded and enslaved the minds of the
people.'[79]

Fr Thomas was doubtless exaggerating, not only refusing to distinguish between the practice of individual and *en masse* pledging, but
also in making no reference to the difficulties of following up the pledge
organisationally. There was little indication given of how stretched
and over-worked the sixteen missionary friars were in attempting to
effect short-term change in such a hurry and on such a scale. The more
sober reality was reflected in the analysis of those who were involved
at grass-roots level. Thus the following was the conclusion of one of
the missionary friars as early as 1906: 'In my opinion it becomes a
question of combining the mission crusade and effecting real, as distinct
from superficial, external spiritual work or dropping into the shade in
another year or two.'[80] This was precisely what happened. Little had
been learnt from the mistakes of Fr Mathew. The constant emphasis
was on short-term surface work, which was always justified on
patriotic or social as opposed to strictly religious grounds, with little
consequent discernment when it came to choosing suitable candidates
for receiving the pledge. In this, they fundamentally differed from the
approach of Fr Cullen. Nevertheless, combining their nineteenth-century
heritage, in the form of the legacy of Fr Mathew, and with the
endorsement of the hierarchy, they could quite legitimately claim in
early twentieth-century Ireland to have established their own
contemporary niche in the temperance movement, and by their own
reckoning, in improving the moral climate. Thus in 1906, Fr Paul could
boast of the following interesting piece of Dublin social history:

> A system of administering justice obtains in our vicinity that is unsur-
> passed in Europe. The magistrates instead of sending certain criminals
> to gaol or impoverishing them all the more, by a fine, send them to us
> for the pledge and a certificate. It is not an unusual spectacle, about
> midday, should one of the fathers be slow in answering his bell, to find 3
> policemen in the hall, with 3 delinquents sent up by the magistrates to
> take the pledge. These poor culprits are generally from the lowest
> stratum of society, and in a condition, the most pitiful, if not revolting,
> with cut faces, black eyes, dishevelled hair, tattered garments, and
> feeling the instinctive shame of the Bridewell. We have never inquired
> how far the system was a success. We are generally very busy and we
> sometimes give the pledge in a hurry, simply through a sense of charity
> or compassion, and let them off . . .'[81]

Significant also in the context of contemporary Catholic temperance
action was the role of the diocesan clergy, both individually and
collectively. Given that the organisational emphasis of temperance

work was focused on the parish, success or failure depended on the extent of the priest's support. This is something which clearly emerges from the experience of the Capuchin missionaries at local level. It was also a factor of which Fr Cullen was acutely aware. It would be inaccurate to suggest that Catholic priests automatically saw the temperance field as an intrinsic part of their ministry. Some did, but many more did not. This is reflected, for example, in the observation of James Gannon that 'Fr Cullen found perhaps his sternest censors and critics in the Society itself. To many he seemed Jansenistical [a belief in the perverseness of the natural will and its inability to do good] in his outlook.'[82] This was coupled with his own exacting spiritual demands which led him to be harsh in equating his own worth as a priest – he is quoted by Gannon as having said: 'There are bad priests, tepid priests, good priests and holy priests. I fear I am only in the third class.'[83]

Presumably he was aware that there were also drunken priests and sober priests who had to be careful in case they appeared fanatical in their denunciations of excess. As with most things, they waited for a lead from the Hierarchy – an article in the *Irish Ecclesiastical Record* of 1901 stated baldly that priests were obliged to oppose the further granting of drink licences because, according to the anonymous author 'the pronouncement of the Bishops on the undue multiplication of public houses – which was not lightly made – puts the matter outside the region of controversy.'[84] This was wishful thinking, but would not at that time have unduly perturbed Fr Cullen. Ensuring that the next generation of priests would be familiar with the pledge and enthusiastic parish promoters of sobriety was of more concern at that stage than tackling the licensing laws. To this end, he organised a Pioneer centre in Maynooth College in 1901 and frequently referred to it thereafter as one of the Association's most pivotal and important centres. The previous generation of Maynooth student priests had by no means been abstemious when it came to alcohol, and neither had they been encouraged to be. The new attempt to inculcate a sober ethos at Maynooth was greatly aided by the appointment of Fr Peter Coffey as Professor of Philosophy in 1902. Coffey was to become a fearsome temperance advocate, though he differed from Cullen in that his emphasis was very much on the social and economic implications of drink abuse and the ethics of prohibition, but he certainly shared the belief that it was essential to encourage temperance among the new generation of priests. Significant in this context was the formation of the Father Mathew Union in Cork in October 1901. The Union was designed specifically for abstaining priests, and administratively consisted of a president, a vice-president from each ecclesiastical province, and a council consisting of one member from each diocese and one member from each participating religious order. There was to be an annual General Meeting to assess progress, suggest temperance plans and confer on temperance subjects generally. The FMU had mixed fortunes. It was never an outright success, but rather limped along, achieving moderate regional reform in some parts but facing a wall of apathy in most other areas. A valuable source has been left in the form of their published annual reports which provide an insightful and remarkably frank overview of the problems facing temperance reformers in the first two decades of the century. The personality of the combative and intellectually adroit Dr Coffey, who almost single-handedly set the Union's agenda, shines through year after year, as does the utter frustration at the fact that most priests had no desire to join.

While Fr Cullen was a member, he was not particularly active in the Union, and though he studied their activities very closely, there was never any question of the Union becoming closely linked to the Pioneer Association. As with other temperance bodies, Cullen watched, but at a distance. In the context of its relevance to the Pioneers, the Union merits examination because, as with the aborted Capuchin crusade, its brief was too wide and differed from the more stringent lines laid down by Fr Cullen. Almost immediately after its inception, the patrons of the Union found themselves in the difficult position of having to define their methods, and quantify drink-induced sin. In 1902, Bishop O'Riordan, the first Patron of the Union, felt that the work was necessary because the organisation Fr Mathew had left in his wake was rude and unformed. He went on: 'Moreover, I own that I have a sort of instinctive suspicion of Total Abstinence work done midst the beating of drums and the applause of the platform . . . I doubt if the movement will ever secure wide and permanent success until we have realised that the sin of intemperance is immeasurably less than the sin through intemperance.'[85]

From the beginning there were differences of opinion concerning the message which it was appropriate to spread – should the physical dangers of alcohol be emphasised or was there a need to hammer home the moral and spiritual implications? In 1904 the Union claimed a membership of 250 (40 regular clergy, 210 secular clergy representing eight orders and twenty-three dioceses). These were not inspiring figures, and the following year the Union could only claim twelve new members. Union members, and the more influential church figures who sometimes addressed the annual meetings were quite open about the pitfalls inherent in temperance work and propaganda. There was a continual recognition of the danger of appearing extreme, on both social and religious grounds. This was encapsulated at the 1906 AGM

in Sligo, when Bishop John Clancy of Elphin, pronounced the following:

> In the first place our teetotalism must not be aggressive. The Church that
> imposes celibacy on us as a precept and consecrates it as a vow does not
> oblige us to be Total Abstainers and we must not become more zealous
> than the Church of Christ. Again, teetotallers must not lay the flattering
> unction to their souls that, because they are teetotallers they are, therefore,
> superior to all others. That is one of the heresies of our time, and the
> sooner it is consigned to the limbo of uncelestial repose the better.[86]

What was even more revealing at these gatherings was the view from
the ground. Parish priests were clearly as capable of being frustrated
by their religious peers as they were by suspicious and unco-operative
flocks. More priests still drank than abstained. But just how much were
they drinking and what damage was it doing? In 1907, Fr Ger Nolan, a
parish priest and member of the Union, drew attention to the following:

> Clerical scandals have sometimes happened in regard to drink. These
> things become known and make a deep, indeed an almost ineradicable
> impression. Good example, on the contrary, while less obtrusive, is
> happily more common and consequently less oppressive. Moreover,
> deep down in the popular mind there has been up till recently – though
> it is gradually disappearing with the advance of anti-clericalism- some
> kind of notion that the imbibing of spirituous liquors is somehow part
> and parcel of the clerical routine.[87]

There were also frequent disagreements as to whom to blame. Some
priests felt that publicans were active promoters of drunkenness and
were deserving of boycott; others felt that the Church's prohibition of
meat-eating on certain days of the year should be spread to drink also.
Coffey, in the initial years of the Union, saw temperance work in Ireland
at this time as drifting, with temperance positions being won and then
lost again. Perhaps utter delusion played its part also. One of the chief
characteristics of the temperance environment at this time (and this
was another factor of which Cullen was conscious) was that for every
initiative which was taken, there was frequently an individual who
had an alternative idea. In 1910, Fr J. Hynes, a priest in Galway, detailed
the activities of the 'St Patrick's Temperance League of the West', which
had been founded in September 1909 after a decree enacted in 1907 by
the Provincial Council of Tuam. The standing committee for this
endeavour consisted of Dr Thomas O'Dea, Bishop of Galway, and five
priests who concluded with wide-ranging ambiguity that there should
be a temperance league for all of Connaught and catholics should take
either the anti-treating pledge and a temperance or a Total Abstinence
pledge, accompanied by a preaching crusade.[88]

There were fanciful claims as to the League success. It had been claimed that 95 per cent of the Catholic people of Connaught had taken some form of the pledge. Fr Hynes was more sober in his assessment, estimating that 80 per cent of women and children had been pledged and 50 per cent of men, but that overall, only 25 per cent were still observing. While there had been a decrease in whiskey consumption, this was attributed to Lloyd George's budget (which had increased the duty paid on whiskey), rather than to the ploughing of a temperance furrow. Moreover, according to Hynes: 'It is generally admitted that the ultimate success of the league depends on the bishops than either the priests or the teachers.'[89] This was hardly a hopeful conclusion given that most members of the Irish hierarchy were not actively interested in temperance work, even if they did occasionally lend their names to condemnatory statements. But perhaps what was really sabotaging these endeavours was what reformers habitually despaired of – the widespread belief in alcohol as a panacea for all ills and joys. This was not just a religious problem, but a social one:

> Generally speaking alcoholic drink in one form or another is still regarded as useful in every illness, beneficial to one who is cold or wet, invigorating for the man engaged in hard work, and indispensable in times of joy, if not in times of sorrow. Boys who have left off school, particularly those in towns, still not infrequently regard the taking of a bottle of stout or a small whiskey as evidence of manliness and as a proof that the leading strings are broken and the state of manhood is entered on.[90]

In the following years, the Union also turned its attention to the need for legislative reform, disgusted by contemporary figures which revealed that 7,190 pubs in the country had a valuation of under £10. A standing committee of the Union proposed complete Sunday closing, the prominent display of a summary of laws and offences and fines to be paid for breach of licensing laws, and another proposal urged that girls and women be prohibited from entering pubs or being served, and 'that young girls or women be not eligible for position of barmaid – those already holding position excepted.'[91] The Union also stressed the need to ban the sale of methylated spirits in chemists. In the wider context of the drink problem, it drew attention to the need for different classes of inebriates to be housed in different institutions. It was pointed out that the only certified inebriate reformatories in Ireland for Catholics were the St Patrick's reformatory in Waterford, with provision for forty male inmates, and the St. Brigid's reformatory in Wexford with provision for sixty female inmates. The Union was perhaps putting the cart before the horse. Despite proposing wide-ranging legislative initiatives, it had to be pointed out that within the Union itself, it was 'altogether inadequately officered', that the useless pledging of entire congregations was still the most preferred temperance option, and that, as Coffey pointed out, there was utter apathy when it came to the teaching of the next generation. He concluded that there was 'a bottomless abyss of difference between prevention and cure'. He also indicated the class bias of much of the temperance reformers, or their determination to influence the future leaders of the country, by suggesting that the priority should be to focus on such educational institutions as Clongowes, Castleknock, Rockwell and Blackrock. Whatever about the majority of the contemporary Irish remaining immersed in drink, it was deemed imperative that the future leaders be sober and holy, but this was encouragement under the cloak of admonishment: 'What an immense gain it would be to the temperance cause if the social classes which they represent, the rulers they are destined to join, could show more numerous instances of light and leading in the practice and advocacy of Total Abstinence than they actually do!'[92]

In time, Coffey revealed that he was more blatantly politicised when it came to the question of drink reform than were many of his religious counterparts. This was not surprising. He had previously provoked the ire of the Catholic establishment by writing about the Catholic church and its responsibility towards the working class, expressing his sympathy with the cause of Christian socialism which was to continue until the 1920s. Though now more directly concerned with the drinks trade, during the First World War it was quite clear who he blamed, and it was not the drinkers. During the War the issue of compensating publicans who would be compelled to forfeit their licences was a particularly contentious subject. Coffey, at a Union AGM castigated

> . . . The government which has been itself the subservient tool of a rapacious liquor traffic and because they have been hitherto as helpless and submissive as the lambs being led to the slaughter . . . What guarantee have we that we are not embarking on the policy of compensating a hydra-headed monster which will accept compensation for every head we cut off, only to grow two more heads for the compensation received.[93]

However, as with most of these temperance issues, unanimity of opinion was not in evidence. Coffey was an extremist, more extreme, for example, than Fr Aloysius, a Capuchin, and another high-profile temperance advocate as well as patriot priest. He urged compensation to be granted on the grounds of natural justice, reminding Coffey that publicans had a legitimate trade and needed to earn a living. He also pointed out that Irish landlordism, however corrupt, could never have been abolished without compensation. Another contributor to this debate, Fr Beauchamp, estimated naively that it would take only £20 million to buy out the drink trade 'whereas the state had given out £98 million to buy two-thirds of the whole land of the country.' Fr T. O'Ryan, however, believed that Guinness alone was worth over £20 million.[94] The following year, more diverse opinions were heard on the merits of prohibition and extinction, with or without compensation. Once again, the temperance reformers had broadened the terms of the drink debate, and had discovered that they could agree on little, except for the stark and most salient fact – that, although it was claimed that there were 1,000 abstaining priests in the country, there were not enough temperance activists on the ground, and education on the subject left a lot to be desired, despite the fact that the National Board of Education had introduced a short syllabus of temperance lessons into its Health and Habits programme which was already compulsory.[95] In 1917, other priests had local rather than national concerns on their minds. One resolution read as follows:

> That since the prevailing custom whereby total abstaining priests have to pay equally with non-abstainers for alcoholic drinks, clerical conference and retreat dinners militates against the practice of total abstinence among the clergy, we recommend the diocesan branches to consider how this custom might best be continued and to make representations accordingly to the proper diocesan authorities.

The resolution was rejected as being petty, materialistic and not sufficiently concerned with spiritual matters.[96] Nonetheless, Coffey, who dominated the proceedings of the FMU during these war years, preferred to concentrate on the ethics of total prohibition, and what was considered a contemporary press boycott of temperance activities (which was perhaps indicative of disinterest among readers concerning the subject as well as the need not to alienate potential advertisers). By 1920 the Union claimed a membership of 600, though it insisted there were about 1,000 abstaining priests in the country, roughly one third of the Irish priesthood. These were not heartening figures for those in the vanguard of the movement, although there were optimistic noises made about the fact that the overwhelming majority of newly ordained priests at Maynooth were taking the Pioneer pledge. Even so, by 1920, in the twentieth annual report of the Union, Fr J.J. Kennedy reported that most branches 'had not much to boast of in the way of energy or activity'; reiterating the message that those priests who did not drink, merely abstained and did nothing to promote the value of abstention, and that younger priests could often be 'deterred by the carping spirit sometimes manifested by non-abstaining priests against temperance initiative of any sort among the clergy.'[97]

Why was Cullen not more actively involved in the FMU? There was little Jesuit involvement in the Union, it being understandably dominated by the Capuchins. Out of the council membership of twenty-three in its inaugural year, 1901, only one was a Jesuit. By 1913 there were only six Jesuits listed. Cullen was certainly interested in the concept, and attended some of the AGMs. He was probably quite legitimately unable to provide much of an active apostolate in this regard given his preoccupation with the Pioneers and his multitude of other projects. But there would have been other reasons. The Union's brief was too wide to satisfy him. Of more importance, Cullen would not have wanted to blur the lines between the Pioneer Association and other abstaining groups. In 1912, Fr Carr of the FMU insisted that because the whole birth, if not concept, of the Union had been so rushed, it was ineffectual. He called for a separate Pioneer section within the Union, but this was felt to be undesirable organisationally, and it was suggested that the bishops would not have been enamoured at this further sub-division.[98] But there would have been other reasons for Cullen's relative distance from the FMU. For a start, he would not have thought it strict enough, or sufficiently evolved from the original Fr Mathew movement, which in private he had described as a movement based on a pledge that was 'easily assimilated and so lightly regarded.'[99] He certainly would not have approved of the plea of the honorary secretary of the Union in 1918, when he suggested that the details of interpreting total abstinence should be left 'to the honour and good sense and intelligence of the branch members'[100] This directly contravened the directives which he issued as spiritual director of the Pioneers, and allowing the members to make their own rules would have been considered a recipe for disaster. One wonders how Cullen would have reacted to a contribution to the eighteenth Annual General Meeting of the Union from Fr Donohue, an executive member from Longford, who got himself into quite a state concerning the abuse by certain Pioneers of the time-honoured custom of drinking Irish coffee:

> The practice is no longer confined to old men, as was alleged, nor is the quantity limited to the traditional 'tea-spoonful'. I have seen young priests wearing their Pioneer badge taking a small quantity of brandy in their coffee, believing, I am sure, that in doing so they were not acting contrary to the spirit of the pledge, nor giving bad example. As time goes on the tea-spoon is discarded and the amount of alcohol grows out of all proportion to the coffee, until the mixture can be more properly described as 'coffee in whiskey'.[101]

Lack of attention to a clear spiritual programme may also have deterred Cullen from closer involvement with the FMU. As a group, it tended to devote more attention to the social, economic and political aspects of the drink problem than to the spiritual. Perhaps this is why he was even more determined to prioritise the spiritual programme within his own organisation. Early in his Jesuit career he had written in his diary that 'I have an ungenerous mental depreciation of other religious bodies – I will endeavour to do something about it.'[102] Whether he did or not is debatable, but his doubts about others merely intensified his own inner spirituality, and perhaps this was reflected in what some felt was his overly narrow and uncultivated approach to the subject of temperance. Lambert McKenna, who by no means idolised Cullen, perhaps summed this up when he wrote that Cullen 'had ordinary Catholic views – only very vividly conceived, ordinary Catholic aspirations only very intensely felt. The moving forces of his life were faith and charity and common sense.'[103] This emphasis on ordinary Catholicism is essential – Cullen was not a priest of towering intellect. He would not have been comfortable debating total prohibition with the likes of Coffey, the Maynooth Professor. Cullen certainly did refer to the issue of prohibition and licensing laws through his own Pioneer column in the *Irish Catholic* newspaper, but in doing so he had total control of the subject and could continually reduce the arguments to the spiritual domain – the *raison d'être* of the Pioneers. Cullen did occasionally share platforms with the likes of Coffey, but only in a national context.

The First World War made a huge impact on the temperance question, and while it marked the beginning of the decline of the numerical strength of temperance organisations in Britain, it did raise the profile of such issues as Prohibition, Compensation and Local Option. These debates coincided with the National Catholic Total Abstinence Congress All Ireland demonstration staged at the end of June in 1914. Opening the congress, Dr Gilmartin, the Bishop of Clonfert, insisted that temperance was a political, social, medicinal but above all a religious and moral issue. The tone was one that would have suited Cullen:

> The one extreme is excess: the other extreme is not total abstinence. The other extreme is the ranting of those people who hold that alcohol is intrinsically bad and should never be touched . . . I don't think it is saying too much that temperance societies which include moderate drinkers are unequal to the task of making Ireland sober.[104]

As a polemicist, Cullen came into his own when writing his weekly Pioneer column in the *Irish Catholic*, which he wrote from February 1912 until October 1921, two months before his death. Lambert McKenna alluded to Cullen 'occasionally overdoing his role of tribune of the plebs,'[105] and this was vividly demonstrated in this column. The column was aimed specifically at the Pioneer membership, or those waiting in the wings, and was dynamic, aggressive, at times provocative and on occasion utterly sanctimonious and self-righteous. It was written by a man utterly convinced of the righteousness of his cause – while McKenna referred to Cullen's preoccupation with the political and civil turmoil of the years 1916–21, he also quotes Cullen as saying that 'the only thing wrong about Ireland is the excessive amount of drinking going on.'[106] This summed up the mood underpinning the Pioneer column, where week after week, whilst continually emphasising the spiritual side of the pledge sacrifice, Cullen also sought to place Irish standards of living, cultural evolvement and social and political development, past and future, in the overall context of drink. The direct and simple message was that excessive drinking left no fabric of Irish life undamaged, and it was everyone's patriotic duty to tackle it. In his first column, he insisted he was writing as the director of an organisation with a membership of 225,000 members. It was an extraordinary figure and a proud boast, given that the movement was still in its infancy. Cullen's aggressive writing must be seen in the context of an era of journalism which was belligerent, personalised and at times scurrilous, as seen in such publications as Arthur Griffith's *United Irishman*, James Larkin's *Irish Worker* and D.P. Moran's *Leader*. Right from the beginning, Cullen was quite explicit about who he wanted as members, in comparison to the catch-all selection methods of traditional Irish temperance societies.

Cullen was apt to make sweeping assertions on the despicable effects of the Irish taste for drink, in the context of the need for education. More often than not he absolved the drinkers themselves from blame due to their social and political subjection.

He also used the column to report on the progress of Pioneer centres around the country, particularly on the need to keep accurate records, enforce entry and membership rules, distribute catechisms and maintain an active administrative structure. He lauded those centres which were seen to be active, and admonished those whom he felt were not making sufficient effort. He dismissed those who viewed the pledge as a part-time undertaking, and indulged in a jocular critique of their lack of moral fibre. In April 1912, he classified the various strands of 'weary wobblers', or those without the character to persevere at all costs. Included in this were continental wobblers (who drank wine on the continent, but not at home), rheumatic wobblers ('they take it inside and outside'), social wobblers ('afraid to say 'no' lest it be remarked'), and 'wedding, christening, funeral and emigrating wobblers'.[107] As a devout nationalist, Cullen was blatantly political when it suited his train of argument, continuing the logic of the 'Ireland sober is Ireland free' philosophy. Thus, in April 1912, he could, write that 'total abstinence from all intoxicating drink furnishes the very best security for the efficiency of our members in the coming Home Rule parliament.'[108]

During the first year of the column, Cullen came across many queries and dilemmas which were to exercise his temperance mind over the following decade. He pronounced on whether or not it was inconsistent for those involved in the sale of drink to wear the pin, the huge amount of expenditure on drink, its link with crime, dispelling myths as to its medicinal value, highlighting the violation of licensing laws and the need for Local Option under a domestic parliament. He also had the capacity to trivialise contemporary tragedies and to make outrageous analogies. When the famous Belfast ship, the *Titanic* sank, he wrote:

> They sank at night into their icy, watery grave . . . and while we breathe a silent prayer of pity for their eternal repose, the awful thought is borne on us that not hundreds, but thousands all around us are perishing in the ocean of drink, and cry in vain for help from those who can, but will not, help them.[109]

In December 1912, the AGM of the Association was held in the St Francis Xavier Hall. Although the Archbishop of Melbourne, Dr Mannix, failed to show owing to illness, he was still referred to as 'Commander-in-chief of the Pioneer forces'. Cullen drew attention, not only to progress, but also to disappointments, and again, in what was to become a recurring feature of his assessments of advancement, he blamed internal rather than external factors – particularly the 'apathy, inactivity and drowsiness of some of our branches and some of our promoters from whom we anticipated more effective help'. In the course of boasting that one fourteenth of the Irish Catholic population had joined the Pioneer ranks he rejected the idea that the 'respectability' of pioneers was an issue of class or wealth, but rather of integrity.[110]

As a columnist, Cullen thrived on targets, whether within or outside his own organisation. His confrontations were based on the need of the Pioneers to know their enemies, and to be able to chastise them effectively, on emotive or more clinically statistical grounds. The First World War was important in this context. He shared the contemporary concerns of nationalists like Patrick Pearse and James Connolly and indeed the view of the British Prime-minister, Lloyd George, on the damage that alcohol could inflict. Cullen tended to turn this into a pointedly political argument. Decrying the tarnishing of the United Irishmen 1798 rebellion by the presence of excessive drink, he referred to the fact that 'England would never have withheld self-government from Ireland if, by her shameful licensing opportunities and laws, she had not first stupefied, paralysed, degraded and disgraced the people she hated and feared.'[111] This sorry scenario was frequently placed alongside the hopes he held for Ireland as a putative state with a domestic parliament, where he hoped a primary concern of indigenous legislators would be to frame laws for the sobriety of the country. Underpinning his concern was the fact that so much money spent in Ireland on drink, which Cullen estimated at this stage was £38,000 daily, was going to a foreign exchequer.

Cullen also developed a near obsession with the medical implications of excessive drinking, and was apt to quote well-known British doctors and surgeons who disapproved of its use as medicine. The importance of hammering home this message was felt to be even more necessary because many medical practitioners still viewed it as an essential part of their medicine cabinet. In 1907, sixteen distinguished doctors had published a pro-alcohol manifesto in the *Lancet*, describing it as a 'rapid and trustworthy restorative'.[112] Cullen informed his Pioneer readership that it was quite the opposite, and frequently sought to dilute the medical jargon by relating it to more populist contexts – pointing to the fact that, for example, athletes performed better without it, the amount of literary giants slain by alcohol, and the responsibility of parents not to pass on the drink habit to their children given that medical research was concluding more and more that alcoholism was hereditary.[113]

Women were deemed worthy of more specific targeting, because it was believed alcohol had the power to do them more damage, it being completely in conflict with their temperament, not to mention tarnishing their roles as mothers ('and spoiling their complexions'). Cullen, it seemed, found nothing more soul-destroying than a hysterical drunken woman. His message was again simple: 'In her case it is unspeakably worse. Somehow or other her degradation is more rapid and her demoralisation more complete. She is bound to drag others down with her.'[114] After the outbreak of the First World War, columns were devoted to the 'deplorable outburst' of female drinking as a result of absentee husbands fighting in Europe and the provision of war pensions.[115] As usual, Cullen did not hold back. In September 1914, he wrote of the babies born to alcoholic mothers:

> When born it is puny, fretful, shrivelled-up and wailing, possibly feeble-minded or an idiot, and fortunately very often goes to swell the infant mortality rate. I say, fortunately, because a baby born with such low vitality could never be a strong or healthy citizen . . . the kidneys are

affected, the liver becomes so hard that it seems to occupy the whole of the lower half of the body, the heart becomes diseased, the flesh disappears until it seems as if the skin were stretched tightly over a skeleton.[116]

Cullen was not alone in depicting the horrors which emanated from a female drinking culture. Many contemporary writers and polemicists did likewise. It was a two-pronged approach – not only were women who drank castigated in a language more ferocious than that used in relation to men, but they were also, alongside their children, graphically depicted as drink's most hapless victims, at the mercy of bestial males. The following was contained in a collection of temperance lessons for schools:

> 'Molly, give me my dinner.' 'John, you know', she replies 'I have no dinner for you. Nobody here tasted food this day. There is not a bit of food in the house. Last night you took away the last farthing.' He gives her a blow in the face with his fist. Poor Pat is hiding in a corner. All his little manhood is aroused at the sight of the maltreatment of his mother. He rises and stands before that mother. His inhuman father lowers him with a kick. His mothers eyes are both blackened. She is knocked down beside her son. The beast returns to his drinking companions.[117]

At the same time, Cullen frequently singled out women as being particularly strenuous and virtuous temperance workers, and expressed the hope that they would use the eventual granting of female suffrage to further this activity. According to the early promoter's card, mixed branches were to be allowed until the organisation was fully developed, after which they would be run strictly on gendered lines.[118] Cullen also relied heavily on the convents (and female religious orders), not only to inculcate a new generation of Irish women with temperance views, but also because of their influence on the wider drinking community. The Annals of the Sisters of Charity reveal for example, not just the work done by individual convents in instilling temperance through sodalities and retreats and Pioneer recruitment, but also that 'Many wives and mothers appeal to the Sisters to use their influence with husbands or sons.'[119] Cullen's singling out of the convents, particularly the active Pioneer centre at the convent in Foxford, County Mayo, which housed the Woollen Mills, was also influenced by the fact that his niece, Sr Stanislaus was a nun there, and he was in frequent contact with her. He lauded the work in Foxford as contributing to civic and patriotic pride, and helping to curtail emigration.[120] On a personal level, the *Model Housekeeping* magazine in 1941, commemorating the centenary of his birth, referred to the influence his own mother and nurse had held over him. A Jesuit writer, Fr Lionel Gallagher referred piously to Cullen's 'trust in the greatness of Irish women' and his belief that they continually needed to imitate Our Lady in their lives in the home.[121]

These views however, were not necessarily shared by some of the more articulate of Cullen's contemporary female temperance activists. Catherine Mahon, one of the few women to share temperance platforms with Irish men in the years before Independence and the first female President of the Irish National Teachers Organisation, called for women to assert themselves more boldly on the temperance question. She believed that unlike Presbyterian or Protestant women involved in temperance crusades abroad, Catholic women had made no progress, nationally or internationally in the cause of temperance, because they hadn't had enough encouragement from 'the nations best and wisest men'. She pointed to the activity of the more militant Women's Christian Temperance movement in the United States and suggested that the Irish hierarchy needed to give women a clear mandate to work in the vanguard of the temperance movement in case, as happened the United States, they would resort to going around 'with a hatchet smashing saloons'.[122] Cullen himself welcomed female suffrage, stating, 'It is to be hoped that they will make better use of it than the men have done, certainly where drink is concerned.'[123]

At regular intervals during this period, Cullen referred to the drink issue in its class context. Many contemporary Jesuits tended to groom and educate a middle class in preparation for future leadership roles, but Cullen was more intent on highlighting miserable slum conditions and the amount of money being spent on drink that could have been used so productively if spent on physical and moral improvement. He continually contended that the majority of crime in Ireland was drink-induced and he decried the fact that there was no native industry in the country other than drink. In this context, he developed a curious fixation with Russia, maintaining that 'Irish Ireland can profitably study the magnificent example given her by Russia.' Romanticising the Russian peasantry, he maintained that after a war-time decree against the production of vodka, they had replaced £100 million a year which the vodka industry had created and had found employment for the 200,000 formerly employed by this state monopoly.[124] At home Cullen insisted that excessive drinking was undoing the work of the labour unions and that lowering consumption of alcohol would lower war-time food prices. He was emphatically pro-allies during the War and predictably placed victory in the context of to drink or not to drink: 'We pay £5 million a day to beat the Kaiser and for £1 million a week we license a power that plays the Kaiser's game by weakening England and keeps back the harvest of victory.'[125]

Cullen's economics may have been crude, but he was clearly motivated by the poverty which surrounded him, particularly the deprivation of children, which led him to continually quote from foreign reports on alcoholic parents retarding the development of their children. He plucked suitably dramatic and arresting figures from contemporary medical journals. Thus in October 1916 he could reveal that from a sample of 1,000 retarded children in Paris, a French sociologist, Bourneville, had found that 62 per cent had alcoholic parents, while in Germany 8 per cent of the children of moderate drinkers died prematurely, and 42 per cent of the children of drunkards suffered the same fate.[126] In his approach to the medical and social aspects of temperance, Cullen kept himself informed, and though at times he may have been selective in his quotations and examples, he did illustrate a desire to highlight the long-term generational consequences of excessive drinking, and in doing so, aside from his clear-cut role as a spiritual mentor, can be viewed as a modern and innovative campaigner in Irish social history. Much of his rhetoric, however, contained illusory references to a need to restore a supposed glorious past, and here Cullen used contemporary cultural yearnings. Thus he wanted to see the 'building up of the homes of Ireland by restoring to them their almost lost ideals of home-life, home happiness, home comfort, home refinement, home industries . . . as they have been in the remote and glorious past.'[127] He invoked similar logic with regard to the hunger for land during this period, regretting the fact that whilst the Irish rural populace were being urged to cultivate as much land as possible, millions of acres were being used for the production of drink. Inner city areas of Dublin were, he contended, also open to the threat of proselytism due to the neglect by drunken Catholic parents of their offspring. The housing of the working class was another pet concern of his, and the language used was emotive as well as economic. In 1921 he referred to men returning to dirty overcrowded tenements, devoid of nourishment and with 'shrill voiced children in constant conflict with a mother grown shrewish before her time.'[128]

While it is undoubtedly true that Cullen also deemed it necessary to instil the middle-class, which would soon be governing an independent southern state, with an appreciation of the value of spiritual measures of sobriety, there was often an undercurrent of resentment that the same middle class did not display an inclination towards redressing social grievances resulting from drink. In 1941, Owen Kelly, who as a student of the Jesuits had been heavily influenced by Cullen, recalled that Cullen 'deplored the fact that many young men, sons of self-made parents, were so spoiled by the latter's' prosperity that you could see them any afternoon 'walking in Grafton Street, smoking a little cigarette, carrying a cane and wearing a high-collar, killing time instead of doing an honest day's work as their fathers did before them.'[129] In his own *Temperance Catechism*, designed for schools and colleges, Cullen reminded those he had won over to temperance from the savings resulting from their total abstinence, 'to make competent provision for the future and let them never forget to help the poor.'[130]

As has been mentioned, the duration of the Great War, and the corresponding changes in the way drink consumption was debated, both in economic and social terms, was not lost on Cullen – or indeed, on the other main players in the Irish temperance movement. The war could be used by the temperance lobby to suit its own ends. Having Lloyd George as Prime Minister with his impeccable anti-drink credentials, in the best tradition of Welsh religious non-conformity, was an added bonus. The president of the Father Mathew Temperance Association, Fr Sylvester, was suitably dramatic, announcing in the 35th annual report that the question of temperance 'has been raised to the dignity of a great national and international question, which the first statesmen of Europe are endeavouring to solve. It required this disastrous and bloody war in Europe to bring home to cabinet minister and crowned heads the havoc that unbridled indulgence can work among a people.'[131] The issue of war-time curtailment of drink practices culminated in the large-scale debate which was engendered by prohibition – the 18th amendment to the United States constitution on January 16, 1919. ('After one year from the ratification of this article, the manufacture, sale or transport of intoxicating liquors within, the importation thereof into, or the exportation thereof from the United States and all territory subject to the jurisdiction thereof is hereby prohibited'.) Cullen's attitude to the subject of Prohibition was suitably disingenuous. While he agreed that it was extreme, and professed that Ireland was not ready for it, he wasted no time in praising what he naively or deliberately exaggerated as its wondrous effects elsewhere.

In the long term, prohibition did immeasurable damage to the International Temperance movement, as it associated formal abstention with compulsion and tended to equate pledges in the popular mind with fanaticism. However this was not in evidence at this stage. In 1917 Cullen reported with glee that Italy, Switzerland, Belgium, Holland and Denmark had all abolished the manufacture and sale of absinthe, while in Greenland, Iceland, the Faroe Islands and Romania, popular votes had been passed endorsing prohibition.[132] Likewise, he extolled the example of what he (wrongly) believed was a 'rather dry' Russia, where, despite the proliferation of illicit stills, 'dry Russia, with little bloodshed, brings about a wonderful revolution, one of the greatest events of the great World War.'[133] It was an issue which dominated his column in 1918, as he praised the dry states of America, where lack of alcohol was equated with industriousness and prosperity, and in Canada, with moral and economic virtuousness. Even as late as 1920, he wrote that prohibition was on trial 'and the movement advances'. Referring to the subsequent controversy he insisted that 'it is not, as some think, an emotional movement.'[134] Rather than directly recommending it for Ireland, Cullen preferred to quote others on its supposed working of miracles, quoting the editor of the *International Record*, George Haytor, as stating that it had been the result of an international recognition of the need to get the best out of life in the best possible way, and involved the 'awakening of the social consciousness in every sphere of human activity'. In relation to Ireland, Cullen admitted that prohibition 'does not seem at present to commend itself to the minds of the people or of those who hold the reins of power' and he preferred to press more strongly for the system of 'Local Option' which allowed, by popular vote, the rate payers of a given locality to decide on drink's availability.[135]

Cullen's refusal to endorse Prohibition in an Irish context was not only a recognition that it did not sit comfortably with mainstream Catholic teaching, but also showed an awareness of the hostility towards others who endorsed the idea. Fr Coffey of Maynooth, now president of the umbrella organisation the Catholic Total Abstinence Federation, had initially rejected the idea of the nationalisation of the drink trade in a public debate with a colleague of his, Fr Cleary, believing there were less expensive temperance experiments which would be better suited to Ireland. But in the same year, 1918, in a paper on the ethics of total prohibition, he rejected the view that it was merely 'a crazy American fad'. Whilst he admitted that he was not looking at the practicalities of legislating for it in Ireland, he believed its momentum could not be discarded, given that, at this stage, Prohibition laws were actually in force in each one of the five continents (in Africa, the prohibition of spirits had been adopted in the Belgian Congo in 1890). He admitted that Irish Catholics saw Prohibition as 'extreme, remote and unpractical', if not bigoted, but finished by writing 'of course there is anti-Catholic bigotry mixed up with it. But for this regrettable development Catholic abstention from the movement has given the opportunity'.[136] The heated reaction to this veiled endorsement of Prohibition for Catholic Ireland, however, may explain why Cullen remained less explicit in print, whatever his private views. He did not want the Pioneer Association to become embroiled in internal Church dissent, given that the movement he was directing was already a controversial subject within Catholicism. Many Catholics, both at an academic and popular level, resented the extremism of Prohibition, deriding a failure to distinguish between the use and abuse of alcohol. Attacking Coffey in the pages of the *Irish Ecclesiastical Record*, Fr J.M. Prendergast accused him of being disingenuous and abstract, believing that if Coffey's logic was extended, no limit could be set to the state's suppression of personal liberties. Reading between the lines it is also probable that Prendergast thought Coffey was being heretical:

> It is assumed that cold, detached, scientific accuracy, the *uberfange wissenschaftliche* view which the Germans of the higher criticism delighted in assuming as their own, is all on the side of the prohibitionists while the others are necessarily biased by inherited prejudices, personal liking for the winecup and a great unwillingness to see the question objectively . . . There is something radically wrong about any movement which makes it criminal to do outside the church door what the good Lord has commanded to be done within, as a supreme remembrance of him.'[137]

Temperance was also of relevance to those whose livelihood depended on the sale of drink. Cullen was cautious in this regard. Unlike his successors, he did not spasmodically attack the licensed vintners. Rather, he reserved his ire for the brewers. As a trade, the licensed vintners had a history of effective organisation and were powerful lobbyists and were understandably sensitive about attacks on the trade, particularly given the amount of attention focused on the abuse of complex licensing laws. In 1922, in a review of the previous eight years, they were self-congratulatory on the healthy and sound condition of the trade, and expressed the belief that 'during all the disasters which threatened us, we had the support and backing of all fair-minded persons, as instanced particularly in 1915, when the conscience of the entire country, even life-long temperance men, revolted against the now famous budget of that year.'[138] Mindful of their own business interests, the licensed vintners declared themselves squarely against drunkenness and asserted their willingness to stamp it out. Reacting to a Father Mathew Temperance Association resolution regarding the flouting of licensing laws, a recurrent feature of this era, they preferred to point the finger of blame at the operators of shebeens and bogus clubs, and licensed grocers who flouted laws by selling drink for consumption on the premises. The trade presented itself as being the object of attack and misrepresentation, particularly during the war years.

The licensed trade was not deprived of the ear of senior Church figures, and this was to be the case throughout the century. Church as well as government was quick to hear their views, given their status and economic importance. In 1916, Dr Harty, Archbishop of Cashel, was happy to receive a deputation from the vintners after certain temperance lobbyists had publicly called for a drastic reform of the licensing laws, but had declined to mention compensating publicans for licences which could become redundant. Accusing the temperance advocates of wanting all and giving nothing, they insisted that the abuser of drink was also their greatest enemy, but that the temperance lobby was being sweeping and excessive in its demands. Harty received them sympathetically, suggesting that the issue of compensation should be referred to in future temperance meetings. In reality, the publicans were in a strong position in rejecting extravagant temperance claims, given that Ireland was a small homogeneously Catholic country, where the majority of the sellers of drink were of the same religion and background as the drinkers, and indeed the abstainers. This was the card that the vintners played, and it explains why figures like Cullen, despite occasional lapses, were relatively slow to target them directly. There were to be further clashes in the future, particularly when it came to determining successive governments' attitudes to licensing laws. But for the present, in addressing the Archbishop, the publicans tugged at patriotic heart-strings:

> There are about 17,000 license holders in Ireland. More than 95 per cent of them are Catholics. We are almost to a man drawn from the farming classes, and at the time we were put to the business by our parents, it was really the only road open to us, with perhaps the unattractive alternative of emigration . . . There is very little between the interests of true temperance and the best interests of the legitimate licensed trader in Ireland.[139]

What exactly did these wider debates mean to those whom Cullen termed the ordinary foot soldiers of his Pioneer army? In reality, they were invited to settle on a much narrower agenda. Cullen invited centres to submit reports to the *Irish Catholic*, so that he could single out individual centres for praise and in some cases chastisement, and to provide him with general material for his column. A key insight into the working mechanics as defined by Cullen himself is provided by the first minute book of the Saint Francis Xavier male centre in Gardiner Street. Cullen, with his deep historical consciousness, and perhaps with an eye on his own place in Irish history, as well as having an eye for strict detail, routine and rules, urged all the Pioneer centres to keep minutes of their meetings. In 1912 he had appointed a working council consisting of seven laymen, presided over by Thomas McCabe and Thomas Woods. The early minutes of this council, under the spiritual direction of Cullen, reveal not only an emphasis on prayer, but also the need to be utterly vigilant in screening potential members, and the need to extend the organisation to schools 'especially the Christian Brothers' schools'. After a lengthy discussion on procedural matters, it was also decided in April 1912 'that in the case of persons who had recently taken intoxicating liquors, the badge should not be given until after a preliminary trial period of three months, such period to be subsequently taken into account as a portion of the two years probation'.[140] In this light, the minutes give an insight into the difference between the populist nationalist rhetoric used by Cullen and others in addressing public meetings and writing propaganda, and the administrative deliberations which were centred around the traits of caution and strictness. Cullen had also devised a scheme where each centre was required to complete a 'query sheet', with details of exact membership and the activities of their centre and return it to Dublin. In 1913 he also insisted that the registers of each centre should be inspected periodically to ensure that the rules were being properly kept. He also placed himself in the role of mediator of disputes. A row in the Kingstown working council was discussed at a meeting in October 1913, and Cullen sought to quell the disturbance personally, although the minutes do not make it clear what the row was about. On this occasion, the row culminated with threats of legal action, though Cullen warned that if legal action was taken in the name of the Pioneer Association the centre's diploma of affiliation would be withdrawn. At the same meeting, efforts to appeal to the patriotism of the Pioneers were not successful:

> A letter was considered from the Manchester Martyrs Celebration Committee [most likely a front for the Irish Republican Brotherhood] in which the Society was invited to take part in the demonstration on Sunday 23 November and the secretary was directed to reply that as the members of the Pioneer Association were not attached to any particular church it would be impossible to secure their attendance as an organisation.[141]

On a more mundane level, the council in Gardiner Street also dealt with the practicalities of fashion-conscious Pioneers who were made aware that 'in cases where a member requests a second pioneer stud for use in his Sunday coat, the council will allow same, it to be marked on register.'[142]

The minutes are riddled with the personality of Cullen, and the agenda was very much his own. Absolute strictness about the ban on alcohol was the order of the day, and defaulters were unceremoniously dismissed. Some of the entries are redolent of judgements delivered in district courts. Cullen was capable, it seems, of provoking a strong ethos of vigilance on the part of council members. Many defaulters reported themselves, though it is fair to suggest there was pressure at work as well as their own consciences, the fear of God, and the terror that they may have been spotted drinking by other Pioneers. Most of those who defaulted seem to have done so in times of illness, which was indicative of the widespread use of alcohol for medicinal purposes, even amongst abstainers, as well as the deceptive use of illness as an excuse for clandestine imbibing, which would explain Cullen's consequent preoccupation with dispelling the myth of its medicinal worth. A typical entry for 1919 was as follows:

> Defaulter, Mr James Gibbons, reported himself as having violated the rules by drinking hot punch when sick, not ordered by a doctor . . . returned his emblem and was duly entered: first offence.

In the same month another entry read:

> A reply from Mr Fred Bowass re: being a defaulter was considered unsatisfactory, the secretary being directed to write to him again, requesting him to answer yes, or no, to the charge preferred against him.[143]

From Cullen's perspective, it was important to have accurate figures of membership, both to satisfy his claim that he was presiding over a nation-wide movement and to bolster propaganda. On one level the figures were astonishing and demonstrate that there was a widespread belief in the value of abstention from drink for spiritual reasons. At the close of 1914 Cullen estimated the membership at 280,000. This was an estimated figure, but with the development of administration, including the system of returning query sheets, he was able to detail exact membership. By the close of 1918 he revealed that there were 256,506 registered Pioneers in Ireland (with 11,674 of those in Dublin), accounting for 284 affiliated centres.[144] The following year the number of affiliated centres had risen to 295, with an overall membership of 277,554.[145] By the end of 1920 the figure had increased to 280,554.[146] In numerical terms it was a triumph for Cullen. As regards expansion, an interesting feature of his Pioneer work at this juncture was his vision for Pioneer organisation in other countries, no doubt inspired to a large extent by his previous missionary work abroad, where he had witnessed a multitude of social problems which he attributed directly to excessive drinking. Having used his Jesuit connections abroad, he was able to report in 1918 that there were Pioneer centres operating in England, Scotland, The United States, Australia, South Africa and Switzerland, encompassing a small combined membership of just under 2,000.[147] Ultimately, Pioneer endeavours abroad were not successful at this time for reasons which will be discussed below. The main problem was the difficulty of supervision and lack of manpower. Cullen always emphasised the need for absolute uniformity in the administration of all Pioneer centres, at home and abroad. An indication of the difficulties involved in this had appeared as early as 1912, when it was recorded in the minute book of the SFX council that 'the advisability of having a separate depot and governing council for America was also considered, but the council deferred coming to a definite decision.'[148]

Despite the impressive membership figures, Cullen and his successors faced an uphill battle. Ireland was by no means steadily transforming into a sober nation. The country was literally overflowing with pubs, and Cullen estimated in 1918 that there were 16,678 pubs in operation.[149] He continually referred to the Pioneers in the context of the future, particularly in the few years preceding his death. On one level his self-defined legacy was simple. He wanted none of the Pioneer rules to be changed. He reiterated constantly that he wanted a continuance of the absolute strictness, believing the Association could only flourish using his methods. He did not believe he was fanatical, and in this he was not alone. In 1913, in the *Irish Ecclesiastical Record*, an article on alcoholism had appeared, written by Fr W.J. Mulcahy. His refutation of the charge of fanaticism on the part of those dedicated to sobering Ireland mirrored Cullen's own view:

> It is a cheap device to brand the temperance movement as fanatical. Now, I deny that it has a single feature of fanaticism in it, for it is based upon physiological principle, chemical relation, the welfare of society, the laws of self-preservation, the claims of suffering humanity and on all that is noble in patriotism, generous in philanthropy and pure and good in Christianity.[150]

Nevertheless, in retrospect, it is perfectly accurate to describe Cullen as single-minded to the point of fanatical in his attitude to drink. In this he was a product of his environment. He drank wine until the age of thirty-four, but when he converted to abstinence he did so with an unique passion and commitment. Some of his diatribes against those given to excessive consumption seem in retrospect not only fanatical but uncharitable. His method involved the use of hyperbolic semantics, with the intention of putting the fear of God into those who had sinned through intemperance.

But Cullen had a strong social conscience and an empathy with the working classes and showed more awareness of social problems than many of his contemporary clerics and his middle-class successors. In his derision of the drunkard, he was consistent, having made it clear at the outset that the Pioneer Association was not interested in the reclamation of drunkards. On a personal level, Cullen's inner spirituality was towering – so much so that Lambert McKenna in his weighty biography devoted half its contents to his spiritual life.[151] It was this spirituality which Cullen also wanted to direct in a practical and organisational way. In a letter to his niece in 1911 he insisted that the Pioneer movement could only work if it was 'properly and passionately backed'.[152] His belligerent writing style was perhaps designed to compensate for the fact that, as the Bishop of Ferns, Dr James Staunton, recalled on the centenary of his birth, he had a 'poor and monotonous voice'.[153] Though often suffering ill health he was always anxious to work and to see others improve their lot spiritually, intellectually, morally and materially. Again, during the centenary of his birth, an acquaintance wrote to the Association recalling that Cullen 'embraced everything, doing everything that nobody else did, started every kind of thing – and made them last'. She recalled that when convalescing after an illness in a London hospital in 1916, Cullen was dissatisfied at seeing the patients, many of them wounded soldiers, lying idle. He organised the delivery of the scripts of a few simple plays, trained the soldiers and got them to stage the play, whilst simultaneously ordering knitting needles, crochet needles and thread and 'got the girls to work'.[154]

Reference has been made to the extent to which Cullen wanted the Pioneer Association to plough an individual temperance furrow. In 1920 he explained why, answering the charge that the Pioneers were not prepared to use their numbers to combine with other, more secular, temperance advocates:

> Our answer has been and must for a time continue to be that the Pioneer movement has struck out its own hitherto untried plan, which needs time for fuller development before it is matured to give assistance to other similar organisations. Until a large army of temperance workers and recruits is mobilised, our present Pioneer work would run the risk of endangering our special methods and, while getting absorbed into a larger temperance army, lose its power together with its identity.[155]

Despite this, Cullen had occasionally lent his name to more general welfare concerns, even if this involved a politicisation which was supposedly forbidden to the Pioneers as a group. Thus in June 1919 he signed a resolution drawn up by the Catholic Total Abstinence Federation, earnestly appealing that the underground Dáil Éireann tackle the drink problem hoping that 'The paralysis of British rule in Ireland does not allow Ireland's worst domestic enemy, the liquor traffic, to tighten its stranglehold.'[156] Cullen died on December 6, 1921, and was said to have been elated, on the verge of death, to hear of the signing of the Anglo-Irish Treaty. It was the job of his successor, Fr

Joseph Flinn SJ, to guide the Pioneers in the new independent state. Flinn had absolutely no intention of changing the methods.

NOTES

1   PAA, Cullen to Mr Rosney, 15 November, 1898
2   ibid. to Flinn, 20 November, 1914
3   PAA, Cullen's Introduction in SFX Minute Book
4   PAA, Handwritten profile of Anne Egan
5   ibid. Lizzie Power
6   ibid. Mrs Mary Bury and Sr. Columba to Fr Mulligan, 28 September, 1961
7   ibid. Mrs A. M. Sullivan, and Cullen 's address to Cork rally, 1911
8   John Dunne, *The Pioneers*. Lambert McKenna's work did not even see fit to name them.
9   J. Halpin, *The Father Mathew Reader on Health and Hygiene* (Dublin 1907)
10 P.J. Gannon, *Fr James Cullen* (Dublin 1940)
11 PAA, Cullen's introduction to SFX Minute Book
12 ibid.
13 ibid.
14 ibid.
15 James Cullen, *Temperance Catechism* (Dublin 1892)
16 There is no mention of temperance in Walsh's correspondence in the Dublin Diocesan Archives.
17 PAA, Cullen's Introduction in SFX Minute Book
18 PAA, Pioneer Association explanatory leaflet [c. 1905]
19 ibid.
20 PAA, Rules of St Brigid's Total Abstinence Sodality for women (Dundalk 1907)
21 ibid. Pioneer Association explanatory leaflet [c. 1908]
22 ibid.
23 ibid.
24 PAA, James Cullen's address to AGM, November 20, 1904
25 ibid. Minute Book of yearly pledge branch, July 7, 1913
26 ibid. Various extracts
27 McKenna, Fr James Cullen, p. 32
28 PAA, Hand-written manuscript, penned. in the last year of Cullen's life
29 ibid.
30 PAA, Mansion House address, 1903, and explanatory leaflet, 1905
31 · PAA, Cullen's Introduction in SFX Minute Book
32 PAA, Cullen's address at the Rotunda, 1904
33 William Mandle, *The GAA and Irish Nationalist Politics 1884–1924* (London 1987)
34 ibid.
35 Richard Stivers, *A Hair of the Dog: Irish drinking and American stereotype* (New York 1976) p. 149
36 Kevin Kearns, *Dublin Tenement Life: An oral history* (Dublin 1994)
37 L. Paul-Dubois, *Contemporary Ireland* (London 1908)
38 McKenna, *Cullen*, p. 97 and p. 327
39 ibid. p. 326
40 Andrew Sheppard, 'The Irish Parliamentary Party, the Irish Licensed. Trade and the politics of the 1909 budget' (unpublished. MA thesis, UCD,1983) p. 19
41 ibid.
42 ibid.
43 Madeleine Humphreys, 'Jansenists in high places: A study of the relationship between the liquor trade and manufacturing industry and the Cumann na nGaedheal government 1922–32' (unpublished MA thesis, UCD 1991) p. 178
44 Cullen, Foreword to *Catechism* 1892
45 Sean O'Casey, *Juno and the Paycock* in *Three Plays* (Dublin 1980)

46 Irish Messenger series, *Temperance Handbook*, n.d.
47 J.C. MacErlain , *Whither goest thou? Or was Fr Mathew right ?* (Dublin 1910)
48 Lambert McKenna: 'Theological aspects of the pledge' *IER*, 1907
49 ibid.
50 IER, Correspondence concerning *abuse at wakes*,1917
51 PAA, File on centenary of Cullen's birth, 1941
52 Andrew Reed, *The Temperance Problem and the Liquor Licensing Laws of Ireland* (Dublin 1906)
53 ibid.
54 ibid.
55 B.R. Balfour, *The Irish Licensing Question* (Dublin 1902)
56 Reed, *Temperance problem*, letters to conference
57 ibid.
58 Cullen, *Temperance Catechism*, 1892
59 William Lawson, 'Public house and licensing reform' in *JSSISI*, vol. 11, 1902
60 Sheppard, *Irish Parliamentary Party*
61 PAA, Cullen's Introduction in SFX Minute Book
62 ibid.
63 PAA, *Rules of St. Joseph's Temperance Hall*, Longford, n.d. [c.1900]
64 Capuchin Archives, B 10/7 (2) Bishop Sheehan to Fr Provincial December 10, 1905
65 ibid. Memo in response to increased. drinking, October 1901
66 ibid. Booklet outlining object, means and constitution of Fr Mathew Association
67 ibid.
68 CA, *Temperance Rallying Songs*, published. by the Fr Mathew Record Office, Church Street [c.1905]
69 ibid. Box B 10 (7) 9 'Fr Mathew Association and the Bishops' Commission to the Capuchins, 1906'
70 ibid.
71 ibid. Fr Paul to Fr General, February 28, 1907
72 ibid. Fr Thomas, 'The intemperance sermon'
73 ibid. Reports, Ballyforan, 1906
74 ibid. Athleaque, n.d.
75 ibid. Achill, November, 1906
76 ibid. Ballygat, n/d
77 ibid. Box B10 (7)
78 Report from Fr Thomas to General Curia, May 7, 1912
79 ibid.
80 ibid. Ballygat, December 1906
81 ibid. B 10 (7) 9. Fr Mathew Association and the Bishops' Commission, by Fr Paul, 1906
82 Gannon, *Cullen*, p. 17
83 ibid.
84 Written by 'Anti intemperance', IER 1901
85 Father Mathew Union, Published. Annual Reports, 1902
86 ibid. Sligo, 1907
87 ibid. Armagh, 1908
88 ibid. 1909–10
89 ibid.
90 ibid.
91 ibid. 1910–11
92 ibid. 1911–12
93 ibid. 1914–15
94 ibid.
95 ibid. 1916–17
96 ibid. 1917–18
97 ibid. 1919–20
98 ibid. 1911–12.
99 PAA, Cullen's Introduction in SFX minute Book.
100 FMU, Annual Report, 1917–18

101 ibid.
102 McKenna, *Fr James Cullen*, p. 96
103 ibid. p. 388
104 *Official Record of National Total Abstinence Congress*, Dublin 1914
105 McKenna, *Fr James Cullen*, p. 19
106 ibid. p. 32
107 ibid. April 6, 1912
108 ibid. April 20, 1912.
109 ibid. June 8, 1912
110 ibid. December 14, 1912
111 ibid. January 11, 1913
112 G.P. Williams and G.T. Blake, *Drink in Great Britain* (London 1980), p. 31
113 PC IC, September 6, 1913, November 22, 1913, December 13, 1913
114 ibid. December 21, 1912.
115 ibid. October 31, 1914
116 ibid. September 12, 1914
117 W.H. Adair, *Temperance Lessons for the Schools* (Dublin 1920 Edition)
118 PAA, Early promoter's card, n.d.
119 Sisters of Charity Archives, Annals of St. Helen's convent in Blarney, 1911–15.
120 PAA, Postcard to Sr Stanislaus, December, 1908
121 PAA, Extract from *Model Housekeeping* 1941
122 Catherine Mahon, *Women and Total Abstinence* (Dublin 1920)
123 PCIC, November 29, 1919
124 ibid. February 5, 1916
125 ibid. September 16, 1916
126 ibid. October 14, 1916 and October 21, 1916
127 ibid. February 17, 1917
128 ibid. January 15, 1921
129 PAA, Owen Kelly to Flinn, c. 1941
130 James Cullen, *Temperance Catechism*, (7th edn 1925)
131 CA, 35th annual Report of Fr Mathew Association
132 PC IC, January 13, 1917
133 ibid. October 6, 1917
134 ibid. October 16, 1920
135 ibid. July 2, 1921 and September 3, 1921
136 Peter Coffey, 'The Ethics of Total Prohibition', *IER* 1918
137 Donal Dineen, 'National Prohibition and Local Option', *IER* 1919
138 Licensed Vintners Association Archives, LVA Annual Reports, 1922–38
139 ibid. 1916
140 PAA, SFX minute book, January 17, 1912
141 ibid. November 24, 1913
142 ibid. April 30, 1914
143 ibid. February 24, 1919
144 PC IC, December 28, 1918
145 ibid. November 29, 1919
146 ibid. January 22, 1921
147 ibid. December 28, 1918
148 ibid. 11 July, 1912
149 ibid. February 2, 1918
150 Fr W.J. Mulcahy, '*Alcoholism*', *IER*, 1913
151 McKenna, *Fr James Cullen*
152 PAA, Cullen to Sr Stanislaus January 26, 1911
153 ibid. Theatre Royal Centenary Address, 1941.
154 PAA, Centenary File, Mrs Leary to Flinn, September 18, 1941
155 PC IC, March 6, 1920
156 FMU, 20th Annual Report, 1919–20

CHAPTER THREE

An Independent Irish
Catholic Crusade

It is merely absurd that a country struggling desperately to find its feet should attempt to maintain in proportion to its population twice as many licensed houses as England and three times as many as Scotland. The statistics for individual towns are still more startling. In Charlestown and Ballaghaderreen every third house is licensed to sell liquor; Ballyhaunis, with a total population of a thousand, has a drink shop for every twenty of its inhabitants and Strokestown and Mohill run it close with one for every twenty-six . . . how many of these towns can boast a bookshop, a gymnasium, a public swimming bath or a village hall? Throughout the greater part of a rural Ireland such things are still looked on as ridiculous luxuries, and the mark of social progress is demonstrated by the opening of two public houses where one would normally suffice . . .

George Russell (AE), 1925

Let your resolution be like wrought iron. Close the door forever on drink. Lock and double-lock the door and fling away the key. You will be astonished at the blessings that will troop after you.

Irish Messenger of the Sacred Heart, 1926

The death of Fr James Cullen and the passing of the Pioneer leadership mantle to Fr Joseph Flinn, coincided with the signing of the Anglo-Irish Treaty, and an independent twenty-six-county state. Given Cullen's patriotism and hope that a domestic parliament would be not only sympathetic to temperance ideals, but be demonstrative in pursuing the abstainers' agenda, it was understandable that Flinn felt obliged to aggressively carry the crusade into a new era. The 1920s was characterised by an increase in activity and propaganda as the Pioneer leadership sought to equate southern Irish sobriety with independent national ideals. It was an ambitious agenda, and despite the frequent reiteration that the Association was primarily a religious movement, it involved the Jesuits adopting a decidedly political stance when it came to drink as a national issue of legislative concern. It also involved open confrontation with the licensed vintners, viewed as, though not admitted as, the Pioneers' natural enemies in the lobbying corridors. In the context of the 1920s it was seen as quite legitimate to attempt to wed the religious ideals of the Pioneers to the broader political environment. Underlining the blurring of these aims was a fundamental conservatism, reflected in Flinn's belief that the only way the Association could flourish was by remaining steadfastly loyal to Cullen's original aims and rules. Flinn was central director of the Association until 1943. He could be scathing, politically precocious and downright insulting in the pursuit of his agenda as well as being deeply pious and spiritual. It is crucial to emphasise that this was perfectly normal given the position he held in 1920's Ireland. He was certainly not alone in his pursuit of a country that was sober and intensely Catholic.

There was a broad consensus in the early years of independence that Ireland as a country was drinking excessively and beyond its resources. It was a view held by many church leaders, politicians, cultural revivalists and those with a concern for law and order. It was undoubtedly the case that the period of the Troubles (1918–23) had exacerbated the drink problem, aligned with a general breakdown in law and order, and consequently, it was believed, a decline in the moral climate. In 1921 a local IRA unit in Mayo had resorted to placing a penny tax on stout sold in local pubs. A Dáil Éireann local government official had rightly questioned the legality of this move, but had welcomed it as contributing to a climate of temperance.[1] This was naive wishful thinking – it is much more likely that the IRA was taking blatant monetary advantage by taxing the most popular form of entertainment in Ireland. Likewise there were frequent reports of wide-scale abuse of licensing legislation by both publicans and customers. It was uncertain who exactly had the authority to enforce licensing laws, given the confused contemporary political climate and the creation of the new Civic Guards in 1922 to replace the Irish Republican Police and the Dublin Metropolitan Police.[2]

In applying a Pioneer agenda for the new Free State, Flinn encountered many of the same barriers as Cullen. There was still a hostility within certain sections of Irish Catholicism concerning temperance and its manifestations, which often made Flinn defensive and paranoid that Pioneer rules were not always being adhered to internally, or were being undermined externally. The decision by the Cumann na nGaedheal administration to tackle the Irish drink question legislatively, through Intoxicating Liquor Commissions and Licensing Acts in 1924 and 1927, highlighted differences in the approaches of various temperance groups, some of which had a broader social and political brief than the Sacred-Heart-based Pioneers. It also brought the temperance lobby into conflict with politicians who would intermittently admonish their extremism, resenting what they classed as a self-righteousness, a refusal to deal with specifics and practicalities, immune as they were from the realities of legislating. Likewise it led to a bitterness between themselves and the licensed vintners with a flurry of caustic exchanges.

Nonetheless, Flinn was in many ways extraordinarily successful. He never departed from the language and ideals articulated by Cullen, and effectively tapped into the increasing religious and cultural homogeneity of the country to expand Pioneer membership by emphasising the spiritual gains to be garnered from abstention. He also succeeded, through annual gatherings at both adult and juvenile level, and through commemorating Pioneer anniversaries, in mobilising Pioneers *en masse*, cleverly manipulating a certain Irish Catholic penchant for outward mass celebration (or at times triumphalism). He also succeeded in securing powerful allies for his cause, particularly those with a shared interest in an improvement in the moral and religious tone of the new state, for example, the enthusiastic endorsement of the Pioneers by Eoin O'Duffy, the new Chief Commissioner of the Civic Guards (later the Gárda Síochana). Flinn was remarkably active and 'hands-on' in his approach to the administration of the Pioneers, and this was compliemented by a rigorous strictness. Alongside this, he sought to develop the social side of the Pioneer movement, by encouraging musicals, entertainments and excursions, though again, under the strictest supervision. The writer John Dunne, in commemorating eighty years of the Association was later to rightly sum up Flinn's attitude as one of 'uncompromising strictness'.[3] He continually used the Pioneer column in the *Irish Catholic* to enunciate his Pioneer philosophy. Immediately after the founder's death, Flinn pinned his colours firmly to Cullen's mast:

> But what of the future? The future will be as the past has been. The master is gone, his pen is still, his tongue silent, but his work lives and please God shall live . . . In no uncertain terms he declared the lines on which the Pioneer Association was to be carried on – the same lines, the same rules, the same spirit with which he had worked and with which he had triumphed. That is the master's wish. His wish is law.[4]

With regard to membership, the figures seem to reveal a slowing down in the immediate post-independence period. The Sisters of Charity had estimated that between 1902 and 1925 they had sold 617,750 Pioneer pins. The trends for individual years were more interesting – in 1920, 50,000 pins; 1921, 29,000, 1922, 26,000, 1923, 31,000 and 1925, 25,000. They had finished their hastily scrawled memorandum by estimating that, in the light of these figures 'There must be at least 300,000 Pioneers.'[5] Though it is impossible to be exact, it is likely that this was an inflated figure. In 1925 Flinn, perhaps eschewing the vigilance of Cullen in this regard, revealed that he did not have exact membership figures, but that he was quite satisfied that membership was approaching 300,000.[6] This may have been slightly duplicitous on his part, but the probable membership was slightly in excess of 250,000.

There were certain aspects of the temperance question which exercised Flinn on a regular basis. He was a regular participant at the meetings of the Father Mathew Union, which continued to pursue its goal of priest-sponsored community sobriety. In an address to them in 1922 his focus was primarily religious, proffering the view that temperance teaching in schools could not be confined to scientific, medical, social, political or economic factors. He explained that the Pioneers 'had no time for mere philanthropy', but were engaged 'in a battle against man's passions', and that religion, based as it was on foundations that did not change or depend on the changing world of scientists, was the most solid base from which to build temperance. He summed up the Pioneer philosophy in its purest form: 'To urge that the supernatural must dominate our whole efforts, that we as priests must see intemperance primarily as a sin, that as a spiritual evil it must be fought by spiritual methods and that our motives must be predominantly supernatural'.[7]

This narrow interpretation was not necessarily shared by the other members of the Union, who still preferred to focus on the issue in all its manifold forms – this could involve the decrying of the legislature for failing to deliver temperance legislation; the association of the evil drink with a foreign-imported dance craze, or the fact that, as Fr Stokes of Dundalk claimed, in extolling the virtues of prohibition and playing the racial card, the Irish relationship with alcohol was different to other countries. While Irish women who drank were 'the exception', and compared favourably with the promiscuous, slovenly, ill-kempt drunken wives of English working-men, and the tippling society belles, with Irish men it was a different case:

> The Irishman suffers from the defects of his qualities . . . the creeping whining Saxon under the influence of alcohol draws like a snail within his shell: the habitual canniness of the dour and stolid Scotchman never deserts him. Only the Irishman unfolds himself and consequently makes a fool of himself for which he must pay in some form or another.[8]

At the same meeting, however, what vexed Flinn more was the Irish Catholic's ambiguous relationship with temperance, when he referred to the deliberate turning of blind eyes and the active concealment of the drink problem. It annoyed him that younger priests were not as staunch with regard to temperance as they had been in the previous fifteen years, and 'what troubled him most was the occasional experience of a Pioneer centre run by the laity in a parish with a total abstaining priest, or even two, who never gave it a word of encouragement or recognition.'[9] This was to be a recurrent irritation for Flinn, and under-lined the importance of distinguishing between those who didn't drink and those who were abstaining Pioneers. In the environment of the 1920s and 1930s, Flinn saw it as a ludicrous loss of opportunity as well as lazy and selfish that there was a constituency in existence who did not drink but would not actually promote the Sacred Heart devotion.

Flinn preferred to let others use Pioneer platforms to express views held by himself, feeling it was more convenient and diplomatic if he did not express them personally. Thus at the 1922 AGM in the Theatre Royal, Dublin, the chief address was made by Canon Lyons of Ardee, who insisted that 'the fatal defect in all non-Catholic temperance movements is that they are cold and soulless. They operate from fear chiefly.'[10] Interestingly, in the same address Lyons made reference to the need for Pioneers to be politically active, to tackle the conspiracy of silence with regard to the abuse of intoxicants, and in particular, he urged women who were 'being dragged from the sanctity of their home' into the turmoil of political life to 'strike at their age-long enemy "John Barleycorn" if they must come out to vote'. Again, perhaps with a measure of cunning, as the central director of an avowedly non-political movement, Flinn was quite content to use the services of others in exhorting Pioneers to relate their spiritual activities to direct political action. Perhaps there was a recognition by Flinn that in the moral climate of Ireland in the 1920s, and more specifically the drink climate, and the practical need to counteract it, a supernatural philos-ophy would not quite suffice – but it was better if this tacit acknowl-edgement came from somebody else. Thus Lyons asserted:

> In this very grave crisis every Pioneer is bound to make his power felt as a political factor, to influence law-making and law-keeping in favour of temperance. Up till recently at all events, we Irish were credited with political instinct and with a knowledge of how to make the most of a vote. For the moment the vote has fallen on evil days.[11]

The primary concern was a reformation of the licensing laws, in particular, a reduction in the number of licences as well as control of opening hours. Reform in these areas inevitably invited further questions such as compensation for lost licences and the position of the *bona fide* traveller. Other dilemmas included whether prosecutions for trivial offences in relation to licensing laws be should be left to the discretion of individual judges and the consequent reaction of publicans. Thus, the concerns of the government, and in particular of Kevin O'Higgins, Minister for Home Affairs (later Justice), who was to initiate reform, were numerous. Regarding its outlook in 1922, the Licensed Vintners Association insisted that all that was necessary was an enforcement of old laws with 'possibly some slight modification regarding the opening hours'.[12] They were acutely conscious of two developments. First, the temperance deputation to the government earlier in the year, which had focused on the need for executive measures during the transition from foreign to domestic rule to deal with abuses regarding the non-observance of closing hours, illicit distilling and the granting of occasional licences. Second, they were concerned at a resolution proposed by Sean MacEntee TD early in 1922 regarding the setting up of a Commission of Inquiry, composed of representatives of the Dáil, the vintners and temperance organisations. In the subsequent election of June 1922, however, three of the seven Dáil representatives had failed to retain their seats and since then no action had been taken by the Dáil. It was doubtless more preoccupied with national security than with national drunkenness. Nevertheless, the Vintners Association were on the defensive, insisting that during the troubled period the real problem was with bogus clubs and shebeens, an accusation which was to be repeated throughout the decade: 'We consider it is the best tribute to those engaged in a difficult business that so very few abuses have been apparent . . . As citizens and large ratepayers it has always been the aim of the Trade to guard against drunkenness or disorder.'[13]

It is clear from Department of Justice files that the government, under increasing pressure to act, took the issues seriously. In a 1923 memorandum it was stated quite bluntly that licensing law reform and its attendant challenges was 'practically the biggest and most urgent social problem that there is before the government, but by reason of the far-reaching question of policy which it involves, it cannot be dealt with successfully or thoroughly until an Irish committee or commission sifts it to the bottom.'[14] The department was not alone in expressing this view. The *Irish Times* insisted that logical, systematic and scientific reform was needed, and that the government should 'think out its problems beforehand and build the social structure of the Free State, from the first milestone, like a Roman road.'[15] The government was already examining the idea of reducing the number of licensed premises through compensating publicans, in the light of figures which revealed that in England and Wales there were 86,722 licensed premises (a ratio of 1 for every 415 of the population), in Scotland 56,841 (1: 695), and in Ireland 16,396 (1: 263). In the same memorandum on licensing reform the Civic Guard commissioner, Eoin O'Duffy, expressed his preference for the abolition of *bona fide* trading, the regional uniformity of opening hours, and a stricter control of private licensed clubs. With regard to illicit trading, he felt 'this is the universal enemy'.[16] Most district judges and state solicitors shared his view that the bona fide trade should be abolished, while in his personal file on licensing questions, the secretary of the Justice Department, O'Cinnéide, was particularly concerned about the illicit distillation of poteen, which was causing distress to the more remote western districts with the result, he was informed, that both children and adults were 'dead drunk.'[17]

From the government's perspective, negotiating a middle path through the licensing maze was hazardous. A proposed shortening in the opening hours from 9.0 a.m. to 10.0 p.m. would be considered too short from the point of view of the rural publicans, and too long to satisfy the temperance advocates. There was also the need to be practical, for, as O'Higgins pointed out, 'in social legislation the one thing you have to keep before you is the possibility of effective enforcement'.[18] In this context, it was believed that a complete uniformity of opening hours was impractical – for example with regard to theatres it was noted that 'if the bars were closed at 10 o'clock there would likely be a stampede at about 9.45 which would seriously disturb both the performers and the members of the audiences who remained in their seats', and would lead to the audience 'swilling themselves in the corridors and lavatories.'[19] The Department of Justice proffered the view that the bona fide travellers had continually abused their position, and that it was accepted that any restrictive legislation would arouse the ire of the licensed trade ('They are now vested and not to be disturbed.'). Of one thing the Department was certain, that with new legislation and the imposition of stricter penalties for breaches of codes 'the Police will have a lively time for a period to come.'[20] This was later to be reflected in acrimonious correspondence to the Justice Department from irate hotel owners in Cork, who insisted that hoteliers on the south side of the city were obliged to keep their doors shut on a Sunday while hoteliers on the north side kept their doors open all day – the Chief Superintendent however, responded unsympathetically by insisting that hotel owners wanted it both ways 'in as much as they wish to keep their doors open and at the same time to be immune from police supervision.'[21]

An important factor in the spear-heading of legislation was the determination of Kevin O'Higgins to effect change and his persistence in spite of opposition. In 1923 he stated: 'We need a genuine licensing code, not a bewildering maze of statutes and decisions, which, while creating offences also provided ingenious means of escape for unscrupulous people, and for people otherwise honest but who were driven to lie and worse in the struggle for existence.'[22]

This was a balanced and fair summation in the climate of the 1920s. It perhaps belies the simplicity of the interpretation which views licensing legislation during these years solely in terms of enshrining Catholic morals legislatively. While the Department of Justice was determined that they would place National interests above the interests of the licensed trade, they equally felt that Catholic temperance societies could display pettiness, lack of cohesion and a dearth of evidence to back up some of their more fantastical claims. The Department's personnel had a tendency to refer to 'what would be regarded as fair by ordinary citizens'[23] and this frequently was a compromise between the conflicting demands of the licensed trade and the temperance reformers.

In reality, as historian Madeleine Humphreys has skillfully demonstrated in her thesis, the Cumann na nGaedheal administration was more than capable of tackling the licensed trade as an interest group. While the revenue was of paramount importance, there was still a determination to regularise the trade, despite the fact that the 15,339 recorded convictions for drunkenness in 1914 had been reduced to 6,862 by 1925.[24] The 1924 Licensing Act, particularly the sections dealing with compulsory endorsement of licences after conviction for an offence, and the position of district justices in their application of this law (they had been far too lenient), 'clearly symbolises O'Higgins' acute anxiety that the judiciary should understand its subservience to the state while the publicans would know their 'privileged' monopoly demanded exceptional responsibility', and that publicans could no longer stave off legislation on 'nationalist' grounds as had been the case at the time of Lloyd George's crusade earlier in the century.[25] Arguments continued over questions of regional uniformity, bona fide, a proposed break in trading between the hours of 3.0 and 5.0 p.m., and the discretion of judges. Despite O'Higgins' concessions to the trade the government did succeed in ensuring a cut in the trading hours. What was even more interesting in the context of a new state struggling to find its feet, were the attempts to define excessive drinking. The *Irish Truth* magazine proclaimed itself in favour of temperance (as did most publicans), but also in favour of 'natural justice' for the liquor trade, and expressed an abhorrence of prohibition, which it insisted was 'a quack remedy which has been proved to have as many obnoxious reactions as the evils which it professes to cure.'[26] It continually lambasted the expense of drink in Ireland, excise duties on spirits and attempts to smother distillers, quoting figures which revealed that while lavish benefits were being given to those involved in the production of sugar beet, the excise on a proof gallon of whiskey had been increased from thirty shillings in 1918 to seventy two shillings in 1920. Temperance advocates provoked its vitriol. Some months later it proclaimed: 'Temperance is a virtue not beyond the reach of any man. But there are none more intemperate in temper, in speech, in unreason and uncharitableness than those who denounce the temperate drinker as an enemy to society'.[27] Those who sought compromise between the two extremes, however, attempted a more balanced, if vague definition. Kevin O'Higgins, speaking in the Dáil in defence of licensing reform, contended that he was not hostile to the licensed trade, or indulging prohibitionists masquerading as temperance reformers. He attempted to answer the question of whether Ireland was becoming more sober:

> That of course is a question of angles. What is excessive drinking? I do not take it that excessive drinking means that you fall over a man every five yards on your way home. If we are drinking beyond our resources there is excessive drinking. £17.5 million was spent across the counter on drink in the financial year 1925–6. Is that excessive drinking? Some people would say no. Some people would say very differently. At any rate I object to the criterion that drunkenness and drunkenness alone is to be the test of whether or not there is excessive drinking.[28]

The Licensed Vintners' Association, in bemoaning what it perceived as punitive legislation, was tetchy and defensive, and frequently looked for its own targets, particularly chemists who sold spirits, illicit distillers and private clubs which it characterised as 'gigantic drinking shops with the difference that they had no restrictions or limitations of any sort or kind'. It also criticised excessive duties on spirits, and its chairman in 1925 expressed the view that the government was 'travelling too fast on a subject that the old regime avoided as long as possible'.[29] In February 1925 the Vintners' Association called an all-Ireland meeting in the Mansion House in Dublin to protest at its lack of representation on the new Intoxicating Liquor Commission, set up by the government to propose feasible changes in the licensing laws. Con Kennedy, the chairman of the LVA was elected to the Senate that year as was a previous chairman, Fanning. This was seen as an illustration of the Association's political muscle, and the absence of elected temperance advocates was seen by them as a proof that 'there was no face behind the demands of the teetotal fanatics, who up to the present seemed to have stampeded the executive by their noise.'[30] At a licensed trade conference the following year, they condemned Irish licensing legislation as 'harsh, unjust and ill-conceived', but in the same year expressed the need for a more unified approach on the part of the vintners owing to their present 'chaotic' condition. After the General Election of 1928 which saw Fianna Fáil take their Dail seats for the first time the new Chairman of the LVA, J.P. O'Neill, expressed the belief that the Dáil was now representative of the whole country with the result that the 'prohibitionist mindset will not be allowed to prevail.'[31]

How did the Pioneers deal with these various strands of the drink question in the 1920s? The Pioneer column in the *Irish Catholic* took on a new vigour and purposefulness during this period, as Flinn and his fellow Jesuits became more comfortable with their role and the need to issue orders to over 400 Pioneer centres. Clearly, the aim was to focus on the saving of souls, while demanding practical and legislative action to reform the moral climate of the country. At the Association's AGM in 1924, a Kilkenny priest, Fr O'Keefe, summed up their agenda:

> We are total abstainers not because total abstinence benefits health, prolongs life and saves money but because it saves souls and makes atonement. The people will not submit it to any oligarchy. Under article 48 of the Constitution the people have the right and the power of dealing with this matter. They should get a chance then, of saying whether they are satisfied or not with our present licensing laws.[32]

As well as inviting political action based on the 1922 constitutional provision concerning the right of the people to petition for national referendums, economic arguments were also frequently employed; principally the idea that as a comparatively poor country, Ireland could scarcely afford extravagant expenditure on drink. In typically combative mode, Flinn was scathing about those deemed to have succumbed to the drink lobby. After the passing of further licensing legislation in 1927, which again reduced the hours of opening, as well as deriding those who had demanded a reduction in the tax on drink, he wrote: 'A number of deputies, stampeded or intimidated, sacrificed Ireland's interests to the interests of a trade, sacrificed thousands of homes to the prosperity of those whose votes and influence they desired, sacrificed the interests of souls to the interests of dividends and bank balances.'[33]

The Department of Justice was also receiving correspondence from Pioneers during the 1920s, particularly with regard to putative legislation, though this could not in any sense be described as representing a co-ordinated or focused campaign. Tragedy could sit quite comfortably beside farce in this sense. In November 1925, an outraged resident of Mountjoy Square drew attention to the excessive drinking in private clubs, particularly that of the Army and Veterans' club, and bemoaned the fact that 'going to mass on Sunday mornings one cannot walk on footpaths without slipping into the vomit left by some drunk after his debauch in this veteran's club.' Interestingly, regarding breaches of the 1924 legislation prohibiting the sale of drink after 10.30 p.m., one of the chief offenders was the Catholic Commercial club in O'Connell street.[34] On a lighter note, incensed members of the Desmond Gaelic Football club complained to the Minister for Justice in June 1925 after Gárdai had raided their club 'during a game of rings'. The club did not even serve intoxicants and the secretary pointed out that of a membership of sixty-six, fifty-five were total abstainers.[35]

The most recently released files from the Department of Justice, concerning the Intoxicating Liquor Commission of 1925 reveal the particular concerns of individual Pioneers. Canon Lyons, the Parish Priest of Ardee in County Louth, suggested that while farmers were perhaps drinking less, good nature and charity continued to cloak and hide 'the quiet steady drinking that goes on, and it is a fortunate family that hasn't a family skeleton in the shape of an immoderate drinker.' His most pressing concern, however, was with the amount of women drinking, and the manner in which they drank. It was the articulation of a widely held temperance viewpoint, which had gathered momentum since the First World War, where women, it seems, were both saints and demons in the lexicon of temperance propaganda:

> Mixed houses tempt women and enable them to get drink and bring it home with their groceries and get it marked down as 'soap' or 'candles' in the pass book. The women of Ireland are magnificent in their sobriety – but there are still too many women drinking, especially in the towns. And I consider one drinking woman productive of more harm than say twenty drinking men. It is true that there is not much drinking amongst women in the country, but there is a great deal more than most people think, because it is of its nature secret.[36]

The issue of mixed trading was also of concern to Flinn, who in a letter to the Department, was anxious to get information for the Commission on the issue of structural separation (effectively preventing the sale of alcohol in grocer's shops) and Sunday closing which was now in force in Northern Ireland, and which he insisted was working well in that jurisdiction.[37]

It was not surprising that the temperance lobby was busy extracting and collating information on the various drink issues, given that it now had an opportunity, through the Commission, to press the abstainer's case. The problem was that they could rarely agree on the targets of their campaign. Contemporary debates on the nature and impact of Prohibition in the United States during this period, hindered their determination to carve out an acceptable Irish Catholic temperance programme. It is probably true, as pointed out by Madeleine Humphreys, that during this decade 'there was a perception among many that Ireland was a society of Distillers and Brewers with a supporting trade which had an exceptional degree of power as an interest group, in the political arena.'[38] It is also true that those now governing had, as previous members of Sinn Féin in the heady years before the Treaty, piously asserted that temperance had to be at the core of Irish nationalism. A pamphlet entitled 'The Ethics of Sinn Féin', published in 1917 contained the following:

> Independence is first and foremost a personal matter. The Sinn Féiner's moral obligations are many and restrictive. His conduct must be above reproach, his personality stainless. He must learn the Irish language, write on Irish paper, abstain from alcohol and tobacco . . . Give good example: make examples of your life, your virtues, your courage, your temperance, your manliness, which will attract your fellow countrymen to the national cause.[39]

Perhaps this was viewed as a compulsory honouring of the social legacy of such as Padraig Pearse, and the Pioneers continually held him, and later Kevin Barry, as exemplary Pioneer models for any self-respecting nationalist abstainer. Some clearly took cognisance, certainly in the short term. C.S. Andrews recalled his own views and those of like minded republicans in the Post-Treaty years, but the extent to which they were representative is questionable: 'We held strongly to the social ethos of republicanism in that we were puritanical in outlook and behaviour. We didn't drink. We respected women and knew nothing about them. We disapproved of the wearing of formal clothes.'[40]

Yet there was perhaps an element of the new breed of the ruling Catholic middle-class who, while disavowing excessive drinking and faced with the task of state-building, resented what they saw as the extremism of the Pioneers and their tendency to portray themselves as moral martyrs. The field was certainly not to be left open to the Pioneers in terms of influencing what were effectively political decisions. They were succeeding in slowly transforming the Irish attitude to drink in a personal way – the *Irish Independent* noted in 1924 that 'Already even the man in the street subconsciously distinguishes between a man with a pledge and a Pioneer.'[41] However, this rather academic assertion belies their relative ineffectiveness politically.

The opportunity to influence the Commission was embraced with vigour by the Irish temperance movement in April 1925. During seventeen sittings, evidence was heard from fifty-three witnesses. The Catholic Total Abstinence Federation rolled out their star performer, Fr Peter Coffey, whose basic temperance thesis was that certain restrictions on private freedoms or natural rights were justified in the interest of the common good. But as far as some of the inquisitors were concerned it was a thesis filled with holes and ambiguities, as the following exchange indicates:

J.J. Hogan (Chairman): 'What does the word temperance mean in your mind? Does it mean total abstinence or moderation in drinking?'

Coffey: 'It means both.'

Chairman: 'It cannot mean both.'[42]

This is not to suggest that Hogan was hostile to the temperance advocates. He was in fact quoted as saying that 'having regard to temperance matters in other countries, you are very moderate in your demands. I think you base them on reasonable and sensible considerations.'[43] But he did believe that total abstinence was a matter for the individual and could not be legislated for. Another member of the Commission was annoyed at Coffey's generalisations on the need for the plain drinkers of Ireland to suffer for the common good, and the fact that while Coffey as head of the CTAF insisted that temperance halls had been built all over the country to provide alternative forms of entertainment, he did not have the figures 'and would not like to give a guess'. Likewise, he claimed ignorance regarding the opening hours of public houses. Perhaps inevitably, certain extremists appeared on behalf of the temperance lobby and their views did little to endear them to the Commission. One such example was Fr T.W. Ryan, parish priest of Rollestown and Garristown, who gave evidence on behalf of the Irish Association for the Prevention of Intemperance. Presenting himself as a pastor whose temperance was a product of contact with society's victims, he saw himself as a practical antidote to the cerebral and theoretical Professor Coffey. In reality he came across as an extreme prohibitionist:

> It is very easy for a person to go into a chemist's shop with a doctor's prescription or a bogus one and get a bottle of wine and get advised by the chemist to take it too . . . In America in one day they eliminated 177,779 public houses without giving any compensation. I hold that they have a perfect right to do it . . . If the state considers it useful the state might take a field-glass from me, if they wanted it for war purposes and they have the right to do it.[44]

If the Commission was becoming tired with conflicting attempts to define temperance in a practical way, the chairman was even more incensed by a report in the *Irish Independent* in June which gave an account of a CTAF meeting which had aired criticism of the Commission, insisting that it was refusing to hear further evidence, even though the Federation felt it was imperative that Fr Flinn give evidence on 'specific points not hitherto dealt with.'[45] The furious chairman, Hogan, described the report as 'inaccurate and untrue', and deeply resented the slur, believing he had heard all witnesses patiently and fairly. Bristling with sarcasm, he pointed out that 'we cannot sit here forever hearing rival parties contradict one another . . . I would like to say further that we did refuse one temperance witness who came forward and had nothing further to add to the evidence already given except the practical and sane suggestion that we should close Guinness's Brewery.'[46] The Capuchin archives reveal that this was the evidence of Mr Dunne, a member of the CTAF and a trade unionist whose argument was based on the premise that given the capital invested and the profits made, the liquor trade gave less employment than almost any other industry, and that while London public-house employees were working 59 hours a week, their Dublin counterparts clocked up 80 hours.[47] The CTAF was at a rather low ebb at this stage with 33 executive members but with an effective membership of just 15. Out of a total of 351 affiliated branches, 145 had paid no affiliation fee since 1923. The Federation was strongest in the Armagh, Ossory and Clogher Dioceses. By the mid 1920s it had come to the conclusion that although there was a need for scientific temperance research, a central temperance library and an information bureau, the Federation had failed to sufficiently mobilise public opinion on the issues.[48]

Flinn, however, in his capacity as a member of the CTAF was called to give evidence. The chairman had described him as 'a missionary priest who has considerable experience of the country'. In a letter to the Department of Justice he had said he would speak on behalf of the CTAF 'but still more as a priest whose daily work brings him into contact with intemperance'.[49] His evidence commenced with the reminder that the Pioneers did not endorse prohibitionism, and that his primary purpose was to speak for the victims of drink, particularly those living in the tenements of Dublin slums. He also drew attention to the widespread abuses of licensing laws prevalent in the drinking clubs in the city. With regard to the licensed trade itself, Flinn couldn't resist presenting the Pioneers as an Association making sacrifices for the Irish downtrodden in a society where drinkers and abstainers came from the same background:

> We are here as absolutely disinterested witnesses. Many of us working in the temperance cause are working against our own families and those

dear to us. Fr Mathew in his work smashed and ruined his own family and many a temperance worker today is injuring his own. We are opposing vast moneyed interests; we have no animosity against them . . . but their aims and ours differ.

He then went on to play his personal trump card: 'With regard to the publican, I regard it as a perfectly legitimate trade. I was born in a public house myself.'[50] Flinn was adamant that pubs should be closed on a Sunday, which he believed was 'perfectly drastic'. The *bona fide* trade and the operation of illicit shebeens, he also regarded as an outrage, and that, limited Sunday opening hours in all areas would be the lesser of two evils. He also emphasised that his opposition to Sunday trading was also based on trade union worries about the issue. In his evidence there was a strong undercurrent of resentment about the class divisions in Irish society, particularly the idea that hotels taking advantage of more indulgent licensing regulations because they could serve drink with food were in effect endorsing legislation which favoured the rich. Interestingly, in the light of some of the material appearing in temperance literature, Flinn denied that drinking was widespread amongst women in Dublin, and that morally, people in the capital had become more 'self-respecting' in the previous few years.[51]

Given his customary vigour in denouncing drink abuse, Flinn's evidence was quite muted. He was keen to avoid the charge of extremism, and perhaps his relatively temperate language was a response to some of the more hyperbolic offerings of the temperance witnesses who had gone before him. In retrospect it can be seen that there was a danger of temperance advocates falling between two stools – being accused of being either too extremist or too vague. It was a difficult balancing act, but overall, the central director would not have been happy with how the abstainers' case was digested by the Commission. The text of the report of the Commission seemed to sum up a fairly widespread public or official view of those who crusaded on the drink question. It is important to highlight it as it posed a fundamental question for the leaders of the Pioneers: Was membership of the Association to be primarily a private and internal matter, or should it be politicised and harnessed to a wider agenda?

> The evidence which we received from temperance societies was substantially the same. Their proposals included complete Sunday closing, the reduction by one half of the number of licenced premises in An Saorstat, the abolition of mixed trading, the suppression of wine licences and the further restriction of registered clubs. We found that some of the witnesses unfortunately had little practical knowledge of the problems with which they were dealing. In putting forward their proposals they

> did not seem to have asked themselves the vital question: What
> restrictions will the ordinary citizen accept as reasonable and what
> results will these restrictions produce? We were disappointed that we
> received from these witnesses little assistance on what appeared to us
> the most important question of all, namely the hours of opening. In
> practically every case they admitted that they had not studied the
> question.[52]

This view of the temperance lobby in official circles was not confined
to Ireland. In 1929 the Royal Commission on Intoxicating Liquor in
Britain also indicated that evidence offered suffered from a lack of co-
ordination and was diffuse and repetitive. The Commission believed the
one thing on which all temperance advocates were agreed – local
option – would merely drive drinking from the public house into the
private home, and not decrease the level of consumption.[53]

It is difficult to assess the general feeling among the ordinary rank-
and-file Pioneers towards these national debates, and the attempts by
the Pioneer leadership to make its voice heard. At a local level, Flinn
was as much concerned with ensuring that the strictness of Cullen's
methods were not forgotten and he reiterated them at every possible
juncture. There were many activists in the Pioneer ranks, but these were
more likely to be of a spiritual rather than a political bent. Despite
academic debate concerning legislation and the ethics of such issues as
prohibition, it is more likely that the religious ideal of sacrifice and
devotion to the Sacred Heart struck a much more resonant and
tangible chord with the majority of Irish Catholics. Guidance concerning the salvation of souls and imitating the suffering of Christ was
staple practice, and much more digestible than the complex nightmare
of licensing codes. The message was that being a Pioneer was not
solely about philanthropy:

> . . . In rescuing from the power of the evil souls that, through frailty or
> malice would begin and persevere in grievously sinful habits of drink,
> which ultimately might lead them to hell . . . there is a tendency to
> ignore or to slight the very people who, of all others, need these helps
> and warnings most, namely the Working Class, the poor, the factory
> hands . . . [54]

They could also read of the religious credits they were stacking up
through the recital of the Heroic Pledge – indulgences of 300 days with
a plenary indulgence once a month for members who had recited it
daily for the whole month, with extra indulgences for those who had
procured new members.[55] Flinn was exceptionally vigilant in ensuring
that the Pioneers stuck to their primary task and equally aware of the
danger of adaptation of the rules. When a new centre was affiliated, or

attached to a particular church or religious house, its form and structure could not be altered in any way without the previous approval of the Central Director. Juvenile centres were required to meet monthly for fifteen or twenty minutes, the meeting consisting of a decade of the rosary, a simple talk on the evils of drunkenness, the renewal of the pledge and a verse or two of a temperance hymn. During the 1920s Flinn bombarded the membership with provocative questions, constantly distinguishing, as had Cullen, between active or 'real' Pioneers, and non-active members.

The promiscuous distribution of badges was utterly condemned and councils deemed to be slack or remiss were denounced for insulting the memory of Cullen and charged with arrogance in believing they could adapt rules that had taken three decades to perfect. Yet in running such a tight ship, Flinn had a tendency to court controversy. This was owing not only to his strictness but also to his concern, occasionally bordering on the paranoid, that the work of the Pioneers was continually in danger of being undermined, maligned or misunderstood. The underlining message was that one defaulter or fraudulent member could do ten times the damage of those who did not join at all. This was evident in the minute book of the Gardiner Street SFX male branch of the Pioneers, where Flinn's personality, as well as the direction in which he wished to take the Association, shone through. In June 1921, another local Jesuit, Fr Thomas Murphy, had been appointed Spiritual Director of the branch, but most of the meetings of that year were postponed for want of a quorum, and overshadowed in the following year by political strife, civil mayhem and the death of Fr Cullen.

In attempting to consolidate the movement in the 1920s, Flinn faced many challenges, not least in attempting to dictate the parameters of the Association's brief, as had been witnessed during the Intoxicating Liquor Commission. A common problem was the need to provide alternative forms of entertainment to the pub. In 1926 the Mount Argus centre was anxious to form an athletics union, but the proposal was eventually rejected by the Central Council – 'There being a danger of endless trouble and anxiety, the amount of energy needed, the drawing up of rules etc., the enforcing of same, and finally the financial side. In a word, such a union would be unworkable.'[56] The following year, the Association failed to secure the use of Croke Park for a proposed Pioneer Annual Sports and the concept was abandoned.[57] Despite these setbacks, Flinn and his council were keen to organise Summer excursions for Pioneer members, not just to entertain themselves, but also to illustrate that Pioneers were perfectly capable of socialising without alcohol, and to repudiate the charge that they were killjoys. Preparations for such outings, which catered for 750 members in 1926, were laced with caution coupled with absolute vigilance. Flinn was convinced there were those who falsely procured badges to take part in these excursions, a fear which was occasionally realised. In May 1928, a letter was sent from the Central Director to Castlebar, Milltown, Tuam, Ballaghaderreen and Ballinrobe centres in Mayo. Flinn's language was becoming increasingly dramatic, and the letter was a perfect illustration of his penchant for admonishing guilty parties in the strongest terms. In retrospect the incident seems highly theatrical, but perhaps must be seen in the context of a new state emerging from civil war and indiscipline:

> ... As you know, our enemies are on the watch. Nothing pleases them better than to be able to cast a doubt on our genuineness. We must not give them the shadow of a chance. You will remember I made that point clear in three letters to the centres and emphasised it week after week in the Pioneer column of the *Irish Catholic*. Now what happened? Some centres, in defiance of these express instructions, allowed persons who were not Pioneers to travel, with the result that *three drunks* entered the station at Galway that night to return with the Pioneer centres that had brought them. This did positive harm to the movement. For these reasons we have definitely decided that, as far as this year is concerned, we shall not take on our excursion any but those for whose presence on the trains our excursion committee is personally responsible.[58]

Intermittent embarrassments aside, Flinn and his council, particularly John Lang, the most prominent lay member and a key administrator, were determined to increase the public profile of the Pioneers. A perfect opportunity for mass mobilisation was the silver jubilee of the Association, celebrated in June 1924, and commemorated later that year in a sophisticated and detailed publication. It was an elaboration of what was essentially a dual Pioneer strategy – private religious devotion coupled with the periodic mass mobilisation of members. It was estimated that over 10,000 Pioneers and 200 priests marched from Parnell Square in the centre of Dublin to the Royal Dublin Society in Ballsbridge, accompanied by nineteen bands. The previous year the Pioneer council had set in motion a procession committee, a railway and catering committee and even a pen and needle committee. It was a unique opportunity for propaganda during which 9,764 photographs of Cullen were distributed. Dr Gaughran, the Bishop of Meath, called it 'the greatest sermon on temperance preached in Ireland since the great days of Fr Mathew'. While most of the banners were religious, socio-economic and political concerns were also reflected on some of the placards, a feature which in the future would be prohibited by the Pioneers. Headings included: 'Suffering wives want better licensing laws', 'Mixed Trading must go', 'More drink for father, less food for children'; 'Live for your country, but live in sobriety'; and '£64 million spent on drink in Ireland in 1921 and 1922'.[59]

Another interesting feature was the gender and age profile of the participants, there being more women than men, and a mixture of both very young and old. This may have been pleasing to Flinn in the abstract: the veterans of Irish temperance symbolically passing the torch to a new generation of the Catholic middle-class who, it was hoped, would navigate the ship of the new Free State to a sober shore. There was also a determination to make it an all-Ireland affair, reflected in the presence of a sizeable contingent from Ulster. It also represented another opportunity for the stalwarts of Irish temperance to share a platform articulating a new temperance agenda as well as reiterating familiar battle-cries. This was reflected in the address of the Jesuit, Fr P. Gannon, whose message was that the country as a whole needed to reassess all its national aims in the light of its changed political status, beginning with the urgency of curbing excessive drinking, which he insisted was on the increase. He traced this slothfulness back to the rejoicings after the Allies' victory in the First World War which tarnished all classes, and where there was 'Champagne in the big hotels and wealthier households, and still more copious flowing of whiskey and porter in the backstreets and public houses.'[60] Gannon went on to stress the need for educating the youth in temperance as a virtue in a strictly Catholic sense, attributing the weakness of the Fr Mathew movement to the fact that it was non-sectarian. As was now almost customary on these occasions, women were singled out as having a special niche, particularly given their recent enfranchisement.

'Much is expected from the women in this matter. It is Ibsen I think who has somewhere said of one of his characters: "He was invincible, the women stood behind him." If the women stand behind any move-ment that movement is ultimately invincible.'[61] Basing the success of the Pioneers on the notion of exclusivity, Gannon got carried away, and gleefully remarked that Pioneers who had arrived for the pro-cession without their membership pins had not been allowed to march and had to watch from the side: 'The Pioneer without his badge was thrust forth into extreme darkness, or to be accurate, onto the footpath.' The largest contingent on the march was from Meath, and their patron, Bishop Gaughran, preferred to keep the theme simple: 'Ought not everyone of us to be filled with a holy zeal to blot out from the face of Erin the stain that attaches to it the world over?'[62]

The line-up of speakers was carefully orchestrated, as were the attendant banners, to provide a mix of Catholic assertiveness (suitable dry runs for the Catholic emancipation centenary celebrations in 1929 and the Eucharistic Congress of 1932) and the social and secular aspects of the drink question. The President of the Catholic Total Abstinence Federation, Fr Coffey, demanded that Catholic principles be reflected in licensing legislation, and urged that a referendum on the issues be held in accordance with the Free State Constitution of 1922.

Behind the scenes, however, the relationship between the CTAF and the Pioneers disintegrated as the decade wore on. In December 1929, a dispute arose between the two groups over a proposal to give the Federation a column in the *Irish Catholic*, similar to that of the Pioneers. Flinn did not approve of what Coffey referred to as 'dual control' of the Irish temperance movement and described his attitude as ill-conceived and 'unbending'. There was also a dispute over affiliation fees. Flinn threatened to withdraw the Pioneers from the Federation and to personally resign from the executive, which he did the following month.[63] A letter to Coffey, in his usual style, set out clearly his grievances, and his desire to see the Pioneers plough a solitary furrow in the temperance field of activity, once again highlighting the differing agendas of the Catholic temperance movements and, in particular, Flinn's belief that CTAF propaganda suggested that the Federation alone could do temperance work. Flinn insisted: 'Misleading pressure is being put on centres to make them join the Federation', the impression being created 'that outside the Federation centres are but helpless parochial units'. He rejected the idea that the Pioneers could not set their own spiritual and social agenda, and took exception to the propaganda methods which were being used in the CTAF's new column in the *Irish Catholic*, particularly the idea that unless all Catholic total abstainers were federated, the whole movement would perish.[64] Another bone of contention was financial, with Pioneer centres confused as to whom they were paying money – the Pioneer Association or the Federation. The Pioneer Association had a strict rule about finances: 'The levying of affiliation fees and subscription on Pioneer centres is causing difficulties and creates an anomalous position. The Pioneer association in the thirty-one years of its existence has never asked any affiliation fee, either annual or on the affiliation of a centre' Even more interestingly, Flinn took exception to CTAF circulars urging 'external action with regard to parliamentary representatives'.[65] This was despite the fact that Flinn had regularly allowed other Pioneers to articulate the same message on Pioneer platforms. The dispute brought to the surface traditional tensions on the methods necessary to foster a culture of temperance. There was an elitist hue about the Pioneers which doubtless irked the likes of Coffey, who would have preferred a politically populist campaign which did not distinguish between differing brands of abstaining Catholics.

Another interesting contributor to the 1924 Jubilee celebrations was the bombastic Eoin O'Duffy, Chief Commissioner of the Garda Siochána, and an enthusiastic promoter of the Pioneers within the Gardai rank and file. In O'Duffy, the Pioneers had a strong if utterly unpredictable ally, one who would later become not just a fascist, but a fascist with a fondness for guzzling whiskey. The Pioneers' involvement with the Gardai was a perfect illustration of their tendency to target specific professions or interest groups with a view to getting those with high-profile civic responsibilities to make abstention from drink respectable and attractive. (They also actively cultivated links with the Army, but this was to be fraught with difficulties).[66] At the Jubilee, O'Duffy had been lavish in his approbation of the association's credentials: 'It is a declaration of real merit, the outward sign of a sterling straight man. It will prevent even the attempt to undermine your character as a public servant, or your manhood as one of Ireland's sons. Become a pioneer. It is an order of merit.'[67] At the 1922 Pioneer AGM, Flinn had delightfully pointed out that O'Duffy had given special permission for the Pioneer pin to be worn openly on the garda uniform and that there were already 200 pledged members in the force. Addressing gardai at Collinstown in that year, O'Duffy had been quoted as saying that 'we have now got a comparative measure of freedom but quite a lot of people interpret this to mean freedom to drink more.'[68] The importance of intemperance was given particular emphasis by O'Duffy from the start of the force as demonstrated by General Order no. 14 – a memorandum sent to all ranks in 1922 concerning intemperance in the force. It is a document which again captures the flavour of the 1920s, particularly the hopes, fears and often extremism of those charged with the task of shaping the new state's future, in this case in the area of law and order. There was clearly a worry that the drunken garda was a parasite on the good reputation of his comrades, and in turn, a fear that the average citizen would have little respect for the new force, which, at the time this memorandum was circulated, had enlisted only half of its recruits:

> Ireland requires and deserves a sober police, and Ireland, so far as I can help, is going to have that essential. In the main, the Civic Guard is, I am glad to say, a sober body of men but . . . A certain proportion, not by any means a formidable fraction of the Guard is developing or has developed a certain notoriety for drinking and frequenting the company

of tipplers. The Guard must not forget they are on trial . . . a police officer who has developed a taste for spirituous liquors is always a corrupt official . . . The stolen visits to public houses are noted with an even greater care than the open violation . . . The disease is infectious. Evil communications corrupt good manners, and the drunkard, a scourge in every walk of life, is particularly obnoxious in the uniform of a public servant . . . No man of any rank who is addicted to drink will be permitted to remain a member of the Civic Guard. This is a penalty which will be rigidly enforced.[69]

However, the practicalities of establishing a robust Pioneer centre for the gardai to match the sentiments of the Commissioner were not so clear-cut. Originally there had been an attempt to start a branch by Fr Horan in Newbridge, and in McKee Barracks under the direction of Fr Hurley. In 1923 a centre at the Phoenix Depot was inaugurated under the spiritual direction of the chaplain, Fr McAuliffe, but after the cessation of this chaplaincy in 1925, the gardai Pioneer branch came directly under the control of the Central Council. It was an inauspicious start and Flinn found that he had to adopt a hands-on approach. Despite his urgings, it wasn't until 1931 that serious discussions took place at branch meetings. The primary concern at this stage, according to the minute book was the prevalence of 'suspected cases of disloyalty to the regulators of the Association' with a concomitant repetition of the rules, particularly aimed at instilling the strict code in young gardai with impending allocation to rural stations.[70]

Despite Eoin O'Duffy's glorious march to Rome with 400 gardai in 1929 to an audience with Pope Pius XI, and the equally enthusiastic reporting of the event in the Pioneer column in the *Irish Catholic*, further references to the consecration of the Phoenix Park Garda Headquarters to the Sacred Heart and spiritual retreats in the depot,[71] this depiction of solidity belied their minute book which revealed a distinct lack of success during these years. In 1932 it was noted that members were continually neglecting to wear their emblems, and in 1934 there were constant complaints at 'recent disgraceful conduct at night in depot by Gardai under the influence of drink', and an unadopted proposal to curtail the entrance of younger members of the force to the canteen.[72] Between 1936 and 1940 only one Pioneer meeting was held each year, though the Pioneers' relations with the force remained strong, and was to undergo a resurgence the following decade, under the impetus of Flinn's successor, Fr Sean McCarron.

Another interesting feature of the Jubilee of 1924 was the publication of an appendix in the commemorative publication, containing facts and figures of the drink issue in relation to the economy and society of Ireland. This was a tried and trusted method in temperance propaganda, and was one Cullen himself had frequently employed. In reality it was a simple juxtaposition which involved pronouncing on the poverty of Ireland and the miserable conditions in which its poorest victims lived, and placing this alongside the vast amounts spent on drink and the profits thus generated, and in turn, the narrow distribution of these profits. When addressing the Pioneer AGM in 1930, P.J. O'Mara felt it necessary to point out that Guinness stock was worth £40 million, and noted wryly: 'I think you may take it that Irish Breweries are still good investments'.[73] In the Jubilee publication, Guinness profits for 1913 were quoted at £1,125,202, but by 1924 they had risen to £2,389,624. Expenditure on drink in Ireland between 1913 and 1922 was estimated at £224,446,543, while excise receipts for 1923 were quoted at £16,488,000. Between 1893 and 1922 110,727,979 gallons of spirits were consumed by the Irish and it was estimated that in the Irish Free State in 1924 there were 15,270 licence holders.[74] In Cork there were 476 public houses, and it was noted caustically that 'this appalling total of one public house for every 160 Corkonians does not include clubs, off-licences, chemists' licences, hotels, army and civic guard canteens. It was also noted with incredulity that 'A Dublin public house was sold a few years ago in two lots for £35,000.'[75] Economic historians have to a certain extent vindicated the temperance case by illustrating that the drinks industry was not a large employer. In 1926 there were 16,189 men employed in the Irish food industry, 13,257 in the clothing sector but only 8,107 in the drinks industry. By 1936 the number employed had been reduced to 6,351 men with only 543 women employed.[76] By 1938 industrial employment in the Free State had risen, but brewing showed a fall in both employment and output, particularly after Guinness acquired the Park Royal Brewery near London to offset the burden of protective tariffs.[77]

The reality was that temperance did not impinge significantly on an industry such as Guinness, and indeed those in charge of the formidable brewery advocated temperance and moderation, in keeping with Protestant Nonconformist moral teaching. Guinness Senior Lord Iveagh, for example, believed that advertising was positively vulgar and it had cost the company dear in certain parts of the United States, after the repeal of the Prohibition Amendment when the idea that 'Guinness is good for you' had been successfully legally challenged. Paradoxically, temperance advocates may even have helped an industry like Guinness, particularly when much temperance propaganda was directed at the evil effects of spirits rather than stout.[78] Despite this, Guinness was occasionally in the Pioneers' firing line. Flinn insisted at a meeting of the Father Mathew Union that one of the real difficulties in educating the youth was the propaganda of the brewers, and he drew attention to the practice of the company sending crates of stout to doctors in England 'recommending it on the score of the health-giving properties it possessed for young mothers.'[79] The Sisters of Charity in Waterford in charge of the Pioneer branch at the convent had also been prompted to comment on advertisements which appeared in newspapers to the effect that if doctors would supply the names and addresses of their convalescing patients a neat package of one dozen bottles of stout would be sent to each. The Sister writing the annals wrote curtly, 'Anything to act as bait.'[80] In any event, the Pioneers were even less impressed when Eamon de Valera, who though no longer an abstainer had suggested, in keeping with his protectionist philosophy, that Ireland should drink more of its own beer. Flinn was outraged: 'De Valera said that at the present time the brewers are engaged in an intensive campaign to "get more customers" in England . . . We are asked to do the same in the name of patriotism . . . The happiness of homes and the souls of men are more important than even the coffers of state . . .'[81]

Given the wider debates that were raging in Ireland in the 1920s and 1930s concerning the impact of foreign social imports – particularly what was termed 'the dance craze' – it was inconceivable that the Pioneers, dedicated as they were to domestic moral purity, would not make their voices heard. In 1923, £855 had been raised through subscriptions and invested in a Free State loan in the names of Fr Flinn and John Bury, a prominent lay Pioneer for the purposes of promoting the Pioneer club with Jim Bird acting as secretary. The aim was to provide a suitable arena for dramas and recitals, in keeping with Cullen's original aim that the Association would provide effective alternative entertainment to the public houses. In 1928 the treasurer felt that the discomfort of the building prevented the Pioneer hall from seriously competing with other theatres, but he insisted it had been proven that the hall could be 'much more than merely self-supporting'.[82] A few years later, a letter was circulated soliciting funds for the erection of a Cullen memorial hall, under the auspices of Fr Thomas Finlay SJ. Interestingly, Finlay, a contemporary of Cullen's, reverted to the language previously used by Cullen regarding the purpose of such halls – 'Principally for the purpose of forwarding the religious and social betterment of the working class'. Likewise P.J. O'Neill buttressed his plea for funds for the same project by suggesting that such an amenity 'may contribute in some measure towards improving the homes and home-life of our people and thereby help to arrest the disaster of continued emigration.'[83] This project never quite took off. Flinn seemed to be equally concerned with reiterating the need to preserve Catholic values and the standards of conduct as was demonstrated in a memorandum of his from 1925, entitled 'Socials':

> It is vitally important that socials etc. should be carried out as, not merely to defy criticism, but to be really worthy of a grand Catholic body and be a headline that others may safely copy. While, thank God, our own socials have been as near the irreproachable as possible, it has been remarked of late, there has been a tendency towards *shorter skirts, lower necks and sleeveless frocks*. Fr Flinn feels that he has only to call attention to these points. Members inviting lady friends will kindly intimate to them Fr Flinn's wish on the matter – while the Lady members of the Dramatic Society will doubtless set a faultless example. This notice is all the more important on account of a pastoral letter on dancing which is to be read in every church in Ireland on the first Sunday in Advent.[84]

This was also an issue which came to dominate Catholic periodicals and the proceedings of the Father Mathew Union, of which Flinn was an active participant. It was raised at the Annual Meeting of the FMU in 1927 when Flinn suggested that vigilance committees were needed to monitor what was termed 'all night jazz dancing', inevitably accompanied by drinking. Flinn also drew attention to the damning verdict of 'A wide and representative mass of impartial testimony' which he contended was contained in a contemporary French publication '*Ici on danse*' which had caused quite a stir in France. This was a good example of Irish Catholic social theorists making use of continental thinking in order to adapt it to Irish concerns.[85]

Clerics were particularly concerned with dancing in rural areas where it was felt effective supervision was more difficult. Given the concerns of the hierarchy and a number of leading Irish Jesuits, the issue was artificially propelled to the status of a national threat, an understandable development in the context of the protective ethos of this era, though historians have critically questioned the canon of Irish social and cultural priorities at this time. Louis McRedmond, an historian of the Irish Jesuits, noted that during the struggle for independence, the Jesuits gave the impression of being able to remain above political tensions (something which is reflected in Pioneer minutes and correspondence) and that they could command a hearing on the economic and social questions of the day. But he also points out that 'The Irish Church stood in quite desperate need of solid theology, cogently reasoned argument on every question that was not of faith', and that in this regard the Jesuits failed to contribute, undermining their ability to 'mitigate the worst excesses of triumphalism.'[86] This is a view shared by Desmond Fennell, who complained of little vision to give the practical work done by Catholic clerics coherent and human-istic purpose.[87] For a Jesuit like James Devane, as enunciated in an article in the *Irish Ecclesiastical Record*, dance halls were merely a cloak for the surreptitious supply of drink that facilitated orgies.[88] The *Irish Independent* also quoted Devane expressing the view that excessive drinking was an inevitable product of a new commercialised indi-vidualism, while Fr Brophy, Parish Priest of Newbridge, referred to dance halls at Athgarvan in Kildare as 'Synagogues of Satan.'[89] Even the *Irish Times* deemed it necessary to refer to the 'baneful effect of drink and low dance-halls upon rural morals.'[90] The Catholic hierarchy did not always make intemperance a prominent issue in pastoral letters at this time, preferring to focus on the threat of the dance itself, but Archbishop Byrne in his Lenten Pastoral of 1934 did refer to the fact that 'drink went a long way towards breaking down the barriers which modesty and purity have built up to keep the passions under restraint.'[91] These Catholic social concerns about dance and the attendant drinking were eventually reflected in the passing of the Dance Halls Act of 1935 which sought to make it more difficult to obtain licences.

Underlying the temperance agenda regarding dancing was, prin-cipally, a concern with the preponderance of women who were begin-ning to drink more openly, a development which it was felt sullied the Irish social fabric, and was more damaging both individually and nationally than the drinking of men. Once again, women were assigned a dual status in the temperance debate -- as both hapless victims of male drinkers and, if they drank themselves, as pernicious perpetrators of a heretical female drinking culture. Initially, the men could be blamed for luring the women into sordid temptation, as when Fr Lawrence at the celebration of the Golden Jubilee of the Father Mathew Total Abstinence Association recorded:

> We find young men, the devil's agents, going to dances in motor cars, which they carefully lock because they contain a plentiful supply of liquor. After a few turns on the floor they invite their girl partners out for a rest in the car. Hundreds of girls have been led into drinking habits in that way and the same is true of almost every centre of population in Ireland.[92]

More often than not, however, the women were presented as culpable in their own right, asserting what was seen as a hideous new-wave libertarianism. In 1931, at the annual FMU meeting, Fr Rice from Drogheda referred to what he termed a 'modern problem', a new type of Irish woman, liberated by the effects of war and suffrage and adopting a catalogue of male vices:

And thus, when women lighted the first cigarette it was only a matter of time till she called for a cocktail. But few of us had noticed these things. . . . Recently when the Serpentine was thrown open to mixed bathing, it was a girl bearing an Irish name who won the gold medal offered for being the first to show her disregard to the canons of modesty . . . Drink and dancing, women and wine – ill-accompanied surely. What can one hope for the future? Like our Yankee friends it leaves us guessing. If there will be more money for hats there will be cash to spare for cocktails too. Unfortunately, from our experiences in other matters, we must incline to hold that temperance for a woman cannot be anything less than total abstinence. Those women who have acquired the cigarette habit have made a whole-time habit of it. Where a man would be content with a single cigarette, the lady must smoke a packet. Of course, they cannot help it, it's the way they are built.[93]

Fr Flinn was more anxious to express the Pioneers' concern with the prevalence of drinking among shop-girls 'who nowadays must have a bottle of wine at their social parties.'[94] A few years later in Tipperary, the concern of Fr Moriarty of Cashel was the young girls of the motor-car owning class 'openly entering hotels and calling for whiskies and soda.'[95]

The attacks on women drinking were frequent, sustained and virulent. Male clerics could get extraordinarily emotive in attempting to fathom what some perceived as a social revolution. The Pioneer column in the *Irish Catholic* was another forum for a public airing of the issue. A fitting example of the female's dual status was contained in a report of the Dublin AGM of the Pioneers held in the Theatre Royal in 1932, under the watchful eye of the recently appointed Spiritual Director, Fr Timothy Halpin SJ. Women, it was contended were gentler and sterner, but could scarce get the balance right. A prominent Dundalk Pioneer, Fr Stokes, elaborated on the fact that women were the greatest allies the temperance body had: 'I am not forgetting that many women keep their male relatives sober, even total abstaining by a species of persuasion that could hardly be described as "gentle".' But he went on to wax bitterly about the other extreme – the advent of the modern girl:

You know the type I mean, a feather-headed immature creature who talks a lot about being independent, emancipated and 'napdoddle' of that sort. She deems it essential to throw – to use no stronger word – conventionality to the winds, to toss off as many glasses of champagne as her befuddled admirers, and swallow cocktails with the best of the simpering hobbledehoys who are the young bloods of this age. Fortunately, the modern girl with her boasted independence and emancipation from parental and other control is alien to the Catholic and Irish mind. That safeguard, great though it is, in many cases does not suffice, for quite a number of foreign influences have found their way into our midst and made themselves felt. At all events the modern girl is a cross-channel importation, and you will be well advised to place upon her a prohibitive tariff . . . The man who enters the matrimonial state with the modern girl and hopes to make a success of it needs to be more than a magician. For one thing, he is an incurable optimist.[96]

The Pioneer hierarchy also considered it necessary to cultivate the support of Irish nuns in the crusade against this perceived female immaturity, given the responsibility the nuns had for the education of young Catholic girls. Cullen had always insisted that the temperance work could not be done without them, and Flinn continued to emphasise this reliance. The convents used similar tactics to others: ensuring the establishment of Pioneer centres for girls to join at a young age, and instilling the horrors of excessive drinking, particularly in the light of their future roles as mothers and wives. The annals of the Sisters of Charity convents illustrate that Pioneer centres, retreats directed by Jesuits, sodalities, prayer meetings and temperance lessons formed an essential part of the girls' religious instruction. Fr Cullen had often insisted that one young mother saved from the curse of intemperance meant a generation saved. This was a message continually repeated at the Lady Lane convent in Waterford, where in 1933 Fr Sebastian, a Franciscan, addressed the Pioneer students with horror stories of 'the very poor districts of the West where in times of scarcity the mothers try to still the babies' cry of hunger by using poteen in the bottle where no milk can be got.'[97] While the girls who were educated in these convents were young, the temperance message was frequently framed in the context of their future duties. Those who failed to take or honour pledges were singled out as representing an insult to Irish girlhood and charged with letting their fellow pupils down, as evidenced in another report from Waterford during this period:

> It was gratifying to hear that at a dance given lately by a business company, our girls proved staunch in spite of provocation and ridicule. One girl, not a Pioneer, was a guest and had never tasted drink but pressure prevailed, and 'just one cocktail will not do you any harm', succeeded in getting her caught. She took one, liked it, took two, three and then four and served as a source of lewd banter when she stood up and declared the heel had come off her shoe and, excitedly refusing to dance, she limped herself out of the room. It would have been well for her if she had the Pioneer principle to save her from the first downward steps . . . [98]

What of the men and the stereotype of excessive male drinking, particularly among bachelors in rural areas? Pioneer propaganda was rather ambiguous on this front. They had pulled off something of a

coup in 1929 by getting a prominent publican and senator, Thomas
Toal, to chair their annual meeting in the Theatre Royal. Toal had
insisted that the Pioneers were not prohibitionists or intent on damaging the licensed trade, believing the conscientious publican could do
a great deal to promote temperance: 'He had never been ashamed to
wear his Pioneer pin behind the counter, and in that capacity he would
often give sound, and at times stern, advice to those who were going
to their own destruction.'[99] However, this was a once-off. In reality,
Pioneers were discouraged from entering pubs (presumably many
wouldn't have been interested, in any case), and this was reflected in
the minutes of the SFX centre in Dublin. In 1933 the new spiritual
director, Fr Tim Halpin, went to the trouble of checking what Fr Cullen
had said concerning Pioneers entering pubs, and the Council came to
the conclusion that 'applicants should not be informed that whiskey
sauce and co. were allowed. Neither should it be mentioned that
Pioneers could enter a public house and treat friends.'[100]

More nightmarish than a preponderance of Pioneer pins in public
houses, was to find a supposed Pioneer boasting loudly about drinking exploits, and it is quite clear from the records that almost all those
who defaulted were males. This falling by the wayside was not always
as private as the Pioneer hierarchy would have wished. In 1936 a press
report concerning a Mr P. Belton, a registered Pioneer, appeared
detailing his voyage to Spain to the Irish Christian Front, quoting him as
saying: 'I drank on Tuesday last in the Bay of Biscay, the first bottle of
stout in my life and since then my beverage is the "creamy pint".'[101] An
outraged Central Council refused to countenance, or disregard such
open rebellion on the part of their more high-profile members. They
demanded an explanation, and in a subsequent letter, Belton admitted
his guilt, left the Association and presumably carried on drinking.[102]

On a wider scale, it was difficult to challenge the many roles drink
fulfilled, particularly in the lives of Irish males. Treating, or the buying
of rounds, was still in some cases an essential part of the small-town
economy, and could reveal the solidarity of certain groups within the
social system. Richard Bales, an American sociologist who sought to
analyse the heavy drinking of Irish males, revealed that attitudes
towards excessive drinking, reflected in economic terms, song and
custom, were manifold, though not all essentially negative.[103] Likewise,
Conrad Arensberg, who with fellow American anthropologist Kimball,
had settled in a rural Clare community in 1937 to record typical Irish
rural life, recalled the local attitude to drinking:

> Where drunkenness begins to interfere with the primary family system
> and its economic base rather than facilitate its preservation, it is

condemned. Short of that drunkenness is laughable, pleasurable, somewhat exciting, a punctuation of dull routine to be watched and applauded and drunken men are handled with care and affection.[104]

Also in this context, the drinker's attitude towards the Pioneer or teetotaller was ripe for dissection. It has often been suggested that heavy drinking among rural males was a key safety valve in the release of sexual tensions, or as a substitute for meaningful physical and emotional relationships. Arensberg insisted that the view expressed by lower middle-class men was 'that the teetotaller is a menace to society, because he is the man who is likely to prowl around the streets getting girls into trouble and destroying their character.'[105] Needless to say this was not an analysis which the Pioneers sought to dwell on in public in the 1920s and 1930s. It was certainly interesting that the observation came from a foreign scholar who insisted on dwelling in the community he sought to analyse; though it is also revealing that he chose to relate these insights in conversation with other scholars rather than in the published form of his work.[106]

A Presbyterian temperance advocate in Northern Ireland was more explicit about the social consequences of the sexual proclivities of heavy drinkers rather than teetotallers. John Hunter drew attention to the prevalence of venereal disease in men who drank excessively, because under the influence of drink a man was 'more liable to yield to temptation which he might otherwise regret'.[107] Although Pioneer propaganda, in common with so much of the Catholic literature of this era was often concerned with issues of sexual purity, more attention was given to political and military purity in the context of the true patriotic Irish male. Included in the newspaper cuttings collected by the Pioneer Council during this period was an undated transcript of a press article which claimed that de Valera in 1921 had insisted on the importance of Irish soldiers keeping fit and thus not drinking, and stated furthermore: 'It is reported on reliable authority that during the Truce and Treaty negotiations, General MacCready (The commander of the British forces in Ireland) when asked why the English had failed to subdue the IRA, had answered that they "were too bloody sober".'[108]

The Pioneer Council's determination to prove that Irish entertainment and socialising did not have to be based on the presence of drink, occasionally brought it into dispute with other organisations. In the Gaelic Athletic Association, the Pioneers felt they had a benevolent partner, helped by the fact that one of the Association's key administrative figures, the general secretary, Paddy O'Keeffe, was a committed Pioneer, and many of the players were abstainers. As has been mentioned, GAA publications had included temperance as one of the key components in the make-up of the true Gael, which historian W.F. Mandle saw as an attempt by the GAA to adapt British Victorian standards to Irish sporting and cultural pursuits. The leadership of the Pioneer Association sought to develop this argument , not just through encouraging sport within the Pioneers but also through lauding the GAA at every available opportunity, and equating their aims with the temperance agenda, in terms of providing healthy alternatives to drink-based entertainment. They were still faced with the unpalatable fact, however, that GAA events were often closely followed by celebratory or mournful drinking sessions. This led to controversy in 1933, when the GAA accused the Pioneers' most prominent supporter among the Catholic hierarchy, Dr Patrick Collier, Bishop of Ossory, of using a Pioneer platform to insinuate that it was behind demands for increased opening hours and drinking facilities to accompany GAA matches. In a letter to Flinn in December 1933, Collier denied that he had slandered the GAA, insisting that he had classified them as 'sober, temperate and self-respecting', but that the licensed trade had used their activities as an excuse to demand increased drinking facilities. He suggested that the GAA should have taken the opportunity to disclaim the licensed trade's demand, believing that silence on its part was tantamount to consent. The secretary of the central council of the GAA accepted that after this clarification 'the air was now clear', but refused to be drawn into correspondence with the bishop.[109] Flinn himself was normally a resolute defender of the GAA, frequently singling out particularly memorable matches with an eye on how many of the team members were Pioneers, establishing a tradition his successors developed with gusto. At the 38th Father Mathew Union AGM in 1938, he referred to reports of drunken disturbances following an All-Ireland final at Croke Park and insisted: that he had himself 'seen a couple of people drunk and several under the influence of drink on the Sunday of the GAA final in Dublin. These people however could not have been at Croke Park and had nothing whatever to do with the GAA . . . '[110]

Throughout the 1930s, the Licensed Vintners' Association continued to spar with the Pioneers. The LVA's annual report for 1932 included the usual resentments against temperance propaganda, with an insistence that in no other country was there such implacable hostility against the trade. According to its figures, convictions for abuse of the licensing laws were the smallest per head of any population in the world, and arrests for drunkenness had fallen from 9,906 in 1900 to 910 by 1931. The vintners also deplored the fact that the national festival, St Patrick's Day, was 'celebrated in sack-cloth and ashes', though, they contended, the majority was opposed to the closing of licensed premises. They conveniently recalled Arthur Griffith's comments of 1921, when he had equated the closing of the pubs on St Patrick's Day with an affront to working-class people.[111] The following elaboration of the LVA's frustration revealed a business feeling under siege from the purveyors of Pioneer ideals:

> The activities of the various temperance bodies abate not a jot, and a stranger unacquainted with the actual conditions would be excused for thinking that the country was steeped in drink. Resolutions of the various temperance leagues and societies asking for further restrictions flow merrily forth and scarce a day passes without press reports of some of these people's activities. The explanation is not far to seek. It is that in reality there is no temperance in the literal sense of the word. All the efforts of these people tend in one direction only and aim at one goal, and that is total suppression of the liquor trade. If the laws were such that licensed houses were open only four hours a day, they would still be active as ever. The more they get, the more they want. Under the act of 1924, only eight short years ago, the legal hours in the Metropolitan area were reduced by twenty-four hours per week, and the 1927 Act, with the establishment of the afternoon closing hour, sliced off an additional six hours per week. In other words, within eight years in the cities of Dublin, Cork, Limerick and Waterford, no less than thirty legal hours per week were taken from the trade . . . [112]

Throughout the decade the vintners attributed drunkenness to the operation of bogus clubs, and the fact that chemists were openly selling lethal 'Red Biddy' wine. They reiterated their call for St Patrick's day opening and complained that rural people travelling to Dublin for GAA matches were being deprived of refreshments in public houses. In 1937 they trumpeted the fact that only three members of the LVA had been proceeded against by gardai for breaches of the licensing laws, a record in the history of the LVA.[113]

The Pioneer leadership was implacably opposed to St Patrick's Day opening. In April 1931 representatives from over 300 Pioneer centres had been present at a rally in the Gaiety Theatre to express their opposition to a proposed change in the licensing laws in this regard, with the sanction, but not the presence, of six members of the Catholic Hierarchy. The meeting was later celebrated at that year's AGM by Flinn: 'Our protest was emphatic, it was national, it was Irish, it was Catholic.'[114] Their protest was based on the belief that drink had denigrated and desecrated the feast day in the past. Originally, opposition to the opening of pubs had been inaugurated by the Gaelic League in 1904, and at the invitation of the Archbishop of Dublin, the LVA had agreed to close pubs on St Patrick's Day. An offer from the Chief Secretary, George Wyndham, to pass a law to this effect was declined, it being preferred to keep it at the level of a voluntary sacrifice. The Dáil had subsequently legislated for it in 1927. At the Gaiety meeting Pioneers now referred to the demands of the LVA 'as unjust as they are grotesque'.[115] The Association was also quick to point out that this was in no way a sectional protest, highlighting that both the Leinster Convention of the GAA and the Gorey branch of the Gaelic League had voted against St Patrick's Day opening.[116] Those speaking from the Pioneer platform on this occasion pulled out all the stops. They were keen to remind the audience that this would be an All-Ireland protest: 'The Pioneer Association knows no partition, no border. Where the honour of Ireland and the interests of the Sacred Heart are concerned, a united Pioneer Ireland will register their emphatic protest.' Fr Murnane, the parish priest of Greystones sought to strike an emotive chord by claiming that all the leaders of the 1916 Rising had been Pioneers, while Senator Laurence O' Neill, referring to the architect of the 1924 and 1927 Licensing Acts, Kevin O'Higgins, who had since been assassinated stated: 'If there was no other reason for keeping the public-houses closed on St Patrick's Day, respect for the brutally murdered Kevin O' Higgins should be sufficient.'[117]

A report of the meeting in the *Irish Times* revealed that Fr Aloysius of the Fr Mathew Total Abstinence Association took a decidedly political line, fearing what he called a revival of "tap-room" politics, and deriding those who were prepared to hide behind a party whip on the issue. For Aloysius, who had also frequently criticised the existence of a Dáil bar, it was a simple issue of nation being above party.[118] On this issue, the Pioneers could not avoid entering the political arena. This was reflected in the minutes of the Central Council of January 1932 where Pioneer councils were instructed to send candidates in the forthcoming election a circular asking them to state if they would oppose the proposed opening of pubs on St Patrick's Day. All but two of the respondents were in favour of retaining the ban, 'but in the event of the matter going to a vote, they should vote with their party.'[119] However, it is not clear how many potential TDs replied, as no copies of the letters have survived. Those who had proposed the opening of pubs on St Patrick's Day were not successful at this juncture, but the Pioneers were patently not comfortable, or indeed effective, as political crusaders. In the *Irish Catholic* after the election of 1932, they printed what they announced was an incomplete list of TDs from the three largest political parties who were members of the Association. The list contained only eleven names, and the experiment was not repeated, and undoubtedly many Pioneer Dáil deputies would have resented the implication that their membership would oblige them to vote in a particular way on certain issues.[120] Neither were Pioneer politicians rushing to share Pioneer platforms. An analysis of the programmes of the Pioneer AGMs between 1922 and 1942 reveals that only one politician was prepared to chair the meeting that was in 1938 when the Chairman of the Senate, Sean Mac Giobuin accepted. The only other prominent lay people who accepted this task during this period were D.F. Correll, President of the INTO, who chaired the AGM of 1936, and Paddy O'Keeffe, General Secretary of the GAA, who chaired in 1942.[121] Fr Flinn was keen to be seen as impartial and to prevent others stirring up party political based rivalry within the Association. The following was noted concerning a ship excursion to Galway by a group of Dublin Pioneers: 'amid the shouts and greetings to those on the Liner, one party cry was uttered, all repetition of which was peremptorily stopped by Fr Flinn, with the emphatic word that on a Pioneer excursion no political cries of any kind whatever will be permitted.'[122]

Flinn could justify the Pioneer's participation in the St Patrick's Day campaign by asserting that it was a religious and national rather than political issue, and he continued to pressurise politicians by sending a resolution concerning the subject to the Minister for Justice and urban TDs in December, 1933.[123] The Pioneers were not immune from other political controversies of the day. In 1936 the *Irish Press* reported that at a communist rally at Rathmines Town Hall in Dublin, there were members present wearing the Pioneer pin with the communist emblem attached. The Central Council felt the reference was 'most uncalled for' but decided to 'take no action'. Later that year, however, a letter appeared in the *Evening Herald* appealing to all Pioneers to subscribe to a 'Pioneer fund crusade to equip and maintain field-ambulances in Spain' during the Spanish Civil War. An incensed Fr Flinn disowned the advertisement and insisted that whoever was responsible had no authorisation to use the Association's name, and that he, personally, as Central Director, had complete control over all Pioneer requests and literature.[124] Likewise in 1937, Flinn insisted that a list of the 12,500 Dublin males, who had been admitted to the Association or probationary ranks between 1902 and 1935 was strictly confidential: 'And may not be used by anyone for any purpose whatsoever without the express permission of the Spiritual Director. He said that different people e.g. heads of missionary bodies on various occasions, directly or indirectly, had tried to get hold of or have use made of those lists for non-Pioneer purposes, e.g. for collections.'[125] At a more local level, regarding the 'political status' of the Association, Flinn's categorisation of the Pioneer general meetings as 'spiritual and national' had brought him into conflict with trade unionists in 1933, who wanted the staff of the Theatre Royal in Dublin, rather than Pioneer stewards, to supervise the event, the idea being that Pioneers were depriving the Theatre Royal employees of their legitimate income. This Flinn regarded as 'unreasonable. Our meeting is not an entertainment.'[126]

Regarding the North, while it was true that the Pioneer movement was an all-Ireland affair, and while Flinn, as had Cullen before him, frequently singled out Pioneer centres in the north for special mention, particularly those centres in areas of Protestant majorities, he avoided making blatant political references to partition. Others on Pioneer platforms were not so circumspect. At the 1930 AGM an address was made by Mr J. Henry, a Nationalist MP in the northern parliament and president of the Newry Pioneer Association. At the 1931 AGM, which was chaired by a Belfast priest, Fr Taggart, Fr Aloysius of the more openly republican Fr Mathew Association 'declared that they in the Pioneer movement did not recognise partition and would end it at the first opportunity', though it was telling that these remarks were reported in the *Irish Independent* and not the *Irish Catholic*.[127] Flinn certainly kept himself abreast of what was going on in Northern Ireland and frequently recorded with a degree of satisfaction the establishment of new centres, reminding his Pioneer audience that it was in Belfast that Cullen had first introduced the concept of the 'Heroic Offering'. Equally, evidence of intemperance was just as likely to be admonished in the Six Counties – in 1935 he reported the following:

> In the last week we had in the 'Six Counties' courts a prosecution that justifies Father Cullen's prohibition of home-made wines that we are so often told are quite harmless. A farmer's wife was summoned for making, for sale, a rhubarb wine containing 22 per cent spirits!!!! Despite her explanation that it was home made from a recipe in an old cookery book, she was fined £500, mitigated to £125 . . . [128]

Desiring essentially to be a self-contained entity, the Pioneers were not particularly comfortable with sharing the temperance mantle with other groups. They had successfully tapped into a formula which allowed them to penetrate the inner lives of ordinary Irish Catholics, though as private minutes and correspondence reveal, this was not done without organisational difficulties and courting controversy. Nonetheless, as was witnessed in relation to issues such as licensing legislation, co-operation with other lobbyists was intermittently approved. Another small, though active temperance group at this time was the Irish Association for the Prevention of Intemperance, a group established in 1878, and dominated by Protestants, Quakers and Presbyterians. Meeting monthly in Dublin, in Bewley's Cafe, there was always some Pioneer presence on the executive, though its presidency was eventually taken over by the ubiquitous Fr Coffey of Maynooth, largely due to the reluctance of anyone else to take on its leadership. In the late 1930s the IAPI compiled data on the legal aspects of the drink question, attending district court hearings concerning applications for licences, and highlighting the perceived inefficiency of the gardai in enforcing licensing laws. Their particular concern was the bona fide provision of the licensing laws, widely abused and denounced by Pioneer and IAPI member, Fr T.W. O'Ryan as 'a fraud . . . The three-mile limit', he said 'was fixed at a time when the donkey was the fastest mode of travel '[129] Another prominent member, Harold Eason, the chairman of Eason's booksellers, insisted that the Association had no axe to grind, and stated, conforming to traditional Protestant thinking, that they merely wanted to see the country 'sober, industrious and happy'. However the Minister for Justice, whom they frequently harangued, conveniently passed the responsibility to the Garda Commissioner.[130] A typical IAPI AGM during this period revealed an active membership of only thirty-six, including twelve women, five clerics of different denominations and four doctors. Flinn was not an active member, but in 1939 the IAPI was in contact with the Pioneer Association concerning the compilation of figures for the consumption of drink in Ireland, and various court cases concerning the drink question.[131]

Whether due to the multitude of his other commitments, or because he did not want the Pioneers to follow this secular route, Flinn did not seem overly keen on immersing himself in the toils of the IAPI. He was not a stranger to the legal world. In 1936 he informed the Central Council that he had received a solicitor's letter on behalf of a publican in Baldoyle, who claimed he had libelled him. Baldoyle's publicans were frequently abused by temperance reformers for their alleged breaches of the bona fide provision. The case against Flinn was not pursued. The following year Flinn was in Dublin District Court with the secretary of the Dublin branch of the Gaelic League, Michael O'Foghludha to oppose applications for increased drinking facilities at dances in the city centre, and it was recorded in the SFX minutes that they 'had much effort in lessening the relaxation sought.'[132] His choice of court partner seemed to indicate that he was more comfortable working with the leaders of groups whose aims he felt were more in keeping with the ethos of Catholic cultural regeneration which had emerged in the late nineteenth century, and of which he could legitimately claim the Pioneers were a part. At this hearing, as reported in

the *Irish Catholic*, O'Foghludha's testimony was the sort which would
have struck a chord with Flinn:

> He testified that during the last four years the Gaelic League had held
> 144 dances on Sunday nights at the Mansion House, which had been
> attended by 106,640 people, an average of 740 each night. He had been
> responsible for those dances and could say that they did not supply
> drink, nor did they allow anyone to have drink; that in the four years
> only three persons were found under the influence of drink and they
> were ejected; they had received no complaints from the Guards about
> illicit drinking and the man in charge of the cloakroom said that he
> never discovered any bottles after the dances.[133]

Strains had occasionally surfaced between the Pioneer ideal and
those involved in other pledge-based associations whose guidelines
were not quite as strict. Flinn defended this at a Father Mathew Union
meeting by arguing that people would not understand the arguments
of abstainers unless they were absolutist about teetotalism. He was
undoubtedly annoyed about what he saw as the arrogance of the
Kerry Branch of the Father Mathew Union in passing a resolution
criticising the Pioneers who

> by condemning such apparently innocuous beverages as raspberry wine
> and blackberry wine is playing into the hands of the alcoholic party and
> is leaving the field clear for the three stock alcoholic beverages: beer,
> wine and spirits . . . it would be more appropriate to allow the highest
> percentage of alcohol which will be innocuous from the temperance
> viewpoint.'

The Kerry branch also felt it necessary to point out that 'there is a very
appreciable alcoholic content in sour milk'.[134] Flinn would not consider
proposals such as these under any circumstances. For him, the whole
point of the Pioneers was that it was uncompromising. Not only did
he personally feel that this was the right path, but it was also in line
with the clear instructions of Fr Cullen. For the Association to bend the
rules in reaction to the many beverages, some alcoholic, some not,
which were coming on the market, would have been regarded by
traditionalist Pioneers as a vulgar surrender to commercialisation.
Neither would Flinn have agreed with the conclusion of Fr Peter
Coffey in 1938 that 'it was better to leave the decision to the common
estimation of men and to the honour of the individual members.'[135] In
the same year Flinn disagreed with a proposal that the FMU adopt the
Pioneer pledge. It was on this ground that Flinn felt more comfortable,
as it was during these debates that the Pioneers emerged, through the
strictness of their rules, as different from other temperance groups,
and, he undoubtedly believed, more religiously and spiritually

motivated. It was a much more comfortable playing field than negotiating with government ministers concerning licensing legislation.

This may explain why in the late 1930s and early 1940s there was evidence of a more concerted shift for the Pioneers, away from the secular concerns of politics and legislation towards the spiritual programme of the Association, and in particular educating the youth in pioneer ideals. This may explain why so many people joined the Association. Madeleine Humphreys has suggested that the Association 'did not seek to create a culture of temperance on a wide scale'.[136] This was not the case for the first forty years of the Association's existence, given its constant preoccupation with what were presented as national ideals, and wedding them to the Pioneer principle, but a narrowing of focus was in evidence as time progressed, though this was to be temporary rather than long-term. Humphreys writes that 'conversations with those who were members in the 1930s and 1940s recall an organisation where one felt special.'[137] This was cultivated by the policy of mobilising Pioneers in large groups and actively targeting young audiences, but in a narrow way, thus maintaining an element of elitism which was deemed to be essential. There was nothing spontaneous about this. It was carefully staged and orchestrated through the organisation of general regional meetings, visits to schools and retreats which formed an essential part of the Jesuit legacy. It was certainly helped by the fact that, according to the Jesuit Fr Halpin, assistant spiritual director in the late 1930s, up to 75 per cent of the newly ordained priests at Maynooth were 'rabid Pioneers'.[138] The proliferation of retreats at this time, particularly those encapsulating devotion to the Sacred Heart, was the corner stone of the Ignatian principle that 'the word of God should be proposed to the people unremittingly by means of sermon, lectures and the teaching of Christian doctrine.'[139]

Initially, the Pioneers could demonstrate their faith at wider Catholic celebrations, in particular the Catholic Emancipation centenary celebration in 1929 and the Eucharistic Congress of 1932. On both these occasions, owing to Congress rules, Pioneers could not participate as a body, but the events were still enthusiastically embraced. Flinn noted in the *Irish Catholic* in 1929 that 'It is the Mass that matters, the Mass, the grand central act of our religion.'[140] For the Eucharistic Congress the Pioneers organised a simultaneous all-Ireland meeting of Pioneers in the Theatre Royal, presided over by Archbishop Kelly of Sydney, a contemporary of Fr Cullen. Though not actually assembled as a body for the Congress itself, Pioneers were continually reminded that it would still be the most representative gathering of the Pioneers ever held.[141] In terms of pursuing a separate Pioneer agenda, the organisational logic was to replicate these national Catholic celebrations on a smaller scale and to institute them as a particular Pioneer specialty. This was vigorously embraced in the late 1930s, and became an integral part of the movement. The Pioneer Column in the Irish Catholic assiduously reported these frequent gatherings, and regional AGMs.

More frequent targeting of youthful audiences was helped considerably by the appointment of Fr Leonard Gallagher SJ as assistant to Flinn in May 1937. He was given the specific task of targeting schools nationwide. Gallagher's emphasis was strictly on the spiritual, with the simple question posed to children – 'Is my own house in order?'[142] Sacrifice and devotion to the Sacred Heart was presented as something that needed constant faith, courage and generosity and was coupled with illustration of the social and spiritual horrors which were caused by excessive drinking. In 1938 there were 1,700 children at the annual Theatre Royal rally, and Fr Gallagher inculcated the simple message that they were defending precious Catholic territory in the same patriotic way the great warrior Cuchulann had done. The inculcation of elitism was accompanied by literature that stressed that they should confine themselves to a select few, and that there could be no neutrals in the crusade. The children were reminded that Jesus had said to his apostles at the Last Supper 'you are they who have remained with me in temptation.'[143] Specific groups in universities, colleges and convents were also targeted, and the Pioneer message was communicated in simple terms by well-known public figures such as Senator Margaret Pearse, who saw the Pioneer's self-denial as an antidote to the deplorable lack of penance in contemporary Catholic life, with an onus on colleges to provide not just academic, but social leadership as well.[144] Belfast was also targeted, and in 1940, 4,000 Pioneers in Newry were addressed by Dr Edward Mulhern, Bishop of Dromore. Pioneer membership was presented as patriotism flying in the face of persecution. Referring to sectarianism, he remarked that 'In many parts of the country the fact of being a Pioneer marked that man as a suspect in the eyes of the English military. Cases occurred, and Newry was one; where the Pioneer registers were seized by police and military and were never returned.'[145]

By 1940 the great majority of the 835 active centres were parochial mixed centres under the control and direction of secular priests. More specifically there were nine centres in religious houses, eight in the ecclesiastical seminaries, sixteen in Diocesan colleges, thirty in boys colleges and secondary schools, four in senior teacher training colleges and University Colleges, Dublin and Cork, sixty-three in convents and boarding schools, and four centres for nurses in hospitals. In the year

1939–40, a record eighty-two new centres and 24,000 members had been recruited which seems to suggest that Flinn and Gallagher's tactics were paying dividends. By 1941 there were 900 centres.[146] Throughout the decade Flinn had been vague about exact membership figures. He did refer to 'our 250,000 members', but in the late 1930s the annual average recruitment of over 20,000 probationers and Pioneers meant that membership was closer to 300,000.

The messages hammered home to new Pioneers fell into a ready pattern: the rules of the Association, the need for spiritual self-sacrifice and devotion to the Sacred Heart to counteract paganism and individualism (Fr Gallagher contended that the outbreak of the Second World War was the consequence of a craze for pleasure without care of the consequences).[147] There were also reports of Pioneer excursions, denunciation of excessive drinking, particularly at Christmas and other festive occasions and the commemoration specific dates, such as the celebration of the centenary of the Heroic Offering in Belfast in 1939. Here, Bishop of Down and Connor, Daniel Mageean, addressing five thousand Pioneers, eight hundred of them from Dublin, in McRory park, declared: 'Fifty years ago, we deserved the reproach of 'A drunken nation'. Today we do not, but there is still much to be done.'[148] Year after year, Pioneers were also reminded on the official programmes of the AGMs never to lend their pioneer badges: 'It should be their pride to prevent their honoured emblem getting into the hands of those who, for self-interest are willing to use the badge of the Sacred Heart to cover a lie.'[149] Those guiding the Association still had a need to identify enemies. Flinn's method was to praise what he saw as zealous devotion and to simultaneously berate those not perceived to be pulling their weight. He singled out university students as being probably the most important Pioneers because 'they would be future leaders in every phase of the nation's life.'[150] But those deemed to have shirked their responsibilities could be subjected to scathing outbursts. In January 1939, Aodh de Blácam, in his 'Roddy the Rover' column in the *Irish Press* had humorously drawn attention to a leading Pioneer lawyer who claimed he took a noggin of Brandy, three eggs, stew and whiskey to cure his influenza, claiming he had not violated his pledge as it was for medicinal purposes.[151] In response, Flinn dismissed the story, claiming he was not aware that there were any leading lawyers who were Pioneers. But where *were* the lawyers?

> Incidently, the non-existence of leading lawyer Pioneers makes one query why it is that the professions as a whole, and what people are pleased to call the 'better classes', are not more strongly represented in the Pioneer movement than they are. Take the annual meeting of 4000

pioneers, all pledged to self-sacrifice and denial for the sake of the Sacred Heart. We have there, in their thousands, the workers, men and women, but where are the doctors, solicitors, lawyers, the big business men, the grand ladies? Can it be that the ordinary working man and woman are more capable of sacrifice for the Sacred Heart and its interests than those more favoured with the goods of the world?[152]

Likewise, Pioneers were urged to treat statistics concerning drink and its effects with distrust, scepticism and disdain. This was part of a Pioneer philosophy which was based on the notion that those who were not Pioneers were involved in a giant cover-up to deny the reality of Irish alcoholism. In the annual report of 1938, legislation had been demanded to counteract the threat posed by drinking clubs:

> Doubtless in a day or two we shall be told that we are completely wrong. Did not Mr Rutledge in his prison report, published recently, tell us that in 1937 only 339 persons were jailed for drink, the lowest number on record. But does any honest man fancy for one second that 339 represents the number of people drunk last Christmas Eve in Dublin? Does that represent the number of those drunk in their homes? Does that represent those put to bed drunk in hotels or elsewhere? Does that represent young ladies brought home in taxis from dances, cocktail or sherry parties? No. The figure 339 means nothing. It does not touch the fringe of the evil.[153]

Another organisational endeavour at this stage, though still only in its infancy, was the desire to expand the Association overseas. This was an understandable development in the context of the mushrooming of the Irish missionary movement, the high point of which had been the establishment of the Maynooth Mission to China in 1916. During the following two decades there was a huge increase in the number of indigenous institutions established specifically for missionary activity, including the development of a medical mission.[154] In seeking to take the first practical steps towards making temperance a direct component of these missions, Flinn was carrying on the legacy of Cullen who had made strong, if vague references on the need to inculcate sobriety in tandem with the religious instruction which the Irish were adapting abroad. In 1928 Flinn could report that an application to start a centre had been received from a native tribe in Ashanti in Africa. Flinn was suitably vague and could only wonder flippantly: 'This application causes a difficulty, where are the black men going to put the pioneer pin when they get it?'[155] But correspondence files concerning attempts to inaugurate the Pioneers in Australia in the 1930s reveal that getting Jesuits to establish the Pioneers abroad was fraught with difficulties. Irish Pioneer values and methods did not sit comfortably on foreign shores. Flinn's contact in Australia, Fr O'Hehir, had explained that Australian priests rarely drank the cordials forbidden to the Pioneers, and in 1932 had suggested a modification of the rules which set the tone for a heated row at the Jesuit Retreat house in Rathfarnham when O'Hehir visited Ireland. An unrepentant Flinn was utterly opposed to any change in the rules and insisted that setbacks were due to a failure to emphasise pioneer motives, that he was convinced relaxation 'could kill the PTA in a short time' and that what was needed was 'the whole hog or nothing.'[156] The difficulty was that the cordials taken by Australian priests, and forbidden to Pioneers, were a recognised 'total abstinence drink' in Australia, and it was contended that forbidding them would drive away up to sixty model Pioneers in Richmond. Flinn would not countenance this, and was still smarting from the experience of his dealings with Fr Lockington, whom Dr Mannix, Archbishop of Melbourne, had assigned to promote the Pioneers in the diocese, which Flinn insisted he did by introducing 'a maimed form of the Pioneer Association.'[157]

Another obstacle highlighted by Fr O'Hehir was the difficulty of getting Catholic theologians in Australia interested in the concept, given the traditional association of temperance with Protestants. But O'Hehir continually returned to the issue of what the Pioneers could and could not drink. In 1934 he wrote from Victoria that the students of the Corpus Christi College in Verribee 'baulked at the Pioneer strictness regarding lime juice and lemon-squash cordials'. Three years later, it seemed that little had changed. Fr Stephenson, based in the Saint Francis Xavier College in Victoria, informed Flinn that due to the hot climate and a lack of suitable drinking water 'bars do a great trade', but that coupled with this 'the majority of priests throughout the country give us very little help. The chief movers in the matter are a couple of young priests, just ordained.'[158] It did not augur well for the future of the Pioneers abroad.

The Pioneer Association needed heroes and role models to sustain the idea of Pioneer membership as belonging to an exclusive, clean-living and patriotic club. The publication in 1925 of Joseph Gwynn's *Life of Matt Talbot*, a bestseller, provided an attractive introduction to a Pioneer who since his death and subsequent deification by the Catholic establishment was a household name. The author was keen to point out that the life of this 'saint in overalls', whose moral character after his alcoholism and pledge was above reproach, proved that his message was relevant to all Irish people, and that his self-sacrifice was a microcosm of all that was best about 'the true types of our people and not the wretched degenerates which a so-called National Theatre presents to the world as types of Catholic Ireland.' The simple message about this man, who was presented as humble and apolitical, was that he was ordinary, the subtext being that all Irish Catholics could become sanctified in their own way – 'A saint has been described as one who, in order to please God, does his ordinary duties extraordinarily well.'[159] This was also the message propagated when the Informative Enquiry into the Reputation for Sanctity of Matt Talbot was opened in 1931. The Archbishop of Dublin was keen to point out that this was about the exaltation of the lowly and the glorifying of the humble, and that 'every priest whose mission has taken him amongst the poor of Dublin will have come into contact with many lives of marvellous holiness.' Devotees were warned, however, that while private devotion to Talbot was legitimate, public images of Talbot adorned with the insignia of sanctity were not because 'any attempt to anticipate the church's judgement by showing premature public liturgical honour would seriously impede the case.'[160] Flinn frequently referred to Talbot at Pioneer meetings as a staunch Pioneer and 'their Dublin working man, their brother Pioneer.' In the same breath he would refer to Fr William Doyle SJ in the hope that he too would be canonised as a role-model Pioneer. Doyle was renowned for his personal physical sacrifices, and microscopic examination of soul and conscience, and had been killed during the First World War when acting as a military chaplain. At an academic level, Alfred O'Rahilly in his biography of Doyle was adamant that 'the extremist or specialist has an important spiritual function in the world. He is not to be regarded simply as a deper-sonalised and generalised model for our mechanical imitation. He symbolises and incarnates man's perennial aspiration towards God.'[161] Fr John Sullivan SJ was another hero, and much was made of the fact that he jettisoned the opportunity to become an Edwardian gentleman of leisure in favour of prayer and self-sacrifice.[162]

While the Pioneer column in the *Irish Catholic* was not overly sympathetic to trade unionism or left-wing politics in general, in January 1941, Jim Larkin and the Workers Union of Ireland were singled out for praise for a notice at their annual New Year's Eve dance in the Mansion House which prohibited those under the influence of drink from entering, or staying on, the premises.[163] Larkin, though not a Pioneer, had since the beginning of his trade union days in Liverpool, called for restrictive licensing legislation. He equated excessive drinking with the oppression of the working classes and denounced its disastrous effects on the wives and children of labourers, a stance which had earned him the loyalty of workers' wives. A contemporary recalled that Larkin's methods of policing morals in this context were forthright: 'More than one drunken docker went head first down the steps of Liberty Hall with Larkin the propelling force. He was usually looked upon by those he chastised, when they sobered up as "only talking right" and "being for their own good".'[164]

Kevin Barry and Patrick Pearse were continually presented to juvenile Pioneers as fitting examples of the ideal patriots. However their biographers did not mention the Pioneer Association's contribution, if any, to their lives. While Pearse undoubtedly disliked and disapproved of drinking, Ruth Dudley Edwards merely placed this in the general context of a 'priggish and intolerant young man', who as well as abhorring pubs was 'indifferent also to food.'[165] Kevin Barry was seen as an even more appropriate role model in the eyes of the Jesuits, given his status as an ex-pupil of their Belvedere College and his reported confession on the eve of execution offering his life for the atonement of his sins in conjunction with prayers to the Sacred Heart. Contemporaries referred to him as 'a complete teetotaller', while his biographer, O'Donavan, suggested he was 'fond of a bottle of stout now and then'. Either way, the Pioneers of the 1930s would certainly have glossed over the fact that Barry may have died with the smell of alcohol on his breath – the dinner ordered for him under sentence of death, as recorded by the medical officer at Mountjoy, consisted of two pounds of potatoes, half-a-pound of bread, three-quarters of a pound of beef and one small bottle of stout.[166]

Other high-profile Pioneers, though undoubtedly committed members in the 1930s, had different attitudes as to what membership entailed. The Legion of Mary founded in Ireland in 1921, consisting of a central governing body, regional councils, weekly meeting praesidiums, and engaged in the sanctification of members through prayer and charity, had much in common with the Pioneer Association, and thrived during this period of the Catholic Lay Apostolate, as encouraged by Pope Pius XI. Like the Pioneer Association, the first four members were women, although there were clearly times when the Jesuits felt it was in competition with their female Children of Mary Sodality. The public figure most associated with the Pioneers was Frank Duff founder of the Legion of Mary, a committed Pioneer who wore a pin, according to his biographer 'as much to identify himself as a committed Catholic as to show concern for temperance', but also because alcoholism had affected his family to some extent.[167] Duff was later to admit, in a letter to the central director that he had committed one of the cardinal Pioneer sins by holding his meetings along lines that were unorthodox.[168] Nonetheless, unlike the Pioneers, physically and spiritually rescuing the victims of alcoholism was a part of the

Legion's work, though there was undoubtedly much overlap in membership of the two. It was not all black, as recounted by Leon O'Broin:

> Frank also promoted the temperance movement and would take alcoholics down to the Mount Mellary, which was then regarded as a recovery centre. A veritable folklore had built up around 'the cats', a local pub not far from the Abbey, where the hard goer had the chance of a final drink before he entered, but whose very nearness became a source of agony to him while drying-out inside. Frank's experiences, as he revealed them to me, were utterly hilarious.[169]

Similar tales were recounted about another unconventional though committed Pioneer, Canon Hayes of Bansha in Tipperary, and founder of the rural self-help group, Muintir na Tire, later to become a key speaker at Pioneer rallies. In keeping with the spirit of his primary concern, MNT, Hayes was quick to stress the social side of Pioneer membership, and indeed as a curate incurred the wrath of his parish priest in Ballybaden in Limerick by organising socials. Hayes was enthusiastic about the positive contribution to Irish society of pubs and moderate drinking. His biographer Rynne recalled, 'He acquiesced in the Pioneer rules, but did not make a fetish of them. Sometimes his actions were unconventional, such as taking off his Pioneer pin and sticking it in the lapel of a drunk who had alleged he would never drink again. He was the friend of alcoholics, seeking them out to encourage them . . . '[170] Fr Flinn would hardly have approved.

The ultimate hero and inspirational role model, however, remained the Association's founder, Fr Cullen. Whether through the weekly Pioneer column or AGM addresses and programmes, his words, deeds and reflections were repeated constantly by Fr Flinn and the Pioneer hierarchy. This took on a special resonance in 1941, the centenary of Cullen's birth. Flinn, though regretfully having to abandon the idea of a mass rally in his memory owing to war-time travel restrictions and rationing, recalled Cullen's memory publicly and privately with an eye to his possible future canonisation. In 1941 a Radio Éireann broadcast on the life of Cullen by Flinn concluded: 'You talked with him, you received kindness at his hands, or perhaps you had differences with him. You know stories about him. You have letters of his. Write and tell me all you know about him.'[171] Though the response was rather muted, one woman in Dublin recounted the alleged cure of a man with tuberculosis through the intercession of Fr Cullen. Another woman, then resident in England, claimed that Cullen had twice saved her from drowning in Dublin. The 1941 AGM took the form of a centenary celebration with Dr Staunton, Bishop of Ferns, at the helm. Here, Cullen was placed in an international context, in the company of

St Margaret Mary and Pope Pius X, in spreading devotion to the Sacred Heart to Ireland.[172]

The centenary was in many ways Fr Flinn's parting shot. He was suffering increasingly from ill-health which was undoubtedly exacerbated by the pace at which he worked. He died in May 1943. The previous summer the assistant director, Fr Leonard Gallagher, who had done Trojan work in the schools and colleges, died prematurely at the age of forty-three. In 1936, John Lang, probably the most influential lay member of the Pioneer Central Council, and who for twenty years had controlled admission to the SFX centre, had passed away. Some solace however was provided by the elevation of two prominent Pioneers to bishoprics in 1943 – Dr Eugene O'Callaghan of Clogher and Dr Daniel Cohalan of Waterford and Lismore. The issue of licensing reform was still to the fore in the final year of Flinn's tenure as central director. With over 40,000 new members that year, more vigorous opposition could have been expected, but it did not materialise, probably through a combination of Flinn's fading dynamism and the recognition, based on previous experience, that political confrontation did little to advance the standing of the Pioneers. The 1941 Bill, nevertheless, was criticised in the Pioneer Column. Despite the welcome abolition of the bona fide anachronism on weekdays, the Bill also provided increased facilities for Sunday opening and St Patrick's Day opening, and made no attempt to lessen the number of licences. It was referred to at the AGM that year as 'A crippled child.'[173]

Flinn had certainly succeeded in consolidating and enhancing the profile of the Pioneers, though this was not without some bruising experiences. He certainly succeeded in keeping the original aims of Fr Cullen to the forefront at all times, even though this became more difficult as the legislative, religious and social parameters of the drink question changed during the 1930s and early 1940s. Flinn had been quite happy to be utterly conservative on the basic tenets of Pioneer membership, though he combined this with an acute recognition of the need to give the Pioneers a higher public profile through mass mobilisation and the vigorous targeting of new, particularly youthful, audiences. In many ways he was of a traditional school that simply equated extremism with being extremely in the right. In this, he was very much a product of his environment and shared the conventional Catholic belief that there was a need to copper fasten political independence with a strict reinforcing of Catholic teaching and morality. Allowing for this, he was also careful to characterise the Pioneers in the overall temperance landscape as being unique, special and patriotic. Fr Sean McCarron, who had been appointed assistant central director in late 1942, took on the role of central director. He was another demonstrative man, sometimes spoken of, through a mixture of fear and admiration as 'the Bull'. Speaking at the 1942 AGM he came across as being as conservative as his predecessor, declaring:

> They had fought for centuries for freedom and they had achieved a partial freedom. Now there was danger that they might, of their own free choice, accept a standard of morality which the persecutions of centuries could not force upon them. Growing up in Ireland there was a social life cheap and foreign to their culture.[174]

In many ways, however, this was deceptive rhetoric. As central director, and one who thrived on confrontation, McCarron had his own identity and a distinct agenda for the Pioneers which involved a change of direction for the Association on many fronts, as he guided them through their third, and most glorious, phase.

NOTES

1   NAI, Department of Local Government and Public Health, 21/19, October 17, 1921
2   NAI, Dáil Éireann Files, 14/6, March 1922
3   Dunne, *Pioneers*, p. 24
4   PCIC, December 17, 1921
5   SOCA, Anon., A record of the number of badges distributed
6   PCIC, December 12, 1925
7   FMU, Reports, 1921–22
8   ibid. 1922–23
9   ibid.
10 PCIC, November 27, 1922
11 ibid.
12 LVAA, Annual Reports, Outlook, 1922
13 ibid.
14 NAI, DJ, H47A, Licensing Law Reform, March 19, 1923
15 *Irish Times*, January 9, 1924
16 NAI, DJ, H47A
17 ibid. DJ H47C, D and F
18 Senate Debates vol 3 col. 1122 November 26, 1924
19 NAI, H 47 (6) Licensing legislation, 1923
20 ibid. DJ H47A
21 ibid. DJ, H291 (43) June 30, 1925
22 ibid. DJ, H47A
23 ibid. and DJ, H47 B
24 Humphreys, 'Jansenists', p. 7
25 ibid. p. 53
26 *Irish Truth*, vol. 3, no. 4, August 29, 1925
27 ibid. October 16, 1926
28 Dáil Debates, February 16, 1927, col. 522
29 LVAA, LVA minutes, vol. 22, January 20, 1925
30 ibid. November 16, 1925
31 ibid. March 1, 1928
32 PCIC, December 1, 1924
33 *Irish Independent*, December 21, 1924
34 NAI, DJ H291 (32), March 24, 1925 and November 21, 1925

35   ibid. June 5, 1925
36   ibid. DJ,Intoxicating Liquor Commission (69), June 25, 1925, released 1996
37   ibid. DJ ILC (74), 24 July, 1925
38   Humphreys, 'Jansenists', Introduction
39   Quoted in Kostick, *Revolution in Ireland: Popular militancy 1917–23* (London 1996) p. 11
40   Tom Garvin, *Nationalist Revolutionaries in Ireland 1858 –1928* (London 1987)
41   *Irish Independent*, June 18, 1924
42   National Library of Ireland, Minutes of Evidence, Intoxicating Liquor Commission, April 6, 1925 R.21/13
43   ibid.
44   ibid.
45   *Irish Independent*, June 15, 1925
46   NLI, ILC, Minutes of evidence, R 21/14, June 16, 1925
47   CA, Copy of Dunne's paper
48   CA, Catholic Total Abstinence Federation of Ireland, Report 1923–26
49   NAI, DJ ILC (74) June 24, 1925
50   NLI, Minutes of evidence, ILC R.21/14, June 16, 1925
51   ibid.
52   *Report of the Intoxicating Liquor Commission* (Dublin 1925) p. 4
53   Blake and Williams, *Drink in Great Britain*, p. 124
54   *Messenger of the Sacred Heart*, February 1924, October 1925, May 1923
55   ibid. February 1924
56   ibid. April 30, 1926
57   ibid. July 26, 1927
58   ibid. May 12, 1928
59   PAA, *Pioneer* Silver Jubilee edition (Dublin 1924)
60   ibid.
61   ibid.
62   ibid.
63   SFX minute Book, December 31, 1929
64   ibid. March 21, 1930
65   ibid.
66   See below, p. 139ff
67   *Pioneer* Silver Jubilee Edition, (Dublin 1924)
68   PCIC, November 27, 1922 and January 5, 1923
69   Garda Museum, General Order no. 14 to all ranks, Intemperance, n.d.
70   PAA, minute book of Garda Pioneers, March 13, 1932 and November 11, 1931
71   PCIC, December 9, 1929
72   PAA, Garda minute book, June 19, 1932 and March 4, 1934
73   PCIC, December 9, 1929.
74   *Pioneer* Silver Jubilee edition, Appendix, Drink in Ireland, Facts and Figures
75   ibid.
76   Cormac O'Grada, *Ireland: A New Economic History* 1780–1939 (Oxford 1994) p. 397
77   Mary E. Daly, *A Social and Economic History of Ireland since 1800* (Dublin 1981) pp. 150–151
78   In conversation with Peter Walsh of the Guinness Museum
79   FMU Reports, 1929–30
80   SOCA, Waterford Annals, 1929–35
81   PCIC, October 7, 1933
82   PAA, J. Bird's Report on the Social Club, 1927–8
83   ibid. Letter soliciting funds for memorial hall, n.d.
84   ibid. Memo 'Socials' by J. Flinn, November 9, 1925
85   26th FMU Reports, 1926–7
86   McRedmond, *To the Greater* pp. 274–80
87   Desmond Fennell, *Changing Face of Catholic Ireland* (USA 1968) p. 201
88   James Devane, 'The Dancehall', *IER*, vol. 7, 1931
89   *Irish Independent*, August 19, 1929
90   *Irish Times*, March 2, 1929

91 Grace McCarthy, 'Moral and political attitudes of the Catholic Hierarchy: An analysis of Lenten Pastorals 1932–45' (unpublished MA thesis UCD, 1989)
92 *Irish Independent*, October 23, 1930
93 FMU Reports, 1930–1
94 ibid.
95 37th Annual FMU Report, 1937–8
96 PCIC, December 3, 1932
97 SOCA, Annals of Lady Lane Convent, Waterford, 1929–35
98 ibid.
99 PCIC, December 7, 1929
100 PAA, SFX minute Book May 24, 1933
101 ibid. November 25, 1936
102 ibid. December 30, 1936
103 R. Bales, 'Attitudes towards drinking' in Pitman (ed.), *Society Culture and Drinking* (New York 1962)
104 ibid. In conversation with Arensberg
105 ibid. p. 166
106 He chose to reveal this to Bale.
107 John Hunter, *The Temperance Problem in Northern Ireland* (Belfast 1925)
108 PAA, Typed manuscript of a press report, c. 1921
109 ibid, SFX Minutes, Collier to Flinn, December 6, 1933
110 FMU Reports, 1937–8
111 LVAA, Annual Report, 1932
112 ibid.
113 ibid. Annual Reports, 1933–7
114 PCIC, December 7, 1931
115 ibid. April 7, 1931
116 ibid. April 11, 1931
117 ibid. April 18, 1931
118 *Irish Times*, April 24, 1931
119 PAA, SFX Minutes, January 27, 1932 and February 24, 1932
120 PCIC, November 1932
121 PAA, AGM Programmes, 1922–42
122 PCIC, June 16, 1934
123 PAA, SFX Minutes, December 27, 1933
124 ibid. January 29, 1936 and September 19, 1936
125 ibid. July 28, 1937
126 SFX Minutes, August 25, 1933
127 *Irish Independent*, November 23, 1931
128 PCIC, April 27, 1935
129 PAA, Irish Association for the Prevention of Intemperance, Minutes, March 23, 1939
130 ibid. April 27, 1939
131 ibid. November 23, 1939
132 PAA, SFX Minutes, February 24, 1937
133 PCIC, April 2, 1937
134 FMU Reports, 1935–6
135 ibid. 1937–8
136 Humphreys, 'Jansenists', p. 147
137 ibid. p. 187
138 PCIC, July 2, 1931
139 McRedmond, *To the Greater*, p. 239
140 PCIC, June 1929
141 ibid. May 1932
142 ibid. December 9, 1937
143 ibid. May 19, 1938, and also Mathias Bodkin, *The Heroic Offering: A talk to young Pioneers* (Dublin 1942)
144 PCIC, March 14, 1940
145 ibid. June 27, 1940

146 PAA, Annual Report, 1940 and PCIC, December 18, 1941
147 PCIC, May 27, 1940
148 ibid. August 24, 1939
149 PAA, Annual Reports, 1927–42
150 ibid. Annual Report ,1940
151 *Irish Press*, January 1, 1939
152 PCIC, January 19, 1939
153 PAA, Annual Report, 1938
154 Hogan, *Irish Missionary*, p. 111
155 PCIC, December 1, 1928
156 PAA, O'Hehir to Halpin 1932, and Flinn's 'Notes on Australia'
157 ibid. Memo on Australia
158 ibid. O'Hehir to Flinn November 6, 1934 and Stephenson to Flinn, August 20, 1937
159 Joseph Glynn, *Life of Talbot* (Dublin 1928) p. vi and p. 177
160 IER , vol. 38, 1931
161 Alfred O'Rahilly, *Fr William Doyle SJ* (London 1925) pp. xv–xvi
162 Mathias Bodkin, *Port of Tears: the life of Fr John Sullivan SJ* (Dublin 1953)
163 PCIC, January 9, 1941
164 Emmet Larkin, *James Larkin: Irish Labour leader* (London 1965), p. 161
165 Ruth Dudley Edwards, *Patrick Pearse: The Triumph of Failure* (London, 1979), p. 120
166 Donal O'Donavan, *Kevin Barry and His Time* (Dublin, 1989) p. 122
167 Leon O'Broin, *Frank Duff: A Biography* (Dublin ,1982) p. 38
168 PAA, Frank Duff letter to Daniel Dargan, n.d. [c.1962]
169 O'Broin, *Duff*, p. 9
170 Stephen Rynne, *Father John Hayes* (Dublin 1960) p. 133
171 PAA, Transcript of Flinn's Radio Broadcast, 1941
172 ibid. Bride Rooney to Flinn, October 21, 1941, PCIC, November 27, 1941 and December
     4, 1941
173 PCIC, December 12, 1942
174 ibid.

CHAPTER FOUR

Aggressive Domination

We do not believe in Prohibition. We believe in temperance and we believe spirituous liquors are not diabolical things at all. It is the abuse of them that is the trouble . . . I am reminded that when I was a girl there was a man working for my family and he took his whiskey neat. When someone thought it would be a good thing if he were to mix it with water he said that he would not do so. He had an iron stomach and the water might rust it. For that reason he drank his whiskey neat. We gave him good whiskey and he lived to a ripe old age. I have nothing to say against whiskey. I think whiskey is a very good thing, if taken in moderation.

Senator Helena Concannon, 1946

A bird never flew on one wing – of course not. But that is hardly a good argument to make you have a drink which you would be better without. It is so easy to slip from one drink, to three, to more, and yet to do so is to court disaster more grievous than that of the bird which tries to fly on one wing.

Pioneer Advertisement, 1946

The 1940s and 1950s were the decades in which the Pioneer Association seemed to triumph. Despite Fr McCarron's use of the language of continuity as he familiarised himself with his new role, he soon developed a new and dynamic rhetoric which was illustrative of the increased role the Association attempted to play in Irish society. While the fundamentals remained – devotion to the Sacred Heart through strict abstinence – the context in which the traditional Pioneer aims were manifested changed, as did the membership, which at least on paper, approached half a million by the end of the fifties. It was an extraordinary figure for such a small country, and the Pioneer chiefs continually framed their ideals in a national context by equating membership with a particularly devout and public form of patriotism. It was an era of mass public Pioneer rallies and celebrations, most notably the Golden and Diamond Jubilees in Croke Park in 1949 and

1959. Yet this careful orchestration of public and religious triumphalism necessitated a simultaneously increasing concern with secular issues. The Pioneer Association had to become more explicitly a business. This involved not only acquiring more personnel, but also taking a stance on the numerous debates on drink issues. It also involved the Pioneers in an ambitious, though, as will be seen, frustratingly flawed attempt to establish the Association outside Ireland. It was in areas like this that the Association could fall between the two stools of active pressure group and vast religious sodality, an invidious position which was to haunt them in the following decades. In one sense, McCarron was eminently suited to the task: religiously, a staunch traditionalist, but with an eye for secular relevancy, and the need to modernise. In this, he showed himself to be more adaptable than his predecessors. But there were inconsistencies. The Pioneers still failed to become remotely politically effective. Although they never explicitly claimed this to be part of their agenda, in practice there were times when it could not be avoided. Writing in 1978, Bernard McGuckian, the central director, noted about McCarron:

> With his own gifts it is not inconceivable that he could have led it into a preoccupation with humanitarian, philanthropic or even political issues. On drink legislation for instance, he was fearless in expressing himself. But he never allowed anything to deflect Pioneers from their primary commitment to personal prayer and self-denial, freely offered to the Sacred Heart of Jesus.[1]

This, however, is a simplification of the difficulties faced by the Pioneers, even at the time of their greatest success, and glosses over the gulf between their often triumphalist rhetoric and their inability to influence in a practical sense.

There was still a marked hostility to the Pioneers from certain quarters and a school of thought persisted which did not deem temperance a particularly suitable or relevant form of Catholic Action, even amongst the Catholic Hierarchy. An ambiguity about what exactly they stood for remained, despite their ability to throng Dublin with devotees marching gloriously to Benediction at Croke Park. But propaganda was seen to pay dividends. In terms of galvanising people, the robust McCarron was an unqualified success. Through careful cultivation of both young and old, he demonstrated the ability to make the association extraordinarily attractive to prospective members. He used many traditional arguments and methods, including the targeting of enemies and the inculcation of a certain paranoia, but he also created new means, and different forums. This mix of old and new was what made him so effective. But was this Catholic action or

Pioneer action? With regard to the wearing of the pin, McCarron insisted in his revised version of the *Temperance Catechism*, that 'Persons who object to the wearing of it are not thinking with the mind of the Church.'[2] This was the kind of categorical pronouncement which could be resented by even the most pious of non-Pioneer Catholics. But even officially it seems the Pioneers were not easily classified. In the *Catholic Workers' Handbook* of 1942, there was no mention of the Association under the section 'Catholic Social Movements' (which included the Legion of Mary and the St. Vincent de Paul Society). Instead they were listed under 'other Social Organisations'.[3] In essence, as the Association increased its membership, and as it saw it, its mandate, its very size led it to be more defensive about its worldly significance, or as its critics saw it, its lack of significance. Thus in the Summer of 1944, readers of the *Irish Catholic* learned that 'one of the principal aims of the Pioneer movement at the moment is to dispel utterly false notions about our standards, motives and ideals'. It was stated baldly that the Association was not against drinking, was not a social organisation and was not pursuing a vendetta against anyone.[4] This, however, was not a momentary preoccupation. McCarron became almost obsessive over the next decade with dispelling what he saw as disingenuous, hurtful and uncharitable insults or myths about the Association. He clearly found it frustrating that there were so many ideas in circulation, many of them contradictory, about an Association whose aims, in theory at least, were clear-cut and simple. The problem was that the original rhetoric of the founder did not necessarily correspond to changed external environments. The irony was that many of the insults flung at the Pioneers were almost invited. They too had indulged in their fair share of disingenuous, hurtful and uncharitable moments, which were inevitable given how closely temperance and excess existed side by side in such a small country. For the time being, the middle ground rarely got a look in, and this certainly suited McCarron. As he saw it, the Pioneer movement was growing, but so were the evils it sought to combat.

McCarron's initial concern was to sharpen the administrative side of the Association, to re-inject vigour into the stalwarts who may have been tiring and to convert a new generation. He encouraged a more active participation. An interesting departure in November 1944 was his announcement that with regard to the AGM 'a new feature in this year's concert programme will be a question time.'[5] He continually emphasised the necessity of rules, and was quite disgusted to discover at his own SFX branch the following year 'that none of the council members held a copy of the rules for the guidance of members.'[6] He was also determined to pluck a thorn in the side of his predecessors – the fact that the government had persistently refused to allow members of the Irish Army to wear the Pioneer pin on their uniforms. The Pioneer leadership not only saw this as an anomaly, particularly when the gardai had full permission, but also as detrimental to the Pioneer quest to get the pillars of the community to set an example by wearing the emblem. A serious drink problem among army personnel was viewed as an urgent malaise worthy of spiritual remedy. In June, 1922, a Pioneer centre had been established at the military camp in the Curragh, but was found unworkable. In 1934 another attempt was made at Renmore station, but the frequency with which men moved from post to post, coupled with demobilisation, rendered it ineffectual. Representations had previously been made to consecutive Ministers for Defence, in an attempt to persuade them to drop the ban. Richard Mulcahy in the 1920s had turned down the request, but, according to Flinn 'the proposal scarcely got a fair chance at that time, being put forward by one who had no right to speak for the Association.'[7] Frank Aiken had also proved unwavering, but there was hope that his successor, Oscar Traynor, himself a Pioneer, would be more receptive. Flinn urged Fr Carey, the Army Chaplain in the Curragh, to use his influence, but in October 1940, Traynor rejected the idea on the grounds that it could open the floodgates to similar requests from other associations. This was despite his own abstinence and being, in his own words, one 'whose tendencies would be towards acceding to rather than refusing the requests.'[8] There were still thwarted attempts to establish centres at Lullymore Camp, Griffith Barracks, Renmore Barracks, Enniskerry and Portobello, but given the premium placed on the wearing of the badge, and with the granting of indulgences being dependent on it, Flinn refused to abandon his mission.

Given his ill-health and subsequent death the issue was left temporarily in abeyance. But in July 1943, in a clever tactical move, McCarron arranged a meeting with Traynor to discuss the issue, and brought the formidable Senator Margaret Pearse, a staunch Pioneer and sister of the dead patriot. McCarron wrote, with understatement, that 'Miss Pearse and myself were frank.'[9] It was a sentence which undoubtedly camouflaged what may have been heated exchanges, but working in their favour was the fact that along with Pearse, the Chief-of-Staff of the army was also on their side. Traynor relented and agreed that from September the Pioneer pin could be worn on the uniform. A jubilant McCarron wrote to Traynor: 'Your courage in granting the permission will not be forgotten to you by our members throughout the country'.[10] In the light of reports of increased drunkenness in the army, it was seen by the Pioneers as a well-overdue concession. In April, 1943, a Special Order on the subject of discipline and drink, by Major General Costello who commanded the First Division in Collins Barracks, Cork, had been hard-hitting and explicit, with distinct echoes of Eoin O'Duffy's criticisms of the gardai two decades earlier, though in this instance there was more of an air of tragedy:

> No officer would willingly take into his unit an inmate of a lunatic asylum . . . any man who gets drunk, in the military sense not merely renders himself ineffective as a soldier, he becomes by reason of the loss of his reasoning power and self-control, exactly like the lunatic . . . We have a case in which a soldier under the influence of drink took a revolver, entered a billet and shot two NCOs dead in the presence of a roomful of his comrades. Our units have lost many fine officers over incidents which have had their origin in drinking to excess or drinking on duty. Even if no more serious consequences have occurred, Officers have had to be got rid of because excessive drinking has led to debt as well as incompetence. Many men whose lives have been ruined by VD owe their downfall to drink . . . '[11]

This was exactly the type of evidence which McCarron was looking for. A few months later, after he had procured a copy of the order, he wrote to General Costello, expressing a desire to visit in order to form a Pioneer branch. In response, Costello welcomed the initiative, though he felt the need to point out that he was not an abstainer and that 'it would be unfair to the troops under my command to suggest that they are more lawless or prone to drunkenness than those of other commands.'[12] Following McCarron's visit, forty soldiers at the barracks took the Pioneer pledge.

The difficulty of spreading the Pioneer gospel in the army ranks, however, was reflected in truculent correspondence between Central Office and various military chaplains. McCarron was fearful that army Pioneer groups would not be the absolute models of sobriety he envisaged, unless strictness and uniformity were inculcated from the outset. Fr Robert Higgins in the McKee Barracks admitted 'we have many opponents', but instead of elaborating in that direction, he was effusive in his assessment of the potential rather than the reality of the rate of membership in the army:

> A soldier with a Pioneer pin is something you feel like going down on your knees and thanking God for. It is a challenge to the world. The Total Abstinence Association means a lot to the soldiers' wife and children. They have more nourishment, better clothes and better homes and above all the good example of a temperate father.[13]

Nevertheless, the facilities officially provided in Officers' and NCO's messes and canteens for the consumption of drink continued to flourish. Fr O'Riordan of Baldonnel summed up the attitude of many when he attested to McCarron that he had always fought shy of Pioneers because it seemed too exalted an ideal for the average man and certainly for the average soldier, given that most of his colleagues would be drinking.[14] There was also a ludicrous suggestion from Fr McLoughlin, chaplain to the Collins' Barracks in Dublin (he was not a Pioneer which made his suggestion even more incredible), 'that the button which closes a soldier's breast pocket have the Pioneer emblem imprinted on it, so that the soldier must cut it out if he wishes to drink.'[15] Understandably, this was not a proposal seriously considered by Central Office. The relationship of the Pioneers with the army was at best, an uneasy alliance. It was as much a problem of administration as anything else. McCarron was frequently worried that he was not getting enough information, in the form of correspondence, as to how the various Pioneer centres were faring, particularly those in the outer army posts. Never slow to express his annoyance with those who did not correspond frequently, McCarron was discovering that he did not have the same degree of control over the army Pioneers as he did with the gardai. There was also a resentment from certain chaplains that he did not appreciate the military way of life. His complaints about irregular meetings merited the following sarcastic response from Fr Thomas Smyth in Clonmel in late 1943:

> I can well imagine that your business methods have been greatly shocked by the irregularity of my correspondence. Before passing judgement however, an idea of army life might help you to appreciate the many difficulties that one has to contend with in the provincial military posts. You may think that we enjoy the stability of the metropolitan stations, but let me assure you, nothing could be further from the truth.[16]

It was fitting that the phrase 'business methods' was being employed in relation to the Pioneer cause and serves to illustrate the degree to which expansion necessitated an increasing concern with secular and administrative aspects. In 1944 the Pioneers acquired offices in Upper Sherard Street, near Mountjoy Square in Central Dublin. It was part of a wider scheme to stabilise the Association administratively. This led to confrontation with the Sisters of Charity who had looked after the ordering and dispatching of Pioneer pins since the foundation of the association in return for which they received a contribution towards the maintenance of their orphanage. For some years McCarron had found the sisters' work, under the direction of the ailing Sr Josephine, unsatisfactory, and he drew attention to the haphazard distribution of pins which had given rise to many complaints. Clearly, in the eyes of McCarron, some complaints were more significant than others. As well as bemoaning a spate of unanswered letters, ill-kept accounts and a failure to deal with correspondence in proper rotation, he wrote: 'Priests, who called personally, and frequently had no right to badges at all, were given preference over centres who had ordered by post, and in one case a Bishop.'[17] McCarron decided to air the issue with the Reverend Mother of the convent, though he later described this as a 'chance meeting'. What developed was clearly a rather uncomfortable exchange, with McCarron lamenting the decline in the standard of the sisters' work, and the Reverend Mother suggesting he do it himself. 'Fr McCarron, rather to her surprise, agreed to do so.'[18] McCarron's subsequent letter to Sr Josephine was as curt as it was ungracious, given the workload she had carried since the era of Cullen: 'If I remember rightly you were just forty years in charge of the Pioneer supplies. I am arranging to have forty Masses said for your intentions.'[19] This did not end the matter, and clearly there was a residual bitterness which affected the relationship between the Pioneers and the sisters. The following year the Pioneer contribution to the orphanage was refused, according to McCarron, because of 'a misunderstanding of our motives', but according to Sr Columba, 'As our help in the association *has been withdrawn* any profit which might accrue from it should not be accepted by us.' A few weeks later Sr Columba felt it necessary to assure McCarron that 'our help has not been withdrawn in the way of prayers. I thought this was understood.'[20]

McCarron had a particular preoccupation with increasing the profile of the Association as a means of revitalising areas that were experiencing depopulation. But, in May 1945, he drew attention to sparsely populated areas that were showing very large increases in membership, and voiced suspicion about the genuineness of many of these members, writing in the *Irish Catholic* that he would prefer the Association at a standstill than 'growing in the wrong way'.[21] He was also keen to hammer home the desirability of administering a temporary pledge, particularly for those whom he believed were too immature to grapple with, or appreciate the severity of the life-time pledge. In doing so, he tentatively questioned the wisdom of the rule which allowed for full adult membership at sixteen years of age, and admitted to his own SFX Council that 'he would like to make minimum age for probation seventeen or eighteen years but that he was slow to alter the original rules'. His solution to this was to encourage the temporary pledge, unless the putative young members had 'close and constant contact with a Pioneer'.[22]

As with the First World War, the Second World War was accredited with providing the occasion for a loosening of morals and over-indulgence in drink, and again women were singled out. Women drinking were still placed in a category infinitely more detestable than that of men. The Pioneer column was frequently reserved for comment on the onslaughts of 'The Modern Woman', where modernity was equated with their tendency to frequent many of the new 'lounge' bars without shame. As usual there was an onus on the women to provide virtuous and religious stability at a time when the world was being divided by material vice and greed in the form of war:

> The general intention of the Apostleship of Prayer for the month of August is that maidens living in the world excel in the virtues especially necessary at the present time. This intention, which carries with it the approval of the Pope is one which must appeal to all who have at heart the desire to see fostered in our own times the traditional sense of modesty and reserve which throughout history has been the mark of Catholic womanhood.[23]

The column was quite specific about the belief that, with pubs becoming increasingly attractive, people were inclined to drink more and indulge in the sin which followed. This accusation was resented by the Licensed Vintners Association who presented the improvement in the standards of comfort in public houses, or what they termed the 'public house movement', as contributing directly to temperance. The vintners also quoted the Royal Commission on Licensing in England and Wales, 1929–31, which had suggested that the improved public house was a deterrent to insobriety. Specifically, the LVA resented temperance advocates busying themselves with the valuation of the increased number of lounge bars which they saw as contributing nothing 'to the arrest of a social development which is only one of the obvious results of the industrial-cum-urban and cinematic civilisation of which we are now a part.'[24] Righteous indignation was the order of the vintners' day as they grew tired of being lampooned as accommodaters if not instigators, of moral decline. They still presented themselves as, if not champions of temperance, at least facilitators of moderation, and their analysis of abstainers' diatribes were laced with contempt. In his report of 1945, the Chairman of the LVA, George Brady, drew attention to the tact and diplomacy that had been necessary during the war to convince people that whiskey could not be supplied in as full a measure as formerly. He then asserted that vintners needed to have a voice at government level to counter black propaganda:

> We have been subjected to vicious, ill-informed, and offensive reproach from certain sections of the press. Our members are much more interested in the good conduct of their business and the preservation of

a high moral tone, than the self-constituted moral censors blinded by fanaticism and bigotry. The informed public-house movement which has made such headway in the last twenty years ensures not only comfort for patrons, but cultivates an atmosphere for social intercourse, conversation and discussion. The last man the publican wants to see on his premises is the immoderate drinker who is his own worst enemy and a nuisance generally.[25]

But the vintners rarely referred to the women whom the Pioneers portrayed as the main beneficiaries of the increased comfort of pubs. A willingness to expose the modern Girls' embracing of a new culture of toleration led some Pioneers to scour the Press seeking out references to 'fallen women', or models of insobriety, and ultimately objects of pity who were letting the women of Ireland down. In this quest they came up with the occasional gem. In the same year as Brady's address they published an extract in the Pioneer column from a piece which had appeared in the *People's Weekly*, drawing attention to a headline which trumpeted the feats of a female civil servant, aged twenty-five, who had become a pint-drinking champion in a pub eight miles from Dublin. This woman, described as 'slim and attractive' had knocked back eight pints 'and she did not seem any the worse for it. She said it's a system – you just keep your head.' The woman did not want her name to appear in print in case her mother would find out. The Pioneer column caustically remarked 'At least she has some respect for her mother if not for herself.'[26]

During the post-war period, the Pioneer leadership continued to decry the increased consumption of drink and frequently pointed to other countries where, it was maintained, consumption had fallen. Simultaneously they drew attention to the shortages of basic foodstuffs, which was still prevalent in Ireland. Typically, and simplistically, they went as far as to suggest that the choice was between famine and beer. The questions were unrelenting: if Poland's Minister for Supplies, Sztachelski, was curtailing the use of cereals in the production of beer, why could Sean Lemass not do likewise? Why couldn't Ireland match the French initiative in combating alcoholism by promoting 'dry' clubs? Why couldn't Ireland reduce its beer production in parallel with America and Britain in the post-war years?[27] The expansion of Dublin suburban housing schemes at this time was another concern, particularly given the applications being made to the Dublin Corporation Housing Committee to provide attendant licensed premises. The Central Council of the Pioneers was adamantly opposed to these applications. In November 1945, a conference was summoned by the Housing Committee and a decision was made not to allow the licences to be processed though this was later overturned by the courts.[28] Opposition had also been expressed by the trade unionist, James Larkin, who the following year insisted that, not only was Dublin Corporation corrupted by publicans, but that there should be no representatives of the drink trade on any legislative body, in the same way that clergy were not entitled to become members of county councils. He also accused the Catholic Church of being 'too squeaky, too mealy-mouthed about attacking the liquor trade'. The vintners in retaliation caricatured Larkin as a 'power-drunk' trade union secretary.[29]

There was opposition in the same year to a Bill designed to provide for the sale of liquor at turf clubs, with the Minister for Supplies, Lemass, anxious to provide for what he termed the 'ordinary needs' of the bog cutters. The Pioneer Association got a commitment from Senator Margaret Pearse to move an amendment on the Bill in the Senate to curtail the sale of alcohol but she quickly succumbed to pressure from her party colleagues in Fianna Fáil to drop it. She merely pleaded that alternative refreshments be provided, with Lemass pointing out that legislation was not necessary to ensure this ('There should be a roof on the canteen but it is not necessary to make it law'). The Pioneers in this instance, as often happened on the political stage, were presented as carping begrudgers. All that Senator James Tunney, a Pioneer, could mutter was 'God help the poor Pioneers who have to sleep in the same rooms along with these fellows who drink.'[30]

McCarron was constantly looking for new ways of expanding the Pioneers. Some were more successful than others. He was anxious in particular to establish centres among what were perceived as areas of special influence in Irish society – government circles, civil servants and the gardai were frequent targets. Certain civil servants in the Department of Education and the Department of Posts and Telegraphs were active in this regard. But other initiatives could be thwarted. In 1946 it was recorded in the minutes of the Central Council that McCarron:

> had received a suggestion from Mr Rooney – *Irish Times* golf correspondent, that a golfing society confined to Pioneers might be formed and that its influence would be considerable in clubs visited by the members. After a full discussion it was agreed that the disadvantages might outweigh any temporary good such a society might have and in consequence the project did not meet with approval.[31]

The *Irish Times* also found itself excluded from another preoccupation of the Association that year. In March 1946, there was a meeting of the Central Council to discuss a proposal from a wealthy young Dublin businessman who (though wishing to remain anonymous) was anxious to fund an advertising campaign promoting temperance. It was decided to go ahead with the project, confining the advertisements to the *Irish Press*, the *Irish Independent* and the Catholic weeklies.[32] The Association was careful about how it delivered its message, and there was a recognition of the need to avoid the charge of extremism. In this, they showed insight, by concentrating on traditional and typically weekly scenes in pubs countrywide, the language that was used, and the need to question drinkers' habits by pointing them gently in the direction of the *Temperance Catechism*, which, it was stressed, would answer their queries in a common sense way, and without exaggeration. In all, nineteen advertisements were inserted from May to December, 1946. In what was superficially a secular campaign, readers were reminded that the ads had been paid for by 'a young man, still in his twenties, and by the way, not a Pioneer'. The following were typical examples:

> Q. 'Is it ever a mortal sin to become partially drunk?
> A. If you drink at all that is a question of importance to you. You will find it answered in the *Temperance Catechism*.'
> 'Is there ever an obligation in conscience not to stand another person a drink?'
> 'Has human respect, through the fear of being thought mean, ever caused you to stand a drink that you know you should have had the courage to refuse?'
> 'Tamper with the foundations and you endanger the whole structure of a building. Are not the drinking habits of so many women today eating into the foundations of morality on which the whole structure of social life is built?'[33]

In retrospect, McCarron believed the ad campaign had succeeded to a certain extent in framing temperance in a positive light, but not enough to justify the continuance of the scheme.[34] The *Temperance Catechism* referred to was McCarron's updated version of the original Cullen book. Most of the research and work involved in its rewriting had been done by Jim Bird, a prominent lay member of the Central Council. It was McCarron's attempt to reiterate traditional temperance arguments about the spiritual consequences of excess, whilst courting modernity in terms of how alcohol should be contextualised. Always underpinning his thesis was a warning which drew attention to the dangers of 'bad company'. In his introduction, McCarron mentioned that he had submitted the text to a prominent Dublin doctor who had approved the sections dealing with the medical and physical consequences of alcohol intake, and that 'care has been taken to avoid anything like exaggeration in presenting the matter, so that its contents may be taken as trustworthy.'[35] Taken in its entirety, the Catechism mirrored the Pioneer's wider aim of forming an exclusive club, and the logic presented was that moderate drinking could and would only lead to one thing – excessive drinking. Balanced conclusions were not on the agenda, despite a preface disclaiming exaggeration. Another subtext was that those who did drink aimed solely at getting non-drinkers to start drinking. It fitted neatly with McCarron's constant message to secondary school students – that ultimately it was a sneering and condescending peer pressure which would persuade many to take a drink they did not desire. It was a negative message, but consistent with McCarron's determination to split Ireland into two distinct camps in relation to drinking. He urged those who were committed to keeping the pledge to 'avoid the company of those who might tempt us to be unfaithful'. Likewise, hospitality drinks 'could hardly be described as a friendly act'. In short, offering a social drink was a declaration of malicious intent:

> Q. Can drink, even if not taken to excess, lead to sin?
> A. Yes, because the company and places in which people normally indulge in drink are themselves frequently occasions of sin for those persons, and often a temptation to drink to excess.'[36]

For younger children, McCarron was later to provide a short Temperance Catechism for primary schools. The message was similar, only further simplified, though perhaps ironic, given McCarron's reluctance in private to see people so young taking on the responsibility of a long-term pledge: 'The two principal causes of intemperance are bad example and bad company. The best thing to do with regard to alcoholic drink is to abstain from it completely.'[37]

On assuming office, McCarron sought to revive the Garda Centre which had lapsed into oblivion. Like his predecessors, he praised the Gardai as representing all that was best about the Irish State. But in courting the Gardai he had another agenda – the specific targeting of trainees with a view to pressurising them to be utterly vigilant about the enforcement of licensing laws. Simply put, Gardai Pioneers had duties above and beyond those of the ordinary Pioneer. Having taken over the spiritual direction of the Phoenix Park Depot himself, McCarron was relentless in addressing this point, and with urging the recruits to stand firm in the face of taunts from Gardai who drank. There was plenty of hostility within the force to the Pioneers but this did not stop them agreeing 'to request the authorities to place an official car at the disposal of Fr McCarron in future on his visit to the Depot'.[38] The Pioneer centre was required to meet on the first Sunday of every month, and discussions 'dealt with the difficulties young men would be faced with postings to the country with special reference to the enforcement of the licensing laws'. McCarron warned them 'about the attitude which would be shown by some of their fellow members, but urged them to be steadfast', an implicit reference to the fact that the editor of the *Garda Review* was believed to be actively hostile towards temperance matters.[39] In imploring them to seek the company of other Pioneers, McCarron regarded the final meeting of particular batches of recruits, before they were posted to various stations, as the most important. The drink culture, as he saw it, touched on almost every aspect of their lives, present and future:

> Fr McCarron referred to the recent suicide of a member who thought he had no other way out. This was a fatal mistake, because there were always other ways. It is to be feared that intoxicating drink played a part in the member's untimely end. Fr McCarron spoke of the danger of members putting themselves under a compliment to publicans. They had no longer freedom of action. Enforcement of the licensing laws was part of the job which members of the force undertook to do and were paid for doing. He referred to the huge amount of money being spent on drink and that there was no doubt but the drink element entered largely into practically all crimes committed.[40]

Regular Pioneer readers of the *Irish Catholic*, however, were spared such detail. In March 1948 it referred to the sixty three 'towering and handsome' young men in the Garda Depot received into the Pioneer Association and referred to one who 'every morning, before he goes on duty, can be seen leading his two little children by the hand, down to school. A simple and homely gesture, it has made a deep impression on many north-side citizens who recognise in the uniformed garda on point duty, the father who is devoted to his family.'[41] This was a typical Pioneer journalistic tactic, to combine the tragic with the edifying – this particular piece came in the aftermath of a series of columns which had blamed drink for the neglect of underfed children, an increase in the drinking habits of young children, the custom of treating or the buying of rounds, the evil of the drunken dance, and the fact that while CIE could not change its engines from coal to oil burning fast enough to combat shortages, leaving the rail transport system almost at a standstill, the Guinness company had succeeded in obtaining sufficient equipment to change from coal to oil burning to increase production.[42]

The Association also continued the policy of organising regional rallies, touring the secondary schools, and generally keeping the movement oiled in as many diverse districts as possible. By the end of 1945 they claimed a membership of 350,000 and 1,165 affiliated centres. Seventy-one new centres were added the following year. It was a steady progression, and the rallies to which they were invited involved well-known priests like the Jesuits, Fr Robert Nash, Fr Leonard Shiel and Fr John Hayes of Muintir na Tire to speak at annual meetings and to indulge in deliberate theatrics. Addressing 5,000 delegates at the AGM in the Capitol Theatre in 1946, Fr Nash thundered: 'I am here to make those rafters ring with a mighty protest against the iniquitous enemies of Jesus Christ who engage in this foul business of selling after hours and selling drink to those who are in no fit state to take it!'[43] Interest in the annual meetings was such that from 1947 onwards two meetings were held simultaneously in Dublin, to maximise the effect of the theatrical set-pieces. The minutes of the Central Council reveal that there was a certain resentment against country delegates being allowed to reserve seats – the breakdown of delegates in 1947 was 2,500 members in the Capitol Cinema, 4,100 in the Theatre Royal with approximately one quarter of those being country delegates.[44]

Given the enthusiasm and publicity which these meetings raised, it is interesting that at the lower administrative level the Association was still relatively antiquated. The Pioneer hierarchy relied on a voluntary network of seven or eight committed lay Catholics to handle admission to the SFX council, nationwide publicity material and distribution of badges. The part-time Assistant Director, Fr Gallagher, as well as having responsibility for promoting the Pioneers within the schools also had to ensure the return of the annual 'Query Sheets', which had to be completed by each individual Pioneer council giving details of membership and progress. In late 1943 due to an increased office work-load, a group of voluntary women Pioneers was formed to help with the dispatch of Pioneer pins – they were replaced the following year by the first official part-time staff member of the Association. Jim Bird, a voluntary worker and central council member, was a typical example of one who devoted his life to Pioneer activity. In effect, from 1923–44 he had been the only Pioneer 'staff' member – until 1927 he had laboured in one of the parlours used for confessions on the corridors of the SFX Church in Gardiner Street, and as McCarron noted wryly in 1947, 'this arrangement had obvious disadvantages, as it meant, for instance when confessions were being heard, he was displaced.'[45] By 1948, with the acquisition of new offices in Sherard Street, a more concentrated staff arrangement included a secretary, clerk and three women helpers, as well as the acquisition of a second-hand Ford car. As late as 1950, however, central council members were still complaining of having to receive applications for membership in a dull and draughty kitchen in Sherrard Street, with the added irritant of music-loving neighbours who clearly were not remotely interested in Pioneer ideals: 'Mr O'Connell protested to the people in the next room, but was told to go to hell. He did not think that the loud-speaker, or the manner in which he was received by the people in the room, was in keeping with the spirit of the work we are engaged in.'[46]

These were inconveniences which McCarron believed were part of the general sacrifice which Pioneer membership and work entailed. He believed that these voluntary contributions underpinned an ethos which the Association could ill afford to lose. Cullen too had been adamant, when establishing the Association that no money would be solicited except for pins, and certainly no affiliation fees. McCarron stuck to the view that the Pioneer Association was a business, but a spiritual one, and even though temperance concerns were becoming more secular he stuck rigidly to the anti-material line: 'Perhaps the more generous supply of funds would allow of more publicity, but the spiritual aspect of the work and its independence would suffer. There is no doubt that as the Association now works it accomplishes far more effective and lasting work than if it had great wealth behind it.'[47] In the same year he admitted to his Provincial that the Association's finances were healthy, showing a profit of £500 on the previous year's work. Two years later, in a similar letter, he urged the Provincial to appoint him an extra assistant and requested to be relieved from his priestly church duties due to his increased work load.[48]

Perhaps the scale of the work was partly because, in terms of the wider temperance movement, the Pioneers effectively had the field to themselves. The FMU rarely featured publicly in temperance debates during these years. The Irish Association for the Prevention of Intemperance was still active, albeit on a tiny scale. The IAPI bristled with elaborate ideas and some flamboyant personalities, but had neither the personnel nor the status to be remotely effective. It was still a mixed group of Quakers, Presbyterians and prominent Church of Ireland businessmen, like the booksellers Walter Hanna and Harold Eason. Hanna had suggested in 1944 that the IAPI should affiliate with the Pioneer Association but was informed that 'we have often tried to get the Pioneers to help us, but that this association is not total abstinence, whereas the Pioneers is.' Another measure of indifference was that, of the 300 questionnaires sent to Dáil candidates before the 1943 General Election on their attitude to temperance, only 30 bothered to reply.[49] In the same year the veteran Fr Peter Coffey had resigned as president owing to ill-health. The IAPI was desperate to keep him on 'on the understanding that he would not be asked to do any work or be given any trouble, his name being valuable to the association, and no other person in view that could be approached to succeed him.'[50] In many ways the IAPI were very advanced in their views on drink – in 1949, for example, they were demanding that a blood-test be introduced to deter drunken drivers, an idea well ahead of its time. They also frequently saw the Northern Irish Government as having a far more enlightened approach to the issue of temperance education. But few seemed to be listening. At their 1947 AGM twenty were present and twenty-two sent apologies. They also found it difficult to attract new activists, most of the members still being relatives of prominent late-nineteenth-century temperance advocates. Although the IAPI remained in existence for the next forty years, by 1950, an executive member, Mr Connor, was admitting that 'sometimes it appeared to him that the work they are doing for the cause is like throwing back the tide with the assistance of a pitchfork.'[51]

In the early days of 1948, the Pioneer column in the *Irish Catholic* had saluted a Pioneer member of the Offaly County Council, Paul Fanning, who had announced that the Pioneers were 'neither pussy-foots nor prohibitionists', when rejecting a resolution from Fermoy urban council protesting against increased tax on beer and tobacco. The column congratulated him on defending his stance against the taunt of another councillor that 'the Pioneers did not count for very much.'[52] Two weeks later the Pioneers of Nenagh were similarly hailed for opposing a proposed scheme by Nenagh urban council to recon-struct the town hall with the inclusion of a licensed bar.[53] The following month, after the General Election which had brought the first coalition to power, the Pioneer column highlighted the Pioneer membership of Oliver J. Flanagan, TD for Laois-Offaly, who had secured the highest number of first-preference votes in the country, and the membership of Joe Blowick, Minister for Lands in the new government and leader of the Clann na Talmhan party.[54] It was likely that their election had little to do with their Pioneer activities, but it was a fitting year for those directing the Association to try and link itself with local and national politicians, as it was the same year in which a thunderous row erupted over a proposal to allow for the general opening of pubs on Sundays.

Public houses had been closed legally in all areas except the five exempted boroughs since the passing of a licensing act in 1878. In 1906 Sunday trading in the exempted areas had been reduced by two hours, only to be increased in a 1943 bill by a further hour. In the Summer of 1948 a Private Members Bill, proposed by two Fianna Fail Deputies, Martin Corry and Michael Sheehan, proposed to allow for the general opening of public houses on Sundays. As a Private Members Bill there was never any realistic chance of it succeeding. Nevertheless it started a debate which illuminated the manner in which the Pioneer

Association would attempt to mobilise opinion to undermine legislation which they believed was a direct affront to the type of work they were engaged in. Later in the year, Corry was to insist that not only was the law preventing the opening of pubs on Sunday widely disregarded, but was blatantly discriminatory against rural people living outside of the five exempted metropolitan areas: 'Everybody knows that the law is practically in abeyance at present, to use a very common phrase in this assembly. I am not a drinking man, but I break that act every Sunday of my life.'[55] The ensuing debate was the usual hotchpotch of parliamentary exclamations of righteous indignation, personal insults and irrational craw-thumping. Oliver J. Flanagan predictably appealed to Pioneers to rally their forces. Others resented the preaching on the morality of drinking, and while Sean MacEntee was accused of lying about the volume of drink he consumed, Patrick Cogan, a TD from Cork insisted there was a deficiency in Cork soil which made Corkonians more thirsty than the rest of the country, particularly on a Sunday. But Corry stated that he was only seeking to give legislative credence to what was already the practice – allowing the Bill to progress would merely mean people walking in the front door as opposed to the back door of a public house on a Sunday as was now the case.[56]

Corry was undoubtedly accurate in his estimation of a widespread disregard for this law, and the tendency to turn a blind eye, but the jocular banter of Leinster House was a far cry from the detached and orchestrated campaign of opposition which McCarron was intent on. It was an interesting dilemma. In theory the Pioneer Association was strictly non-political; indeed, in theory Corry could have been a Pioneer in proposing the Bill. As Cullen would have put it, it would have been against the *spirit* but not the *rules* of the Association. But McCarron was adamant that the issue of Sunday opening could not be ignored. Ultimately, the Catholic hierarchy, in what J.H. Whyte called an 'unexpected intervention' effectively killed the momentum by emphasising their complete opposition to Sunday opening as a violation of the Sabbath and an affront to Canon Law,[57] but this was not before the Pioneers mounted a campaign of fierce opposition. McCarron had sent a submission to the Taoiseach, John A. Costello, maintaining that aside from the violation of the Sabbath, which was reason enough to repel the Bill, convictions for drunkenness had risen from 2,803 in 1942 to 4,891 in 1947, and that prosecutions for violation of the licensing laws had increased from 10,045 in 1942 to 15,333 in 1944. He also maintained that expenditure on drink had increased from £13,176,188 to £20,723,985 between 1942 and 1945, coupled with an estimation that the valuation of licensed property had shown a 600-

per cent increase since 1939.[58] McCarron had clearly done his temperance homework, but other Pioneer members preferred to restrict their arguments to religious issues. A resolution sent by the Dundalk centre to local TDs stated simply: 'I need not remind you that in 1917, at Fatima, Our Lady emphasised the necessity of observing the Lord's Day as a means of working off the wrath of God.'[59] In the Pioneer mind, at least within the Pioneer hierarchy, closing *all* pubs on Sunday would effectively meet the argument that there should be equal facilities for all. What were equally interesting were the responses elicited from politicians on this issue. In June 1948, a member of Fine Gael, Seamus Ó Cinnéide, had written to McCarron explaining that a lot of party members were still bitter against the Pioneer Association because they had remained mute when the price of the pint was the issue. Nevertheless, he urged McCarron, because this issue was more fundamental, to get 'your Fine Gael friends' to block the first reading of the Bill.[60] McCarron's lengthy reply gives an insight into how he saw the priorities of the Association with regard to certain legislative matters. While maintaining that he would prefer not to have to enter public controversy, he continued:

> Although the bill does not enter into political issues, it becomes very difficult to steer clear of these once controversy on a matter before the Dáil begins. You will appreciate that the Pioneer Association is completely non political and that it would be fatal for it to enter into the political field. In this matter however, where there are catholic principles involved, if it is necessary to do so, I will use every means, even with the danger of being misunderstood, to fight the bill . . . The principle of taxation of alcohol is admitted. The question of what the tax should be is not a question of principle but of expediency. It would have been impossible for us to have taken sides in that question without being accused of being political.[61]

It was one of the most significant letters McCarron wrote during his tenure as central director. Allowing for his sincerity, he was being inconsistent and not a little disingenuous. The Pioneer column in the *Irish Catholic* for example, had frequently voiced its support for making drink more expensive. Likewise, he had no hesitation in hailing those Pioneers who used their political positions at local level to oppose decisions concerning the provision of drink facilities. Seemingly, the rules could be bent depending on McCarron's audience. Also surprising was the inflated sense of urgency, if not impending doom, emanating from this correspondence. Given that the Bill had no chance of success, he was perhaps exhibiting a certain political naiveté. The *Sunday Chronicle* later admitted that after the bishops' intervention 'even publicans don't know which way to jump.'[62] McCarron duly met the Taoiseach, but in correspondence with a fellow priest admitted that it hadn't been of much help and that it would be more useful to exert pressure from outside the Dáil.[63] There was a clear sense that even among pious Catholics in the Dáil there was little stomach for the Pioneers acting as a third political force. There would certainly have been resentment at the kind of message delivered at a Pioneer rally that those who supported the Bill were not worthy of ever again receiving a vote from a Pioneer. This was uncharted territory for the Pioneers and it showed in terms of the responses they received. Many would have seen them as having tunnel vision in their approach to a complex issue. The reality of the Irish drinking culture meant that equating the pub solely with intemperance was a stance which could easily backfire. The response of Dan Breen, veteran War of Independence hero and Fianna Fáil TD was typical. While praising the Association for what he referred to as its 'great work', he implied that the Association was out of touch with the feelings of ordinary Irish rural citizens:

> I have an open mind on the matter, and I would like to get some solid and concrete evidence of why the rural people should not have the same laws as the city people. Why should a man be forced to leave his own town, village or parish to get a drink if he felt like having one on a Sunday? I have felt this 3-mile limit from his home as stupid, or worse still his getting a drink over a wall and be forced to rush it in case a Guard may come along and catch him taking it on or near the licensed house. I have lived in countries where the licensed houses are open all the 24 hours for the 7 days of the week and I must say I saw no drunks, unless an odd Englishman or tourist wanted to fling his money about.[64]

Even the Bishop of Derry was not particularly impressed with the campaign of opposition, feeling that the real question to be addressed was not what the law was, but whether or not it was enforced, his main concern in this regard being a preoccupation with cross-border traffic on a Sunday as northerners travelled to pubs in the South.[65]

McCarron was also leaving himself open to being used by the likes of Ó Cinnéide, who insisted that the Opposition was financed by publicans and black marketeers. He was not impressed with what he saw as McCarron's lack of vigour, noting 'I'm losing faith in you. You cannot see the wood from the trees. You're an ultra conservative.'[66] McCarron's response was curt, and again revealed his discomfort with being the pawn of more seasoned political operators: 'I am sorry that you find the ways of the Pioneer Association so conservative. However its whole purpose would be endangered if it allowed itself to become entangled in political issues or dependent on political patronage.'[67] Even within his own ranks, the debate on Sunday opening was an occasion for expressions of political partisanship, which would have further reminded McCarron of the tightrope he was walking. He got involved in a row with Fr W. Allen SJ, of the Jesuit mission to China, who, in a letter to McCarron had heaped abuse on TDs who were Pioneers and silent on the issue, singling out one who, he insisted, had gloated over the defeat of De Valera in the Civil War, contending that if one was to assess tax and agricultural policies 'the present mongrel government shows every sign of being a pro-brewers government.'[68] Whether due to a personal leaning towards Fine Gael, in common with many Irish Jesuits, or because of the petty and spiteful tone of Fr Allen's contribution, McCarron was livid. He berated him for his attack on the government, and for introducing politics into Pioneer correspondence, insisting that the Pioneers gave respect to all elected governments because 'it could not maintain its position as a religious organisation if it did not recognise the proper foundation of authority and government.'[69] Nonetheless, Fr Allen, noted for independent views, insisted on having the last word, maintaining he was 'Happy to be a political priest of God and even a political Pioneer! However you may rest at ease. I have no doubt you will see to it that I do not get much scope for advocating such revolutionary ideas from any Pioneer platform or publication.'[70]

Bishops like O'Callaghan of Clogher and Staunton of Ferns were sympathetic, and insisted that the Hierarchy were unanimous in their opposition to Sunday opening. Perhaps the problem was that certain individual Pioneers, encouraged to write to their local TDs, could get slightly carried away in what was such a highly politicised country. In September, while McCarron was on a visit to Rome, his newly appointed, and much less demonstrative assistant Fr Daniel Dargan SJ was attempting to put reins on a Fr Gleeson, resident in Meath Street, Dublin, who revelled in writing what he called 'scorchers' to local TDs. Dargan tried to reason with him, explaining that 'it is overstating the case to say that our brand new government is now going to sell the rural families, wives and children to the devouring molock of liquor.'[71] In his response to the Association, Erskine Childers attempted to portray himself as a temperance martyr, revealing the gulf between politicians with an eye on the electorate and Pioneers with an eye on spiritual salvation: 'Your Association will be aware that although I am not a teetotaller I courted unpopularity by saying publicly many times that four glasses of stout instead of five would hurt no-one, and this during the General Election.'[72]

In truth, there were few spiritual arguments in sight and the Pioneers were learning a valuable lesson about Irish politics, that in most instances policies were not to be wedded to religion to the extent that they would have wished, despite the ability of the hierarchy in this instance to abort the debate. In dismissing a protest against the proposed bill from Cashel Urban Council, the Limerick County Council summed up the attitude of many: 'After all, if these Christians look back they will see that St Paul recommended a little wine . . . It is the most silly thing that has ever come before the council . . . There is much more damage done by the people who are afraid to have a drink than by those who take too much of it.'[73] With few exceptions, the relative silence from Pioneer politicians made it clear that few had the stomach to play Pioneer politics and this was in keeping with the original theoretical *raison d'être* of the Association. When the vote on the Bill was finally defeated in February 1949, its original sponsor, Corry, revealed that since taking a stand in favour of Sunday opening he had received 168 letters on the issue from temperance activists, though another TD, Patrick O'Reilly, rejected the charge of intimidation, insisting that the Pioneers had kept quiet on the issue and could not be classed as bigots, as they 'did not set out to put a muzzle on anyone not anxious to take the pledge of the Association'. The vote was 65–41 against.[74]

Another Dáil deputy, Dr Patrick Maguire, had noted that there had been no 'pow-wow' on this occasion between the Pioneers and the licensed vintners. The vintners had been curiously mute on the issue, despite certain portrayals of them in temperance literature as sponsors of Satan. The truth was that they were more concerned at this stage with legislation already in existence, particularly the Industry and Efficiency Prices Bill of 1947 and supplementary budgets which they regarded as nothing short of bureaucracy gone mad and a worrying extension of what they termed 'the Managerial State'. The publicans did, however, enjoy quite a cosy relationship with the Catholic hierarchy. After an interview with the Archbishop of Dublin, Dr McQuaid, the secretary of the LVA instigated a fund raising campaign on behalf of Italian Catholics to help in their forthcoming election campaign, and succeeded in raising £2,800.[75] McCarron felt that the opening of pubs on Sundays was an issue of sufficient importance to warrant a meeting between himself and the honorary officers of the Licensed Vintners Association. He reiterated that the statement of the Catholic Hierarchy was binding in conscience, or as was penned in the *Irish Catholic*: 'The Licensed Trade in Ireland is practically 100 per cent Catholic. It was generous and prompt in its response to the recent appeal for help in the Italian election. One would like to see it as generous and as prompt in its response to the Holy Father's recent appeal for the sanctification of the Sunday.'[76]

But the vintners had other contacts, and were in touch with one whom they described simply as 'a Cork cleric', and chose not to rely on the interpretation of McCarron, but 'to rely on the Cork clerical authority', though the specific advice given was not recorded'.[77] In a deputation to the Minister for Justice in April 1948, reference was made to the fact that rural members of the LVA were becoming increasingly restless about the LVA executive's failure to oppose Corry's Bill, but the overall impression is that they were biding their time. The Minister himself contended that Corry's Bill was wholly mischievous in intent and that it was 'in fact quite frankly impossible for him to bring his government into open conflict with the hierarchy.'[78] The issue was by no means buried. The LVA were also in contact with the Father Mathew Union with a view to a future proposal for Sunday opening which would be acceptable to the Catholic Hierarchy. McCarron had also met the FMU, but was more concerned with allegations that Beamish and Crawford were financing the campaign for Sunday opening. There was no concrete proof of this, but it was enough for McCarron to send the LVA a caustic letter which further embittered relations. He also requested a copy of their constitution: 'Is the LVA a secret organisation whose constitution may not be given to any but its own sworn members, or is it that you are ashamed of it or afraid that it will not stand up to critical examination?'[79] There is no record of a reply to this letter, but it was significant that two years later the vintners were more than happy to subscribe to a fund to help finance the Jesuit College at Milltown, which had been damaged by fire.[80]

During 1949 the Pioneer Association was much more concerned with internal considerations. This was the year of the Golden Jubilee of the Association, and as early as 1947 McCarron and the Central Council had turned their attention to the most appropriate way of celebrating the Cullen legacy. Although not envisaged on a lavish scale at this time, it was ultimately to evolve into the biggest public celebration of Catholicism seen in Ireland since the Eucharistic Congress of 1932. It was a major triumph for the Association and set a precedent for the mass mobilisation of Pioneers. In other ways, the display at Croke Park was a microcosm of the utterly comfortable dominant position of the Catholic church in Irish society. Although it was specifically a Pioneer celebration, the manner of its presentation was not exclusive. It was a further illustration of a religious and political nationalism which actively demonstrated the Irish Catholics penchant for communal devotion. More than a day out, it was seen, not just by those with a temperance agenda, as a sign of a healthy and virile church, and the fact that it was held in the grounds of the GAA's Croke Park was further illustration of the homogeneity of Irish society at this time. It was presented as a cumulative linkage of Ireland's many heritages, all pointing in the same direction. On the eve of the rally, the *Irish Press* leading article revelled in drawing together these various nationalist strands:

> Tomorrow the Pioneer Total Abstinence Association ceremony commemorates a great work for the Irish people. Amidst the miseries of the last century too many of our people yielded to the solace of drink. . . But they earned for us, with the lively help of British propagandists, the ugly title of the 'drunken Irish'. To the work of rescuing the nation from the degradation which threatened it, many movements contributed. The political and national struggles of the period helped to make the people more manly and self-reliant, whilst the organising of athletics, particularly by the GAA, was also of great assistance. But it was undoubtedly the spiritual movements that were able to do the most lasting good. The man who is trained in self-denial makes the best citizen. In the finest National movement in Ireland in our time, the volunteers eschewed drink and it is noteworthy that in that movement none of those weaknesses appeared which had wrecked earlier military organisations. Tomorrow's ceremonies then, are as important as any that have been held in Ireland.[81]

Despite this unbridled triumphalism, the finished product – over 80,000 Pioneers in Croke Park of Mass and Benediction – had not been arrived at with ease. It took two years of careful orchestration and intricate administration to mobilise on such a scale. The original estimated attendance had been in the region of 20,000. As early as December 1947, McCarron was able to announce to the AGM that the association had secured the use of Croke Park, no doubt helped by the fact that Paddy O' Keeffe, the General Secretary of the GAA was a prominent Pioneer and had presided over Pioneer meetings in the past. Generally speaking the Pioneers had a good relationship with the GAA and were never slow to equate Pioneer membership with the enhancement of athletic prowess. There had been the occasional hitch, as when in 1945 they had decried the practice of teams having to use the facilities of pubs in the absence of changing rooms, or worse still, a GAA raffle in which the first prize was 'A pint a day for a year' ('Surely there could be found some more dignified and uplifting way of getting funds?').[82] The location secure, it was up to McCarron and others to guarantee the attendance of as many as possible. Getting young people, particularly women, to attend was seen as vitally important in the context of parading a future generation of Pioneers. There was a strong emphasis on the celebrations providing a fitting occasion for wider school Pioneer reunions, for example. Some of the circulars, such as the following, sent to past pupils of St Louis' convents, sought to present attendance as a pressing obligation:

> We feel that it is up to us, past pupils of St Louis Convents, to assemble together in all the splendour of our really magnificent numbers. We think that we owe it to the Pioneer Association which has done so much for us. We owe it to our country, on whose present-day womanhood the slur of intemperance has been cast, to show that, for the few who drink to excess, there are thousands who, on the contrary, have surrendered to God forever their right to take any drink whatsoever. Surely we owe it especially to our own nuns, to say mass together under the St Louis banner and to let the country see, in our demonstration of loyalty and strength, that we are grateful under God, to the sisters for all they have done, so unselfishly, and so thoroughly, for us. Can we count on you?[83]

The celebrations were also to include a Mass for children in Dalymount Park on the Saturday, and a special meeting of Pioneer priests on the following Tuesday. The response of the Catholic Hierarchy was, at best, lukewarm. The Archbishop of Dublin's permission was necessary for all the planned events. McCarron first wrote to him in August 1948, and after two months awaiting a reply, had to write again, only to wait a further two months for a reply. The original date planned, June 19, clashed with the octave of Corpus Christi, and had to be changed to June 26. Archbishop McQuaid was informed by McCarron that 'we could have no interest in a meeting which would be a mere temperance rally in the sense of being anti-drink.' In April 1949, he had revised his original estimated attendance from 20,000 to 50,000. The original choice of Dublin Castle for the Benediction ceremony was thus deemed too small, but McQuaid refused permission for the ceremony to be performed on O' Connell Bridge, as it had been during the Eucharistic Congress of 1932. McQuaid also turned down a request to preside over the ceremonies himself, claiming he would 'be so occupied' with more pressing matters.[84] McCarron had originally earmarked five members of the Hierarchy to be included in celebrating the children's' Mass, the Croke Park ceremony and the priests' meeting in the Mansion House – Bishops Walsh of Tuam, Kyne of Meath, Dunne of Dublin, Collier of Ossory and O'Neill of Limerick. His list however had to be drastically revised. Kyne refused, writing: 'I fear that such a recent convert might not be the best choice to speak. A convert too, not so sure of his strength of resolution who may let you and the cause down in the future.'[85] Likewise, the Bishop of Ferns, Dr Staunton, refused on the grounds that 'I am not a Pioneer and it seems presumptuous to attend the meeting of Pioneer priests.'[86] Others pointed to the inconvenience of having to travel to Dublin on two consecutive weeks, because there was a meeting of the Hierarchy in Dublin the week before. Archbishop Walsh also tried to avoid attending, by suggesting the Association approach the Archbishop of Cashel who 'is a Pioneer and would fit the bill much better than I could'. A fretting McCarron begged him to attend, noting 'how much more than most of the hierarchy your Grace has done to promote our work while the Archbishop of Cashel has not been so consistent and active.' He also pointed out that the matter of inviting bishops to attend Pioneer meetings was a delicate one, having to be authorised by McQuaid in advance, and as he had already been approved by McQuaid, McCarron was loathe to ask approval for another change. Walsh reluctantly agreed.[87] Bishop Collier of Ossory was much more enthusiastic, agreeing to attend the priests' meeting at the Mansion House because he would already be in Maynooth, and while attendance at the meeting would necessitate a late homecoming to Maynooth, which might have been frowned upon: 'The occasion justifies a late homing. In any case we will hardly be suspected of roistering.'[88] Eventually, Fr Hayes, founder of Muintir na Tire, was chosen to deliver the address, an event he described to his biographer as 'the greatest occasion on which I was ever asked to speak'.[89] In truth, he was chosen by default. There was an air of panic about the letter McCarron sent him, which unlike the gushing and obsequious formality of correspondence with the Hierarchy, read ' I want you and I want you badly to do a job for me.'[90] It was remarkable that the Pioneers could not get a commitment from a solitary bishop to address such a vast Catholic gathering, and clearly this was a source of consternation. Dr O'Connell, the secretary to McQuaid, had clearly made some reference to this when approaching McQuaid about the issue. Two weeks later, McCarron saw fit to write to him, rather cryptically:

> With regard to Fr Hayes, you can be perfectly at ease. I told him the matter had not been put to His Grace and that what you said was your own idea and was in the strictest confidence. I am very sorry that you have been put to such trouble and caused such anxiety about the whole matter.[91]

Despite the circumstances of his recruitment, Fr Hayes was probably a wise choice. A seasoned orator, he also had the populist touch through his grassroots experience in fostering community and rural development. In this kind of experience he was a world removed from the hierarchy who kept a significant distance between themselves and their flocks. The reality was that most members of the hierarchy would have been nervous in addressing such a large crowd. In any event, not many of them were Pioneers.

Another major concern was the necessity of providing enough transport. The plan was to have everyone in place at various assembly points, all within five minutes of Nelson's Pillar, and then to proceed from O'Connell street and march eight deep to Croke Park. Special county committees were formed to orchestrate the travel arrangements, though as late as two weeks before the appointed date a panic-stricken letter was sent to J.C. Courtney, Chairman of CIE, by the exasperated co-ordinator of travel arrangements, exclaiming 'the position is almost impossible. We have no certainty of any buses, no knowledge of times of buses, no idea of fares, no guarantee of a link up with railheads.'[92] There was also resentment towards the GAA Munster Council for fixing June 26 as the date for the Cork versus Tipperary Munster Hurling Final replay. It was an example of arrogant begrudgery given that the GAA had put Croke Park at the disposal of the celebrants free of charge. The Munster Council politely pointed out that it had gone out of its way to avoid a clash of dates, to allow the Pioneers to monopolise CIE trains. The chairman of the council also noted: 'I should have mentioned that many of our best members are travelling to Dublin and that I have spoken to Pioneers all over Munster and did not find any wavering in their decision to do likewise.'[93] The Department of Education agreed that salaries would be paid to Pioneer teachers if they did not make it back in time for school on Monday, on condition that they had the permission of their school managers.[94] Pioneers were encouraged to march in vocational groups, and particular emphasis was placed on the importance of a good turnout from Dublin centres. The Pioneers had been requested to ensure that celebrants refrained from smoking in Croke Park as matches and cigarettes thrown on the pitch would destroy it, though in official circulars this was changed to the unusual request that 'as the celebration is completely religious those taking part are requested not to smoke'. Banners carrying anti-drink slogans were also strictly prohibited. There were stern regulations regarding the bands performing music for the service with an instruction that 'in performance [the music] must be of a sufficiently high standard that will obviously do credit to the Association.'[95] A week before the event, a request by the Order of Malta to be positioned at the church altar for Benediction, because the Archbishop of Dublin was their chaplain, was rejected by the Rally Committee on the grounds that 'it would be invidious to make any distinction between the four first-aid organisations.'[96]

June 26 turned out to be one of the hottest days of the Summer. From an organisational point of view the commemoration was an unqualified success, reflected the following day in extensive front-page press coverage and aerial photographs. Estimates of the numbers who attended stood at 100,000, distorted in subsequent years to up to 120,000, though the lower figure was undoubtedly more accurate. The messages of the speakers were kept simple and direct: primarily the idea that this was by no means a mere temperance rally, but a strictly religious celebration. Nevertheless, in the private drafts of his Croke Park speech, McCarron had adopted a two-pronged approach – to emphasise the patriotism of the movement and also their ordinariness which was sanctified by sacrifice:

> Names spring to our minds, names of men like Matt Talbot, Fr John Sullivan, Fr Willie Doyle, Padraig Pearse and his brother Willie . . . men different in a thousand ways yet alike like this: that they have worked and lived and died bound by the rule of prayer and sacrifice under the banner of the Sacred Heart of Jesus. Members of the Pioneer Association . . . your lives are ordinary lives, yet they have been lifted out of the rut of the common-place by the Heroic Offering. This is a great occasion, when for the first time ever the Pioneer Association as a body has been enabled to meet around the altar to receive Christ's own blessing in the Benediction.[97]

The *Irish Times* quoted Fr Hayes as having denounced the persecution of the Cardinal of Hungary, while the *Irish Independent* focused on his spiritual message of combating a world steeped in materialism, and wrote of the sweetness of the vibrant swelling unison as the Heroic Offering was communally recited. 'The majority were women and quite a large proportion young girls . . . It is well for Ireland that within her shores there thrives so well organised and so unselfish a body of devoted men and women.'[98]

The Association glowed in the aftermath. There were a few however, who were not impressed. A week after the ceremonies, a disgruntled Irish speaker wrote (in English) to the Association expressing annoyance that 'from start to finish, as far as I heard at any rate, not one solitary word of the Irish language was introduced into the proceedings. If even a decade or two of the five in the Rosary were said in Irish it would have satisfied most people.'[99] It was left, however, to the brilliantly erratic, and alcoholic, Myles na gCopaleen to tear strips off the Association in his characteristically witty, and incisive manner. He lambasted the cowardice of CIE in allowing the seaside rail service from Amiens Street to Bray to be brought to a standstill by the Pioneers, particularly when the weather was so fine. In his column *Cruiskeen Lawn*, he elaborated:

> The Temperance movement, here as elsewhere, is a strictly bourgeois neurosis. Dublin's working man with his wife and four or five children

intent on spending a day at the seaside does not have to journey to Croke Park to prove that he is not a slave to whiskey. If he can manage one pint of porter a day, it is the best he can do and that pint will not blind his senses as to prevent him seeing the impertinent character of CIE's order that yesterday he must stay at home because the organisers of a scene of unbridled pietistic exhibitionism must have the transport to which he is entitled. I can recall nothing comparable to yesterday's procedure and I hope somebody will examine the legality of it. If the abstainers are entitled to disrupt transport in their own peculiar and selfish interest, there is in our democratic mode no reason in the world why the drinking men of Ireland should not demand and be given the same right. Let everybody stay at home because the boozers are in town! And one final word. Temperate connotes restraint, the avoidance of extremes. The pressurising of uncertain CIE and GNR bosses to hound the common people out of their trains – presumably because a refusal would mean these bosses were 'communists' – is in itself an unparalleled example of extremism, class warfare and tyranny. I would advise these Pioneer characters that there is more in life than the bottle, that fair play to others is important and that temperance – taking the word in its big and general value – is a thing they might strive to cultivate a bit better . . .[100]

NOTES

1   Bernard Mc Guckian, *Pioneering for 80 Years* (Dublin 1978), p. 7
2   Sean McCarron, *Temperance Catechism* (Dublin 1945)
3   *Catholic Workers' Handbook* (Dublin 1942)
4   PCIC May 31, 1944
5   ibid., November 16, 1944
6   PAA, SFX Minutes, January 29, 1945
7   ibid., Flinn's Memo re Army, August 18, 1940
8   ibid., Oscar Traynor to Flinn, October 30, 1940
9   ibid., Memo by McCarron detailing meeting with Traynor July 29, 1943
10 ibid., McCarron to Traynor
11 ibid., Memo by Major General Costello
12 ibid., Costello to McCarron, April 25, 1944
13 ibid., Fr Higgins to McCarron October 20, 1943
14 ibid., Fr Riordan to McCarron, September 24, 1943
15 ibid., Fr McLoughlin to McCarron November 11, 1943
16 ibid., Fr Thomas Smyth to McCarron, November 30, 1943
17 PAA, McCarron, Memo on progress of Association, 1947
18 ibid.
19 PPA, McCarron to Sr Josephine, November 24, 1944
20 ibid., McCarron to Sr Josephine November 24, 1944, and Sr Columba to McCarron, July 8, 1945 and July 24, 1945
21 PCIC, May 17, 1945
22 SFX Minute Book, July 29, 1947
23 PCIC, August 8, 1944
24 LVAA, LVA Annual Report February 2, 1946
25 ibid., Annual Report, 1945
26 PCIC, April 11, 1946
27 ibid., April 11, 1946, May 2, 1946 and July 15, 1946

28 PAA, Memo by McCarron, 1947
29 *Irish Independent*, March 29, 1946 and *Licensed Vintners' Guide*, vol. 11, April 1946
30 Senate Debates, vol. 53, November 27, 1946; ibid., December 11, 1946, col. 248
31 PAA, Central Council Minutes, January 8, 1946
32 ibid., March 19, 1946
33 *Irish Press, Irish Independent, Evening Herald*, May–December, 1946
34 PA, McCarron, 1947 Memo on Progress
35 McCarron, *Temperance Cathecism*, 1945
36 ibid.
37 Sean McCarron, *A Short Temperance Catechism for Primary Schools*, (Dublin 1951)
38 PAA, Garda Minute Book, May 6, 1946
39 ibid., April 14, 1946 and October 13, 1946
40 ibid., January 6, 1947
41 PCIC, March 11, 1948
42 ibid., April–December, 1947
43 ibid., November 28, 1946
44 ibid., December 4, 1947
45 PAA, McCarron, Memo on Progress, 1947
46 ibid., SFX Minutes, October 27, 1950
47 McCarron, 1947 Memo
48 McCarron to Provincial, January 4, 1949
49 IAPI Minute Book, June 22, 1943 and March 23, 1944
50 ibid., January 23, 1944
51 ibid., March 30, 1950
52 PCIC, January 8, 1948
53 ibid., January 15, 1948
54 ibid., February 26, 1948
55 Dáil Debates, November 17, 1948, vol. 113, cols. 41–126
56 ibid.
57 J.H. Whyte, *Church and State in Modern Ireland 1923–70* (Dublin 1971), p. 177
58 PAA, 1948 File, Submission to Taoiseach
59 ibid., September 15, 1948.
60 ibid., Ó Cinnéide to McCarron June 11, 1948
61 ibid., Mc Carron's response, June 12, 1948
62 *Sunday Chronicle*, November 7, 1948
63 PAA, ibid., McCarron to Fr Ryan, July 1, 1948
64 ibid., Dan Breen to McCarron July 8, 1948
65 ibid., Bishop of Derry to McCarron, June 18, 1948
66 ibid., Ó Cinnéide to McCarron, July 1, 1948
67 ibid., McCarron's response, July 2, 1948
68 ibid,. Fr Allen to McCarron, June 4, 1948
69 ibid., McCarron's reply, June 5, 1948
70 ibid., Fr Allen's reply June 7, 1948
71 ibid., Dargan to Fr Gleeson, September 19, 1948
72 ibid., Childers to McCarron, September 21, 1948
73 *Limerick Leader*, October 30, 1948
74 Dáil Debates, February 17, 1949, vol. 114, cols. 225–257
75 LVAA, Minutes vol. 30, April 17, 1948 and April 22, 1948
76 PCIC, July 29, 1948
77 LVAA, Minutes, November 2, 1948
78 ibid., April 22, 1948
79 PAA, McCarron to 'Christy', June 7, 1948
80 LVAA, Minutes, November 28, 1950
81 *Irish Press*, June 25, 1948
82 PCIC, September 13, 1945
83 PAA, Jubilee Circulars, 1949
84 ibid., McCarron to McQuaid, April 25, 1949 and McQuaid's response, May 29, 1949
85 ibid., Kyne to McCarron, March 5, 1949

86   ibid., Staunton to McCarron, May 29, 1949
87   ibid., Walsh to McCarron February 24, 1949 and McCarron's response, May 1, 1949
88   ibid., Collier to McCarron, May 21, 1949
89   Rynne, *Hayes* p. 153
90   PAA, McCarron to Hayes, April 13, 1949
91   ibid., McCarron to O'Connell, April 27, 1949
92   ibid., Fee to J.C. Courtney, June 12, 1949
93   ibid., Munster GAA council reply to Cahir Pioneer centre June 7, 1949
94   ibid., Department of Education Secretary to McCarron, May 15, 1949
95   ibid., Official Circulars and instructions and Central Council Minutes, May 30, 1949
96   ibid., Central Council Minutes, June 21, 1949
97   ibid., Draft of McCarron's speech
98   *Irish Times,* June 27, 1949, *Irish Independent,* June 27, 1949
99   PAA, Fr Myles Allman to McCarron, July 1, 1949
100 *Irish Times,* June 27, 1949

CHAPTER FIVE

The 1950s

The traffic in drink is not like the fish and chips business where a
man stops when he has enough. In this country drinking does not
mean the satisfaction of a natural thirst.
Michael Browne, Bishop of Galway, 1959

For a decade so under-researched, the 1950s has entered the realm of
Irish historiography surprisingly distinctly defined. Phrases and words
such as 'stagnation and crisis', 'malaise and morass' and 'drift' loom
large.[1] Clearly, much of this labelling is based on the economic stagnation which characterised Ireland during this decade and the attendant
emigration which dealt a blow to the national psyche. Such labels,
however, ignored much in the 1950s that was changing. For the Pioneer
Association, this was particularly true. In the early part of the decade
membership continued to expand. By 1952 they were claiming that
one hundred new members were joining every week. And yet it was a
decade which brought challenges. A high level of drink consumption
continued unabated again highlighting the closeness of the two
extremes of abstinence and excess. There were further challenges to
Pioneer ideals as licensing issues were tackled legislatively and socially.
There was also an increased recognition, and definition, of the concept
of alcoholism, and new associations, such as Alcoholics Anonymous,
sought to deal with drink abuse in an increasingly practical, scientific
and medical manner as opposed to a solely spiritual approach.

The Pioneers had difficulty in adapting to these shifts in consciousness. They continued to pursue their traditional aims, and mass public
devotion to the Sacred Heart continued to be encouraged, culminating
at the end of the decade in another massive Croke Park Rally to
celebrate the Diamond Jubilee of the Association. For McCarron, the
agenda for the 1950s was dual. He said the Pioneers needed to rely on

166

spiritual weapons and 'systematic and external activity'.[2] In pursuing this, he had the support of two young assistants, the Jesuits Fr Daniel Dargan and Fr Kevin O'Carroll, who between them travelled the country week after week addressing regional Pioneer rallies. There was continued emphasis placed on the belief that the Association offered the best solution to intemperance and that the Pioneer pin was essentially just another badge of Irish identity. Theoretical intellectual and spiritual justifications were eschewed, in favour of propaganda which depicted Pioneer membership as the most natural and desirable thing imaginable. The following passage which appeared in the *Irish Catholic* was typical:

> Travelling by train to the West of Ireland recently, I was pleased to see the Pioneer badge so much in evidence. Passengers of all types wore it, some elderly, some young, some well-dressed, others obviously poor. At one station where there was delay, another train moved up alongside. The engine stopped. The fireman turned and looked out at us. The Pioneer badge was in his jacket. At another station, a junction, the station master, driver and another CIE official stood for a while in friendly conversation. All three were adorned with the badge.[3]

For every passage such as this, there were as many which were defensive in tone, penned in the knowledge that the drink culture in Ireland was as strong as ever and that there was a certain section of Irish people to which the Association would never appeal. There was nothing uniquely Irish about this. In America, for example, a cosmopolitan middle class was less likely to support temperance. Here, efforts to link the abstaining mindset to extremist forms of neo-populist indignation were not successful. Temperance had a rather negative connotation, particularly among sections of the upper middle class.[4] In terms of the class structure in Ireland, there was little attention given by the Pioneer Association to the isolated rural hard-drinking bachelor, who, because he did not fit in with the familial and generational identity of the Pioneers, remained a strange and enigmatic underground caricature. This was a central feature of Monsignor O'Brien's facile, but often entertaining, survey on the impact of Irish emigration in the 1950s, where excessive drinking was viewed by practically all the contributors as having a central role in retarding Irish development, to the extent that O'Brien could refer to the drinking bachelor as 'the strangest species of male on the face of the earth . . . Instead of engaging in the social life common to men and women in other countries the Irish bachelors spend their evenings in the pubs.'[5] Drink was also suggested to sublimate their sexual desire, thus reinforcing the low level of marriage which was also contributing to population decline. In the view of Sean O'Faolain it was also a form of invert sexism: 'Look at the way in which a man can drink Lough Erne dry and it is not called a binge, but if a poor woman gets a cold she is told to cure it with butter milk boiled with onion.'[6] Excessive male drinking was seen to put women off the idea of marriage, and within marriage, as a pastime from which women suffered from most of the ills and few of the pleasures. As Arland Ussher accurately pointed out, there was a culture of toleration at work in Ireland which saw excessive drinking as entirely respectable, just because it was gregarious.[7] It certainly did the Irish male no favours in terms of their social development. Critics of the Catholic Church in Ireland poured cold water on the degree to which the Pioneer Association was in any position to tackle this problem. The American anti-Catholic polemicist, Blanshard, derided the fact that it needed a reformed alcoholic and undeclared saint in the form of Matt Talbot to fight alcoholism, while in reality, heavy drinking was the Irishman's confession that he was not mature enough to face life as a moral adult.[8] This was a view shared by latter-day sociologists, such as Tom Inglis: 'The pub became the place where men displaced their sexual frustration through a competitive compulsive pattern of drinking. If the school was the penitential house which characterised the trans-formation of Irish society in the first half of the nineteenth century, the pub became a type of perpetual secondary school for males.'[9]

Nevertheless, in keeping with established patterns, it was the women rather than the men who were targeted in Pioneer circles. This also seemed to be a favourite theme of a few members of the Catholic hierarchy during the 1950s in their addresses to Pioneers. In late 1950, Dr Collier, Bishop of Ossory, was asking girls to boycott dances because a refusal to attend would render the socials unfeasible, warranting the closure of bars.[10] Two years later, the Bishop of Meath, Dr Kyne, the same bishop who in a private letter to McCarron, had doubted his own long-term ability to keep the pledge, also drew attention to the increased number of Irish women drinking. At a rally in Mullingar, he contended 'in the case of the girls who go away to work in the bigger towns and who indulge in drink, the case is not so much moral weakness as mental insufficiency. They look for their models in the cheapest elements of society.'[11] Again, these patriarchal developments were not confined to Ireland. Feminists in England contended that women may have been attracted to temperance movements for their own reasons and wants, including a desire to assert themselves emotionally and financially, not merely seeing temperance solely in terms of defending hapless female victims.[12] Perhaps for some women membership of the Pioneer Association was also a means for females to enjoy each other's company, though the Saint Francis Xavier centre in Dublin didn't seem to think so. In 1953 the SFX council expressed a desire to see more men taking part in Pioneer excursions as they were becoming unbalanced, with too many women travelling, which the council believed 'detracted from the enjoyment of the outing'.[13] One wonders was it the women themselves who expressed this feeling. Pioneers writing about women were utterly unambiguous in asserting that females succumbing to drink were infinitely worse than drunken men, particularly in the context of the home.

In 1947 the idea of publishing a Pioneer magazine as the official organ of the association was first aired. By the following year it became a reality and was an immediate success as it sought to convey the traditional messages in an innovative way with plenty of colour, humour and human drama. With the variety of temperance advocates who contributed, it also helped to broaden the parameters of debate within the Association, which in time would elucidate inconsistencies and expose a certain tunnel vision in established temperance thinking. In the context of women, the magazine gave Pioneer commentators an opportunity to elaborate on the most ghastly sin a woman could commit. One of the regular features was the coverage of court cases which dealt with crimes committed as a result of excessive drinking. The following appeared in February 1949:

> Yesterday it was a husband who wrecked a home through drink. Today it is a wife, and a far more serious problem is this. For if the man of the house chooses to forsake his responsibilities for the lure of the bottle, the wife may generally be relied upon to try and keep the family and the home together. If he leaves her, well, so long as he still contributes a reasonable amount, the final, fatal tragedy may be averted and one day, a chastened father may return sobered and resolved to renounce alcohol once and for all. But, when the wife and mother is victim of this wretched disease, the case is far more serious. The home without a woman, or with a drinking wife and mother is rudderless, miserable, reckless. Even if father is steady and tries to carry on, what can the best man in the world do against a woman who is an incorrigible drink addict? Almost inevitably comes the break up of the home, and more often than not, the break is permanent.[14]

Despite this sexism, the magazine could be dynamic, innovative and eclectic. This was important in terms of relating Pioneer membership to the reality of varied human experience. It also gave the moulders of the Association a wider brief in terms of tackling temperance issues on a social, political and economic level, highlighting developments outside Ireland and reiterating spiritual tasks and gains. The magazine in the 1950s developed a regular pattern – a well-known celebrity, actor, singer, GAA stalwart, radio commentator – on the front page proudly sporting a Pioneer pin, an editorial elucidating the *raison d'être* of the Association, articles dealing with the scientific and medical aspects of alcohol, coverage of court cases, political comment, particularly with regard to drink legislation, instruction to councillors controlling Pioneer centres, cartoons, fiction, history and even a film page. It was also part of a growing consciousness of the need to use different forums for propagating the ideals of the Association.

There was also an agenda during the 1950s designed to facilitate the dispelling of a widespread perception among non-Pioneers that the Association's members were anti-social in eschewing the most popular form of socialising in the country. In March 1950 an advertisement appeared in the *Evening Mail* about a temperance social club under the auspices of the Pioneers. When the Central Council discovered this, the advertiser was admonished for using the Association's name without authorisation and was forced to write to the eighty-eight people who had replied explaining that the ad had been inserted under false pretences.[15] It was a salutary lesson for one who had dared to take an individual initiative with regard to Pioneers providing entertainment for themselves. As has been seen, this was one of Cullen's original aims in raising funds for the SFX hall and Social Club. Although in theory the Gardiner Street Jesuit Community owned it, in practice it was run by the Pioneers. The Pioneer Club was overseen by a committee of eight and a spiritual director, who in the early 1950s was Fr Troddyn. Originally the spiritual director had appointed all council members, but in 1952 Fr Troddyn allowed for three of them to be elected. He defended the amount of control he had in the running of the club, believing that 'this is common experience, even in the most democratic of societies.'[16] In 1954 the club had a membership of roughly one hundred, mostly working-class and single men who had a deep involvement in other charitable societies, such as the Saint Vincent de Paul. Troddyn saw their function in these terms: 'They help the Association by showing people, who are very ready to think otherwise, that Pioneers are not pussyfoots who do not know how to enjoy themselves properly. In brief, [Pioneers] have a name that is both honoured and attacked: they will try to give further reason for the honour and show up the misguidedness of the attacks.'[17]

At this time the club, having been found structurally unsafe, was forced to find new premises in Mountjoy Square. This had resulted in fierce rows about the actual ownership of the club, with the superior of the Gardiner Street Jesuit community furious at having to undertake the task of locating suitable new premises. Drama had always played an important part in the development of the club, in keeping with Fr Cullen's wish to see the club produce theatre which was 'constructively national'. Not all the drama, however, was confined to the stage. Pioneers, whatever about their spiritual edification, were not immune from heated artistic temperaments, and unseemly rows characterised the drama committee's proceedings during the 1950s. In 1955 there was accusations of vote rigging at elections to the drama committee, while others disagreed with the choices of the spiritual director, Fr Troddyn, due to the fact that the previous year's pantomime preparations had consisted of 'bickering, loud arguments and criticisms without a vestige of helpful or sensible suggestions' which were 'a nightly occurrence in the dressing room'.[18] As agreement could not be reached on the composition of a new council, the entire council resigned, a development which did not seem to unduly perturb Troddyn – he simply wrote in the conclusion to his report that 'the whole committee resigned and I appointed a new one.'[19] Troddyn himself, however, was also under suspicion at this time, being suspected of committing a heinous crime in the realm of the Pioneer movement – allowing non-Pioneers admission to Pioneer social events. This rule was somewhat sacred within the Association, and according to Troddyn, McCarron had suggested to the Provincial that not enough vigilance was being exercised. The fact that Troddyn was not a Pioneer himself deepened the suspicion.

There was something rather farcical about a non-Pioneer having to take the responsibility of keeping non-Pioneers out of social events. In many ways the Pioneers were solely to blame for the impression that they were socially snobbish. The 'Rules for Socials' issued by the Central Council in the 1950s illustrated a certain paranoia that existed within their ranks, as if they were expecting at any moment to be invaded by sneering boozers intent on flinging empty stout bottles. The rules dictated that the secretary of the local Pioneer centre had to stand at the door, identifying all those entering, ensuring they were adorned with the pin. Under no circumstances could alcohol be given to the band, and 'each centre is instructed to have a real social – not merely a dance.'[20] On the sporting front, in 1953, a Pioneer Club sports ground had been acquired at Santry with facilities for tennis, cricket and football. To be allowed membership, women had to be the members' wives, sisters or helpers in the Drama Society. Inside, permission was sought 'to provide the modest card games: Solo, fifteen and twenty five. Gambling games, poker, pontoon and banker are strictly prohibited. Should anyone contravene the rules there will be no second chance.'[21]

Outside Dublin, it was assumed that in terms of social entertainment, the same rules would be adhered to, although the Pioneer leadership in Dublin could not keep the same vigilant eye on proceedings. This led to an extraordinary turn of events in county Derry in 1956 in Leckpatrick, when the local Pioneer centre was suspended by Dr Farren, the Bishop of Derry, over an unauthorised céilí, advertised to be held by the Pioneer centre. The episode did more to highlight the hostile attitude of some members of the hierarchy and the effects their admonishment could have on a faithful flock, than it did to highlight any 'wild streak' lurking within the ranks of the Pioneers. The bishop informed the parish priest a week before the céilí that the Pioneers had violated a diocesan statute by inserting an unauthorised advertisement in the church. He also wanted to know 'since when did the Pioneers start running céilithe and dances'.[22] The local curate, Fr Marren, who was also spiritual director of the centre although not a Pioneer (this was allowed under Pioneer rules, if a Pioneer spiritual director could not be found), sought to distance himself by insisting that he had never been properly appointed. He in turn approached the woman whom he believed had inserted the notice. She sent her account of events to McCarron:

> Fr Marren met me literally on the doorstep of the Sacred Heart Church and told me we were suspended. He has got a rather warped or sarcastic sense of humour. There were women passing at the time, I considered it rather out of place, so being flustered I lost my temper and told Fr Marren off. I'm in a bit of a fix, as he called at me that I wasn't telling the truth.[23]

In Dublin, McCarron was horrified at the prospect of a row developing with the bishop. As far as he saw it the Pioneer Centre had no option – 'It is our duty to accept his ruling in the matter, simply, and without criticism.'[24] This did not take account of the outrage felt in Derry, and certain Pioneers had no intention of being silenced or subservient at the expense of their personal dignity or the truth. The girl's father, also a member of the suspended Pioneer centre, took the bishop to task in a hard-hitting letter:

> Not being spineless or a 'yes' woman, she defended herself. Perhaps your Lordship could imagine the impact this would have on a young girl (She did not insert the offending ad). The congregation, not understanding the cause of the commotion, naturally put individual interpretations on the unedifying scene and the cause of it. Dame rumour then took over and duly amplified your edict, so that your Lordship's despicable method of promulgating a profound announcement has cast an opprobrious stigma on a young promising life. I respectfully submit to your Lordship

that to send such a message by phone and ask a priest to deliver it by word of mouth instead of it being issued over your Lordship's signature is – just not manly. If your Lordship has a 'chip on the shoulder' towards the association, say so and purge the feeling of pique and petty jealousy, instead of making a scapegoat of a curate. If it is a sin or crime to organise a céidhli mór under the patronage of a Pioneer centre it will, I am sure, when made public, surprise many. Being the 'woman of the house' I can ill spare her, but I have sent my daughter on a short holiday to get away from the stuffy parochial atmosphere and to fortify herself for your Lordship's next blow . . . As being under disgrace, any parochial activities will be taboo for her during life, she will cease forthwith participating. However good her intentions, they could only have a boomerang effect. I shall convey to priest friends of the Diocese that they may consider our house 'out of bounds' lest they too might incur your Lordship's wrath with its dire consequences.[25]

This 'Battle of Derry' was a far cry from the relative tranquillity which had been associated with another mass mobilisation of Pioneers. As 1954 was the Marian Year, the director of the Association chose Knock for this particular outing. It was another occasion in which intricate orchestration was of paramount importance. The flying of the National, Pioneer and Papal flags in Knock in September was another illustration of the Association's status as a representative Irish Catholic body. The High Mass was presided over by Archbishop Walsh of Tuam and the ceremonies included Stations of the Cross, Rosary and Benediction of the Blessed Sacrament. The death of Jim Bird during the preparations, who had been General Secretary of the Central Council since 1923, was a blow to the organisation of the pilgrimage but the *Irish Catholic* was still able to report an attendance of 50,000. The following week, Fr Doherty, one of the assistant spiritual directors, sought to inflate the figure to 70,000.[26]

The chief problems were those of transport, with CIE carrying 30,000 pilgrims on 24 trains and 207 buses, though pilgrims were advised that discomfort was not to be a cause of complaint – those travelling 'realising that they are making a spiritual pilgrimage will accept any discomforts or inconveniences that may arrive, offering them to the Sacred Heart with their other Pioneer sacrifices.'[27] Pilgrims were also informed lavatories 'may be used in emergency only' – this was an interesting reference as it was the culmination of lengthy correspondence in 1954 between the organisers in Knock and Central Office. Fr Malone in Knock had initially suggested segregating the sexes, but this was rejected by Central Office who saw it as impractical 'and that the provision of lavatory accommodation was therefore essential on the grounds of efficient organisation and of decency', and that if people were prevented from relieving themselves after travelling such distances 'it will be with some measure of embarrassment on the part of ladies at least.'[28] Having agreed to call in the Army to provide portable toilets, the priority was then one of location – it was essential to ensure the toilets would be screened from the Blessed Shrine. Correspondence in the aftermath of the pilgrimage was dominated by McCarron's hard-nosed business sense, with his insistence that as traffic instructions, parking and stewarding had been supervised by Gardai Pioneers, under Chief Superintendent Henry O'Mara, at the Association's expense, and as CIE had recognised their application for equity with regard to commission earned as a result of transport costs, the onus was on the reluctant Ulster Transport Authority to do likewise. There was also gratitude that the employees of the Drogheda bus depot, who were on strike over staff appointment disputes, had been prepared to lift their ban for the duration of the pilgrimage.[29]

Further mobilisation got underway in 1956, this time to commemorate the centenary of the death of Fr Mathew, the Capuchin temperance crusader of the nineteenth century, in June 1956. As was usual on these occasions, hyperbole abounded, McCarron in his circulars insisting that 'Fr Mathew himself gave the pledge to five million Irish people and two million of other nationalities.'[30] As orchestrated by a regional Cork rally committee, which expected an attendance of 60,000, the route was through the centre of Cork city, ending in the Mardyke grounds. As Cullen was often presented as the natural successor of Fr Mathew, it was seen by the Pioneers as much their celebration as any other, particularly given the fact that they were the only temperance association which had the membership and the organisational experience to make an occasion like this viable. The central reason for participation, as pointed out by contemporary circulars was 'as Fr Cullen always wished it to be remembered that he owed so much to the example and inspiration of Fr Mathew.'[31] Despite the insistence that the thirty-two counties would be represented, Belfast was suffering from rally fatigue, and the response from their centres 'had not been big enough to justify running a train'.[32] Once again, despite McCarron's proud boast that the Pioneer Association was now a Catholic Action organisation representing half a million members, confirmations, visitations, and general lack of interest ensured that the now customary invitations to twenty-one members of the Catholic Hierarchy elicited only three positive responses, with Collier, Bishop of Ossory, though he could not attend, the only one to elaborate and actually give encouragement. Bishop Mageean in Belfast, despite refusing the invitation, acknowledged that 'apart from the deluxe invitation card you offer to provide hotel accommodation and transport for me. You certainly have done it big.'[33] Bishop Lucey of Cork, as he was on home turf, had agreed to preside, but was adamant that he did not want to give any formal speech. The generally non-committal nature of the Hierarchy's correspondence was summed up by the curious response of the Bishop of Achonry, Dr Fergus: 'perhaps it will do, at the moment, if I say that I shall go, if I possibly can and if I find later that it is not possible, I shall let you know.'[34] The GAA as usual lent a helping hand by ensuring there would be no fixtures in Cork on the same day. John O'Callaghan, Commandant of the Collin's Barracks in Cork was responsible for stewarding, and in a letter to a Dingle band leader, revealed how strict instructions were in terms of who had to get priority. 'There is a very strict instruction about playing in the Mardyke grounds. Only the band of the Southern Command will play during the ceremonies, therefore, your band will cease playing on entering the Mardyke grounds.'[35] Another major fear was that the Provincial of the Capuchins in Ireland, Dr James, due to give the address and notoriously long-winded, would bore the audience, though in a letter to Fr Dargan, he accepted 'it would be unpardonable in the circumstances to exceed the thirty minute limit.'[36]

Pioneer exclusivity was again stressed at all times. Fr Coffey, the chief Pioneer organiser in Cork city, wrote to Dargan on the necessity of keeping a 1.00 p.m. Mass in St Patrick's Cathedral on Sunday a secret until the last minute, lest it be darkened by hangovers: 'I am rather afraid some of the late Saturday night men here may take advantage of it.'[37] Likewise, a resounding refusal was the response of the Central Council to the following request of a Kilkenny Pioneer, who was obviously out of touch with the organisation's rules: 'We have been asked by a few parishioners, who, though not Pioneers are very good-living and temperate, whether they would be allowed to travel to Cork on the Pioneer train on Sunday next to visit relatives. They would not, of course wear badges or attend the celebrations.'[38] The address of Dr James focused on the contribution to temperance of Fr Mathew and his skill in ensuring a permanent place in the social history of Ireland, withstanding the laws of change and the vicissitudes of time. McCarron spoke of the duties of the Pioneers in the context of giving spiritual protection to emigrants. Perhaps it was also a measure of the progress which it was felt the Pioneers were making that McCarron could say with a degree of satisfaction: 'It is not then my purpose to convert you from evil ways, but rather to strengthen you in a virtue already adopted as your own and practised in your lives.'[39]

If it is true, as has been suggested above, that the 1950s has been associated with gloom, there is also a sense in which a more inquisitive culture was emerging, which was to set the tone for the more probing and culturally diverse 1960s. The debate on drink and temperance was inevitably affected by this, particularly in relation to access to drink facilities and with regard to defining alcohol and what constituted alcoholism. In the long run it was a debate which undermined the Pioneer agenda. There were also other challenges facing 1950s Ireland, and by extension, the Pioneer Association, chief among them emigration. In Pioneer propaganda emigration was at times seen not only as a grave social and economic challenge, but also as a fundamental threat to the spiritual security of Pioneers, often simplistically presented as the danger of succumbing to pressure in a foreign environment and falling by the wayside. It was something which both the *Pioneer* magazine and the Pioneer column in the *Irish Catholic* referred to continually. In November 1951 the magazine noted that it was 'painfully clear that in too many cases emigration is but a prelude to defaulting from the Pioneer ranks',[40] with members urged to seek out fellow Pioneers abroad. There was also the necessity to overcome what McCarron presented as hostility to the Pioneers abroad. In England he wrote of valiant Pioneers having to force their way through 'misunderstanding and prejudice and opposition'.[41] In 1955 it was suggested that as many as 35 per cent of Irish emigrants were dropping the practice of their religion and that this often had its origins in drink abuse.[42] In light of these threats, both supposed and real, there was a determination to make the Pioneers more than a purely Irish movement. Expansion was beset by many problems, as had been demonstrated by the unsuccessful attempts of the 1930s. But the real thrust in this direction was made in the 1950s, and it warrants scrutiny, not just to highlight the difficulties inherent in expanding abroad but also the extent to which it illuminated in an international context, the limited appeal of Pioneer methods. Much of the correspondence which deals with this international effort is laced with confusion, disagreement and resentment. This is not to undermine the Trojan work which was done by particular individuals, both religious and lay, in attempting to establish solid foundations for international Pioneerism, but more of an indication of the difficulty of adapting the Pioneer framework to countries not as homogeneously Catholic, and indeed small, as Ireland. In the mid 1940s, McCarron, through appeals to the Assistant General, Fr Durge, had been anxious to recruit more Jesuits to spread the Association's wings. However, although the Provincial of the Jesuits was not that enthusiastic, he did not want to be seen to dictate the wider Jesuit agenda, perhaps being mindful of the brakes often put on the activities of other Catholic action groups. He wrote that he wanted to see the Association established in other countries:

> but I doubt that the Society would take the responsibility of recommending it to the Provinces at large. You know how constantly our late Fr General refused, though urgently asked, to engage the Society to promote the League of Mary. He refused also in 1940, to write a laudatory letter to the Knights of the Blessed Sacrament for their 25th anniversary. His reason was that such pious associations, excellent in some countries are less appropriate in others. The temperance association would not likely be accepted, not only in wine-producing countries but also in others.[43]

At this time it was estimated that outside of Ireland's centres there were sixteen in England, six in Scotland, one each in South Africa and Paris, Iowa, Perth and Melbourne. In the early 1950s there was a strong effort to establish the Pioneers in Australia, particularly because Ireland's most famous Pioneer exile, Archbishop Mannix of Melbourne, was at the helm. In November 1950, one of the assistant spiritual directors, Fr Doherty, travelled to Australia to give the effort more structure and coherence. The Australian centre was duly to become the first fully organised external National Council of the Pioneer Association. It was a slow growth. In 1951 there were only 417 Pioneers and by 1955 there were still only 4832, organised in six Dioceses and ninety one primary schools. Doherty, who was assiduous in reporting back to Dublin, was quite specific about the obstacles: 'A 20 per cent Catholic population [with] deep rooted drink traditions which the climate helps and which are fostered by a drink trade largely Irish and Catholic', along with wide-scale violation of a loosely administered Confirmation pledge.[44] Archbishop Mannix had initially given Doherty $1,000 to assist his campaign, but it seems that funding was not the problem, but the extent to which Doherty could take independent initiatives, particularly his desire to adapt the *Temperance Catechism* to suit Australia. 'I'd get the whole thing well vetted here. If I wait for vetting from Ireland I'll miss the bus.[45] Five months later he was still wondering about autonomy, and worrying that the Australian provincial was expressing displeasure about being under Irish control. It was to be a common resentment. There was also ill-feeling about McCarron's suggestion that only Irish priests were helping – this, Fr Doherty contended, 'has annoyed them and helped to convince them of the idea I was trying to rid them, viz. that this is an essentially Irish movement. In the Catholic world here there is a strong complex with regard to things Irish.'[46] Doherty was succeeded in Australia by Fr

Kevin O' Carroll SJ, and there was no love lost between the two, with McCarron frequently acting as intermediary. Doherty did not believe that O'Carroll had the independence of mind to adapt the Pioneers to Australian circumstances, whilst retaining the original rules, while O'Carroll felt that Doherty had not been strict enough. In the Summer of 1953 he insisted that Australian Catholics still associated temperance with Protestantism: 'I avoid all contact with the Protestant temperance people like the plague. Doherty's method of letting the Parish Priest preach instead of him, led to abysmal ignorance of what we Pioneers were trying to do . . . Unlike the early days in Ireland there is no feeling that drink is ruining the country.'[47] He also insisted that older priests refused to run the Association according to the rules, and that the temporary pledge seemed to be associated solely with the drink convert.[48]

O'Carroll's detailed analysis was not submitted regularly. McCarron berated him in subsequent years for not having sent a report to Dublin in two years.[49] There was some progress. By 1959 it was claimed that there were 126 centres in Australia catering for 20,000 members, though it is difficult to assess how many of these were active. There was also a distinct preference for the temporary pledge which would suggest that many simply could not contemplate the life-long commitment. There were difficulties too in New Zealand. By 1956 there were 11 centres with 1,500 members, 800 of them based in Auckland owing to the work of Fr J. McCorry and the support of the Pioneer bishop of Auckland, Liston. But there were problems because of the distance from the Australian National Council and with customs over the importation of badges. Essentially, New Zealand wanted its own National Council. In 1957 McCarron was fearful of New Zealand Pioneer work being taken over by secular clergy, leading to a loss of control by the Jesuits, as well as losing unity of purpose and rule. Eventually in 1959, Fr Hassen, a native Jesuit, was appointed director in New Zealand 'so that a rift can be avoided'.[50] These difficulties behind the scenes were generally ignored in the public presentation of a glorious crusade abroad. But Doherty did admit of Australian distrust of displaying religious emblems. Likewise in his articles in the Pioneer magazine he wrote of the difficulties of the Pioneers in Australia commanding respect, which sat uncomfortably with reports of Australian Catholics being 'moved to tears' by the demonstration of Irish faith at the Golden Jubilee celebrations in 1949, and this while Australians spent £109 million on beer alone in 1951.[51]

America, certainly in the long term, was not to provide much solace either, though an extensive Irish emigrant population ensured that the effort was greater and more geographically spread than in Australia. Many of the same problems were encountered, including the association of temperance with Protestantism and a suspicion of emblems. Added to this, America had the baggage of the legacy of Prohibition which had done untold damage to the cause of temperance and abstinence, particularly among a generation who, having experienced Prohibition legislatively, recalled its utter uselessness, and morally, its damage. The Pioneers had to tread carefully. As early as 1947, Fr Regan, a Jesuit in Missouri, who had been in the Jesuit College in Milltown in 1932, was corresponding with McCarron on the subject, reminding him that 'it is our long American tradition in a hostile non-Catholic atmosphere to avoid external demonstration', and that even Irish Pioneers coming over as visiting or missionary clerics had taken off their badges in response to requests by their Superiors: 'one Rector I know was rabidly anti-Pioneer just on account of the badge.'[52] McCarron refused to give way on this issue, setting a precedent to which his successors were loyal. It was not surprising that they were reluctant to tamper with a rule which had ensured such uniformity and public allegiance in Ireland. He was honest in reply: 'Maybe just now is not the right time to start. I do feel that it would be better not to start until the whole movement with all its rules is capable of being accepted.'[53] The moral dilemma, however, concerning public demonstrations of piety refused to go away. A disappointed Regan was still writing to McCarron two years later: 'Very many Juniors are willing and eager to practice the devotion, but I find none who wish to join the organisation. They maintain the wearing of the pin stirs up needless hostility to the movement. Virtue in America must be the 'hidden violet' type to suit even the ordinary run of Jesuits.'[54]

In Boston, while the Catholic Archbishop, Cushing, had granted permission for the Association to be organised in early 1951, he felt that the pledge was too severe for American youths, particularly because they had not been trained to the same extent in matters of faith as their Irish counterparts. Of more pressing concern, however, was Cushing's distaste of subservience, administratively and spiritually, to Dublin. Fr Tangvey, writing on behalf of the Archbishop, wanted a clear picture of the obligations of the American centre to Dublin, arguing that if Boston could be independent there would be a stronger chance of spreading the Association; if not, it would be confined to Irish emigrants.[55] Cushing, in turn, provoked the ire of Dublin by demanding 500 pins without agreeing to affiliate to the Central Council in Dublin and undertaking to stick strictly to Irish rules, or to make members aware of the various provisions of membership and to furnish Central Office with regular reports of Pioneer work. Cushing was refused the pins. He then became hostile, and in a personal letter to McCarron insisted that he was no longer interested, and moreover that he 'did not want anything to do with the Dublin office. The rules and the details are too much for my approach to a big spiritual need.'[56] It was a frosty beginning.

Difficulties in other American states were not easily overcome. Correspondence with centres in Washington, where a Pioneer Working Council had been formed in 1948 revealed further limitations, exacerbated by the fact that emigrant communities did not remotely resemble the small homogeneous parishes which formed the backbone of the Association in Ireland. In April 1950, Seamus O'Boyle, a Pioneer based in New Jersey summed this up in a letter to McCarron: 'We are like no parish centre in Ireland. We are drawn from the 32 counties and have different ideas from all the different areas.'[57] Others in New York had their doubts about O'Boyle. Two months later another member of the Working Council wrote to McCarron wondering if it was acceptable to have as President or Council members people who were formerly IRA prisoners – a direct reference to O'Boyle.[58] McCarron's reply is not documented, but O'Boyle continued to be active. Three years later another member wrote to head office complaining of rules being flouted, the rigging of elections and abuse of position, most particularly what some saw as the hijacking of Easter Week celebrations by ex-IRA members under a Pioneer Banner.[59] There were 1,100 Pioneers in New York, and it was estimated that 98 per cent of them were Irish-born. They also had different ideas of appropriate entertainment, and there were frequent rows as to the merits of admitting non-Pioneers to Pioneer functions. In Dublin, McCarron and his assistant, Fr Dargan, busied themselves rapping the knuckles of renegade Pioneers who insisted on organising glee clubs and fashion shows which Dargan felt were 'outside the scope of Pioneer activity'. A few years later there was further controversy over the decision to offer a prize of a round trip to Ireland to raise funds in a Pioneer draw, which Dargan felt 'would injure the spiritual aspect of our work and would lessen the respect in which our movement is held.'[60] Not surprisingly, these skirmishes were not relayed publicly in Ireland. By 1959 there were approximately 2,000 members in New York and the image of them as presented in Pioneer propaganda was as shepherds of an idyllic emigrant flock. Rather than concentrate on specific American Pioneer activity, they contented themselves with vague generalisations about the Irish and their children forming the backbone of the Catholic church in the United States.[61]

In the early 1950s there was also a slight interest in the Pioneers in Holland, principally from Baron van Kessinich, formerly president of

the 'Sobrietas' temperance group in Holland and later Mayor of
Maastricht. Full of his own self-importance, the devoutly Catholic and
larger-than-life Baron, who had initially given up drink for health
reasons, sought to initiate a Dutch branch of the Pioneers. In the
Summer of 1951 he wrote to McCarron, and the correspondence again
illustrates the degree to which continental Catholicism was sceptical of
Catholic abstinence: 'Today the only Dutch Pioneer addresses a very
important letter to you, for which he must ask strict secrecy for the
time being towards the Dutch church.'[62] Van Kessinich was initially
concerned with translating Pioneer rules and literature into Dutch in
order to galvanise an elite band of Dutch Catholics. He was not only
content to go slowly, but had little choice. He revealed to McCarron
that Dutch Jesuits were forbidden to wear badges and the Netherland
bishops had warned him not to indulge in open propaganda. A
measure of how impractical and extreme the Pioneer pledge was seen
on the continent was indicated by the fact that the two Jesuits who
began the Pioneers with van Kessinich resigned, the first because he
had accepted a job promoting retreat houses and did not want to
offend by refusing house hospitality, the other because his confessor
had advised him to change sacrifices from time to time. Van Kessinich
also wrote of another Dutch Pioneer, a 'poor girl', who broke the Pioneer
pledge because she was chosen as queen of a local wine-makers festival
and could not be seen to refuse to taste it.[63] There was an element of
farce in these attempts to cultivate abstinence in a cultural environment which placed such a heavy emphasis on drink socially. Perhaps
realising this, van Kessinich preferred to fill his letters with details of
his own life and his impeccable Catholic credentials. He frequently
wrote of his son in a Trappist monastery in Treglen, and in 1951 had
written gleefully of his visit to the Pope with his wife, in his official
capacity as Mayor of Maastricht: 'We make a combined programme,
my wife and I, that she should talk about the fourteen children and I
about the town, my country and the temperance work, especially
about the Pioneers.'[64] By 1954 he had enrolled only fifty members, but
continually requested McCarron to visit. He was also under attack
from some members of the Catholic clergy in Holland and declared
guilty of Puritanism due to his endorsement of the Pioneer rules.

There were eighty members in Belgium, but again, correspondence
was largely taken up with difficulties in translating the Pioneer rules
and adapting them to foreign circumstances. The organiser, Fr Mans,
believed the rules were 'retro-active' and that it was utterly foolish to
forbid non-alcoholic wines, which were taken regularly by abstaining
continental clergy, but under Cullen's now seemingly archaic rules

were deemed taboo. McCarron's response was hardly satisfactory to Belgian priests set in their ways: 'The Pioneer Association does not want to forbid the use of drinks which are not alcoholic. But neither does it want to make a rule so vague that the decision as to whether this drink or that falls under the rules is left to the individual member.'[65] This was the kind of directive issued from Dublin, which those, even of an abstinence mentality, found unreasonable and patronising.

It is important to place resentments about the classification of drink in context. It has been suggested that there was a fear about departing from Cullen's initial list of proscribed drinks. But changing markets and a wider consumer culture had ensured that the non-alcoholic drink market had expanded rapidly, unlike Pioneer rules. This had led, for example, to farcical correspondence with Australian Pioneers wondering if they were permitted to take cough mixtures.[66] It was an issue which troubled McCarron and many other Pioneers. Month after month in the *Pioneer* the ordinary Pioneer faithful sought clarification on the list of banned drinks, or on a new product which was non-alcoholic but in the guise of a previous alcoholic drink. The central council minutes reveal that in early 1951 it was proposed that the ban on 'cordials' should be lifted, because unlike in Cullen's time, they were now mostly non-alcoholic, which meant that a popular drink like the non-alcoholic Cantrell and Cochrane's ginger wine could not in theory be consumed by Pioneers.[67] However, in a display of Pioneer strength (or arrogance), McCarron thought it more appropriate to request the drinks companies to change their labels. Writing to the English drinks manufacturers Rose and Co. concerning their lime juice cordial, he requested that they drop the use of the word 'cordial', or it would remain forbidden to Pioneer members: 'You will realise that these members would offer a big market for your produce if it fell within our rules. A number of Irish manufacturers have ceased to describe their non-alcoholic products as cordial, in order to capture the market which our membership offers them.'[68]

Chemistry was not on the side of the Pioneers. McCarron went as far as to send products like ginger wine and blackberry wine to the public analyst in Dawson Street, Máire MacNeill, for testing. As a Pioneer she was happy to charge no fee but also hinted to McCarron that the lengths to which he was going were utterly far-fetched. Perhaps it was an indication of a still strong insecurity within the Association that he was afraid members would be duped into drinking certain beverages which contained tiny traces of alcohol. In 1954, MacNeill sent him a report concerning Whiteman's Cydrax which contained a minuscule (0.61 per cent) weight of absolute alcohol, but her attached comments were of more interest than the chemical details:

> From this result, and speaking as a chemist, I would not consider Cydrax an alcoholic drink. Speaking as a Pioneer, I would think it a good thing if Pioneers could take what is considered a healthy drink like cider without breaking their promise. I know, and approve of, the strict attitude of the association, but if adhered to too strictly, it could give rise to anomalies.[69]

MacNeill's view would have been coloured by the fact that of all the drinks sent to the office, porters and ciders would have contained the least amount of alcohol. Yet, not surprisingly, her views were ignored. Four years later she was still being requested to test the recipe for electuary, pointing out that it could take up to five years for the treacle in electuary to ferment. Five years later, the Oblate Fathers in the Pius XII University in Basutoland, requested the views of the Pioneer Central Office on a Basotho food called 'Mothoho' of corn, meal and yeast which native Pioneers had forbidden on the grounds that the sour taste was evidence of fermentation.[70]

The arrival of the first European branch of Alcoholics Anonymous in Dublin in 1946 was a critical development in terms of the growing problem of drink addiction in Irish society. Although it is impossible to give an exact estimate of the number of alcoholics in Ireland at this time, it was quite clear that ignorance at all levels of society existed concerning the condition. In one sense the Pioneers were wary of an association which deemed the condition a disease which could be tackled, but not solved, by a mixture of secularism and spiritualism. During the 1950s, prominent American sociologists like Fr John C. Ford, Professor of Moral Theology at Weston College, Massachusetts, saw alcoholism as both a disease and a moral problem, and endorsed the AA's Twelve Steps to conquering the addiction, including total abstinence. Quite reasonably, he argued that exponents of both total abstinence, and moderate consumption should come to terms on a common ground of Christian sobriety, as there were no contradictory principles involved which should make the two movements natural enemies.[71] As early as 1948, however, McCarron had already made a judgement on the value of the AA, when he wrote to an American Jesuit that 'AA will do a certain amount of good but will not be as effective and lasting as the Pioneers.'[72] Nevertheless, it was a challenge to become more educated about the causes and treatment of alcoholism. It was an issue which began to preoccupy the *Pioneer* during the mid-1950s. In January 1956 the anonymous 'Chaunticlere', who compiled a monthly column entitled 'Sober Facts', sought to distinguish between 'the drunkenness that is sheer gluttony and that which is rooted in the disease of alcoholism', while later that year he was insistent that for the pathological drinker the addiction must be considered a sin, at least in its cause and that 'the alcoholic must see in the self-sacrificing priest his best friend, his true counsellor', again illustrating a reluctance to recommend a secular approach to the problem.[73] At the end of the following year an editorial acknowledged that while it could be accepted that alcoholism was a disease which was incurable, people could deliberately abuse the disease label to imply:

> That the victim is no more free to stop drinking than he is to cure himself of heart trouble. Such people blind themselves to the doctrine of free-will and to our Lord's teaching in avoiding sin and the occasions of sin. Their theory is absurd and in fact the vast majority who drink to excess know well that they are doing something wrong and blameworthy'[74]

To be fair, this analysis was a far cry from the stance of the magazine at the beginning of the decade when presenting alcoholism as a disease was depicted as a self-indulgent refusal to confront reality. Then it was not only denied that alcoholism was a disease, but was a complication of manifold personality disorders, and 'as such it pertains not merely to psychiatry but even more definitely to religion.'[75] The logic was blunt – drunkenness deliberately engineered was sinful and as such the most important element of combating alcoholism required religious and not medical treatment. The Pioneer column in the *Irish Catholic* developed this concept, in replying to a hypothetical scenario where a woman expressed the belief that her husband would never be cured, despite repeated prayers:

> Drunkenness can be cured. Every year witnesses conversions from excessive drinking. Of course God listens to and answers prayers provided that these prayers be earnest and persevering. For his own wise reasons, God may defer the giving of special graces to the drunkard for a long time and thereby, amongst other results, develop in those who continue to pray a deep spirit of faith and trust, detachment from the good things in life, zeal for souls and many other magnificent virtues.[76]

Fittingly, these debates on the scale of drink addiction and the methods best suited to tackling it coincided with another re-examination of the licensing laws and access to drink facilities, as well as Pioneer preparations for their Diamond Jubilee which was the occasion for another mass display of Pioneer devotion at Croke Park. On another level there were cracks beginning to appear in the Pioneer armoury, and some of the events of the late 1950s were essentially a prelude to the beginning of a decline in the influence of the Association, and to a fundamental challenge to Irish Catholicism itself – what Patrick Corish saw as the need to honestly evaluate a relatively static community from the point of view of religious practice, but living in a world which was changing rapidly around it.[77] By the late 1950s it was felt, once again, that the licensing laws in Ireland needed to be modified and liberalised. In 1956 a Commission was established with a view to re-examining the many pieces of legislation dating back to the eighteenth century which comprised the licensing code of the state. The Commission, which reported in 1957 was to involve thirty-nine sittings and the hearing of evidence from seventy-one witnesses. Once again, the issues of primary concern were those of hours of trading, the bona fide law and Sunday opening. The last of these was undoubtedly the most controversial. Those with a vested interest in Sunday opening were still reeling from the Catholic hierarchy's thundering statement refusing to countenance the issue in 1950, two years after their criticism of the 1948 Private Member's Bill. John Whyte, in his work on Church and State in modern Ireland made the following observation on the statement:

> Not only was the proposed legislation wrong, but even to make a case for it was wrong . . . It was a remarkable document and it would be hard to find an episcopal statement couched in more peremptory tones for the whole period covered by this book [1922–72]. It was for the time being completely effective in its purpose.[78]

Initially it seems, judging by the evidence contained in the files of the Department of the Taoiseach, it was still too early to broach the issue again. At the end of 1955 the Assistant Secretary of the Department of Justice, Tommy Coyne, admitted that a select committee on licensing laws would be at an advantage over a commission in that it was less likely to be overly academic and its proposals more likely to be implemented. He maintained, however, that the Sunday opening question 'must be regarded as a closed issue' in the light of the Hierarchy's disapproval, and that the present Minister would be haunted by Sean MacEoin's insistence in the Dáil in 1950, as Minister for Justice, that he would not expose himself to the lick of a Crozier.[79] He believed there was no other option but to demonstrate 'that on the facts the canonical prohibition on Sunday trading does not (as they seem to think) apply to the sale of drink in Ireland'. This was a reference to the fact that the 1878 Law prohibiting Sunday opening was a piece of British legislation, which was out of harmony with the culture and tradition of the Irish people, and that prior to 1878 Sunday drinking had existed in Ireland 'from time immemorial.'[80] In the Dáil, Deputy John McQuillan insisted that there was a need for a re-examination of the Sunday opening question, and in presenting the Pioneer Association as unreasonable extremists, noted that in the past 'they threatened to put horns on me and all sorts of things if I supported a bill that would allow the rural dweller to have the same facilities as the city dweller.' In the same debate, A pioneer and Labour TD, James Tully, castigated McQuillan for presenting the Pioneers 'as somewhat in the nature of witch-hunters', while Deputy Corry, who in 1948 had proposed the original Sunday opening bill preferred to detail the abuses and disregard for the law which he saw as the ultimate ass: 'The Sergeant must wait till Mass is over, but when the priest turns around for the sermon, three or four men go out the door and over to the pub where it is "three pints Jack".'[81]

Doubtless there were many TDs who broke what was in effect a lame duck of a law, as did many of their electorate. Conscious of this, it is interesting that the revamped Gardai Pioneer centre of the 1950s was relentlessly prevailed upon by spiritual directors to be specifically resolute in upholding the licensing laws. In 1955 Fr Doherty spoke of the members of the force who did not fulfil their duty in this regard 'and said that at least Pioneers should do so at any cost whatever.'[82] Indeed, in the *Irish Catholic*, Doherty went as far as to write that 'to uphold, protect and enforce the laws of the land is the duty of the Gardai. That applies to the licensing laws as much as to any other part of the general legislation, more perhaps to those laws than to most others.'[83] This, of course, was tunnel-vision delusion. His successor as spiritual director, Fr Smyth, equated this responsibility with the personal behaviour of the Gardai, believing that the position they occupied in public life ensured that what they did would be commented on favourably or unfavourably 'and hence in the matter of drink they should at all times give good example . . . Drink it was said was going to be a problem for each one of them and they must have an attitude towards it.'[84]

Predictably, the Pioneers rallied against Sunday opening. But their arguments had lost some of their potency. They continually referred to the danger of vested interests – the Licensed Vintners' Association – being allowed undue influence in determining legislation. For its part, in 1953, the LVA had convened a special General Meeting of the Dublin City and County section to demand Sunday opening. They had noted that 'if 1.00 p.m.–3.00 p.m. closing were in Dublin City the GAA would collapse. They are afraid if this is put to the Minister and we are out of it, it may give him an excuse [to change the law].' In noting, however, that Dublin was the most unionised city in Europe, it was conceded that while the Pioneer Association would be opposed, more damaging opposition was likely to come from the Vintners' – 'they know their rights under the Trades Disputes Act and these are as wide as a gate.'[85] However, a few years later, the secretary of the LVA was expressing the same fears which had been noted by the Department of Justice – that while they were anxious to recommend the abolition of the bona fide law, on the question of Sunday opening, it was a matter of conscience, and there was a need to avoid 'at all costs' a conflict with the hierarchy. They decided instead to present their case for Sunday opening outside the four boroughs on the grounds of temperance. In any event, many vintners themselves were divided on the issue, some objecting to a Sunday closing time of 9.00 p.m. on moral grounds. They had been heartened by a letter from the Bishop of Achonry on behalf of the Irish Hierarchy which restated that under canon law, Sunday drinking was a violation of ecclesiastical law, but the secretary 'indicated that the third paragraph of the Bishop's letter might give some opening on the grounds that Sunday opening at specific hours to the general public might lead to better temperance.'[86] It was an encouraging sign. While the Hierarchy duly issued a statement rejecting Sunday opening, it was far more restrained than that of 1950, and no longer held that it would be a violation of ecclesiastical law.[87]

The Report of the Intoxicating Liquor Commission of 1957 did recommend limited Sunday opening, from 5.00–9.00 p.m., and the Pioneer representatives on the Commission, Kevin Clear and Dermot O'Flynn, were prepared to yield to this on the grounds that it was in the interest of temperance to have uniformity of opening hours country-wide, rather than solely in the exempted county boroughs. While the report admitted that 11,953 licensed premises were in excess of reasonable requirements, it did not recommend corrective action. What was more surprising was the fallacious contention that 'drunkenness has ceased to be a problem in the state. In 1955 prosecutions for drunkenness totalled 3,782 as compared with 7,165 in 1925 and 45,670 in 1912.' This supposed increased sobriety was attributed to education, standards of living, alternative recreation and temperance reformers.[88] The two Pioneer representatives rightly took issue with this and in a minority report referred to a memorandum submitted by the Pioneer Association in which they reiterated the view that when facilities for drinking were increased there was a corresponding increase in intemperance. Evidence had also been submitted by the Irish Association for the Prevention of Intemperance and Church of Ireland Temperance witnesses. Referring to this varied evidence, A. J. Pinkerton, chairman of the County Dublin Vintners' Association drew attention to what was now a traditional comment on disparate temperance groups offering evidence:

The evidence put forward by the several temperance organisations generally favoured a further restriction of opening hours. These proposals varied from urging complete closing on Sundays, to advocating the desirability of taking drink home where the family could consume it in comfort. The sincerity of the witnesses was beyond all doubt, and the restraint with which the evidence was given seemed to indicate that perhaps there was some misgiving as to what might be the consequences if some of these proposals were put into practice.[89]

The report of the Commission was to provide the basis of the Intoxicating Liquor Act of 1959 but the legislative path was by no means smooth. The Pioneers insisted that the support they had given to the majority recommendation was deliberate, clear-sighted and confident, although they had communicated to the Taoiseach's Office their refutation of the contention that drunkenness was no longer a serious problem in Irish society.[90] It also seems evident that by the late 1950s, particularly with the replacement of Fr McCarron as central director by his assistant Fr Dargan SJ, that there was a school of thought within the Association which felt that licensing legislation should not be of paramount concern and they preferred to concentrate on traditional messages of spiritual enhancement, alternative recreation and the dismantling of noxious stereotypes cultivated abroad about the Irish. Politically, a lot more barriers had to be overcome. Behind the scenes there was still a lot of bickering and bartering to ensure that Sunday opening would be steered onto the statute books in the face of hostility from some of the hierarchy. In one sense it was a critical battle for both church and state as they flexed their respective muscles. A Department of Justice memorandum from 1958 suggested that the Catholic Church would not be opposed to Sunday opening for reasonable periods due to its recognition and acknowledgement that the bona fide law was being widely abused. Informally, the Father Mathew Association agreed that 12.30–2.00 p.m. and 4.00–6.00 p.m. would be acceptable, but that anything beyond that would upset the pattern of family life, 'as well as attendances at evening devotions', and would not be acceptable to the Hierarchy.[91] The following year, however, the Archbishop of Dublin, John Charles McQuaid began to badger the government privately for the proposed wording of the putative bill, with De Valera phoning McQuaid and fudging the issue by suggesting that the government would 'probably' go along with the majority Report recommendation and asking, though he knew quite well, what exactly McQuaid meant by wanting 'relevant documentation'.[92] The Department of Justice had in fact drawn up a summary of expected objections from the Hierarchy which had been communicated through Dr Hammil of Maynooth College, and secretary of the Father Mathew

Union. In a memorandum expressing opposition to Sunday opening, McQuaid made it clear that he was annoyed that no proposals were forthcoming as a basis for discussion.[93] In the event, the government gave in to the pressure and met McQuaid, and Bishop Browne of Galway, and Lucey of Cork. De Valera was adamant that unless there was a definite reason against a particular recommendation, it should be allowed to proceed. The objections of the Hierarchy were as disparate as the temperance reformers had often been McQuaid was concerned about the advent of motor cars being conducive to increased drinking among the youth, and the failure to enforce licensing laws because district justices and gardai were too closely linked socially with offenders, while Dr Lucey bemoaned publicans who consistently served drink to those already drunk. De Valera himself was in favour of Sunday opening between 12.00–2.00 p.m. and 5.00–9.00 p.m. and was pressing them on the issue but they insisted that they would have to wait until a meeting of the full hierarchy. The Department of Justice privately thought it utterly ridiculous to imply that gardai 'should so order their lives as not to have the ordinary social contacts, meeting occasionally hoteliers, publicans etc.'[94] The minutes give an interesting flavour as to the general tenor of the meeting:

> The Bishop of Galway interjected to say that the Catholic Church was against prohibition, and that the Bishops here were realistic in their approach to licensing matters. Dr Lucey said there was no evidence of popular feeling in favour of a liberalisation of the licensing laws. He said that most women, in addition to the large body of Pioneers, the members of trade unions and others were opposed to additional facilities. He said that the government should legislate in respect of normal requirements and not for exceptional occasions.[95]

In the event the government was only prepared to reduce the proposed Sunday times of opening by one hour. A 1959 draft Bill was sent to all bishops, with provision for Sunday opening. McQuaid was seething. In a letter to the Minister for Justice, Oscar Traynor, he stated:

> I do not agree with the terms of the bill. The Government has not seen fit to accept the representatives of the hierarchy. It cannot then be supposed that any view expressed by the Archbishop of Dublin will have any avail. I may however be permitted to say that in my opinion, the bill, even if passed by the usual majority of the government will prove to be in effect a failure.

De Valera's successor, Lemass, decided to ignore his recriminations, and informed the Assistant Secretary, Tommy Coyne, that 'his Grace's letter does not call for a reply.'[96] Even still, later that month, McQuaid was still attempting to influence the final bill. In reality he was more concerned with provisions for a closing time of 11.30 p.m. for week-days, and wanted 11.00 p.m. all year round. Meeting the secretary of the Department of Justice, Berry, ostensibly about other issues (adoption and St Patrick's Institute) he took the opportunity to express his disapproval and to make sure it was conveyed to the government.[97]

This was a very important juncture in church-state relations and has perhaps been unrecognised as such. It also seems to have proved that, if anything, a Fianna Fáil government was more likely to face down the Hierarchy than any other. J. H. Whyte records that it provided the only example of a recommendation from the Hierarchy being simply rejected by an Irish government.[98] It was also a measure of a certain realism within the Pioneer Association that they had been prepared to sign a report at odds with the view of McQuaid, although in any case, the Hierarchy had hardly been the strongest of Pioneer supporters. The Pioneers were perhaps beginning to recognise that they had a limited role, if any, to play in secular and legislative terms, and if the hierarchy was unable to prevent this legislation, the Pioneers were unlikely to be in any stronger a position. The Pioneers could also reject a charge of hypocrisy by insisting that they had never been against drinking, but its abuse. In other ways it was a confused time, with divisions appearing both within temperance groups and the licensed industry itself. Rising above this confusion, Lemass, speaking in the Dáil on the issue, wrong-footed those who were looking for a free vote on the grounds of conscience, and majestically squared the circle of episcopal disapproval: 'Drunkenness is a sin for which men are responsible to a higher court than ours.'[99]

It should be noted, however, that the whole Intoxicating Bill episode was revealing for other reasons. To be fair to McQuaid, as one who was deeply involved in the provision of Catholic social services in Dublin, he was right, as were the Pioneer Association, to criticise the utterly fallacious contention of the Commission that excessive drinking was no longer a serious problem in Ireland. In a letter to the Department of the Taoiseach in May 1959 he had expressed regret that 'in the report consideration is given to drunkenness, not to alcoholism', and suggested that given the increase in the consumption of drink, aligned with a falling population and high percentage of abstainers, it was surely obvious that there was heavier drinking by fewer people.[100] As a result of his comments the Department of Justice queried the Department of Health as to the scale of the problem of alcoholism in Ireland. The reply was a staggering indictment of the ignorance that existed at the highest levels of Irish society concerning drink abuse, and again characterises the ambivalent attitudes to the Irish drinking culture which existed, despite the attempts of the Pioneers: 'Off hand they [The Department of Health] have said it is not a problem in this country: that fewer than 400 persons are received into institutions (public or private) for treatment in any year.'[101]

This was the same year in which the Pioneer Association could claim a membership of nearly 500,000, registered in 1900 centres around the country. The question has to be addressed as to why they were not more successful in rectifying ignorance or in influencing the culture of excess. The reality was that the Pioneers were equally bereft of reliable figures for alcoholism in Ireland, and were not particularly interested. Pioneer devotion was to remain for most a personal piety, undemonstrative and non-confrontational. But if the personal piety had remained the mainstay, by the end of the 1950s the country was changing rapidly. In the same year, 1959, Liam Maher, on the subject of temperance in Ireland, exaggerated the membership of the Pioneers at 600,000, and concluded: 'There is about the Pioneer strictness an asceticism which will always repel the vapid and attract the loyal. There are still Giants in our day'.[102] As the Association headed into its most challenging, and ultimately damaging decade, this was a misplaced optimism.

NOTES

1   See for example, Terence Browne, *Ireland: A social and cultural history 1922–85* (London 1986) and Dermot Keogh, *Twentieth-Century Ireland: Nation and state* (Dublin 1994)
2   PC IC, December 28, 1950
3   ibid., May 7, 1953
4   Joseph Gusfield, 'Status conflicts and the changing ideologies of the American temperance movement' in Pittmann (ed.), *Society, Drinking and Culture* (New York, 1962)
5   John O'Brien (ed.), *The Vanishing Irish* (New York 1956) p. 33
6   ibid.
7   ibid.
8   Paul Blanshard, *The Irish and Catholic Power: An American Interpretation* (London 1954), pp. 79–82
9   Tom Inglis, *Moral Monopoly: The Catholic Church in modern Irish society* (Dublin 1987) p. 181
10 PCIC, December 14, 1950
11 ibid., May 8, 1952
12 Valerie Hey, *Patriarchy and Pub Culture* (London 1986) p. 15
13 PAA, SFX Minutes, March 27, 1953
14 *Pioneer*, March 1949
15 PAA, Central Council Minutes, March 6, 1950
16 ibid., SFX Pioneer Club Memo by Fr Troddyn [c.1953]
17 ibid.
18 ibid., Troddyn to Leo Kenny, SFX Club, May 9, 1955
19 ibid., Troddyn to McCarron, n.d. [c.1955]
20 PAA, Circular re Rules for Socials, n.d. [c.early 1950s]
21 ibid ., Social club, Memo on Progress of Sports Club
22 ibid., Margot Kelly to McCarron, May 15, 1956
23 ibid.

24 McCarron to Margot Kelly, May 16, 1956
25 ibid., B. Kelly to Dr Farren, May 21, 1956 (copy)
26 PCIC, October 17, 1954
27 PAA, Circulars concerning Knock pilgrimages 1954
28 ibid., McCarron to Fr Malone, September 7 and August 28, 1954
29 ibid., J. McCormack to McCarron, September 21, 1954 and McCarron to James Whyte, November 2, 1954
30 ibid., Cork Circulars, 1956
31 ibid.
32 ibid., Memo on travel arrangements, May 23, 1956
33 ibid., Collier and Mageean to McCarron, May 9, 1956
34 ibid., Fergus to McCarron September 11, 1956
35 ibid., John O'Callaghan to Michael Quirke, May 16, 1956
36 ibid,. Fr James to Fr Dargan, June 21, 1956
37 ibid., Fr Coffey to Dargan April 31, 1956
38 ibid., St John's Centre, Kilkenny to McCarron, June 19, 1956
39 PC IC, July 19, 1956
40 *Pioneer*, November 1951
41 ibid., January 1953
42 ibid., August 1955
43 PAA, Fr Durge to Provincial, April 8, 1945
44 ibid., Fr Doherty to McCarron, March 29, 1951
45 ibid.
46 ibid., August 8, 1951
47 ibid., O'Carroll to McCarron, July 3, 1953
48 ibid., September 16, 1953
49 ibid., McCarron to O'Carroll, September 16, 1955
50 ibid., McCluskey to McCarron, November 1, 1956
51 PCIC, October 23, 1952 and *Pioneer*, June and August 1952
52 PA, Fr Regan to McCarron, July 3, 1947
53 ibid., McCarron to Regan, August 1, 1947
54 ibid., Regan to McCarron, June 26, 1949
55 ibid., Tangvey to Dargan, January 10, 1951 and March 8, 1951
56 ibid., Cushing to McCarron, June 9, 1951
57 ibid., Seamus O'Boyle to McCarron, April 24, 1950
58 ibid., Helen Sharkey to McCarron, June 16, 1950
59 ibid., Mary O'Brien to McCarron, March 27, 1953
60 ibid., Dargan to Fr Frederick, May 5, 1953 and October 11, 1957
61 *Pioneer*, September 1957
62 PAA, Van Kessinich to McCarron, July 26, 1951
63 ibid., October 20, 1953 and April 14, 1954
64 ibid., August 13, 1951
65 ibid., McCarron to Fr Mans, February 3, 1953
66 ibid., McCluskey to McCarron, November 1, 1956
67 PAA, Central Council Minutes, April 9, 1951
68 ibid., McCarron to L.Rose, October 13, 1951
69 ibid., Máire MacNeill to McCarron, August 28, 1954
70 ibid., May 7, 1958 and Our Lady's Novitiate, Roma, Basutoland to Fr Smyth, March 23, 1959
71 John Ford, *Man Takes a Drink* (London, 1956) pp. 53–4
72 PAA, McCarron to Fr Regan, Missouri, July 13, 1948
73 *Pioneer*, January 1956 and June 1956
74 ibid., November 1957
75 ibid., May 1950
76 PCIC, January 25, 1954
77 Patrick J. Corish, *The Irish Catholic Experience: A historical survey* (Dublin 1985) p. 230
78 J.H. Whyte, *Church and State*, p. 195
79 Dáil Debates, March 1, 1950, vol. 119, 7, col. 1063

80 NAI, D/T S15990A, Intoxicating Liquor Commission, 1956, Memo by Coyne, Assistant
    Secretary of the Department of Justice
81 Dáil Debates, vol. 153, 3–4, cols. 492–504, 1955
82 PAA, Garda Minute Book, April 29, 1955
83 PC IC, December 18, 1952
84 PAA, Garda Minute Book, September 27, 1958 and January 21, 1956
85 LVAA, Minutes, March 29, 1953
86 ibid., October 19, 1956
87 J.H. Whyte, *Church and State*, p. 327
88 *Report of Intoxicating Liquor Commission* (Dublin 1957) Introduction
89 ibid.
90 *Pioneer*, September, 1957 and NAI, DT S15990B, February 17, 1956
91 NAI., DJ S15990 B, September 19, 1958
92 ibid., DT S16524, May 9, 1959
93 ibid.
94 ibid.
95 ibid.
96 NAI, DT S165243, McQuaid to Traynor, October 28, 1959 and Lemass to Coyne,
    November 3, 1959
97 ibid., Berry Secretary of Department of Justice, Memo on interview with McQuaid,
    November 21, 1959
98 J.H. Whyte, *Church and State*, p. 237
99 Dáil Debates, vol. 178, November 25, 1959
100 NAI, DT S16524, May 9, 1959
101 ibid., Department of Justice Memo, June 5, 1959
102 Liam Maher, *Temperance in Ireland* (Dublin 1959), pp. 19–20

CHAPTER SIX

Challenges from Within
and Without

'Pat' said the Clergyman 'you are at it again. You must keep away
from drink. It is your mortal enemy.' 'Wisha Father', rejoined Pat,
'Wasn't it only Sunday last that your Reverence told us to love our
enemies.' 'Well then if I did' said the Priest 'I never told you to
swallow them.'

Robert O'Neill OFM, *Talks to Pioneers*

Fr Mulligan holds the view that the attitude of Pioneers towards
alcoholics was not Christlike in as much as there was a great lack of
charity shown towards such people. He believes that much of the
criticism of the Pioneer Association has its roots in the 'holier than
thou' attitude which he believes was held by Pioneers in the past.
That must, he said, be shed if we are to get down to more lasting
work.

SFX Council Minutes, May 26, 1966

The 1960s was extraordinarily painful and challenging for the Pioneer
faithful who had guided the Association to its seemingly unassailable
position of the mid-1950s. The changes in Irish culture and society in
this decade have been attributed to many factors, both internal and
external – programmes for economic expansion, younger politicians,
the advent of television and access to foreign influences, changes in
traditional Catholic practice heralded by Vatican II reforms and the
dramatic turnaround in emigration figures. Fergal Tobin sought to
encapsulate these developments in the memorable phrase 'The Best of
Decades'.[1] Perhaps it would be simplistic and trite to assume that for a
Catholic spiritual organisation it would be the worst of decades. It
should be recognised that within the Pioneer Association there were
those who recognised that the Pioneer message and methods needed
to be recontextualised in the light of a rapidly changing society. The
tensions which emerged in the 1960s within the Association had as
much to do with internal recognition of the need to adapt as they had

194

with inevitable external probing. Many of the traditional themes were relevant but there were also new challenges, particularly the difficulties posed by alcoholism, both in terms of defining it as a condition and the attitude the Association should adopt towards it. There was also an undercurrent of doubt that the Association's traditional methods of propaganda could withstand critical probing, to the extent that by the end of the decade the suggestion was floated that the Association be authorised to admit moderate drinkers as members. It did not succeed, but that it came to the surface at all illustrated how rapid the pace of change had become. It also revealed the frustration felt among a liberal wing that it was myopic, obdurate and counterproductive to pitch drinker and abstainer so widely apart.

Yet, the Association was by no means a spent force. It was still used by many as a base to further their own identity, whether or not for strictly religious reasons. A fitting caution against misrepresenting a desire to embrace the pledge was contained in the pages of Hugh Brody's 1973 social study, *Inishkillane*, which sought to document change and decline in the West of Ireland. Taking the pledge, it seems, was as much about modernity as about following traditional paths. Brody noted that the youth were responding positively to the local priest's campaign against drinking:

> It is quite remarkable how many young men in Inishkillane take this pledge seriously, but they do not, despite the argument and theory of the Priest, conceive of it as a religious act, still less as a sacrifice in atonement for humanity's sinfulness. Rather, it is part of their identification with the forces opposing the traditional patterns of social life and social authority.[2]

This is the kind of subtle insight which serves as a warning against limiting debates about the power of the Catholic Church in Ireland to issues of 'tradition' or 'modernity'. On the brink of the 1960s, particularly with the celebration of the Diamond Jubilee in Croke Park in June 1959, the Association managed once again to mobilise on a vast scale loyal Pioneer troops, coinciding with the seventy-fifth anniversary of the GAA. Once again it was a remarkable organisational feat, with a crowd of up to 90,000 in attendance. But the language used in the address of the new central director, Fr Daniel Dargan, typified the fear creeping into Irish Catholicism that traditional practices were under threat:

> Voluntary service, unselfishness, loyalty and perseverance are qualities that are becoming more infrequent, yet they are qualities necessary to the life of a nation. The nation that has lost them is near the verge of decay. Christianity is being assailed. The corruption and decadence of

> this materialistic age are creeping into Ireland and threatening to make
> our people forget that they have souls to save and that they have
> responsibilities to the souls of others.[3]

The rally was also addressed by Cardinal Conway, Archbishop of Armagh, but once again, private correspondence in the lead up to the event pointed to the difficulty of getting senior church figures on board. The tone of the hierarchy's letters characterises an ageing group. Dr Quinn, Bishop of Cavan, wrote: 'It is thoughtful of you to provide transport to Croke Park. I am not quite an "ancient"' but I am nevertheless loath to step it,'[4] while one of the Pioneers' staunchest allies, Bishop Collier of Ossory, felt he was the last of a dying breed:

> I am now in the ranks of the 'old Bishops' in Ireland and my engagements
> must be of a provisional acceptance. But I hope to be with the Pioneers
> of Ireland on the great occasion. I am almost a Pioneer Bishop of Ireland,
> as I took the Pioneer pledge in 1903 with my class at Maynooth on the
> first visit of Fr Cullen, founder, to the college.[5]

The Archbishop of Dublin, John Charles McQuaid, was more muted, highlighting the discomfort of non-Pioneer bishops: 'The celebrations have my best wishes, but especially as you will have Pioneer Bishops present, it would be more honest of me to look on from a distance.'[6] Dargan was keen to have Archbishop Walsh of Tuam to preside over the Benediction. Perhaps because the Pioneers had relatively few allies among the Hierarchy, they tended to exaggerate the commitment and enthusiasm of those bishops who were members. Dargan stressed that he wanted Walsh because 'your Grace has always been such a wonderful friend to the Pioneer Association', but Walsh in reply diminished his acceptance somewhat: 'Candidly I think that you should call on one of the other bishops who have shown more activity in the Pioneer ranks than I have.'[7]

Away from the concerns of the hierarchy, Paddy O'Keeffe, General Secretary of the GAA, aligned himself with the Pioneer cause by ensuring there would be no GAA fixtures to clash with the rally. Dargan's contact in Rome, Fr Henry Nolan SJ, who worked with Vatican Radio, wrote that he was 'delighted to hear that Paddy O'Keeffe turned up trumps again as he always does', but added that Dargan's request to get a few shots of the Pope giving his blessing to the Pioneer outing, to be incorporated into a film of the rally, was beyond his power.[8] Eventually the National Film Institute of Ireland agreed to produce a 16 mm film of the rally, based on a script by prominent Catholic historian, writer and Pioneer, Mary Purcell, and recorded in London. There was a degree of excitement about this self-reliant venture within the Association, and it was significant that in the aftermath of the rally, Radio Éireann's coverage was considered very poor. In order to deal with this and other issues, Fr Dargan showed insight in September 1959 by convening a meeting to discuss how future public Pioneer occasions would be handled.

Whatever about the headline-seeking which such a crowd in Croke Park ensured, the overall feeling was that the mass rally was an idea which had outlived its usefulness and was becoming increasingly impractical. It was suggested at this meeting that a crowd of 100,000 was 'too unwieldy, involving excessive discomfort for those participating and takes too long to reach Croke Park. A more satisfactory plan would be to limit the procession to a much smaller number, say 10,000.'[9] This was a fitting example of Dargan's practical and frank way of assessing such occasions, and was indicative of a departure from the view that the success of such ventures could be based solely on numbers. Another contributor to the post-mortem, a priest from Harold's Cross, seemed to imply that the organisers' and participants' fervent prayers for fine weather may have been a curse: 'Having drawn attention to the weakness in the organising of the Jubilee it is only fair to add that the intense heat of the day caused the tar on the roads to melt and when some of the processionists tried to make off they found their shoes stuck to the road.' A letter from another participant echoed these complaints suggesting that mass parades were an outmoded way of celebrating or commemorating, and that water supplies from 'humble' buckets were 'primitive and insanitary'. The correspondent continued forcefully with unbridled pre-Vatican-II sexism – with regard to the future he felt that it was best to have 'a token number from each centre to consist of able-bodied men only. No women and no children.'[10]

On the surface the Association in 1960 seemed to be robust. According to the *Province News*, an internal periodical for Jesuits, seventy nine new centres had been affiliated in the previous year and the circulation of the *Pioneer* magazine was 42,000 copies a month.[11] The Association was still excessively local in its focus. The tendency was to pinpoint particular events or places and hammer home the message of how Pioneer-dominated the occasions or localities were. A perfect example was the tendency to trumpet the feats of GAA teams who were known to have a majority of Pioneer members, and if the referee at Croke Park was a member, all the better:

> The All Ireland Hurling final between Waterford and Kilkenny which ended in a draw on September 6 was a brilliant and exciting game. The players deserve high praise for the skill they displayed, but much more for their sportsmanship. We are glad to say that quite a number of the

hurlers on both sides are Pioneers. Many compliments have been paid
to referee Gerry Fitzgerald for the adept manner in which he controlled
the game. He is a Pioneer from Rathkeale in County Limerick.[12]

In terms of Pioneer social outings, the following entry was typical of
Pioneer columns of the early 1960s: 'On July 17, Inchigeela, County
Cork was invaded by 600 Pioneers – the largest number of people ever
to be seen in this charming little village with a population of 177
inhabitants.'[13]

On a national level, however, this domination was not evident. The
Association was still concerned with licensing legislation and the fact
that there appeared to be a continued increase in the consumption of
alcohol, which certain vested interests were hoping would be accompanied by an increase in the hours of opening of licensed premises.
While Lemass, as seen below, had been determined to push through the
Intoxicating Liquor Bill of 1960 despite the opposition of the Hierarchy,
there was still much debate on the issue, and it became a convenient
political point-scoring theme. In September 1960, James Dillon at a Cork
City Fine Gael executive dinner, having excoriated Fianna Fáil's economic and agricultural policies went on to slam the Intoxicating Liquor
Bill which he suggested had 'gravely injured publicans and caterers in
our tourist resorts and the amendment of this law is urgently needed
before the next tourist season if the tourist industry is not to follow
agriculture into decay.'[14] The Minister for Justice, Oscar Traynor, denied
that publicans in holiday resorts were losing out:

> Losses if any have been occasioned by the fact that there is now strict
> enforcement of the licensing laws and illicit trading is not now tolerated.
> As I said however in the concluding debates on the bill some months
> ago, I do not expect the Intoxicating Liquor Act of 1960 to be the last act
> of the Oireachtas to deal with licensing hours. That act has been in force,
> however, less than four months and if there is to be any question of its
> amendment the government will require to have evidence of a
> substantial kind as to the necessity for doing so.[15]

Key issues at stake were provisions for the granting of area exemption
orders which had been scrapped by the 1960 Bill. Dermot O'Flynn,
Secretary of the Pioneer Executive Council, and later a Chief Knight of
Columbanus, informed the Catholic Hierarchy of the pressure being
placed on politicians to amend the legislation and called on them to
assist the Pioneers in counteracting what he called the 'organised
campaign'.[16] It became quite a heated debate with the issue of tourism
being used by both sides to vindicate their respective stances. Many
urban and rural district councils passed resolutions demanding amend-
ments on the grounds that afternoon closing from 2.00–5.00 p.m. was

adversely affecting the tourist trade. Likewise the President of the Irish Hotels Federation, O'Carroll, echoed these complaints in the winter of 1960, predicting 'irreparable damage' to the tourist trade if the law was not amended.[17] The *Irish Press* had also referred at the end of the summer season to tourists on a Sunday 'wandering in the rain',[18] while the bishop of Achonry had written to Dermot O'Flynn, 'it is lamentable that the much lauded licensing act is proving such a failure.' The grounds on which he felt it had erred were not spelt out.[19] Fianna Fáil at its Annual Delegate Conference was certainly feeling the heat, where more than 80 per cent of the resolutions passed related to licensing laws, with delegates warning Lemass that he faced election defeat on the issue, and threats that the Attorney General would be served with a writ by county Dublin publicans who were demanding compensation for loss of earnings since the new Act became law. Their anger was given added potency by the fact that cities such as Cork had experienced their biggest ever influx of tourists.[20]

Rancorous outbursts as to the importance of tourists was further illustration of a lack of uniformity on both sides of the drink and licensing hours debate. The *Irish Catholic*, regarding as facile and misconceived the contention that all tourists were drinkers, proclaimed 'one would expect bodies whose chief concern is tourism and tourists to have a better sense of proportion. Such a picture is more a caricature than an accurate presentation.'[21] However shortly afterwards he was flatly contradicted by Dr Lucey, Bishop of Cork, who in an address to Pioneers admitted that 'the published figures for the sale of liquor and convictions for drunkenness over the last few years indicate increased drinking. But these figures are explained by the tourist trade sales and by the increased vigilance of the gardai.'[22] In the Pioneer column of the *Irish Catholic* it was insisted that increasing licensed facilities was tantamount to selling the Irish soul and that, if anything, tourists complained that there was too much drinking going on. Whilst denying that the Association was a pressure group (even though they operated as such in private), at a Pioneer rally in Galway in 1961, Dargan insisted that a proposed extension of hours of trading as envisaged in a 1962 Licensing Act, would encourage longer drinking sessions to which the general public were forcefully opposed. Eschewing his normally moderate approach to these issues, he refuted the idea that there was even anything to debate: 'We are presenting a case that is not only strong but unanswerable. The wives and families of drinkers are not organised and have no easy opportunity of publicly expressing their opposition. Nevertheless, they have rights, just as surely as pedestrians have rights when legislation for motorists is being framed.'[23]

This was one of the oldest Pioneer tactics – when issues of a controversial nature emerged, they frequently played the gender card,
particularly the idea that at a most fundamental level, women would
be the principal victims of any increased facilities for drinking. Publicly,
it was somewhat deceptive. An analysis of the minutes of the ladies' St
Francis Xavier council in Gardiner Street reveal that most of their
discussion was taken up with the reading of temperance catechisms
and the organisation of socials rather than a preoccupation with the
social vulnerability of women in a home marked by excessive drinking.
One of the few recorded decisions from the minutes of 1960 was
probably more representative of the kind of protection of women the
association was concerned with: 'at our last meeting Fr Dargan made a
suggestion to have men helping at the quarterly socials by carrying
heavy trays.'[24] Nevertheless, women were still singled out as having
by far the heavier responsibility when it came to abstemiousness, both
for the present and the future, Dargan reminding schoolgirls in Navan
in 1961 that 'whatever their role in life may be, mother wife or sister of
a drunkard, it is they who must bear the brunt of the shame, poverty
and sorrow which follows excessive drinking.'[25]

In dealing with these issues of licensing, the Pioneers were more
comfortable with indulging in the same kind of propaganda which
they felt had served them in good stead in the past. But the continual
talk of pressure to change laws coming from vested interest, was, at
least from the perspective of the licensed vintners, a crude simplification. Divisions existed within the Vintners also. Branches of the
Irish Country Vintners' Association agreed that closing time should be
increased in their districts to 12.00 p.m. midnight, and sought to
reduce closing hours of dance halls to the same time. In this they
expressed disagreement with the concept of uniformity of hours as
advocated by the Dublin City Licensed Vintners' Association.[26] The
Minister for Justice rejected this because 'while the hours prescribed in
the Act did not have the unanimous support of members of both
houses almost every deputy and Senator who criticised them did so
because he considered them unnecessarily long and not the reverse.'[27]
For its part, the LVA in Dublin since late 1959 had been conscious of
the need to avoid being seen as a vested interest group, and the
Chairman, Patrick Maher, stressed the importance of criticising measures mainly from the consumer's point of view. In private, Maher
believed that increasing opening hours during the week and on
Sundays was 'likely to promote serious moral problems for the
community and to interfere with the normal pattern of family life'.
However by 1962, the new chairman, McSheary, at an AGM in the

Catholic Commercial Club in Dublin, felt that the 1960 Act 'seemed to be working reasonably satisfactorily and that uniformity was the only answer to ordered conditions in the trade', though it was felt that compulsory endorsements were fundamentally unjust and should be left to the discretion of the courts.[28] The LVA intermittently met the Minister for Justice in 1962, but when it came to the issue of opening hours there were 'conflicting views even among the deputation'. The reality for the vintners was that the issues which preoccupied most of their time were negotiations with employees over working hours and time off in the light of changed working hours. These often heated discussions were chaired by the Jesuit, Fr Edmund Kent, from the Workers' College in Ranelagh.[29]

From the outset the Pioneer Association had sought to challenge the close linking of Irish identity to drink. It was something, which they felt by the 1960s, their sheer volume of membership ought to have dispelled, but it lingered, particularly they believed, in the minds of those outside Ireland. The Association was not the only group which was susceptible to sensitivity in this regard, and it became an issue on which the government sought to intervene in late 1960. In June 1960 in *Time* magazine, in an article which was later reprinted in a German Foreign Affairs Bulletin, reference was made to the musical exploits of young German jazz amateurs in the United States, to the effect that 'the idea of a stolid German at a jam session seems at first glance as unlikely as an Irishman at a temperance meeting.'[30] This provoked not only the ire of the Pioneers but also of the Department of External Affairs which was pointedly defensive about what it saw as insulting stereotypes. The Taoiseach, Lemass, responded by requesting the Central Statistics Office to furnish him with comparative details of drink consumption in Ireland, Britain and other countries. The figures, based on the year 1958, showed that in bulk litres, Ireland consumed, per head of population, 64.3 of beer and 1.2 of spirits, while the figures for Britain were 79.1 and 1.1 respectively.[31]

At a speech given to a Muintir na Tire Rural Week at Rockwell College in Tipperary the following month, Lemass chose to interpret these figures in a way that delighted the Pioneers. Given that the government, in terms of revenue, had a vested interest in drink consumption, it was significant as one of the few occasions in which the Irish temperance movement was recognised, and indeed praised, at an official level. The theme of his speech was anti-Irish prejudice:

> One of the most persistent and irritating falsehoods about the Irish is that they are excessive consumers of alcoholic drink. That lie has gone very far afield. Even the BBC Television service rarely, if ever, presents a play about Ireland without the characters moving around in clouds of

alcoholic vapour. The simple truth is ignored, and the truth is that the per capita consumption of alcoholic drink in Ireland is one of the lowest for all countries for which reliable statistics are available, even if one counts against our own people the not inconsiderable intake of tourists. The consumption of beer per head in Britain is about the same as in Ireland, and of wines considerably higher. Of all the spirit drinking countries Irish per capita consumption is nearly the lowest. Of course, there are still many people who take too much alcohol, but the proportion of abstainers is probably higher here than anywhere. One of the most noteworthy features of the Irish way of life – which is the very high proportion of the population who have made solemn pledges to take no alcohol at all, is nearly always ignored by foreign commentators.[32]

Sean Ronan, Secretary to the Department of External Affairs, wrote to the editor of the offending remarks in Time pointing out the high degree of temperance activity in Ireland and succeeded in eliciting an apology which was suitably contrite: 'alas, these clichés about people are beguilingly convenient. It is easier (as the Bulletin is well aware) to label a nation than to know the nation. Facts are perhaps the only remedy.' This prompted the *Evening Press* to bellow the headline 'German apology for drink libel on Irishmen.'[33] Daniel Dargan had been watching these developments closely. He had previously written to the editor of *Time* magazine to complain about the offending remarks, and revealed in a letter to the Department of External Affairs that while the magazine's editor had been prepared to apologise, he had qualified it with a plea for the temperance people to be more self-deprecating: 'Obdurately, however we still say that the expression in question has been raising chuckles for years, especially among Irishmen.'[34] In a follow-up letter, Dargan expressed delight that the Taoiseach, as he saw it, had paid the Association such a handsome tribute, adding that he was happy that 'our Association is helping to maintain the good name of Ireland.'[35] Dargan was also curious as to the source of the Taoiseach's statistics, which had been furnished by the Central Statistics Office. It was an interesting request. Both official government departments and temperance reformers had traditionally found it difficult to produce reliable statistics. In the past Dargan's predecessors had frequently used whatever scraps of information they had solely for propaganda or to selectively back the latest stance the association was taking. The truth was that the Irish government did not have its own statistics. The figures referred to by Lemass had in fact been taken from a Danish publication, with the Central Statistics Office maintaining that they were 'not aware of any International Yearbook from which the required information could be obtained'.[36] It was perhaps not surprising that the Pioneer Association did not use statistics to much effect. Despite its scale, the clear trends in Irish society were towards increased consumption. Others were unimpressed with the assumption that because of Ireland's unusually high numbers of total abstainers, drinking patterns were not excessively heavy. In a letter to the *Irish Independent* in 1960, a reader pointed out that in relation to drink consumption as perceived abroad 'paranoid outbursts against the English are no substitute for realistic policies', and that statistics detailing the per capita consumption of alcohol had little bearing on the scale of alcohol problems in that country, suggesting that the consumption of one hundred pints a day could be divided between ninety-five abstainers and five drinkers.[37] Certainly, the figures in retrospect seemed to suggest an upward curve of drinking as the 1960s progressed, helped no doubt by increased affluence and a proliferation of drinking venues, despite the fact that the Pioneer was able to publish an updated alphabetical list of seventy-two non-alcoholic drinks permitted to *Pioneers*, from 'Applecham to Zip', in the same year that 16,556 women and 14,595 men joined the Association.[38] It was however an inescapable fact that during the 1950s and 1960s most Western nations increased their alcohol intake per person, but international comparison of expenditure proportions was more telling. Alcohol accounted for a high percentage of personal expenditure which suggested that alcohol held a prominent position in the Irish hierarchy of needs, or indeed, it could be asserted that beer was consumed in Ireland as an economic necessity.[39] It may also have been significant that drink consumption had declined somewhat in the 1930s, and by the 1950s and 1960s there was a generation growing up with little personal experience of the excesses their grandparents had experienced. Between 1948 and 1970 consumption of alcohol per person rose 60 per cent from 3.2 litres to 5.1 litres, and consumption increased a full litre per person in the five years preceding 1970. Three quarters of the drink consumed was beer.[40] In 1963 it was estimated that middle-class Dubliners spent only 10 per cent of their income on housing, which was less than they spent on drink and tobacco.[41]

Outright hostility to what were perceived as insulting stereotypes manifested itself frequently in Pioneer publications, particularly when the perpetrators were felt to be completely at a distance from the reality. Fr Edward Murray, Professor of History at the University of Notre Dame in Indiana, castigated his adopted country's shallow presentation of Ireland's drinkers:

> The Irish drink less whiskey per head than the Scots and more cheerily. There are reams and reams of such drivel being written today in foreign periodicals and some of the gravest offenders are the slick Yank maga-

zines. It is a pity that so many American and English journalists yield to the temptation to dip their pens in alcohol when describing Irish habits and traditions. We are neither irrelevant or facetious when we say that it would be more to the point to dip one's pen in Holy water when depicting the usual course of life in the land of Saints and Scholars.[42]

If it is true that abstainers had cause to be disheartened, it is also the case that much of their defensiveness was born of a hostility towards the pledge in a culture permeated by drink, with so much social entertainment centred around the pub. But it was deceptive to believe that it was primarily foreign writers or observers who wrote frequently on the relationship between alcohol and the Irish way of life. Throughout the 1960s the Pioneers counteracted this by painting an idyllic picture of local contexts. The following extract from the *Irish Catholic* was typical:

> We would like to know if any Parish in Ireland can beat the record of Ballintrillick in County Sligo. Ninety-five per cent of the people between the ages of 14 and 40 are either Probationers or Pioneers. There is no public house in the Parish. At the recent successful social over 200 attended. There, we can safely surmise, the peace of Christ reigned during Christmas: there, homes are happy: there the young men and women have done something glorious.[43]

Needless to say, such passages did not reflect the wider picture. Despite the pace of change in Ireland in the 1960s there was a certain stagnation associated with Irish drinking practices and the drinking environment which the Pioneers were powerless to change, and with which writers associated an inheritance which was almost immutable. What was perhaps even more challenging was the idea that the Catholic religion itself could be responsible for this heavy drinking, the idea being that religious faith and belief in the afterlife sponsored an endurance and hardship in the present from which drink was a welcome and almost necessary relief. It was also seen as inclusive. This was the analysis of Maurice Sheehy:

> Intoxicating drink is the Irish anodyne. A fondness for drink, like religion and patriotism, unites and characterises the catholic Irish. It is evident everywhere, in city, town and country, in all social classes rich and poor, educated and ignorant, and, in recent decades in women as well as in men. Irish drinking is heaviest in the country towns where addicts excuse themselves by saying 'there's nothing else to do'. The clergy themselves are apt to share in this 'good man's weakness', and turn a blind eye on Irish drinking habits.[44]

In 1965, Art Gallagher from the University of Kentucky did a follow-up study to the sociological survey of rural life which Arensberg and Kimball had completed in Clare in the 1930s and found that attitudes to drink in rural parishes were much the same thirty years on. Attitudes, he claimed could 'only be defined as tolerant' with drink essential as a means of initiating social contact, especially with strangers. He also found that 'there were no moral sanctions invoked in the discussions about drink.'[45] In his study of the (fictional) western parish of Inishkillane, Brody wrote of drinking patterns and habits being closely aligned to the seasons, with heavy but happy drinking in the Summer and more despondency in the winter among the despairing alcoholic bachelors:

> A drunken man in winter leans more heavily on the bar. He often seeks to draw another drinker or two to his side. Such a group creates a tight circle of privacy around itself – a privacy physically expressed by the arms they lay across one another's shoulders. Then, with faces almost touching, they appear to join closely in evident despair. This despair is not expressed in discussion among the drinkers. Rather, they exchange silence as if it were words, and words in brief expression of the lonesomeness.[46]

Alcohol, it seems was the exception, even within the rigidly defined system of social and sexual mores which defined so much of Irish behaviour. Alexander Humphreys, in his study of the 1960s rural populace who had migrated to Dublin wrote of the typical country-man now settled in Dublin:

> Although he is certain that man's bodily nature with its emotions is at root good, he is rather more suspicious of it and deals with it somewhat more severely. As a result he inclines to a jaundiced view of sex and a generally ascetic outlook which places a high premium upon continence, penance, and in most spheres of life, on abstemiousness.

The sphere of alcohol was presumably not included, as Humphreys acknowledged the 'almost nightly visit to the pub'.[47] Tony Farmar in his study of middle-class Dublin saw the public house in more lyrical and sexist terms – 'as a retreat for the breadwinner from priests and women and where consequently all sorts of comfortable myths could flourish.'[48] On the other hand, one of the first major sociological surveys of rural life – The Limerick Rural Survey, edited by the Maynooth academic Jeremiah Newman in 1966, found that intellectual and spiritual culture was at a low ebb and that while there was a tendency for the better educated and intelligent farmers' sons to spend less times in pubs, as a social revolt against segregation and the bachelor stigma, the drinking den was still very much contributing to the general male malaise: 'The public houses are drab and uncomfortable. There is no provision for anything but hard drinking and a respectable woman would never set foot inside one of these places. Unless there is a grocery shop attached, she never drinks in the local bar'. Added to this was the reminder that 'very few of the older farmers are non-drinkers. In fact there is a tendency to distrust the abstainer.'[49] To compound the gloomy picture, a study was carried out in 1968 which involved monitoring twenty-two public houses in Dublin for two weeks to estimate the number of women and children frequenting pubs – the final figures were 46,574 women and 27,999 children of whom 5,807 were babies in arms.[50] One wonders why the men were not counted also.

Clearly authors were either more comfortable or felt it was more representative to discuss the Irish drink culture in terms of indulgence rather than abstinence. Aside from the sort of scenes witnessed at Croke Park, Pioneer piety, while publicly symbolised by the wearing of an emblem, was for most a personal phenomenon, regarded by many as an extension of their already broad religious practice and not something to be singled out for comment, which could explain why an organisation with such a vast membership received relatively little attention. There were also those guiding the Association who felt that concentrating the recruitment work at schools, even if it was only for short-term gain, was of more benefit than tackling obdurate legislators or depressing pub conditions. Certainly there were new challenges to the Pioneer youth in the 1960s, particularly in terms of varied modes of entertainment, advertising and media and more peer pressure than hitherto, which would explain why many dropped the pledge at a relatively early stage. The Pioneer Association by no means ignored these issues. The *Pioneer* sought to be utterly modern and its popularity was reflected in sales which between 1954 and 1963 jumped from a monthly total of 34,589 to 54,735.[51] Part of this success could be attributed to the inclusion of coverage of sport, film, music and a women's page as well as the ubiquitous religious articles. But it was of equal significance that editorials were frequently defensive, indicating that there was an acute acknowledgement of a tendency to distrust abstainers. Month after month the contention that the association was neither Jansenist nor Puritanical was hammered home. Cardinal Conway pointed out that the tendency was to see the Pioneers as pussyfoots or fanatics, but the reality for him was that 'in Ireland, the very name 'A Pioneer' has come to mean a fine type.'[52] However this was the sort of semantic posturing which irritated moderate drinkers, with the seeming inference that one who drank anything at all was not quite so fine. It was no wonder that the *Pioneer* editorials were frequently born of defensiveness and frustration, though rarely would it be admitted that the damage could be self-inflicted:

> Wrong ideas about our movement still exist. Last month the BBC tele-
> vised an interview on the Pioneer Association. After the discussion the
> BBC interviewee said that he had been surprised to discover that
> Pioneers do not object to people taking alcoholic drink. Many temperance
> societies frown on all use of alcohol as a beverage and he had presumed
> that this was the official Pioneer attitude.[53]

Perhaps it would be facile to suggest that most Irish Catholics felt
they were religiously endowed enough without having to increase
their devotion through further sacrifice, but a trace of this feeling was
articulated by some. As far back as 1949 the writer John D. Sheridan
had insightfully depicted the dilemma of the moderate drinker, occu-
pying the middle ground in a country in which attitudes to drink were
extreme:

> It boils down to this – that the heavy drinker dislikes total abstainers in
> the mass, but likes them in ones. He likes you but he hates me. He likes
> you 'in spite of' and he hates me 'because'. He hates me because I drink.
> He despises me because I want to remain conscious and perpendicular,
> because I stop when the going is good. Please understand that we have
> a grudge against the rest of the world. We resent the sneers of the heavy
> drinker – that prince of bigots – who looks down on us as cute, penny-
> watching apron-slaves, and is forever trying to raise us to his mighty
> stature. Our case against the total abstainer is not so easy to put into
> words, since we envy his high motives and admire his self-control, but
> we think it unfair that we who carry the heavier end of the cross should
> be denied a share of the halo.[54]

It was a dilemma the Pioneers had not been ready or willing to confront. It was a long time before Sheridan was asked to contribute to the
magazine again. When he was finally asked in 1965 the editor 'threw
out the hint that I need not mention the drink.'[55] But his acute observations were becoming even more relevant in the 1960s, particularly as
a climate of relative affluence did not sit lightly with the perceived
austere culture of abstention.

This was brought into even sharper focus with the continued effort
of the Association to make inroads abroad, particularly in the United
States. Whatever about murmurings of resentment against the Pioneers'
self-proclaimed virtuousness at home, it was even more difficult to
tackle America, where hostility to pin-wearing pledge-takers was
blatant, a product of the catastrophe of Prohibition and an assumption
that Catholic abstainers shared the severities of the fundamentalist
Protestant temperance crusaders. The correspondence between the
American Pioneer centres and Central Office in Dublin in the early
1960s can only be described as tortuous, as the Pioneers' attempts to
expand the base of the organisation were repeatedly thwarted. In the

1950s, a temperance advocate in America had suspected that the increased cosmopolitanism of the middle class would render them less likely to support temperance: 'There has been a breakdown in the middle classes. The upper classes have always used liquor. Now the middle class has taken it over. The thing is slopping over from both sides.'[56] Aware of what they were up against, some of the branches that had been established in the 1950s tended to be even more extreme than their Irish counterparts in an attempt to prove their devotion to the Sacred Heart. Some of the American Pioneers travelled to the Diamond Jubilee celebrations in 1959, but before they departed, a member in New York, who wished to travel with her non-Pioneer brother sent the following letter to Dargan:

> I have flown enough to know that even sober passengers need something for the nerves. We can't watch them constantly, nor can we search their luggage. Their word might mean something and then it might not. There will be no liquor served on board as a matter of course. There is only one alternative – a blanket rule issued from Dublin ordering us not to accept a non-Pioneer under any circumstances.[57]

In the light of this attitude it was little wonder that there was a hostility to the Pioneers. There were not only administrative problems inherent in controlling the movement abroad, but also the constant fear that if the Association was not properly supervised it would fall out of the control of the Jesuits, and this sense of urgency punctuated much of the correspondence. Unlike Australia, where the Jesuit Provincialate covered the entire country, in America it was more scattered, and by 1960 Dargan was anxious to establish an American office, staffed by Jesuits to oversee the movement. In 1957 there had been four centres, by 1960 there were twenty-five with an estimated membership of 15,000, which Dargan insisted in a letter to the Provincial was a growth 'entirely spontaneous and without any propaganda from our Dublin office'. However, as he continued, it seemed growth was a double-edged sword:

> At the moment, the matter would seem to be quite urgent. Each day now I am afraid I may receive a request from a Priest-Director of one of the American centres insisting on the opening of an American office. Such a suggestion might very well come from one of the many non-Jesuit local directors and naturally I do not want to see this apostolate slip away from Jesuit control.[58]

The Provincial of the New York Jesuit Province, Fr McGinty, was less than enthusiastic. What he essentially wanted was a casual approach to the pledge to be carried out under the auspices of an established Catholic action group such as the Apostleship of Prayer. The main task for Dargan was to get the majority of American Provincials to agree to the appointment of a national Director for America, but complicating the struggle against American church bureaucracy was the attitude of the clergy to the concept of the movement itself. Late in 1960 Fr Eugene Murphy SJ, Director of the Sacred Heart programme in St Louis, fired the first of many warning shots across the bow of Dargan, the culmination of which was to question the feasibility of the entire American project:

> As I told you, the name 'Pioneer' would have so many connotations here that I think a substitute would have to be found. The other problem is the pin. As I understand it, this is a sine qua non requirement. I am sure that many Americans would never join an organisation in which they had to wear a pin.[59]

Dargan himself was conscious that many American Jesuits were reluctant to get involved in case they earned the label of prohibitionists and he was at pains to emphasise that the Pioneers were not in any sense puritanical nor their aims remotely repugnant to Catholicism, that 'the attitude of a Pioneer to drink is not unlike the attitude of a priest to marriage' and that it could help to strengthen the bond between the Secular clergy and the Jesuits.[60]

From his contact in Rome, Fr Thomas Byrne, Dargan was warned that the American Provincials would drag their heels on the issue, though he was assured he would have support in Rome if the issue came that far. At their summer meeting in 1961, according to Fr Ray Kennedy, one of Dargan's main Jesuit contacts in New York, the Provincials did not want to reject the proposal for a national Pioneer office outright as it was a Jesuit Apostolate, but there was no unanimity on the question of appointing a national director, despite Dargan's promise of financial support. Kennedy urged caution: 'One does not hurry, rush or push a Provincial.'[61] Initially Fr McGinty, the New York Provincial, had submitted a memorandum by Fr John Ford who had argued that the Pioneers were needed in America as a catholic counterbalance to the groups striving for a return to Prohibition, maintaining that the Pioneers were an organisation which 'frowns on campaigning and crusading' and that it was important for good relations between the American clergy and hierarchy not to be closely dependent on Ireland. But Kennedy, writing again to Dargan, concerning a decision to let him visit Ireland for only one month to study the Association, revealed the more prevalent attitude when his provincial 'in a comment made quietly and in a low voice said "it seems hardly worth our investment".'[62] In may 1962 the Provincials rejected the proposal. Thomas Byrne in Rome explained to a dejected Dargan that the American

Jesuits simply did not want another interprovincial or assistancy work with a national office, with McGinty insisting that if it was adopted it had to have the status of an assistancy work 'so you have stalemate, you cannot do anything more at present.'[63]

It was doubtless more than a question of adding layers of bureaucracy. Dargan took umbrage at the fact that a few months later McGinty had travelled to Dublin and had not even bothered to call and see him. But at the beginning of 1963 it was evident that some sort of new pressure had been exerted on the American Jesuits (perhaps from the Jesuit General in Rome). In January McGinty wrote to Dargan informing him that he had discussed the issue with Fr Byrne of the Jesuit assistancy in Rome, and following consultations with his own Provincial they agreed to establish a national office in America with Fr Ray Kennedy as national director. The sting in the proposal was that they wanted the wearing of the pin to be optional, and if not, blackmail was the order of the American day:

> I have seen the violent reaction of some at the mere mention of it . . . so convinced am I of the great good which this organisation can effect in this country, that, should the wearing of the emblem be retained as an obligation I and my consulates shall entertain plans for a similar organisation with a different name and without this obligation.[64]

Predictably, Dargan found this obnoxious and unacceptable. The pin was regarded as being the corner-stone of the Association in Ireland, particularly in terms of inculcating uniformity among members and in publicly emphasising their religious credentials and zealous devotion to the cause. An optional arrangement, it was felt, would trivialise the entire ethos of the movement. Dargan was conscious of the fact that in the beginning Fr Cullen had faced virulent opposition to the wearing of the pin but had weathered the storm and had been utterly vindicated. As he informed Fr Byrne in Rome 'I do not see how we could possibly give way on this point.'[65] Dargan, however, was prepared to compromise, suggesting that Central Office might be prepared to allow for the wearing of a smaller pin or the emblem to be worn on a ring, and in a last act of desperation in March 1963 suggested to Fr Kennedy that the emblem could be 'suspended from a wristlet watch-band'.[66] Alongside this correspondence across the Atlantic there was the more fundamental worry that the American provincials were still not committed, to the extent that some believed that 'the Franciscans might do the job better.'[67] In April Kennedy again wrote to Dargan and explained that the eleven American provincials left office on a 'stagger system', so that six years from then at least one would still be provincial. He had also discovered that of the eleven provincials in

1961–2 only one, McGinty, had been in favour of the American Jesuits embarking on Pioneer work. McGinty's attempt to plough the Pioneer furrow through pressure from Rome, even on a watered-down scale, was clearly on shaky ground.

Although Kennedy cautioned Dargan against putting more pressure on McGinty, he admitted that the idea of two organisations, one with a pin, the other without, would lead to 'great embarrassment for all of us and even rather scandalous competition and ultimate bitterness.'[68] Dargan was anxious to consult with his predecessor, Fr McCarron, who at this stage was on retreat in Northern Rhodesia. Robust as always, he urged Dargan not to compromise on the issue of the pin invoking the memory of Cullen and the opposition he too had faced. Introducing a new element into the debate, he saw the issue in terms of class snobbery. Knowing that Fr Kennedy had himself expressed reservations about the pin, and having discussed the matter with Fr Byrne , he came to the following conclusion:

> My impression of Fr Kennedy is that he is an American snob, looking down on our way of life and our methods. One of the purposes of the badge was to bring members out into the open to combat the social pressure of excessive drinking. The Americans don't want to be associated with anything so crude.[69]

He also reminded Dargan that in the past there had been opposition from Cardinal Cushing and that he had stood firm for the benefit of the Association. By May 1963, both sides were firmly entrenched and in the final letter of the three-year saga, McGinty wrote to Dargan 'I am deeply sorry that it will be impossible to co-operate in this apostolic movement.'[70]

This long-drawn-out episode revealed not only the extraordinary lengths which the Association was prepared to go to elicit a response from America, but also its utter determination to face down senior Church figures in order to safeguard essentials. It was significant that references were continually made to the foundation years, particularly to the idea that Cullen had succeeded precisely because he had ignored and sidelined those who had criticised his concepts and methods. The contemporary leaders of the Association still felt they had to use inheritance in order to guide the Association's future, and given the high membership figures in Ireland, they felt their logic was unassailable. Contact with America was by no means severed, however, despite the failure to secure a national directorate. Individual Pioneer centres in various states continued to operate, but they were always something of a thorn in the side of Dublin's central office. In Washington in 1962, James Madden, an attorney-at-law in New York and treasurer of the

New York Regional Council resigned owing to what he insisted was a misuse of funds, and the antics of the St John's Centre in the city which was continually presented as factionalised and corrupt. Madden presented his case personally to Dublin because 'the minutes give biased, inaccurate and incomplete impressions of meetings.'[71] A newsletter produced by the St John's Centre members revealed that they were ever anxious to present themselves as being even more devoted than their Irish Pioneer brethren and to counteract the charge that they were feckless. A special flight to Ireland which had been sponsored by the New York Regional Council had been advertised in 1961:

> We wish to make it clearly known, that under no circumstances will liquor be allowed on the round trip. It is not our intention to embarrass anyone, but in order to strengthen this ruling, the sum of $20 is being added to the round trip fare. This sum will be refunded upon your return to the US but will be declared forfeit if the liquor ruling is violated.[72]

The minutes of the New York Regional Committee the following year recorded details of a boat trip, revealing that this outrageous paranoia, which would have mortified even Fr Cullen, was by no means isolated: 'John Denihan and John Brennan were appointed to stay with Fr Winters while people were boarding and watch for containers that might be holding liquor. Jimmy Coleman suggested that John Denihan wear his police uniform, but John declined, stating that he had no authority'.[73]

For all their social paranoia, a meeting of the officers of the Regional Committee in 1963 revealed unhappiness that the Pioneers in New York spent most of their time organising entertainment and had neglected recruiting work in the schools and general publicity and propaganda. Seemingly, their dilemma was that 'like many other Irish associations, we have depended on the steady flow of immigrating members which has now slackened off,'[74] confirming the general impression that the Pioneers in America were more often than not merely Irish Pioneers in exile, though with some peculiar quirks. Likewise the Pioneers in Boston by 1965 were writing to Dargan bemoaning the fact that the Centre had moved eight times in eight years and that the Spiritual Director was attending rarely, if at all: 'He might come for five minutes every two or three months . . . I asked the members one night why the group was not coming. They told me that our meeting was just like a public dance – where was the Spiritual Director?'[75] But perhaps the Pioneers in Boston were not faced with the same challenges as the twenty Pioneers in San Francisco in 1967:

> Boys and girls dress alike so that it is difficult to know one from the other. They wear bells and jewellery. Most of them do not work. They share whatever they have with their friends. Seemingly most of them do

not drink – but they take the drugs LSD and Marijuana. They speak of free love with no laws. They have tried to change the name of streets. They are against war. In this land of the hippies, twenty Pioneers meet once a month. Already the Legion of Mary has had contact with the hippies and please God the Pioneers of San Francisco will begin an Apostolate among them.[76]

One of the enduring features of the Pioneers abroad was the degree to which involvement in the councils, especially at executive level was politicised in a way that it was not in Ireland, as if the control or direction of a council conferred special status on the exiled Irish. In Ireland it was significant that a certain degree of apathy existed in this regard during the 1960s. In 1962 there were vacancies for Saint Francis Xavier council positions, and the new spiritual director, Fr Mulligan SJ, felt it necessary to point out 'that the founder Fr Cullen laid it down as a principle that appointments of this nature should be regarded as permanent.'[77] Clearly, many regional centres had decided that this was undemocratic and were apt to elect people to council positions, but the Pioneer hierarchy discouraged this. In February 1962 the Pioneer Column in the *Irish Catholic* had ordered elections of councillors and officials to cease because it was deemed to be the prerogative of the Spiritual Director to make these appointments.[78] In New Zealand, where a national director, Fr Hassen, had been appointed in 1959, Dargan insisted on hammering home this point repeatedly, with the overriding emphasis on the need to retain strict Jesuit control:

> I sincerely hope that you will have no trouble makers to upset you in your work. It is possible that certain people will be anxious to get on to the National Council. A useful point to make to such people is that our bishops and our parish priests are appointed by superiors, they are not elected.[79]

Clearly the feeling was that there was no reason to depart from the wider and well established Catholic administrative practices, but what was even more revealing, and again this underlines the fear of rene-gade or unorthodox Pioneers surfacing, was the view those in charge of the association had of decentralisation. Many of the councils were superficial constructs, though this was only admitted in private. Dargan pointed out that in Ireland, the central directorate consisted of a central director, an assistant central director and eight laymen:

> In practice (and this has been the same since Fr Cullen's time), this group of laymen is more a rally committee than anything else. The laymen are excellent people, most loyal to us and never make any difficulties of any sort . . . In London, New York and some other cities, they have a Regional Committee . . . we want to ensure that the Association does not pass out

of Jesuit hands and so we give no real authority to the Regional Committees. All this is strictly confidential – one trouble that has arisen in New Zealand is that some local centres have without permission gone ahead and had badges manufactured for themselves.[80]

Another problem in New Zealand was that the national director could only partake in Pioneer work and recruitment during vacation from his seminary, and by 1962 there were still only seventeen active centres with a membership of roughly 1,500.

London was not faring particularly better in the early 1960s. Once again, the centres were largely composed of Irish emigrants, and it was seen as an ideal way of meeting fellow emigrants. Pioneer publications during the decade continued to prioritise emigration, both because it was inevitably seen as a threat to the faith, and because of continuing stories about the propensity of Irish emigrants, whether through loneliness or a new found affluence, to drink more heavily. This was attributed to the moral laxity spawned by an alien environment, which could be represented as nothing short of pagan. Much time was also devoted to explaining the importance of the Irish image abroad. In Pioneer propaganda, however, the emigrant challenge was invariably reduced to one single danger. Dargan, who frequently travelled to England to address regional Pioneer rallies, informed his audience in Birmingham in the summer of 1963 that 'the chief cause of failure amongst our emigrants is drink.'[81] Thus the newsletter of the Pioneer London Regional Committee noted how important a visible Pioneer pin was amongst the Irish in England – those with the pin 'are both Catholics and Pioneers and these common factors, will, in time lead them into conversation with each other'. However, the following year, conscious of being overly dominated by the Irish, they were keen to encourage Pioneers to spread the faith wider – 'the next time you come to a Pioneer meeting or social try and bring an English Catholic with you.' The London Pioneers were particularly proud of Major Roache, originally born in Limerick, and now a member of the Vauxhall centre, who recited the Rosary each morning outside 10 Downing Street and at Speakers' Corner in Hyde Park.[82]

Behind the scenes, however, there was continual tension concerning control of the Pioneer councils in certain districts. In April 1963 the secretary of the London regional committee wrote to Dargan contending that the London and Coventry regional councils were 'running on entirely different rules', adding that the decision to exclude non-Pioneers from Pioneer social events meant they were finding it very difficult to attract new members.[83] Coventry was proving even more fractious – this regional committee was composed of three delegates from each centre who were entitled to vote for the executive officers. But clearly for some, elections were the only issue they were interested in. In 1965, three delegates attempted to destroy the AGM by objecting to new procedures designed to sideline those who saw the Association purely as a means of playing small town politics. The secretary of the Coventry committee wrote to Dargan:

> For the past two years the attendance at the hall has been poor – 12–18 members at the monthly meeting, whereas 40–50 members attended the AGM just for the election. The majority of these members would not turn up till the following AGM. In an attempt to improve the attendance monthly, it was agreed by the regional committee at the AGM in October 1964 that any delegate who was absent from three or more meetings would lose his right to vote at the AGM.[84]

On the eve of the 1960s, the Association claimed, through the pages of the *Irish Catholic* that like the Church, it was now a world-wide organisation. It was a bold assertion which contained much fanciful thinking, but in reality was a reference to small Pioneer centres being set up not only in the US and England but also in parts of Africa and South America. The wider Irish missionary movement by 1965 consisted of 7,085 priests, nuns, brothers and laity working in Asia, and Central and South America who were, according to Edmund Hogan, the historian of the modern Irish missionary movement, involved not only in the spread of cathecetics and the administration of sacraments but also schooling, health care and other social and human needs.[85] Alcohol abuse was presumably one of these. As far back as the late nineteenth century the founder of the Pioneers Fr Cullen had referred to excess drinking as being a contributory factor to the demise of colonial African communities. The best the Pioneers could do in this regard was to make a start in the areas where they had missionary contacts. In 1960 progress was recorded in Nigeria, Kenya and especially at the Chikuni centre in Northern Rhodesia where an Irish Jesuit, Fr Bernard Collins, had started a centre in 1958, and which by 1960 could boast 67 Pioneers and 151 temporarily pledged.[86] At the end of 1961 it was reported that 800 Pioneers had attended a South African rally in Kliptown, Transvaal and that 'the different races mingled easily. The majority were African, but present also were Europeans, Indians and Chinese.'[87] Domestic readers were invited to read monumental significance into these small beginnings to the extent that by 1964 they were informed that 'with the founding recently of two branches in India, the movement has now extended to all five continents.'[88] Colouring much of the reporting of these developments was the idea that these colonies were in much the same position as Ireland had been a century previously, ravaged by oppression and deprivation which was conducive to alcohol abuse, and that Irish missionaries with the benefit of the Pioneer phenomenon at home were well qualified for the task of reclamation. It was an ambitious aim, and much of it, as with most missionary work, was dependent on the heroic efforts of individuals.

In early 1966, an Irish Pallotine, Fr Sherry, originally from Monaghan, was reported to have established a Pioneer centre in Mbulu in Tanzania where the ubiquity of the local beer 'Pombe' was responsible for widespread alcoholism, with the result that many who took a temporary pledge were lapsing. It was remarked that 'the making of beer can be done only with government licence, but practically every family gets a licence at times of marriage, harvesting etc.'[89] Drinking in such regions was also often associated with religious ceremony. It was reported in 1966 that, as the drinking of rice beer as part of religious ceremonies conducted by Indian Aboriginals was becoming excessive, Archbishop Kujur of Ranchi had started a Pioneer group.[90] But even in preaching against alcohol abuse, the Pioneers were conscious that prohibition was not a satisfactory solution. In 1956, Fr Sean O'Hanlon MSC, had established a Pioneer centre in Papua New Guinea. In 1966 it was reported that he had been appointed to a government Commission to explore the feasibility of legalised drinking for the natives: 'Prohibition as then practised was undemocratic and discriminatory against the native population. It is interesting to note that Fr O'Hanlon voted for legalised drinking – with, of course, proper controls. The Pioneers are advocates of voluntary total abstinence, not inhuman or compulsory abstinence.'[91]

By the close of 1967 the statistics for the Association's overall standing were also published in the *Irish Catholic*. According to their own calculations there was a total of 2,672 Pioneer centres: 2,152 in Ireland, 159 in Africa, 132 in England, 26 in Scotland, 37 in the USA, 8 in Canada, 3 in Trinidad, 3 in Belgium, 147 in Australia and New Zealand and 1 each in Cyprus, West Indies, Fiji, Philippines, India and Korea. Figures for the distribution of pins, revealed how widespread the wearing of the pin had become. In 1956 108,000 badges were distributed, accounting for 69,000 Pioneer pins, 31,000 Probationer pins and 8,000 temporary pledge pins. In 1966 the overall figure was 132,500. One worrying development, however, were the figures for lapsed centres. In 1957 it had been 24, but by 1966 there were 124.[92]

Overall these figures seemed to indicate a movement which was robust and healthy. Perhaps the Association also felt it necessary to emphasise the scale of membership in the light of the Irish debate on alcoholism which had come into sharper focus in the previous few years. A month earlier it had been suggested in the *Sunday Press* that there were up to 60,000 alcoholics in Ireland, with a resultant 200,000 people directly affected.[93] Perhaps the prevalence of alcoholism and the concomitant call for a more ecumenical approach to a problem which had for so long remained underground represented a fundamental challenge to the Pioneers. They were understandably loathe to admit this initially. They had after all never declared that their aim was to solve the problem of alcoholism or to reclaim problem drinkers, although it is undeniably the case that many reformed alcoholics joined the Association, as did people as a reaction to having experienced alcoholism in their families or peer group. Their persistent analysis of the drink question and the emphasis on salvation through sacrifice in the drink arena also meant that they could not refuse to embrace the debate. It was equally significant that with the rise of a new generation of priests, searching questions on the Association's role began to surface internally as much as externally. As has been suggested in the previous chapter the question of defining alcoholism as a social and moral problem was a challenge to the traditional method of Pioneer propagandising. The Irish Temperance movement was forced to react to international trends, as modern research on the issue threw down new perspectives which, aligned with the mentality of Vatican II reforms, suggested that old attitudes to alcoholism were not only lacking in scientific and medical accuracy but were also devoid of basic charity. This was an accusation which rested heavily with an association which prided itself on the notion of giving and sacrifice. It is true that the Association had at various times been sensitive and defensive, even when at its height. But the questions being asked in the 1960s were conducive to self-criticism, and a chasm began to emerge between those who insisted on following the guidelines laid down by Fr Cullen to the letter, and those who sought to modernise the Association, even if this meant disregarding fundamental rules. Ultimately it was a battle which neither side won and which left the Association falling between two stools.

There had been warning signals, even from some of the Association's more high-profile supporters, that the movement could become a victim of its own success. Dr Lucey, Bishop of Cork and Ross, had suggested that while the Pioneer body was now so impressive that it could be legitimately termed a parish movement, 'the fact of the matter is that the more the temperance movement in Ireland becomes a total abstinence movement, the less hope of reclaiming the drinker. I suggest that the Pioneer who forfeits his or her badge should not be cast off forever.'[94] Two principal themes seemed to dominate regarding the relevance of the drink debate for the Pioneers, and they were almost identical to the gauntlet which Vatican II had thrown down to the wider Catholic community; the need for dialogue and confrontation. Groups like the World Health Organisation and the American Medical Association had come to accept alcoholism as a disease. The establishment of Alcoholics Anonymous in America in 1946 and the establishment of the US National Clergy Conference on Alcoholism in Indiana in 1949 were also signals of a new approach to problem drinking. In Ireland the path to understanding for the temperance lobby was slow and somewhat tortuous. There was no sustained attempt to deal with the issue in the mid years of the century. The *Pioneer* magazine (by the mid-60s it had a circulation of 55,000) was an opportunity for increased probing. Given the format which this often polemical publication took (international as well as domestic focus, not just on drink but on social, cultural and political themes) it was only a matter of time before alcoholism was placed under the spotlight. But the initial signals were not particularly encouraging. Pioneer publications still had a tendency to divorce references to alcoholism from their context to suit their own ends. It involved a crude simplification which pitched the alcoholic as flying firmly in the face of the Ten Commandments. Thus in 1956 the magazine had asserted that doctors 'have isolated if they have not solved, the problem of the compulsive drinker; showing that a distinction must be drawn between the drunkenness which is sheer gluttony and that which is rooted in the disease which is alcoholism.' Harsh a judgement as this was, at least the idea of alcoholism as a physical disease rather than a moral or mental malaise was being floated, if not very wholeheartedly. Much attention was also given to the attempts of the French Health Minister, Mendès France who had formed a special committee to highlight the dangers of alcoholism, and it was suggested that a similar Irish watchdog committee was needed. Again, the focus was overwhelmingly negative. It was noted with a degree of grim satisfaction that 'an actual cirrhotic human liver, preserved in a glass jar was displayed in a busy metro station together with models of the human brain, one healthy, one suffused with alcohol.'[95]

Those relaying what they considered the facts were much happier in dealing with the effects rather than the causes of alcoholism, in much the same way as Fr Cullen had done in his original contributions to the *Irish Catholic*. The incidence of imbecility, for example, was granted to be much higher among children born of alcoholic parents. The other main focus on alcoholism were the sufferers' families, with again, the female being depicted as both the main victim, and, at times, the main sponsor of alcoholism. In 1958 an article appeared, reputedly written by the wife of an alcoholic who had drunk himself to an early grave.

While admitting that, in the final days she had found religion a great source of solace, she felt guilty that she had not been more religious from the outset. The subtext was that she had not done enough:

> I don't know whether it is better to continue living with an alcoholic husband or not. If I had to do it again, I suppose I would continue, but with a great deal more charity, I hope. I know now that in such a marriage there is need for tremendous love and courage. One must forget oneself completely. All I did was blunder through on God's grace.[96]

Four years later a question was posed as to how a woman could get her boyfriend to stop drinking. The answer was absolute: 'After marriage she can never change him. If she tries, she will only drive him to drink instead of curing him – the girl who marries a man to reform him is doomed to failure.'[97]

By the mid-60s there was an acceptance, though not unanimous, that alcoholism was a disease which did not discriminate, with a timely reminder that even in an association like the Pioneers there were thousands of potential alcoholics. Once again, women were singled out, a contributor insisting that 'Alcoholism may, especially in women, be a hysterical reaction, the individual's demand for attention and admiration becoming insatiable.'[98] These extracts seem to indicate that for every step forward the Association took, it could always rely on a sceptical contributor to pull it two steps back, as if a sympathetic analysis of the alcoholic's dilemma would somehow undermine the Association's work, or as if organisations which sought to cater specifically for alcoholics were somehow competitors. Many Irish Jesuits were keeping an eye on what was happening in the United States, particularly with regard to the priest's role in alcohol problems. Fr John Ford, a prominent American sociologist, had deliberated on this subject in an address delivered to the first Pastoral Institute on Alcohol Problems at Notre Dame University in April 1959. Highlighting the relatively raw understanding of the condition, Ford had admitted that he could not specifically define alcoholism, referring to it as 'a drunkenness plus something else'. As to whether it was a sickness or a sin 'that is a sort of lawyer's question. You are asked to choose between the two. Why can't it be both? I think that it is both.' Ford accepted that alcoholism involved a sickness of the soul and a certain moral delinquency, but that the moral responsibility of the alcoholic for his drinking was diminished somewhat. He saw AA's contention that alcoholism was a sickness as paradoxical in that the remedies they prescribed were 'nothing but a programme of mental and spiritual regeneration'. Ford's principal message was that Catholic priests had to realise their limitations in attempting to understand alcoholism and to co-operate with groups such as AA.[99]

This was a message which was to assume more relevance to the Pioneers in the coming decade, though the difficulties of definition remained. Perhaps more worrying to the Pioneers was that those who accepted these arguments often seemed to believe that there was little need for a separate Catholic body to deal specifically with alcoholism because they would have to build it up along much the same lines as followed by AA. In the domestic context, a publication by Fr E.F. O'Doherty and Dr Desmond McGrath, *The Priest and Mental Health*, was the product of a conference held in Dublin in 1961. In terms of its analysis of the Pioneer Association, it was a hard-hitting demand for a changed mentality. It was suggested that treating certain diseases and mental illnesses as a disorder of the spiritual life was 'a facile aim to cross fertilize the priest and the psychiatrist'.[100] It accepted that alcoholism originated from a personality disorder but that it was crude and simplistic to pin its origins to a single and specific form of personality disorder. Interestingly, the authors also focused on alcohol abuse in the priesthood (a by no means insignificant problem, though one on which the Pioneers rarely broached), suggesting that, as clerical life was a relatively lonely one, there was a greater opportunity for alcoholism to grow undetected, or the danger of alcohol being used by the priest in an attempt to tie himself closer to the flock he hoped to influence.[101] Another contributor, Sean O'Riordan, suggested that, in working against alcoholism, success had been best in the preventative field, and he singled out the Pioneer Association for praise in this regard. But in another timely message to priests regarding their expectations of the Association, he too presaged the challenge of the 1960s in terms of the exact meaning and significance of a pledge in devotion to the Sacred Heart:

> Seeing as much of the ravages of habitual intoxication as we do, we may be tempted to think that freedom from this plague constitutes a sort of guarantee of sound morality in all spheres of life. In particular, we may expect too much from the Pioneer Total Abstinence Association. Having made their Heroic Offering they should, we may think, be sound and solid Christians in their whole manner of life. But it is unreasonable to look for so much from any one radical renunciation made, even for the highest motives, by a Catholic young man or woman. Absolutely faithful to their Pioneer promise, they may still be insecure or immature personalities in other ways, and may fail accordingly. Drinking is very often a symptom of a deeper personality problem or disorder. The fact that the release of drinking is precluded by membership of the Pioneer Association leaves the personality problem or disorder if it is present in an individual case, just where it was – and it may well break out in other ways.[102]

O'Riordan had touched on a dilemma that some of the more restless souls in the Association, anxious to redefine the aims and methods of the Pioneers, were feeling. The Pioneers were perhaps open to the charge that they were reading too much into their membership by viewing it as a blanket solution to present and future threats, thereby denying the diversity of the normal Catholic psyche and creating exclusivity. In this context it was not insignificant that their tried and trusted methods of recruiting youngsters were coming in for criticism. In 1966 they found themselves on the defensive over allegations that they were forcing children to join the Association. Their qualified defence was extraordinary in terms of its utter arrogance – 'We do not think the practice is widespread. We doubt if there has ever been violence used to force children into one or another section.'[103]

Debates of this kind opened up clear divisions between tradition and change, which was frustrating for the old guard. A key figure was Fr Mulligan SJ who had been appointed assistant spiritual director in 1955. During the course of the 1960s he effectively waged a one-man campaign in an attempt to make the priorities of the Pioneers more secular and, in his view, more relevant to a society that was changing rapidly. Mulligan was initially concerned with the problem of the Irish alcoholic, but as he sought to galvanise the Pioneers in the direction of dialogue, he found himself questioning more fundamental Pioneer beliefs and practices which sparked controversy both inside and outside the Association. In the early stages, Mulligan did not speak the language of a Pioneer radical. As spiritual director based in the SFX Centre in Gardiner Street, where he aired many of his ideas, the minutes initially record him making clear 'the real purposes of the Association as laid down by Fr Cullen, founder.'[104] But, at a Cork rally and AGM two months later he took the bold step of introducing two members of Alcoholics Anonymous and urged Pioneer councillors to attend open AA meetings, hammering home his view that membership of AA in no sense conflicted with Catholic principles and could in fact lead to lapsed Catholics returning to the fold. Mulligan's wider reasoning, however, touched a raw nerve:

> I feel that often in the past our aim has been obscured by the many things that have been said on our platforms, things of a political or social nature concerning drink abuses. These things need to be said but they would better have been said from Parliament or from other plat- forms, but because of a lack of formed social conscience among our people it was left to Pioneers alone to say them.[105]

Although Mulligan was trying to sugar the pill somewhat this sort of rhetoric was unprecedented, and it was telling that the Pioneer column in the *Irish Catholic* chose to censor this excerpt in its official report of the meeting the following month.[106]

Mulligan, however, was occasionally in a position to write the column himself, and during the following year he continued with his insistence that Pioneers needed to become conversant with the methods of AA if they were serious about contributing to a culture of temperance. He also contended that legal restrictions were ineffective in curtailing alcohol consumption and that a mitigation of the abuses of excessive drinking would most likely be served by education rather than punitive measures, and that organisations such as The Irish Countrywomen's Association, Muintir na Tire and the Saint Vincent de Paul Society needed to recognise this. The boldness of Mulligan's stride was propelled by his determination to tackle the sacred Pioneer principle that spiritual matters should always take precedence over the social. He saw himself as merely applying the wider process of renewal within the Catholic Church to the Association, the logic being that the Pioneer organisation needed to be subjected to vigorous self-examination and updateing, although he contended that this could be done at this stage 'without changing in the slightest the rules'. Seemingly it was more a question of attitude:

> Where then does the Pioneer Association need to be updated? There has been in the past too much stress on the personal responsibility of the drunkard, and as a consequence a too great readiness on the part of some Pioneers to condemn drunkards. Intemperance is only one of the capital sins and it is by no means the most malicious. Pride is a far worse spiritual malady. Again, some drunkards are compulsive drinkers and therefore their responsibility is accordingly diminished. These people are not necessarily to be blamed for their plight but they are to be helped. So far they have received only spiritual help from Pioneers. They need more. They need sympathetic treatment, social and material.[107]

Mulligan's aim was to create a consensus among established voluntary organisations by adopting a co-ordinated policy of information, and he was accurate in seeing ignorance as the greatest barrier to a wider understanding of the plight of the alcoholic. The tension which this created was explicable in terms of the focus it placed on other aspects of the association. What exactly did it stand for? What did it support and what did it oppose? These simple questions had never been definitively tackled. Although the most demonstrative and insistent in terms of demanding change, Mulligan was not alone. At the Dublin AGM at the end of 1965, Fr Ronan Drury, Professor of Sacred Eloquence at Maynooth College, also expressed the belief that the Association needed to be remodelled, and suggested that it was time to forget protests against licensing legislation and drink advertising, to show more sympathy towards alcoholics, and to eschew the hardline attitude that the safest course for avoiding alcoholism was total abstinence. On the defensive, Dargan responded: 'However much we disliked protestations, he felt that in the past we had performed a social benefit by our protestations.'[108] The question, however, was for whose benefit? The Pioneers had often referred to 'the weight of public opinion' when campaigning against a liberalisation of licensing laws. In reality this was something of a fiction: a large Pioneer membership did not necessarily translate into mass opposition to these issues, and in retrospect, Fr Dargan admitted that the Pioneers' excursions into these areas were relatively futile.[109]

The direction which Mulligan was heading was significant. Essentially he was accusing an organisation which prided itself on its spiritual sacrifices of being uncharitable. A good insight into the persistence with which he pursued his case is found in the minutes of the SFX council. Here Mulligan tested the Pioneer appetite for change, by continually referring to the importance of AA, by questioning members about their attitudes to alcoholics, and in particular, about how the Association could play a part 'in the rehabilitation of alcoholics'.[110] This of course was what Fr Cullen had specifically stated was not the concern of the Association. Charity was a word Mulligan used repeatedly. He did not want to see alcoholics joining the Association and believed that they should instead take a temporary pledge, but for him, an ecumenical approach was necessary, and if that involved the proximity of Pioneers to those drinking pints, all the better: 'He posed the question thus: were we too spiritualised in our general approach? Should we be more forthright or aggressive? It was stressed that there was a need for more dialogue as apostles. It was suggested that members entering public houses might be an example of such.'[111]

Mulligan was heavily influenced by international developments, not just at the level of change within the Catholic Church and the quest for inclusive religious dialogue, but also by developments in research into alcoholism and the drink culture. Enormously influential in this regard was the *Plaut Report*, a French study that was the culmination of a co-operative commission on the study of alcoholism, which contained a particular emphasis on how to prepare teenagers in a society where most adults drank, and a call for a centre for alcoholism to be established in co-operation with the National Institute of Mental Health. The Report contended that while church groups differed in their positions regarding the moral aspects of drinking, progress could not be made with problem drinkers until the broader questions of alcohol abuse had been dealt with. It contained some important messages which were relevant to Ireland, particularly the view that from the standpoint of education ' a serious difficulty has been created because disapproval of dangerous drinking has been confused with opposition to all drinking.'[112] Stressing the need to see alcohol as a health problem, it criticised prohibition and the longevity of 'therapeutic nihilism' which claimed that problem drinkers could not be helped. Referring to the need to initiate discussion, it called for a variety of co-ordinated treatment approaches to avoid 'the ideological rigidity that still persists in the treatment of problem drinkers'. It also highlighted different races and cultures and how they viewed drink: the Jewish practice of introducing youth to drink in stages and frowning on drunkenness, the widely held view in France that a certain amount of alcohol was necessary for good health, and the Irish drinking culture which was not as closely identified with ritual as in other cultures:

> People brought up in totally abstinent traditions who later take up drinking are more likely to become problem drinkers. This may partly reflect the belief of abstinent groups that all drinking is bound to be excessive. In addition, of course, drinking in such subcultures evokes adverse reactions from the group. Neither a disapproving attitude, as held by some Protestant groups, nor an excessively permissive one, as among the French, appears to be effective in preventing alcoholism. Instead, cultural patterns with built in restrictions and taboos against inappropriate drinking – Italian and Jewish practices for example, are better as models.[113]

While accepting that there was huge difficulty in defining what constituted socially acceptable drinking, and that youngsters needed to be introduced to the idea of appropriate drinking, as against diatribes vilifying alcohol, the report also sought to explode a few myths about temperance promotion: 'This objective, while mentioned in almost all state alcoholic beverage statutes is usually of minimal importance in the day-to-day work of the state authorities. Enforcing laws against the serving of alcoholic beverages to minors and to intoxicated persons is the extent of direct activities relating to the idea of promoting temperance.'[114]

The reforming mind of Fr Mulligan was very much open to what he saw as salutary lessons for the Irish temperance movement. However, the wall of tradition blocked him. At an educational meeting in Portlaoise at the beginning of 1967 he linked his message on alcohol and charity to the wider ethos of renewal as expounded by Vatican II – to return to a charitable reading of scriptures and the Gospel to discover that love and compassion were the very basis of Christian life. He acknowledged that many Pioneers felt the Association would be tarnished by active involvement with alcoholics, but undeterred, he boldly asserted that with other voluntary groups, the Pioneers 'must co-operate in providing half-way houses for alcoholics coming out of prison or hospital and who have no home to go to.'[115] Mulligan was clearly trying to ensure that the Pioneer pin would be viewed as a badge of compassion rather than as a red flag to an alcoholic bull, but his attempts to lay the groundwork for these ideas and the reaction he received illustrate that he faced an uphill task. In 1967 he questioned whether or not the Pioneers should be involved in the condemnation of drink advertising, or whether the Association itself should have a public image, given his responsibility within the Association for public relations. Various views were expressed: 'The Spiritual Director did not agree with these views, and the members could not accept the views of the Spiritual Director'.[116] A discussion paper which Mulligan introduced the following month revealed the source of the tension: 'There was some discussion on his paper and it took a turn towards demeaning attitudes of Catholics stemming from Vatican II. The discussion was exhilarating though it did expose that some thinking Catholics were bewildered about developing trends in church thinking.'[117]

The following month Mulligan showed that he was going to pursue his case either way, when he suggested abandoning the Pioneer prayer as it then was in favour of a more relevant and secular version. None of the council members present agreed and insisted Mulligan wanted change 'for the mere sake of changing and that was not acceptable'.[118] This was a sentiment which was doubtless representative of the Association at large.

What was more challenging at a fundamental level was a school of thought which attributed some of the blame for excessive drinking in Ireland to a stultifying atmosphere within Irish Catholicism which literally drove people to the pub. The Pioneer Association was particularly vulnerable to this charge because of the strictness of its pledge and the habitual sternnesss of its overall attitude. It is interesting that the Fr Mathew Temperance Association continued to operate, but its membership card from the 1960s suggests a much softer approach to abstinence:

> The rules shall allow for moderate use of alcoholic drink on three different types of occasions: 1. As medicine (e.g. punch for 'flu or a spoon of spirits for a sudden pain) 2. In a foreign country: where wine is regarded as part of a normal meal in the same way as tea or coffee here 3. As a toast, one drink is allowed at a wedding, a 21st Birthday, or 25th anniversary of parents' wedding: Christmas Day, and when cup of victory is filled and passed around.[119]

One suspects that Mulligan would have been quite content with rules that were flexible along these lines. What they revealed was the chasm between the continuity in Pioneer practices, considered by many to be its biggest strength, and an opposing temperance view which considered the Pioneer sacrifice too extreme, if not puritanical. As seen by critics it was a perfect example of the kind of institutionalised stringency which was ripe for Vatican II reforms, and from the vantage point of traditionalists, as a shining beacon of sacrifice in a world that sought material indulgence. Fr Robert Nash, the Jesuit writer and retreat director, warned of the developing trend of toning down the hard sayings of the Gospel and the presumption that the spirit of self-denial was not suited to the modern mentality.[120] It was no wonder many Catholics found it painful, given the force with which a new message had been spread. Affluent materialism in the 1960s was not representative of a strand of militant atheism, but rather 'agnostic disinterest in religion' which certainly bred a spirit of criticism, but which also allowed a majority of Irish Catholics retain their devotional practice almost in its entirety. The accusation of a lack of charity could easily be rebutted by pointing to the social and welfare programmes which many clergy pioneered both at home and abroad. Clearly the Church in the light of Vatican II did not lend itself easily to glib generalisations.[121]

There were those who believed that the beliefs and practices of the majority of Irish Catholics were insufficiently theorised, sustained by rule and law, social custom and sense of duty: 'A framework of authority and sanction rather than a personal commitment of mind and heart so that such belief and faith is extremely vulnerable in a rapidly changing society.'[122] During the 1960s critics were to scrutinise these features and chastise a church which was depicted as being unwilling or incapable of serving internal dialogue and self-confrontation and not sufficiently concerned with the actuality of Catholic life: 'The Church and Ireland were not lacking. But they bore no direct relationship to reality. Their degree of insight was that of newspapers, old-style catechisms, nationalist rhetoric, positivistic learning, public-house eloquence and adolescents' dreams.'[123] Michael Sheehy, questioning whether the Catholic Church in Ireland was dying, suggested that the institutionalised church had contributed to Ireland's negative drinking culture by turning a blind eye to excessive drinking, but believed that with the atmosphere of the 1960s 'no doubt the new freedom, and the satisfaction provided by materialist pursuits will reduce Irish frustration, and, as a result, the volume of drinking. Besides, Ireland is fast losing her fine spiritual institution, a vital sense of transcendence, the frustration of which accounted for so much of the excessive drinking of her best sons.' He also suggested that AA's approach to excessive drinking was much more helpful than the Pioneer Association which he erroneously asserted had been established in 1938, and sought to cure Irish drinking habits 'while leaving their cause – human frustration – intact'.[124] This was a lazy critique which divorced the Association from its context and attributed to it an aim it did not profess to have. But the idea of the Church contributing directly to alcohol-induced malaise was embraced by latter-day sociologists:

> 'As much as the church and school served to develop a rigid system of sexual morality, the pub in later life served to maintain this morally, albeit in a more convivial, but nevertheless highly ritualistic and disciplined manner'.[125]

This, however, was a politically correct and unbalanced assessment. There were few who would deny Ireland's comparatively high rates of excessive drinking, though simultaneously, those who compiled the European league tables of drinking cannot always be said to have qualified their analysis by alluding to the country's similarly high abstention rate. It was undoubtedly the case, particularly in depressed rural areas, with low marriage rates and a high incidence of mental illness that there were pockets of utter desolation, to which heavy drinking contributed. But just how representative these areas were was not clear. Some observers were acutely conscious of the danger of tapping into the alcoholic stereotype, to add spice to their literary output, particularly the idea that the common Irish response to all matters of complaint, trivial and grandiose, was to simply have another drink. Donal Connery, an American journalist writing in 1969, admitted that alcoholism was a problem, and that it had a seriously negative effect on relations between the sexes, but he cautioned:

> The pub is a booby-trap however, for anyone trying to take a true measure of Irish life. The fact is that the majority of adults hardly ever set foot in a pub. Most Irish females simply do not drink in public and many never touch a drop in their lives, and among the men there are more total abstainers than heavy drinkers . . . I will admit, as I write this that it is painful to go against form and portray the Irishman as something other than a glorious drinker and an altogether devil of a fellow. None the less, there are far more homes than pubs in Ireland and it is in the homes that one must look for the Irishman as he is most of the time. Away from the conviviality of the pub he's revealed as someone who is extraordinarily ordinary. He leads a far simpler and certainly less sophisticated life than most other Europeans.[126]

Perhaps it was the teasing out of these anachronisms that preoccupied the likes of Fr Mulligan. Certain Pioneers had been conscious – as had other groups such as the Irish Association for the Prevention of

Intemperance – of language or deeds which could be deemed as contributing to the myth that the words 'pub' 'Irish' and 'Catholic' could
be the trinity which best encapsulated national identity. At the same
time as Mulligan was insisting that the attitude of some Pioneers
towards alcoholics was not Christlike, exception was taken to an
alleged statement by the Minister for Agriculture and Fisheries, Charles
Haughey at Maynooth College, that he would like to see pubs becoming
the centre of the social and cultural life of the people.[127] But it was not
only the temperance body whose sensibilities were being offended. In
the same year the licensed vintners objected to the anti-drink rhetoric
used at Pioneer rallies believing they were invidious to the trade and
pilloried hard-working publicans. They insisted on writing to the
Pioneers demanding the factual basis of their assertions. There were
also other matters of concern: 'Reference was also made to the objec-
tionable manner in which Telefís Éireann had portrayed the publican
in the programme "The Riordans".'[128]

By the end of the 1960s, many Pioneers were anxious about the
nature of their role as an institutionalised aspect of Catholic culture
and society. Aside from the obvious personal and spiritual sacrifices
which formed the basis of membership, there were questions about the
extent to which they were a public organisation which was obliged to
take a stance on matters of public concern. Smaller groups like the
Irish Association for the Prevention of Intemperance had a much more
clear-cut agenda in this context. In 1965, for example, they specifically
amended their constitution to include the provision that they were
bound to disseminate information on the nature, properties and effects
of alcoholic liquors, and in subsequent years were particularly perturbed
by what they saw as the favoured treatment in the legal system of
alcohol-based crime. In 1967 they were both incisive and forward looking
in this regard:'The Bill at present before the Dáil was discussed and it
was decided to watch the matter of the Minister having the power to
restore driving licences.'[129] Given the kind of public debate which Fr
Mulligan was attempting to instigate, it was inevitable that the
association would be forced to decide if they had a role in this regard.
In 1963, the Bishop of Clogher, Dr O'Callaghan wrote to Fr Dargan for
advice concerning alleged proposals to build a series of Irish road
motels with drink licences. Dargan replied that a protest should be
lodged with the government and that the licences should be opposed on
each occasion there was an application. He also added the following:
'Unfortunately some elements in government circles seem anxious to
throw off restraint where liquor laws are concerned. Nevertheless the
government is better qualified than any other group to prevent this
abuse.'[130] This was an admission which would not have been made

two decades previously and was indicative of Dargan's tendency to avoid the more militant approach of his predecessor, Fr McCarron. It was also a realistic recognition of the limited ability of temperance groups to influence policy in this area. It was also relevant in the light of Fr Mulligan's criticisms of the timidity of the Association in relation to linking itself to the wider changes prevalent in Irish life.

Early in 1967, Fr Dargan was keen to identify Pioneer priorities, and consulted Fr Mulligan and other prominent Pioneers to attempt to decide the attitude the Association would take in matters public or controversial. It was recorded that:

> The new policy asserts that the Pioneer Association as such will not enter into any such controversies and that no Pioneer in future should express his views in controversial matters as being those of the Association. Each member present expressed his views as to the merits of the new policy and in each case the field covered was wide but very detailed. A number present favoured the policy, whilst others doubted the wisdom of it.[131]

Initially, Fr Mulligan seems to have been an enthusiastic endorser of this new policy, hoping that it would lead the Pioneers down the path of co-operation rather than confrontation. He was particularly keen to ensure that various voluntary groups worked in tandem in education and alcohol abuse. However, he had not waited for the discussion at council level. Ten days previously, presumably in the light of conversations with Fr Dargan, he had written to the Secretary of the Irish Countrywomen's Association urging them to get involved, specifically recommending that they study the work of the American North Conway Institute which had adopted an ecumenical approach to dealing with alcohol abuse, by stressing that social and legal controls were necessary but ultimately alcoholism had to be viewed primarily as an estrangement from God. Mulligan informed the ICA:

> Alcohol education must be non-controversial and because of that and for other reasons, the Pioneer Association has adopted a new public relations policy, namely that the association or anyone speaking on its behalf will not enter into controversial matters like licensing laws or advertising. We shall leave that to others. The problem of alcoholism and education are a community concern. It needs the co-operation of everyone in the state, government departments and voluntary agencies.[132]

But defining what constituted 'controversial' was not simple. If the impression given at this stage is one of consensus it belied more fundamental, and festering, tensions which Mulligan could not or did not want to keep in check. A decision to avoid confrontation was perhaps seen by some Pioneer veterans as a way of opting out of the changes prevalent in Irish society, but for others it still had to be the first step in a process of tackling what they viewed as the archaic basis on which the Association had built so dramatically in the 1940s and 1950s. At another level there was a feeling that the Association, given its still vast membership, was not being accountable, and that meetings or programmes based on a reiteration of outdated temperance catechisms hardly amounted to contributing to a meaningful culture of temperance in a society which was becoming more consumer-driven. As a starting point for those who agreed with Fr Mulligan, renewal within the Association in the context of Vatican II and the need for ecumenism was how the Pioneers could co-operate with problem drinkers. Even Mulligan's tendency to initiate discussion papers was something of a worrying novelty for those who dared not question what were essentially nineteenth-century rules and procedures.

Fr Dargan had, it must be stressed, attempted to accommodate Fr Mulligan. At the end of 1968 an unprecedented meeting was held in Ely House in Dublin, attended by representatives of Pioneer regional councils. The discussion was wide-ranging and Dargan saw it as a milestone in the history of the Association, as the contributors sought to directly confront the ideas and proposals for change which Mulligan had courted – the value and significance of the symbols of the Association, particularly the badge and prayers, its social and spiritual aims, influencing public opinion, and especially, bridging the gap between Pioneers and non-Pioneers. Dargan set the tone, but also set down a marker as to how far proposals for renewal could go, particularly in the light of suggestions that moderate drinkers be permitted to join the Association:

> For some time past he had been urging a greater co-operation between Pioneers and people who drank with a sense of responsibility. It was unhealthy to have a great gap between Pioneers and non-Pioneers. There was a real need to influence public opinion to a responsible attitude in the use of alcohol. A suggestion had been made that not only would we enter more into communication but that we should virtually enrol them as auxiliary members. From the many letters received and from views expressed both by individual centres and Regional committees, it was clear that the feeling throughout the Association was that the idea of co-operation would be favoured but that of Auxiliary membership would not be favoured.[133]

Dargan also suggested that he had been misrepresented in the press on the issue of proposals to admit moderate drinkers, but that the ensuing jolt may not have been unwelcome – the idea of drinking Pioneers was obviously headline grabbing, but he sought instead to steer this in a more constructive and less sensationalist direction. He was also likely to have been influenced by a stern letter from the Archbishop of Cashel, Dr Thomas Morris, a staunch Pioneer who had expressed consternation at the changes being mooted at this time. He informed Dargan that the majority of people he knew were moderate drinkers and did not need to safeguard themselves, but went on 'To organise the moderates would seem to limit their Apostolate somewhat. Their moderation surely extends to other areas of life as well. For the present anyhow, I feel the Pioneers should stand alone.'[134]

Another contributor to the Ely House discussion, Fr Joyce, a prominent Kilkenny Pioneer, sought to pitch past against present, agonising over the clash between total abstinence and the national practice:

> Recently I heard it suggested that the continued success of Fianna Fáil's organisation was due to the fact more than half of the local branch secretaries are Pioneers and therefore are men who have the respect and the time . . . But perhaps the initial success of the movement might now be its greatest weakness. People are inclined to associate its success with its strictness and methods and forget that these were successful because they suited the need and opportunities of the time . . . We have lost the respect of young people in making accusations which are only partially true and at times we have earned their ridicule by saying that evil exists where there is merely a different point of view.[135]

The meeting discussed the age-old challenge – that of an embedded tolerance to excess drinking which was an intricate part of Irish custom. A Jesuit, Fr Michael Sweetman, reminded the audience in an address dealing with renewal, that 'one of the worst tyrannies is the tyranny of Irish drinking customs. So that a man who may only like two drinks is forced to take five or six or double that number, if he is not to be thought mean or anti-social. That is an insane taboo.'

Yet, for all the frank exchange of views, the proposals which emerged were tepid to say the least, and smacked of an Association almost desperate to put itself forward as a useful component of Irish society. It was acknowledged that they first had to deal with poor internal communication. It was also proposed to organise a car-drive service for those travelling to the pub, Pioneer baby-sitting to facilitate young couples to do likewise, and finally that 'We should mix with non-Pioneers and relax and enjoy ourselves with them.'[136]

By this stage, however, particularly for those sharing Fr Mulligan's views, these suggestions, though noble, were too shallow. Mulligan had come to the conclusion that they were merely superficial changes which did not attack the core of the dilemma as he saw it – rule eight of the Association which decreed that the Central Council had no power to dispense with, change or modify any of the rules or to allow any form of compromise about their interpretation. Mulligan regarded this as too legalistic and pharasaical, treating interpretation like army regulations (which was precisely what Cullen had wanted to instil in his 'Soldiers of Christ'). For him, this did not respect individual conscience. In particular, he did not believe that it was always necessary to wear the badge, or to recite a fixed prayer, and forcing people to return badges if they had defaulted he regarded as excessively moralistic. In a letter to Pierce Barrett who also played a role in public relations for the association, he hammered home his case, citing an example:

> Two years ago I received a letter from a priest on the Aran Islands. A woman who got a severe pain was encouraged to take a drop of brandy by neighbours. There was neither a doctor or nurse on the Island at the time, and if there had been they would have been called in. My interpretation then was that she had defaulted and had to begin again. I doubt if I could make such an inhuman and unChristlike decision as I now see it. This is a case where the spirit is more important than the letter.[137]

This was a perfect example of the development of Mulligan's thinking and his insistence on the need to relate rules to the reality of everyday experience. If it made the likes of Barrett uncomfortable, it was because he was essentially introducing a new frame of reference for those working for the association. In his role as assistant director, Mulligan saw himself as there to provide a service, to put at the disposal of the Pioneers the views of experts and to allow them access to a multitude of opinions, so that the Pioneers' personal sacrifice would not be the sole defining ethos of the Association, or as he put it in a letter to a fellow cleric 'let our asceticism be hidden.'[138] This of course challenged the entire identity of the Association given that the public wearing of the pin was designed to be a deliberate and necessary public manifestation of internal piety and sacrifice. The idea that prayer and self-denial were not valid enough reasons for the continuance of the Association in its present form incensed many traditionalists, including the redoubtable Oliver J. Flanagan who viewed a dilution of the rules as a veiled attack on national identity rather than a courageous attempt to initiate dialogue. At a seminar in Cloneygowen, Flanagan, one of the few Dáil representatives who frequently spoke as a self-proclaimed 'Pioneer TD', had the following to say:

> It is my honest personal opinion – and I repeat personal – that the hall mark of every Irish man and woman should be the Pioneer emblem and the Fáinne, because in the grand tradition of our faith and fatherland, temperance, good citizenship, love for our country, its language and culture should and must be our aim. Changes in the modern world are expected but one cannot change the method of giving good example.[139]

This was the sort of attitude which Mulligan felt had to be jettisoned if the Association was to have a future. Despite the impression of a one-man crusade, Mulligan succeeded in provoking dialogue, particularly on the subject of alcoholism. For example, Fr McCarron, who, though no longer central director, still kept a close eye on developments, was sensitive to the charge that the Pioneers had not been sympathetic to AA. In retrospect he insisted that when AA had been established in Dublin in 1946 he had been approached by the organisers and had advised them on how to establish a presence in the country. He was also willing to accept categorically that alcoholism was a disease, even if he stuck to the erroneous view that it could be cured:

> There are many ways the problem of alcoholism can be tackled. Alcoholism is a disease. I have a long experience of it and I feel that it can be cured. I have dealt with a number of cases and have brought them back to being teetotallers. On the way back there is need for help, and, remember I was not always a Pioneer. I knew, by the way they talked that they had the goodwill, but I also feel that they needed the help of God. That is one of the main reasons why I became a Pioneer.[140]

Alcoholism had also become an issue deemed worthy of official government action. In November 1966 the Minister for Health had announced the setting up of an Irish National Council on Alcoholism, and the director, Richard Perceval was not concerned with the merits or demerits of alcohol but the fact that nothing was being done about the prevalence of the disease, which it was estimated, could be affecting up to 60,000 sufferers. As a recovered alcoholic himself, he had insisted that the help of the Pioneers was needed.[141] Some Pioneers, however, showed antipathy to the idea of co-operation. In 1969 Pierce Barrett, in reacting to the suggestion that being a Pioneer involved using one's abstinence to shape the wider community's attitude to drink, wrote the following:

> I do not think that a person who makes the Heroic Offering needs to take a practical or active interest in the problem of drink in order to be a good Pioneer. It was never intended to be other than a spiritual organisation. No great demands are made on us and I see no reason why we should not continue.[142]

On the surface there was a clear gulf between those who wanted to modernise and those wishing to be left in peace. But even amongst those who sought a new departure, there was no consensus about the pace of change. Mulligan always wanted to go that one step further. In Longford in 1969 he insisted that moderate drinking had to be viewed as equally acceptable as abstinence, and he uttered the heretical proposal that it might be equally enlightened to introduce children to alcohol moderately, as part of a Sunday meal, for instance.[143] The reaction of one letter-writer to the *Sunday Press* was typical: 'Will Fr Cullen not turn in his grave? Fr Mulligan should think again before destroying the peace of many a fireside.'[144] However, some private correspondence seems to indicate that there were some more sym-pathetic to Mulligan, if not quite prepared to go to the same lengths. In the same year, Charlie O'Mahony, a Cork Pioneer, rejected the idea that children should be exposed to alcohol, but felt that the wearing of the badge should be optional, and that the long-term aim should be to move from a position of total abstinence to a position of moderate drinking. Life, he felt, had been too easy for the Association 'It is a pity some capable writer does not have a proper "go" at us. I really feel that would do us all a great deal of good.'[145] Sean Haughey of the North Dublin regional committee was somewhat bolder, suggesting it should be optional to wear the badge and that he was in favour of a Pioneer group of moderate drinkers 'maybe at the cost to ourselves of having to drink a few lemonades we could exercise an element of restraint on the more heavy consumers among our friends.'[146] Mulligan's language in turn was becoming harsher. In a letter to Pierce Barrett, a member of the central council, he wrote 'There is a warning in the history of other temperance associations, not so much here as in England and America, where many of them end by losing their appeal and credibility by narrow programmes and ridiculous activities.'[147]

From Barrett's perspective there was worse to come. In May 1969 the *Evening Press* reported that three regional Pioneer centres in the diocese of Ossory had extended their best wishes to the Kilkenny beer festival, a move which had been endorsed by Fr Mulligan, as if to make amends for previous wrongs and harsh anti-drink propaganda.[148] This unprecedented greeting had its origins in a talk which Fr Joyce of Kilkenny had given in Durrow, in which he had criticised the exces-sive drinking which had become an established part of the festival. The festival committee subsequently held an emergency meeting at which seventeen of the twenty-two members were in favour of aban-doning the festival if the local clergy believed it damaging. This was not what Joyce had intended and he proposed a compromise which involved members of the local clergy 'policing' the event by keeping an eye on publicans, underage drinking and providing shelter. Pierce Barrett was outraged. He himself had travelled to Kilkenny and was appalled by the excessive drinking and was 'surprised at the feather-headed conduct of Fr Joyce in thinking up such a course of action' and the lack of courtesy in not informing Dargan what was going on.

However, his real target was Mulligan, and he referred to his endorsement of the move as 'unethical and unfortunate', suggesting that the Association was in danger of being irreparably tarnished: 'This is a personal letter. Please burn it now. You may burn the complete file if you so desire. I send it only that you may be aware of what is going on.'[149]

Needless to say Dargan did not light a bonfire but the episode certainly marked a turning point, with Mulligan deemed to have gone dangerously overboard. Three weeks later, in the minute book of the SFX council of which he was spiritual director, the entry indicated, almost with a sigh of relief, that there was no business transacted that day 'pending the transfer of Fr Mulligan'.[150] Renewal had been swallowed by reassignment.

NOTES

1 Fergal Tobin, *The Best of Decades: Ireland in the 1960s* (Dublin 1984)
2 Hugh Brody, *Inishkillane: Change and decline in the west of Ireland* (London 1973) p. 173
3 PCIC, July 2, 1959
4 PAA, Bishop Quinn to Dargan, May 23, 1959
5 ibid., Collier to Dargan, April 3, 1959
6 ibid., Dunne (on behalf of McQuaid) to Dargan, April 17, 1959
7 ibid., Walsh to Dargan, January 3, 1959
8 ibid., Fr Henry Nolan to Dargan, April 16, 1959
9 ibid., Minutes of discussion, September 17, 1959
10 ibid., Fr Browne to Dargan, September 9, 1959 and Gerry Browne to Dargan, n.d.
11 *Province News*, October 1960
12 PCIC, October 1, 1959
13 ibid., August 8, 1960
14 PAA, Extract from Dillon's Cork speech, September 17, 1960
15 Dáil Debates, vol. 184, October 26, 1960
16 PAA, Dermot O'Flynn, Memo to Hierarchy, n.d.
17 *Irish Independent*, November 3, 1960
18 *Irish Press*, August 5, 1960
19 PAA, Dr James Fergus to O'Flynn, October 26, 1960
20 *Sunday Despatch*, October 16, 1960
21 *Irish Catholic*, October 27, 1961
22 Daniel Dargan, *Talks to Pioneers* (Dublin 1961)
23 PAA, Extract from Galway Rally speech, February 21, 1961
24 ibid., Minute Book of SFX Ladies' Council
25 PCIC, July 13, 1961
26 PAA, Memo from Irish Country Vintners' Association, September 9, 1960
27 ibid., Department of Justice reply (copy) October 10, 1960
28 LVAA, Minutes, vol. 33, February 1959–November 1961, November 15, 1959, November 16, 1959
29 ibid., July 9 and July 31, 1962
30 NAI, DT S16920A, July 8, 1960, Statistics re Consumption of drink in Ireland
31 ibid.
32 ibid., printed in the Bulletin of the Department of External Affairs no. 494 September 12, 1960
33 *Evening Press*, January 13, 1961
34 PAA, Dargan to Sean Ronan, n.d.

35 ibid., February 17, 1961
36 ibid., Broderick, Central Statistics Office, to Sean Ronan, March 13, 1961
37 *Irish Independent*, May 25, 1960.
38 *Pioneer*, April 1963 and PCIC June 13, 1963
39 Brendan Walsh and Dermot Walsh, 'Economic aspects of alcohol consumption in the Republic of Ireland' in *Economic and Social Review*, vol. 2, no. 1
40 Bill Rothwell, *Alcohol: Ireland's Beloved Drug* (Dublin 1990), pp. 25–26
41 Farmer, *Ordinary Lives*, p. 168
42 Dargan, *Talks to Pioneers*
43 PCIC, June 24, 1963
44 Michael Sheehy, *Is Ireland Dying? Culture and the Church in modern Ireland* (London 1968) pp. 204–6
45 Joyce O'Connor, *The Young Drinkers: a cross national study of social and cultural influence* (London 1968) p. 51
46 Hugh Brody, *Inishkillane*, p. 33
47 Alexander Humphreys, *New Dubliners: Urbanisation and the Irish family* (London 1966) p. 26
48 Farmer, *Ordinary Lives*, p. 168
49 Jeremiah Newman (ed.), *The Limerick Rural Survey* (Dublin 1964)
50 Joyce, *Young Drinkers*, p. 41
51 PCIC, August 1, 1963
52 Dargan (ed.), *Talks to Pioneers*, p. 39
53 Pioneer, October 1964
54 Pioneer, June 1949.
55 ibid., June 1965
56 Joseph Gusfield, 'Status conflicts and the changing ideologies of the American Temperance movement' in Pittman (ed.), *Society, Culture and Drinking*, pp. 101–121
57 PAA, Helen Sharkey to Dargan June 2, 1959
58 ibid., Dargan to Provincial, n.d. [c. 1960]
59 ibid., Eugene Murphy to Dargan, October 11, 1960
60 ibid., Dargan to McGinty, March 16, 1961
61 ibid., Fr Ray Kennedy to Dargan, October 7, 1961
62 ibid.
63 ibid., Fr Thomas Byrne to Dargan, June 11, 1962
64 ibid., McGinty to Dargan, January 5, 1963
65 ibid., Dargan to Byrne, February 13, 1963
66 ibid., Dargan to Kennedy, March 26, 1963
67 ibid., Kennedy to Dargan, March 1963
68 ibid., April 1, 1963
69 ibid., McCarron, Chihuni Mission, Rhodesia to Dargan, May 13, 1963 and April 8, 1963
70 ibid., McGinty to Dargan, May 18, 1963
71 ibid., James Madden to Dargan, January 19, 1962
72 ibid., Copy of St John's Centre Newsletter [c. 1961]
73 ibid., Minutes of New York Regional Committee, September 1962
74 ibid., January 1963
75 PAA, Frank and Alice O'Sullivan to Dargan, November 27, 1965
76 PCIC, September 14, 1967
77 PA, SFX Minutes, March 30, 1962
78 PCIC, February 22, 1962
79 PAA, Dargan to Hassen, n.d. [c. 1962]
80 ibid.
81 PCIC, July 18, 1963
82 PAA, London Regional Committee Newsletter, May 1962 and March 1963
83 ibid., Connolly to Dargan, April 29, 1963
84 ibid., McKiernan to Dargan, October 1, 1965
85 Edmund Hogan, *The Irish Missionary Movement: An historical survey* (Dublin 1990) pp. 8–9
86 PCIC, September 1, 1960
87 ibid., December 14, 1961

88 ibid., March 26, 1961
89 ibid., February 3, 1966
90 ibid., August 11, 1966
91 ibid., September 29, 1966
92 ibid., November 2 1966
93 *Sunday Press*, October 1, 1967
94 Dargan (ed.), *Talks to Pioneers*
95 *Pioneer*, April 1956
96 ibid., March 1958
97 ibid., November 1962
98 ibid., May 1964
99 *The Furrow*, vol.2, 1960
100 F. O'Doherty and D. McGrath, *The Priest and Mental Health* (Dublin 1963)
101 ibid., p. 16
102 ibid., p. 53
103 PCIC, August 25, 1966
104 PAA, SFX Minutes, August 29, 1963
105 *Cork Examiner*, October 28, 1963
106 PCIC, October 31, 1963
107 ibid., January 30, 1964
108 ibid., December 16, 1965
109 In interview with author, September 5, 1996
110 PAA, SFX Minutes, August 28, 1964
111 ibid., November 20, 1965
112 Thomas Plaut, *Alcohol Problems: A report to the nation by the Co-operative Commission on the study of alcoholism* (New York 1967) p. 8
113 ibid.
114 ibid.
115 PCIC, February 9, 1967
116 PAA, SFX Minutes, April 28, 1967
117 ibid., May 27, 1967
118 ibid., September 29, 1967
119 CA, Fr Mathew Total Abstinence membership card, 1962
120 Dargan (ed.), *Talks to Pioneers*, p. 132
121 Peter Connolly, 'The church in Ireland since the Second Vatican Council' in *Ireland at the crossroads* (Lille 1979)
122 *Furrow*, vol. 20, 1969
123 Fennell, *Changing face*, p. 190
124 Sheehy, *Is Ireland Dying?*, pp. 204–6
125 Inglis, *Moral Monopoly*, p. 181
126 Donal Connery, *The Irish* (London 1969) pp. 97–100
127 PAA, SFX Mnutes, August 26, 1966
128 LVAA, Minutes, vol. 35, October 4, 1966
129 PAA, IAPI Minutes, January 21, 1965
130 PAA, Dargan to O'Callaghan, September 4, 1963
131 ibid., SFX Minutes, March 31, 1967
132 Irish Countrywomen's Association Archives, Mulligan to Ms Lewis, March 21, 1967, Resolutions, Box 43
133 PAA, Central Council File, Minutes of Ely House Meeting, December 1, 1968
134 ibid., Bishop Morris to Dargan, November 28, 1968
135 ibid., Ely House Meeting Minutes
136 ibid.
137 ibid., Mulligan to Pierce Barrett, n.d. [c. 1969]
138 ibid., Fr Mulligan to Fr John, n.d. [c.1969]
139 *Irish Times*, December 6, 1968
140 *Pioneer*, February 1967
141 ibid., May 1967
142 PCIC, February 28, 1969

143 PCIC, February 28, 1969
144 *Sunday Press*, March 16, 1969
145 PAA, Charlie O'Mahony to Mulligan, May 12, 1969
146 ibid., Sean Haughey, Paper read to Ninth Dublin Regional Committee, April 14, 1969
147 ibid., Mulligan to Barrett, April 1969
148 *Evening Press*, May 23, 1969
149 PAA, Barret to Dargan, June 4, 1969
150 ibid., SFX Minutes, June 27, 1969

CHAPTER SEVEN

Epilogue
Struggling for Status
and Direction

As Minister for Health, however, I must concentrate on the other
section of the community – those who drink and those who wish to
continue to do so. There is no question of condemning young
people. My generation has not by its own performance earned the
right to do that.

Charles Haughey, 1978

The problems facing the Pioneer Movement in modern times are
formidable enough and sufficiently perplexing to drive the whole
lot of you to drink.

Bishop Cassidy of Clonfert, 1982

The Pioneer Association spent much of the next twenty-five years
attempting to grapple with the fall-out from the cultural upheavals of
the 1960s. The Association reacted in a number of ways, some inher-
ently positive, others characterised by the brash confidence and righteousness which had been its hallmark at its height, but which now
seemed sadly inappropriate. Crusading was no longer fashionable,
particularly from the vantage point of a generation which had little
experience or memory of Irish Catholicism prior to the Vatican II era.

The question of what the pin now stood for was open to a host of
interpretations. For many, there was no question of the Association
continuing in its traditional guise as it moved into the 1970s. Drink
consumption continued unabated, which perhaps made the issue of
temperance immediately relevant, but which also deepened the gulf
between those who indulged and those who abstained. The observations concerning the cloud of rejection which settled ominously over
the American temperance movement towards the end of the 1960s
were deeply pertinent to the Pioneers as they moved into the

following decade: 'It is when social movements are ideologically closed to all but the most deeply committed that they most accentuate the schisms and conflicts of the society.'[1] Attempting to chart a middle ground was often deemed to be the only realistic response, but this left the Association with the responsibility of attempting to define moderation in a culture of extreme attitudes to alcohol. Another American observer noted in 1976 that: 'What really matters is that an ethic of moderate drinking is free-floating; it is not embedded in a structure of orientation. There is no organisation or reference group that is built on an ethic of moderate drinking.'[2] The Association had already come to this conclusion in the 1960s, but a feeling persisted, particularly amongst those who wished to see the Association adopt a more secular and liberal stance, that it needed to applaud the moderate drinker, particularly in a climate where the problem of alcoholism was increasingly an issue of national health and well-being. But for others, heaping plaudits on the moderate drinker was tantamount to suggesting that the abstainers were, in effect, intemperate and religiously and ideologically redundant.

The rise in teenage drinking was a recurring theme of this era and it raised familiar questions about the extent to which a group like the Pioneers could give direction, particularly in relation to demands for changes in the licensing laws and the positions adopted by publicans and those involved in the drink industry. Experience had suggested that they were utterly ineffectual in this regard, but an interesting development of the 1970s and 1980s, and ironic given their previous muteness, was the tendency of senior members of the Irish Catholic Hierarchy to lend a helping hand through addresses to Pioneers, and statements concerning the moral and spiritual decline spawned by drink excess. This was a message they could realistically link to other social issues such as the widening gap between rich and poor, unemployment and crime which came into sharper focus during these decades of vast change and inequality.

Another interesting departure was the attempt to negotiate a new Pioneer crusade abroad, particularly in Africa. It was almost as if some of the emerging African countries, many of them with serious drink problems, became a substitute for the barren fields at home, the conditions on that continent being ripe for the sort of temperance momentum Ireland had experienced a century earlier. Those guiding the Association during the 1970s have to be credited with a certain sense of openness to change, if not adventure, and there was certainly much more frankness about not only the aims, but the abilities of the Association. But it was equally significant that in the 1980s a defensiveness began to re-emerge with a consensus that the Association, if only to have a clear identity, needed to return to its spiritual basis, and disregard secular innovations, even if this meant tacitly accepting that its appeal was slight and its longevity open to serious doubt. A return to familiar territory, even if this was the acceptance of the inevitability of decline was perhaps felt to be more feasible than excursions into areas which left Pioneer motives too open to varying interpretations.

The controversy surrounding the public and private utterings of Fr Mulligan as documented in the previous chapter should not detract from what were genuine efforts by Fr Dargan, who was to remain as central director until 1977, to effect significant change in the organisation. Dargan's style was circumspect and was often overshadowed by the tendency of some of his more colourful colleagues to indulge in soundbites which simplified the complications the organisation faced. On the eve of the 1970s his predecessor, Fr McCarron, had announced, somewhat disingeneously, that 'I feel proud in saying we have won a place which is not in opposition to the drinker.'[3] This was in direct response to charges that the Association, over a number of decades had done the exact opposite. At the core of the charge was the wider and persistent theme of the need to reform and adapt Irish Catholicism in an attempt to temper unswerving loyalty to traditional practices. Cultural patterns were clearly changing religious attitudes, not neces- sarily undermining the basic faith of the Irish catholic, but the manner in which they interpreted and practiced their religion. The response of the obdurate Archbishop of Dublin, John Charles McQuaid to the 'Aggiornamento' or updating of catholic practices to prioritise the vocation of the laity, and the Vatican Council's Dogmatic Constitution which depicted the church as a fellowship necessitating a Catholic's personal involvement, was that 'nothing had happened in Rome to disturb the tranquillity of Irish catholic life.'[4]

The Pioneer Association could not afford to indulge in such arrogant and naive semantics, particularly given the fact that, as Desmond Fisher pointed out, Catholics were no longer so prepared to spurn material comforts in contemporary life in order to ensure a higher reward in the life to come.[5] The fact that the leading generals in the Irish Hierarchy had been unacquainted with much of the work of the Continental theologians who had laid the foundations for many of the eventual pronouncements of the Vatican Council did not mean that many of the foot soldiers of Irish Catholicism, including key Pioneers, would be immune to contemplating change, internal dialogue and self-confrontation. Desmond Fennell in 1968 had pointed to the intel- lectual dearth which was concomitant to the illusory idea that Irish religion was exceptionally moral, perfectly catholic, intrinsically spiritual and uniquely cultured.[6] Extending this argument the follow-ing year, the *Furrow* magazine asserted that 'The beliefs and practices of the majority of Catholics are insufficiently interiorised . . . not personally examined and tested and then affirmed or rejected'.[7] Similar questions were now being directed at the Pioneer Association and in the view of Dargan, it was obvious that internal change had to begin before the organisation could face the external challenges of an increasingly secularist and materialist society, in which drink consumption was increasing. Where did it belong? A contributor to the *Pioneer* Magazine in 1970, Des Cryan, observed that 'The Association it must be noted does not fit in as happily and in as integrated a way as it might into our society. It never has.'[8]

Recognising the need for an internal revamp, Dargan had identified the lack of communication and overcentralisation which had come to characterise the Association and its structures in the mid-60s, and had introduced Pioneer Regional Councils (by 1977 there were eighty), which chose delegates to be represented on the central council. The council met quarterly, with decisions based on a majority vote. It was deemed essential at this stage for individual centres, numbering over 2,000, to feel that they were being represented in some way. In 1970 Dargan also took the bold and unprecedented step of introducing a constitution for the Association, a document which was endorsed by Cardinal Conway and sent to all Pioneer centres. This document was accepted by 511 centres which sent voting forms on the issue, and rejected by only 6. The constitution set out the aims of the Association – promoting temperance and sobriety by spiritual means – and the revised administrative structures – a central director appointed by the Irish Jesuit Provincial in conjunction with the Irish Episcopal Conference, a central council composed of delegates from regional diocesan councils, (with six appointed by the central director), with Regional committees and local Pioneer centres forming the base of the pyramid. Each diocese in Ireland where at least six Pioneer centres existed had the right to elect annually from the regional committee one delegate to the central Council. The constitution was presented, and received, as a welcome formalisation of the degree of democracy which had been injected into the Association.

Dargan also sought to encourage a more questioning spirit, partic-ularly in relation to issues which had traditionally been ignored or bypassed, using Central Council meetings as a forum for the exchange of provocative views. Whilst the Association, at the end of 1970 was reported to be toying with the idea of incorporating a renunciation of drugs into its traditional pledge, the *Sunday Independent* had reported that 'The group of modern minded Pioneers led by Rev Thomas Finnegan, President of Summerhill College, Sligo, who advocate that the Pioneer Association should have a pledge against drug taking were given a mild rebuke last night by the Association's Central Director.'

Responding by letter the following week, in what marked the beginning of an uneasy relationship with a media which pounced delightfully on any hint of a shift from traditional Pioneer aims, Dargan denied he had admonished any such proposal and insisted it would be given 'careful consideration'.[9] When the issue was duly discussed by the central council the following March, the majority view was that drugs should not be included in any new form of the pledge, and instead much attention was given to the need for educating the youth on alcohol. This was the beginning of comprehensive debate within and outside the Association regarding underage drinking, which was to dominate the Pioneer agenda for much of the following two decades. Dargan and the secretary to the Central Council, Dermot O'Flynn, had met previously with the Minister for Education on foot of a memorandum which had written urgently of the need to take preventative action precisely because unlike the Italian or Jewish youth, Irish teenagers were not being taught to distinguish between responsible and irresponsible drinking.[10] At the central council meeting the issue was put more starkly: 'For the younger generation, just now, the vertical avenue of prayer has lost its appeal. Should we not have the courage to experiment, to plan something more positive for them?'[11]

Fears in this regard were closely bound up in the knowledge that, as Dermot O'Flynn pointed out in a letter to the Minister for Justice, those under the age of 18 were being served alcohol all over the country.[12] The key problem was deemed to be the archaic licensing laws of the 1920s which had declared it illegal for a publican to 'knowingly supply' a person under 18 with drink, providing the publican with the convenient get-out clause of ignorance, the onus being on the state to prove otherwise. Likewise it was lawful under the 1924 Intoxicating Liquor Act for a 15-year-old to purchase alcohol in an off-licence provided it was in a sealed container containing not less than one pint – again this was legislation which had been designed to facilitate in the past the provision of alcohol for the elderly or immobile who would have been dependent on a younger generation to run errands. But aside from the actual legal aspects, the 1970s presented the cultural challenge to temperance advocates to counter such a promiscuous attitude towards alcohol on the part of youth.

Academic and sociological research seemed to confirm the fears of the Pioneer Association – a detailed survey of Dublin's youth in the 18- to 21-year-old bracket had confirmed that through a mixture of parental influences, peer-group pressure and social, personal and cultural inheritances, the Irish had an ambivalent attitude to drink. Although the survey did not substantiate the stereotype of Ireland as a crude nation of all-embracing hard drinkers, it did confirm that there were two value systems in operation in Ireland in relation to alcohol consumption. The research of Joyce Fitzpatrick seemed to indicate that though drinking was firmly embedded in the Irish social and economic framework, there was also a premium placed on abstinence. But it was a confused premium inherited from a generation whose attitudes to drink were inconsistent. The young people were found to respect abstainers, tolerate moderate drinkers and were wary of excessive drinkers, which seemed perfectly logical, but many of them were also the offspring of parents who, though drinkers, had an unfavourable attitude to drink in general.[13] From the sociologist's perspective, many theories had been put forward as to why there was excessive drinking, although few had been empirically tested, but in conversation with teenagers the impression given was one of uncharitable confusion: 'A further indication of their ambivalent attitude to drink was in their attitudes to the alcoholic. While some of these young people were prepared to call an alcoholic a sick person, nearly two fifths called them "sick and weak-willed" and "sick, morally weak and a criminal"...'[14]

Clearly the new generation had inherited much from the temperance propaganda that their parents, whether drinkers or not, had been grounded in. They were also shown to have inherited an innate sexism, with four fifths of both sexes disapproving of girls their own age drinking. Fitzpatrick, writing in 1972, felt that the solution to these ambiguities was to take the emotional content out of the debate on youth and drink, to cease relying on the simplicities of mythology and demonisation and to begin to distinguish between drinking, drunkenness and alcoholism.[15]

These pertinent observations had obvious implications for the Pioneer Association whose approach in the past had relied heavily on propaganda which was rooted in emotional paranoia, albeit in a religious and spiritual framework. This approach was no longer working to the same extent. The response of the Association, particularly under the influence of the new assistant central director, Fr Bernard McGuckian SJ, was to inaugurate a new movement entitled Renewal and Youth (RAY). The intention was not to replicate the Juvenile Pioneer movement but to reach out, as was recorded in the central council minutes, 'to the 80 per cent of youth who are non-Pioneers'.[16] This was to be done by requesting RAY members to make a promise to abstain from alcohol for four years and to become involved in group educational, recreational and charitable endeavours, or as Cardinal Conway put it, 'It will aim at giving the great mass of the young people of this country the opportunity – from reading, discussion and social experience – to form mature and balanced judgements on the question of drinking.'[17]

It was a bold and imaginative departure, particularly in its independence from established Pioneer methods. There was a concerted attempt, particularly by the vigorous targeting of schools by McGuckian, to give teenagers a chance to hear and see both sides of the drink argument in an environment which was positive and educational. The aim was to get the movement backed by prominent lay people so that 'the basic virtues of truth, honesty, tolerance, friendliness and courtesy could be packaged in modern times.'[18] It was also a realistic recognition that the life pledge did not and would not interest the majority of Irish youth, but that if educated at this stage, when they did begin to drink they would be more likely to become moderate drinkers. Though there were those who feared it would undermine the traditional Pioneer programme, the departure was the culmination of the researches of a sub-committee youth group formed by the central council which divided the youth of Ireland into three categories – those interested in abstinence for life, those prepared to take the pledge up to the age of twenty-one and those for whom abstinence held no appeal whatsoever. Sensibly, it was decided to concentrate on the middle group,[19] and it enjoyed considerable success in the 1970s before fading out in the 1980s.

Perhaps it was also a reaction to the confusion concerning the practice of taking confirmation pledges. In the early 1970s the Catholic Hierarchy were being approached regarding the possibility of confirmation pledges being offered in all dioceses until the age of eighteen. Some had begun to see such pledges as something of an invasion of liberty, particularly when done publicly, and practices in various parts of the country differed depending on the Bishop in question. At the end of 1974, Archbishop Morris of Cashel wrote to Dargan 'I still ask the children to take a pledge at confirmation time with no apologies to champions of liberty.'[20] However Bishop Cahal Daly of Ardagh and Clonmacnoise had been somewhat more circumspect: 'I have myself been experimenting with the confirmation pledge in a mild way, with a view to try to make it more personal and meaningful and for the confirmandia, also more realistic. Instead of having the children recite it collectively and aloud, I have them say it silently and individually.'[21]

At a 1974 Episcopal Conference the question of diocesan confirmation pledges had been discussed, and the variety of situations pertaining in various parts of the country was an indication of the lack of consensus on the merits of pledge-taking, and indeed the pressures operating in some dioceses against the concept of enforced temperance: in the diocese of Ardagh and Clonmacnoise, a pledge was administered until the age of eighteen, in Clogher it had been until the age of twenty-one but was reduced to eighteen and was taken silently. In Cork and Ross the children were simply asked to join the Pioneer Association; in Killaloe it was taken until the age of eighteen and aloud, while in Limerick the pledge had been dropped in the 1960s. In Waterford and Lismore it had been administered until twenty-one but had been jettisoned in 1967 on the advice of local priests, who subsequently were to persuade the bishop to reintroduce it with the wording 'until I leave school'. In Tuam a pledge against drugs was included, while in Clonfert smoking was tagged on. In Dromore the pledge had been dropped in 1970 on the advice of priests and was made the responsibility of teachers, while in Dublin it had also been discontinued in 1970 but there was increasing parental pressure to reinstate it.[22] In 1975 the central council suggested writing to the Catholic Hierarchy proposing that a confirmation pledge be administered until the age of eighteen in all dioceses. For its part, the following year the Association reduced the age of admission to the probationer ranks of the Pioneers from fourteen to twelve, both because of the increased pressure on children to start drinking younger and a resentment among those leaving primary school still being classed as 'Juvenile' Pioneers.[23]

If it is true that there were certain ethical reservations about young people being publicly committed to a pledge it was also the case that the government demonstrated itself reluctant to instigate a system of identity cards to help curb excessive drinking. Other associations, in particular the Irish Countrywomen's Association had long been agitating for such a system of identification, but it was noted after a meeting with the Minister for Justice, Erskine Childers, in 1971 that 'the minute it was mentioned due to the circumstances at the moment we would hear the words "Police State" shouted from the rooftops.' Three years later the ICA was attempting to foist the idea on to the agenda of an uninterested government, although some local communities and parishes had taken it on themselves to issue identity cards.[24] Another grievance was the manner in which television advertisements sought to glamorise drinking in the minds of vulnerable teenagers, or as the ICA put it in a deputation to the Minister for Justice, Patrick Cooney, in 1974, 'Advertisements always depict a he-man with a beautiful girl and a fast car. Why can't we be shown the old man sitting in the corner sick and penniless because of his drinking?'[25]

From the perspective of the Pioneers, the real challenge of teenage drinking lay in confronting a confused generational inheritance – Irish teenagers of the 1970s were not faced with a uniform drinking pattern, but one which was both ambivalent and multifaceted – an adult world in which some totally abstained, some drank pathologically and others only during religious rituals. Some drank at all festive and special occasions, and some incorporated moderate drinking into their everyday lives. It was a recognition of these hybrid patterns which had prompted some Pioneers to urge the Association to adopt a broad and non-judgemental approach to educating teenagers about alcohol. John Leen, President of the Kerry Regional Pioneer Council had in private lambasted the Association for being outmoded, rigid and unscrupulous in dealing with lapsed members, particularly the youth, as the established rules restricted their natural inquisitiveness and need for experimentation. He expressed the view that 'for today's faith-questioning young people, any motive for being a total abstainer should be acceptable.'[26] However there were others during the 1970s who identified in such sentiments a dangerous liberalisation which was tantamount to the abandonment of the concept of sacrifice. Pierce Barrett saw these attempts to lessen the severity of the pledge or the reasons for taking it, as evidence of a growing national inferiority complex which was preventing members from having the courage to display their virtue, leading to public indifference. His stance on the youth question was a desperate plea to retain the trappings of tradition:

> The only way in which we can achieve our aims and promote our Association is to copy the methods of other secular organisations – get them young and train them our way. The idealism of youth can just as easily be channelled into the ways of civilisation and decency as it is presently being diverted into other less admirable activities. I would conclude by asking once again for that support which we once accepted as being our right.[27]

The last sentence spoke volumes about the psychological and cultural shift away from an acceptance of continuity, particularly among a generation who had little experience of the religious homogeneity and strict subservience of Irish Catholicism in the 1950s. Dargan was keen to encourage debate about the most effective means of reaching out to sceptical youths, but he also recognised there were bridges too far. In 1976 he expressed opposition to the views of a British Alcohol Education Officer who had espoused the belief that parents should introduce their children to small quantities of alcohol at an early age, in order to inculcate an attitude of moderation which they would carry to adulthood:

> Fr Dargan said he could see the sense of young people in Italian, Jewish and Chinese families being introduced to alcohol at a tender age, because public opinion rejects excessive drinking in these countries, but that the Irish view of drinking is irresponsible and consequently it would be wrong for Irish families to encourage their children to drink.[28]

Given the spiralling rates of alcoholism and the vast expenditure on drink in Ireland in the 1970s and 1980s, few could dispute Dargan's accusation of irresponsibility. It was to become such a national problem that Dargan's successor, Fr McGuckian, declared in 1979 that it now set the Pioneer agenda: 'As Pioneers our specific concern is to help victims of alcoholic abuse,'[29] a statement which was indicative of a rhetorical restructuring of the Association's priorities and *raison d'être*. The figures were startling. Interestingly, excessive drinking that had traditionally been blamed on poverty was now being blamed on affluence. While there had been a significant decline in alcohol abuse in the early decades of the century – death from cirrhosis of the liver had decreased by 20 per cent between 1908 and 1949 – since the mid-century it had been steadily on the increase. While Irish people in the US and Britain had the highest rates of alcoholism of any ethnic group, at home, Ireland, though ranking high in terms of alcohol-related hospital admission and income spent on drink, nevertheless did not rank high in the international table for alcohol consumption, pro-secutions for drunkenness and deaths from cirrhosis of the liver.[30] This seems to suggest that the culture of abstinence adhered to by many adults contributed to these unusual figures. But perhaps this meant that the drinkers were drinking more. They were statistics which Richard Perceval, the Director of the National Council on Alcoholism found puzzling and illogical. In the years 1960 to 1967 admissions to psychiatric hospitals for drink-related illnesses had risen from 404 to 2,015. There were apparently 800,000 drinkers in the Republic who spent £80 million a year on alcohol in the late 1960s. Seventy-two per cent of male adults and thirty-six per cent of female adults were drinking and 143 million pints of beer were consumed in 1970. Between 1963 and 1972 consumption of spirits rose by 66 per cent and in 1971 £147 million was spent on drink, accounting for 11.5 per cent of total consumer expenditure, and it was estimated there were 66,000 alcoholics in the country. In the same year 614 women were admitted to Irish hospitals with alcoholism or alcoholic psychosis. By 1979 this figure had doubled to 1,152. Alcohol problems among the under twenty-fives in the Republic increased by 360 per cent between 1970 and 1985.[31] This, of course, was only the tip of the iceberg. Compounding the view of the Irish ambivalence to alcoholism, Tim Pat Coogan noted in 1975 that 'what these statistics cannot tell us about is the internal reality of drink's place in Ireland . . . at the time of writing no doctor would dream of putting "Alcoholism" on a patient's certificate such is the ambivalence towards the subject.'[32] By 1980 1.5 million drinkers consumed £700 million worth of drink and it was estimated there were 75,000 suffering from alcoholism. In 1987 there were 83,000 prosecutions for drink offences and it was estimated £1,315 million was spent on drink, or £3.6 million a day, accounting for 12 per cent of total consumer expenditure.[33] There was also a tendency to tolerate a certain amount of mental illness when disguised in the cloak of alcohol. Nancy Scheper-Hughes pointed to the continuing and informal relevance of old Brehon laws which distinguished between 'the intoxication of drunkenness' (Meiscelenna) and 'the intoxication of madness' (Meisce merachta). Alcoholism was perhaps still seen as a safer form of pathology than schizophrenia. In seeking scapegoats within the social structure of rural Ireland alcoholism in an immature and dependent personality was often blamed on the way in which Irish mothers reared their sons.[34]

Obviously these were frightening figures, though arguably they could have been worse if the Pioneer Association had not been in existence – Norway, for example in the mid-1970s, had 90,000 alcoholics out of a population of 4 million.[35] This however was cold comfort for a temperance organisation which could feel its spiritual message being sidelined in the clamour to secularise and psychoanalyse the issue. In the early 1970s prominent Irish medical figures such as those attached to institutions, such as St John of God's, suggested causes of Irish alcoholism, not in terms of distance from God, but in the context of the Irish physical disposition, innate inferiority complexes and endogenous and manic depression. For an Association which had continually depicted drink as demon in the past there was also the charge that its approach was cold and removed: 'In addition, present-day emphasis is more likely than in the past to concentrate on the drinker as a person rather than on the alcoholic drink. This is illustrated by the expression "alcoholism comes in people and not in bottles".'[36] When he was departing as central director in 1977, Dargan recalled that 'Times have changed since I first introduced recovered alcoholics to Pioneer seminars and meetings. Then such a move seemed revolutionary. We were trying to get over the World Health Organisation concept of alcoholism as a disease.'[37]

Within the Association there was also the question of whether or not those who joined had done so because of inherited alcohol problems, or as a reaction to alcoholic relations. In 1971, Professor Peter Beckett from Trinity College, in researching the socio-cultural or inherited origins of alcoholism, attempted to examine any evidence of a hereditary link (with one generational gap) in familial tendency towards alcoholism, and aimed his research at Pioneers who abstained as a reaction to alcoholic parents, and those who abstained on grounds of morality or principle. He suggested that research could prove that the first group could carry an inherited trait for alcoholic abuse. His hypothesis was that rates of alcohol abuse in the offspring (now adult) of lifelong abstainers who themselves had relatives who had abused alcohol would be higher than the rates of abuse in the offspring of life-long abstainers without alcohol-abusing relatives. It was an enlightened attempt to academically and medically examine the fundamental relationship between the two extreme cultures in relation to drink in Ireland, but the Pioneers, no more than Irish society as a whole, were not ready for this intrusion. It obviously touched a raw nerve, and it was minuted by the central council that 'there was little support for the questionnaire on "Is alcoholism hereditary?"'[38] Nevertheless the following year Dargan still maintained that, next to Alcoholics Anonymous:

> The Association that has done most to spread a knowledge and understanding of alcoholism is the Pioneer Association . . . I am not saying that there is not room for improvement in this field, but I am convinced that Pioneers are doing much to remove the stigma from alcoholism and to make it easier for people with drink problems to seek help.[39]

And yet in the very same letter, Dargan touched on the limitations of the Pioneers' relationship with alcoholism:

> While every organisation must be ready to develop and to adapt, it must preserve its essentials. An applicant may be influenced by a number of reasons e.g. fear of becoming an alcoholic, desire to save money. He may foster these motives but he must also include love of Christ. We are not free to abandon our constitutions. To attempt to do so would be a serious violation.[40]

In the light of these differing sentiments, others felt that the Association had to draw a line in the sand in relation to alcoholism. In 1975 Dermot O'Flynn of the central council suggested that 'There could be a hidden danger in a humanistic appeal to good works. We must persevere in our resolve to strengthen and extend the ideals of the Heroic Offering.' A few months later the idea of organising a national collection for alcoholics was rejected by the council on the grounds that the Association needed to put its own house in order and the organisational difficulties inherent in putting such a huge effort into work 'not directly connected with our Association.'[41]

The contradictions remained unresolved. In 1975 Pierce Barrett in his position as PRO for the Association saw his job in terms of 'selling Pioneer ideals to the public', but there was still a residual concern that the language they were using was steeped in an outdated and arrogant definition of their status in Irish society. In 1976 the point was made that 'it was not for members of the Association to use the word "heroic" about themselves and it was now more general practice to refer to the traditional "Heroic Offering" as the "Pioneer prayer" or "Pioneer offering".'[42] But the ambivalence if not indifference to the problem in society as a whole was still thwarting the attempt to carve out a modernised temperance niche. The problem, as Fr McGuckian saw it was that 'Public opinion on the question of excessive drinking is inconsistent. A generally expressed desire for moderation is not accompanied by a willingness to take the steps necessary to achieve it.'[43] This touched on the inertia which persisted throughout the 1970s, and may explain why there was a decided shift to the spiritual in the 1980s either as an exercise in damage limitation, or as a recognition of the futility of attempting to lead. But what exactly were the steps necessary to tackle excess, and did the Pioneers figure in a solution? The Report of the National Council on Alcoholism had duly referred to the Pioneer organisation as 'the largest and most important total abstinent group in Ireland' and its 'sacrificial motivation', but as the report elaborated, it was clear that they were not the most important players:

> The most important step in the prevention of alcoholism and excessive drinking is to change attitudes. This change can only be achieved gradually by a broad based programme of propaganda, information and education in which certain Departments of State, Regional Health Boards, voluntary Organisations, schools, management, Trade Unions and the Medical profession co-operate. Above all, the state must be seen to be concerned and must give the lead in preventative measures.[44]

The idea of 'giving a lead' was one which was returned to frequently, and the state's performance in this regard was nothing short of pathetic. During the 1970s the Pioneer Association made intermittent representations to the government concerning licensing laws which were not being enforced. It was noted in 1973 that 'these representations have been met, not with a denial that the violations occur, but rather the statement that it is impossible to enforce the law.'[45] It was also noted that parents, not publicans, were turning up at meetings to discuss the licensing laws, and the following year the question was asked that 'If publicans and gardai disregard the present licensing laws, was there any reason to believe that they would enforce laws dealing with identity cards?'[46] The Association did not see itself as having the responsibility of drafting new legislation, but merely to point out defects in the present laws and their violation. In 1977 the same message was reiterated to the new Minister for Justice:

> The purpose of the law on underage drinking is to protect vulnerable young people. Ordinary observation all through the 1970s offers sufficient evidence that this purpose is not being attained. Garda authorities in private conversation and occasionally in public have indicated their willingness to enforce the law – their real difficulty is that the existing law is not enforceable. The main provisions of the law were passed over 50 years ago, decades before motorways, singing pubs or supermarkets.[47]

It was by no means solely a Pioneer concern. Two years later, Edward Connellan, Secretary of the Vintners' Federation of Ireland was also calling for a change in the law and more severe penalties for violaters, supporting a recommendation of a Youth Council's Report on Underage Drinking, that the Health Education Bureau convene a working party to promote public awareness of the problem. He was forceful in his conclusion, echoing the rhetoric of a previous generation of Vintners: 'I wish to make it abundantly clear that the Vintners Federation of Ireland has and never will condone the disgraceful practice of underage drinking.'[48] These various appeals seem to have done little to galvanise the state into sponsoring change. In 1984 the Association was still looking for a deletion of the words 'knowingly supply' from the 1924 Act. It was admitted frankly in the same letter that 'Our adult Pioneer membership in the Republic is upwards of 200,000. Yet we have been singularly ineffective where influencing legislation has been concerned.'[49] The following Summer Fr William Reynolds SJ, the new central director of the Association, suggested after consulting legal and parliamentary figures regarding proposals to extend the opening hours of pubs that:

> it is not who the letters come from but rather the weight of the letters which count . . . In the past your TD has approached you seeking your vote and for this reason you have every right to approach him or her demanding some form of justice. I'll leave it to your discretion as to how you approach your TD.[50]

Irish legislators throughout the century had shown little appetite for confronting the complex and often archaic English inheritance which comprised much of the licensing code, and tended to cover up cracks on an ad-hoc basis, leading to a bizarre overall picture. In 1983, the cutting wit of one of the country's most able parliamentary orators, John Kelly, was directed at confusion concerning the interpretation of a 1786 licensing law amid doubts about the legality of serving alcohol in Ireland's National Concert Hall:

> Are we not a great little people? We have managed to license greyhound tracks but we cannot make sure that one can get a convenient drink in all theatres. Above all, we have not succeeded in curing the greatest omission of all in this area, the absence of proper liquor licences in ordinary restaurants. We must be the only country in Europe in which that is so. I don't mind making a parenthetic prediction, that the best business done at Knock Airport will be in the bar – providing some 18th- or 19th-century act will enable Monsignor Horan's company to apply for and get a liquor licence.[51]

Throughout this period the media had also shown itself ready and willing to pounce on perceived cracks in the Pioneer armour or any hint at a dilution of their spiritual foundation. Fr Pearse O'Higgins SJ, the assistant central director in 1969, had been wary of allowing journalists to attend meetings of the Association because 'we had unhappy recollections of subeditors amending *bona fide* material from reporters on the job.' However, at a central council meeting in 1974 it was insisted that the Association had a good relationship with the media, but two years later, in the same setting it was noted that 'Members reported on adverse publicity in newspapers when certain hoteliers used the occasion of a Pioneer social to apply in the local courts for an extension of their license . . . it seemed obvious that certain journalists had seized the opportunity to misrepresent the true situation.'[52] This was as a result of the abandoning of the traditional Pioneer rule that only Pioneers could attend the Association's social events. In 1970 Dargan had accepted that it was ridiculous and illiberal for non-Pioneer partners of members to be excluded from socials, and indeed, deprived of drink. Pat Duffy, through the pages of the *Pioneer*, extended this rationale: 'We should be much better employed congratulating the moderate drinker on his strength of will and saying "have this on me" instead of upsetting him with a load of missionary flim-flam that would drive anyone to drink or worse.'[53] Six years later, Sean Hanrahan, a member of the central council, insisted that an interview he was doing for the Magazine should be conducted in a pub on the grounds that 'the old concept of the Pioneer being a lugubrious poor soul who led a life of miserable privation while his drinking colleagues lived it up in the euphoria of alcohol should be killed off once and for all, and it is up to the Pioneer to do it.' Nevertheless there was still a temptation amongst subeditors to opt for the attention-grabbing headline, 'Pioneers drinking'. The *Evening Press* in 1976 reported gleefully:

> One of the most radical priests in the Pioneer movement, Fr Joyce of Kilkenny, is now throwing in the sponge . . . he was responsible for introducing bars to Pioneer functions in Kilkenny . . . he has appealed to all pioneers to begin to run their own Association. He said 'Pioneers are all the time passing the buck. Well it's about time they copped on to the fact that the Pioneer Association is basically a lay temperance movement with a spiritual tradition. They don't need the priest at all, except as a spiritual adviser. They certainly don't need him as an organiser.[54]

A National Leisure Council of the Pioneers was very active in cultivating the social side of the Pioneer movement, but any Pioneer involvement with routine social entertainment was often depicted by outsiders as the inevitable and welcome triumph of the secular. In attempting to explain to the media a process of re-evaluation or adaptation, Dargan felt that he had often been misrepresented, if not totally misquoted. In a letter to the *Sunday Independent* in 1977 he described as 'absurd and grossly inaccurate', a report which purported him describing the Renewal and Youth movement as 'a moderate drinkers organisation for young people'. He also insisted that he had never said, as the journalist wrote, that 'in the near future it seems that moderate drinking rather than total abstention will be the main aim.'[55]

Some years later journalists were seemingly unimpressed with the perceived hijacking by the Pioneers of the American President Ronald Reagan's visit to Ballyporeen in 1984, as recorded by Fr Eanna Condon, the local parish priest:

> We visited the various sites which the president might include in his itinerary and while in O'Farrell's pub, we were offered Irish Coffee. Local County Councillor Con Donavan was at pains to point out that while holding the drink for photographers, as a Pioneer he would not be drinking it. I identified myself as another Pioneer and Mr Deaver [the presidential adviser] asked how many Pioneers there were in Ireland and before we could reply, a journalist answered in a stage whisper from the back of the group: "Two". . . '[56]

Ironically, at a time when the Pioneer Association was in decline, the Irish Catholic Hierarchy, particularly its younger members, began to be more vocal in their endorsement of the value of abstention, seeing it as part of their wider pastoral duties, particularly towards the youth. In the early 1970s Bishop Birch of Ossory insisted that nothing that modern preventative medicine had to offer could compete with the Pioneer movement, which he saw as necessary to reinforce a traditional and necessary patriarchal stability – 'A girl should be told about her role as gentleness maker in the world and a boy should be told about his role as builder, constructor, provider.'[57] Bishop Fergus of Achonry saw the Association as a useful and essential antidote to the values and mores of a permissive society, while Dr Murphy, Bishop of Limerick, lauded its attempt to change the Irish social outlook on alcohol. Bishop Edward Daly of Derry, though not a Pioneer, also praised its restraining influence 'in a lounge-bar society', while the new Bishop of Kilmore, Dr McKiernan, the youngest of the Hierarchy, was also quick to praise the Pioneer motives. Bishop Cahal Daly of Ardagh and Clonmacnoise was probably the most consistent public advocate of the Association, seeing its sacrificial motivation as its biggest strength in an age of questioning and doubt. Addressing a pilgrimage of nearly 50,000 Pioneers at Knock in 1974, to celebrate the 75th anniversary of the Association, he castigated the expenditure on drink in Ireland and highlighted the need for spiritual backbone in a secular world: 'According to reasonable estimates, what we are spending on church buildings and repairs is only about 2 per cent of what we spend on spirits'. In ensuing years he also placed an emphasis on parental responsibility, suggesting that 'society is not worthy of the teenagers they are educating.'[58] Right into the 1980s Daly was insisting that the solution to excessive drinking lay in prayers of supplication, and that the Pioneers were not anti-drink but pro-Jesus. His urgings were an accurate summation of the defensive stance the Association adopted in this decade: 'If the cry of the Irish nation – a long, piercing, persevering cry goes up to the Sacred Heart, in the end that cry must be heard – above all if that cry be sustained by heroic sacrifice.'[59]

The Association attempted to enlist the help of the Hierarchy in promoting a 'Temperance Week' each year in the first week of Advent, the logic being that in an age when it was so difficult to persuade people to undertake life-long commitments with regard to pledges it would be appropriate to cultivate a temporary but institutionalised awareness each year of the scale of the Irish drink problem. In a letter to the secretary to the Irish Hierarchy, Dargan admitted that 'a difficulty exists as regards the most suitable name for the week. The word "temperance" has a dated ring about it. Today doctors and those engaged in work for alcoholics favour the word "sobriety" . . . '[60] The first Temperance Week was in 1974, Advent being chosen because of its traditional association with conversion. It was also a reaction to a disappointment that many priests had begun to ignore the more traditional Temperance Sunday.[61]

In 1975 the Irish Hierarchy responded by issuing a pastoral letter on Temperance. It was significant in that it marked an increased awareness of the problem, and sought to clearly distinguish between use and abuse. Starting from the premise that alcohol was a gift from God, and suggesting that the Irish in the past had been tolerant of drunkenness owing to their oppressive environment, they distinguished between drunkenness and alcoholism on the grounds that alcoholism was a disease and 'there may be no blame attaching to alcoholism especially if the alcoholic is taking the necessary steps to cope with the problem' Decrying the buying of rounds, advertising and vast expenditure on drink, they also defined temperance as 'a struggle for cultural and social development'. Lauding the efforts of Alcoholics Anonymous they also praised the Pioneers for performing an invaluable service through prayers which needed to be echoed by all Irish Catholics in an exercise of education in self-denial. It also dealt with the thorny issue of the public image of the Irish drinker: 'Are we Irish immature in our attitude to alcohol? Is there a sneaking admiration for the heavy drinker; a belief that no gathering is a success unless many of the people become to a greater or lesser degree intoxicated? Is there a pressure on the individual not to be a spoilsport by remaining sober?'[62]

Pastorals of this kind were not as frequent as the Pioneers wished, and Dargan pointed out to the central council in 1978 that 'as the Hierarchy had published a Pastoral on temperance three years ago, it is not expected to have another in the near future.' In the same year the Association examined other possible avenues, suggesting that the Irish President and Council of State be persuaded to investigate alcohol problems through a Presidential Commission,[63] though this was perhaps deemed by some to be beyond the Association's brief, as in 1973, when the idea of creating an office of a national lay president of the Pioneers had been rejected, as well as a proposal to establish a continuous commission to review rules and aspects of the Association. It was felt that a constant change of rules would prove unsettling and that 'experience showed that a body set up for the purpose of recommending changes was in danger of wanting change for change's sake.'[64]

Instead the Association sought to enlist others to promote temperance in a general way – in 1976, the GAA, for example, agreed to promote a 'No Rounds' car sticker, designed to discourage this established and unrelenting Irish pub custom. Occasionally, politicians would appear on the pages of the Pioneer or on Pioneer platforms to endorse the Association by emphasising its inclusiveness and relevance. Readers were informed in October 1970 that P.J. Lalor, the Minister for Industry and Commerce, and a Pioneer since his youth, had 'won the hearts of drinkers in Ireland a short while ago when he rescinded an order from public house owners to increase prices.'[65] In February 1973 his Pioneer cabinet colleague, Minister for Education Padraig Faulkner, urged a modern approach to the inculcation of temperance values in youth, suggesting that traditional craw-thumping and sermonising in school-rooms would no longer suffice.[66] Oliver J. Flanagan, Parliamentary Secretary to the Minister for Local Government in 1976 could always be relied upon to blow the Association's trumpet. He piously informed readers that 'If I were not a Pioneer I feel I would not be in my present position.'[67] Youthful Pioneers and RAY members had also been subjected to an account of the drinking habits of President Erskine Childers:

> The President said he would repeat his own personal experience and confess that until he was Minister for Health he used to drink four or five spirit drinks over two and a half hour periods at cocktail parties, and without any effect, luckily for himself. He had then decided to take only two drinks and drink soft drinks subsequently and he had never noticed the slightest effect on his capacity for enjoyment, for drawing out peoples' ideas and interests and he experienced no sense of fatigue.[68]

In 1980, the Fianna Fáil Minister for Agriculture, Ray MacSharry, congratulated the Pioneers for providing a forum for the broadcasting of ideas 'that would otherwise, in all probability, never be brought to public attention.'[69] It was interesting that some high-profile figures were being more vocal about the perceived value of the Pioneers. No more than with the Catholic Hierarchy, it was perhaps ironic that they were being paraded at a time when the Association was in decline. But it was also perfectly understandable, as past Pioneer propaganda had been confident, internally regulated and tightly controlled – methods which were no longer seen as viable options in the 1970s.

The Association still wished to spread its message overseas. On one level it made sense to re-inject vigour into foreign endeavours, given the measure of despondency in Ireland. In October 1969 Dargan had expressed a desire to see more progress in London suggesting that an emigrant chapel be deployed specifically to promote temperance. It was a request, however, which overlooked the wider problems facing emigrants – his contact in London had diplomatically pointed out that Pioneer recruiting was almost negligible apart from getting existing Irish Pioneers to join a local English centre. Regarding the proposal to appoint a priest for Pioneer work, the correspondent pointed out that 'If a priest is available, the general emigrant work is more important. In comparison, Pioneer work covers a small problem.'[70] Supervision of far-flung councils remained a troublesome endeavour. In 1973 Dargan wrote to Fr Sheridan, Director of the Pioneers in Australia emphasising concern with rumours that the Australian Central Council wished to become independent of Dublin, and to instigate rule changes – 'In order to enable me to scotch the rumour, will you please give me an assurance that in fact the agreement is being adhered to.'[71] Sheridan's reply, though crafted cautiously, gave pause for thought and was a reminder of persistent attempts, going back twenty years, to shake off the shackles of Dublin control:

> Until I came on the scene the movement in Australia was more than moribund. There was neither an active branch nor even a National Council . . . the national bank balance was only $48 . . . we realise what a tremendous debt we owe to the Irish foundation and would be extremely slow to alter anything. However, in keeping with the trends outlined in Vatican II which encourages local churches, especially in mission countries, to develop their liturgies and movements in line with their own national aspirations, and at the same time insisting that mother nations must allow this freedom, it could be that certain minor rules are more of a hindrance than a help.[72]

In Belgium in 1975, the Pioneer organiser found the Association 'in a sad state of affairs', and in 1977 it was pointed out that since the departure of the Belgian organiser Fr Joe Hassen in 1964 the office of director had changed hands several times, and had since lapsed because 'there was no-one suitable for the post on the seminary staff.'[73] Likewise in Fiji in 1975 the national director had been complaining of a breakdown in communication and pleading for a visit because priests were 'occupied to their full capacity'.[74] A few years later Pioneers in Papua New Guinea were similarly demoralised and dejected, complaining of little support from Sydney or Melbourne Pioneers:

> Papua New Guinea is in need of the Pioneers, more so than Ireland herself, in my opinion. Here, it is not unusual for Seminarians and Deacons to get expelled for being drunk. One was ordained a priest even though he was blind drunk as a Deacon in the Seminary ground; the authorities turn a blind eye to that.[75]

However, there was little point in the 1970s of expending missionary energy on tiny centres which had little realistic prospect of expansion, particularly with missionary priests, nuns and volunteers already stretched to capacity. The response of the Pioneers, particularly the new central director Fr McGuckian, was to launch something of a crusade, particularly in Africa, by personally visiting these areas in order to extend the Pioneer apostolate. In 1978 he embarked on an ambitious tour which included Australia, America, New Zealand, Fiji and Africa, pinpointing in particular potential areas of Pioneer action like Kenya, Zambia, Tanzania and Nigeria. In the early 1980s it could be claimed that Africa was the most fruitful and fastest-growing harvest for the Pioneers with reports from thriving centres in Kenya, Uganda, Zambia, Nigeria and South Africa. Seemingly, many of these newly emergent countries were ripe for a temperance crusade, it being closely linked, like Ireland a century previously, with the need for safety-valves to secure stability and respectability. In June 1980 it was reported that Fr Robert Kelly, the National Director of the Pioneers in Zambia since 1978 was travelling thousands of miles promoting the Pioneers.[76] In August 1984 McGuckian left for another African tour, and the following year it was estimated that there could be up to 100,000 Pioneers in Africa, no doubt aided by the fact that, in comparison to 1950 when there had only been a handful of native Catholic bishops, there were now over 300.[77] It was one of the few Pioneer experiments abroad which seemed robust and it was an indication of the ability of the Pioneer message to be still overwhelmingly relevant in particular circumstances.

At home, as the Association moved into the 1980s, many of the experiments of the 1970s began to dissipate, and with them, a certain inquisitive, if not irreverent ethos which had emerged in the previous decade. There was a decided shift back to issues of faith and their relevance for present and coming generations. Doubt still pervaded Pioneer publications – it was noted in March 1981 that 'It is extraordinary that 83 years after its foundation, many Irish people still entertain strange notions of what the Pioneer movement is about.'[78] At this juncture it was estimated that there were 10,000 Pioneers with over fifty years of membership, 80,000 with over twenty years of the pin and 100,000 others. The Association, in coming to terms with its historical inability to impinge on the wider drink culture in the context of law and social customs, reverted to a positive and essentially spiritual portrayal of Christian sacrifice. Questioning seminars and conferences continued, but the terms of reference were narrowed, and an air of defensiveness pervaded which challenged the notion that there was a responsibility on Pioneers to be anything more than model Christians who had made a personal and beneficial sacrifice. At Knock in 1982, at another Pioneer pilgrimage, the Bishop of Clonfert, Dr Cassidy, referred to the 'mild despondency' hanging over the Association, but reiterated the need for 'the robustness of the supernatural'.[79] Others responded sharply to the critics – in 1984 Fr Gerard McGinty referred to the perception of the Pioneer sacrifice as 'an exercise in Christian masochism' and maintained that 'the Pioneer must collide with and undermine this utilitarian viewpoint.'[80] The following year, Fr Joe Delaney insisted it was a national disgrace that alcohol was still not seen as a serious public health problem and that the ideal of temperance had been watered down and weakened by opponents of the Association preaching moderation – that the Pioneers had in effect been 'intimidated, shamed or reduced into silence and submission'.[81] These sentiments were indicative of a wheel turned full circle, being precisely the charges which critics had levelled at the Pioneer Association when it was at its strongest. In 1985 the new central director, Fr Reynolds, expressed the view that the Association would be better equipped to handle criticism, if not disdain 'if we were more spiritually aware and vigilant.'[82] The impression given was that this could be done by examining the gospel, saints' lives and Christian teaching rather than tackling the obdurate drinker. As late as 1990 Mary Purcell pointed out the reason why historical symbols such as Matt Talbot played such an important role:

> For one thing he was a lay person, and this is the age of the laity in the church. He was a working man. He was for many years an alcoholic and the most recent statistics for underage and teenage drinking have shaken us all. We are living in an age of self indulgence. We need the example of an ascetic like Matt Talbot to restore some measure of self discipline.[83]

The Association remained sensitive to its standing in Irish society. In 1993 the management board of the Association attempted to elucidate on 'What the pin stands for today'. The negative comments revealed that it was perceived as old, dry, prohibitionist, top-heavy with structures and rules, with too many badges and categories and that the base of total abstinence was too narrow for contemporary society. Other criticisms included the emphasis on spirituality, that the the Pioneers were running against an unrelenting tide of commercialism and belonged to 'an era of devotions, sodalities and fish on Fridays' and 'with too many old and serious people involved'.[84] Many of these negative comments were seen as a product of ignorant stereotyping and also, as Fr Micheál Mac Gréil put it, in an address in 1993 on the future of the Pioneers, 'in response to some Pioneers who may unwittingly give the wrong impression'.[85] There was a measure of truth in both reasons. He concluded:

> The spirituality of the Pioneer Association will have to be re-examined in the light of contemporary culture. It has always been a fruitful Ignatian principle that we must begin with the people where they are at the present time. Symbols and practices which no longer make sense to people must be changed.[86]

These remain the religious and secular challenges of promoting temperance in modern Ireland.

NOTES

1 Gusfield, 'Changing status' in Pitman (ed.), *Society, Culture and Drinking*
2 Stivers, *Hair of a Dog*, p. 97
3 *Pioneer*, February 1969
4 Desmond Fisher 'The Church and change' in Kiernan Kennedy (ed.), *Ireland in Transition* (Cork 1985) p. 137
5 ibid., pp. 133–143
6 Fennell, *Changing Face*, p. 197.
7 *Furrow*, vol. 20, 1969
8 *Pioneer*, April 1970
9 *Sunday Independent*, November 29, 1970 and December 7, 1970
10 PAA, Memo to Minister for Education, December 9, 1969
11 ibid., Central Council Minutes March 14, 1971
12 ibid., Dermot O'Flynn to Minister for Justice, July 24, 1971
13 Joyce Fitzpatrick, *Young Drinkers*, p. 51
14 ibid.
15 ibid.
16 PAA, Central Council Minutes, November 14, 1971
17 *Pioneer*, November 1972
18 PAA, Central Council Minutes, June 13, 1971
19 ibid., March 12, 1972
20 ibid., Bishop Morris to Dargan, November 1974
21 ibid., Daly to Dargan, August 21, 1974
22 PAA, Memo on diocesan confirmation pledges, 1974
23 ibid., Central Council Minutes, June 8, 1975
24 ICAA, July 3, 1971 and Report of the Chairman of Procedures and Resolutions, Autumn Council, November 6, 1979.
25 ibid.
26 PAA, John Leen to Dargan, May 18, 1972
27 *Pioneer*, October 1976
28 *Evening Herald*, January 9, 1976
29 John Dunne, *Pioneers*, p. 36
30 Walsh and Walsh, 'Economic Aspects' and Roger Blayney, 'Alcoholism in Ireland: medical and social aspects' JSSISI, vol. 23, 1973–4
31 *Pioneer*, October 1970, September 1971, November 1982, January 1989 and Report of National Council on Alcoholism
32 Tim Pat Coogan, *The Irish: A personal view* (London 1975), p. 99
33 *Pioneer*, January 1989
34 Nancy Scheper-Hughes, *Saints, Scholars and Schizophrenics: Mental illness in rural Ireland* (University of California Press, 1979)
35 *Pioneer*, October 1976
36 Blayney, 'Alcoholism in Ireland' and *Irish Independent*, December 12, 1972
37 *Sunday Independent*, July 17, 1977
38 PAA, Central Council minutes March 14 1971
39 ibid., Dargan to John Leen, May 31, 1972
40 ibid.
41 ibid., Central Council Minutes, June 8, 1975 and November 9, 1975
42 ibid., March 14, 1976
43 *Pioneer*, April 1973
44 ibid., January 1974
45 PAA, Dargan to Cooney, Minister for Justice, July 13, 1973
46 Central Council Minutes, June 9, 1974
47 PAA, Memo presented to Gerry Collins, Minister for Justice, December 15, 1977
48 *Pioneer*, February 1978
49 PAA, Memo to Minister for Justice on underage drinking, August 1, 1984
50 ibid., Circular to Pioneers by Central Director, Fr W.J. Reynolds, May 1985
51 John Fanagan (ed.), *Belling the Cats: Selected speeches and articles of John Kelly* (Dublin 1992)

52   PAA, Central Council Minutes, October 26, 1969 and March 14, 1976
53   *Pioneer,* June 1970
54   *Evening Press,* September 9, 1976
55   *Irish Times* and *Irish Independent,* July 20, 1977
56   *Pioneer,* November 1984
57   *Pioneer,* December 1971
58   *Irish Press,* June 25, 1974 and *Pioneer,* February 1977
59   *Pioneer,* February 1987
60   ibid., Dargan to Bishop McCormack, September 9, 1974
61   ibid., Central Council Minutes, March 10, 1974
62   *Pioneer,* January 1975
63   PAA, Central Council Minutes, March 12, 1978
64   ibid.
65   *Pioneer,* October, 1970
66   ibid., February 1973
67   ibid., March 1976
68   ibid., February 1973
69   ibid., October 1980
70   PAA, John Casey to Dargan, October 1969
71   ibid., Dargan to Sheridan, January 26, 1973
72   ibid., Sheridan to Dargan, February 23, 1973
73   ibid., Fr John Monahan SJ to Dargan, May 22, 1977
74   ibid., James Ross to Dargan, April 17, 1975
75   ibid., Fr Raphael to McGuckian, January 12 1979
76   *Pioneer,* June 1980
77   ibid., January 1985
78   ibid., March 1981
79   ibid., November 1982
80   ibid., September 1984
81   ibid., February 1985
82   ibid., September 1985
83   Mary Purcell, *Remembering Matt Talbot* (Dublin, 1990 edition)
84   PAA, *What the Pin Stands for Today: A discussion document submitted by the Board of Management* (February 1993)
85   ibid., Fr MacGreil: 'The Pioneer of the future', Wexford International Seminar 1993
86   ibid.

Appendix A

MANUSCRIPT SOURCES

Pioneer Total Abstinence Association Archives, Sherrard Street, Dublin
(Uncatalogued)

Central Office Correspondence Files

> Army 1920–43
> Proposed Sunday Opening
> Licensing Act 1948
> Sisters of Charity 1901–48
> 1949 Jubilee
> 1954 Marian Year
> 1956 Fr Mathew Centenary
> 1959 Jubilee
> Licensing Law 1960
> Temperance Catechism and Advertising Campaign, 1946
> Pioneer Social Club and SFX Hall 1905–60
> The Catholic Hierarchy 1952–74

External correspondence files dealing with the establishment of the Pioneers in Australia, Belgium, Canada, England, Holland, New Zealand and the United States, 1924–80

Miscellaneous correspondence and notes of Fr James Cullen dealing with personal and Association matters, 1900–22

Miscellaneous transcripts of addresses, speeches and seminars 1900–80

Father Mathew Union Annual Reports 1901–38

Minute Books of the Central Council 1914–80
Minute Books of SFX centre 1956–80

Minute Books of the Yearly Pledge Branch 1913–25
Minute Books of the Irish Association for the Prevention of Intemperance
    1938–89
Minute Books of the Garda Pioneer Branch 1924–60

Pioneer Magazine 1948–90

Capuchin Archives, Church Street, Dublin

Various Correspondence files dealing with the Fr Mathew Temperance
Association and the Franciscan temperance movement 1905–45

Licensed Vintners' Association Archives, Anglesea Road, Dublin

Minute Books 1900–1970

National Archives of Ireland, Bishop Street, Dublin

Department of Taoiseach Files
Department of Justice Files

Sisters of Charity Archives, Sandymount, Dublin

Annals 1910–50

NEWSPAPER AND PERIODICALS

Evening Herald
The Furrow
The Pioneer
Irish Catholic
Irish Ecclesiastical Record
Irish Independent
Irish Messenger
Irish Press
Irish Province News
Irish Times
Journal of Irish Economic and Social History
Journal of the Social and Statistical Inquiry Society of Ireland
Sunday Independent
Sunday Press
Studies

Appendix B

SECONDARY SOURCES

Adair, W.H., *Temperance Lessons for the Schools* (Dublin 1920)

Arensbert, Conrad and Kimball, S. *Family and Community in Ireland* (Harvard, 1968)

Balfour, B.R., *The Irish Licensing Question* (Dublin 1902)

Bane, Liam, *The Bishop in Politics: Life and career of John MacEvilly* (Westport 1993)

Bland, Joan, *The story of the Catholic Total Abstinence Union of America* (Washington 1951)

Blanshard, Paul, *The Irish and Catholic Power: An American interpretation* (London 1954)

Bolster, Evelyn, *The Knights of Saint Columbanus* (Dublin 1979)

Bodkin, Mathias, *The Port of Tears: The life of Fr John Sullivan* (Dublin 1953)

Bodkin, Mathias, *The Heroic Offering: A talk to young Pioneers* (Dublin 1942)

Brody, Hugh, *Iniskillane: Change and decline in the West of Ireland* (London 1973)

Browne, Noel, *Against the Tide* (Dublin 1986)

Brown, Terence, *Ireland: A social and cultural history 1922–85* (London 1986)

Canning, Bernard, *Bishops of Ireland 1870–1987* (Dublin 1987)

Casey, John, *Temperance Songs and Lyrics* (Dublin 1896)

Coffey, Peter, *The Nationalisation of the Irish Liquor Traffic* (Dublin 1918)

Connell, K.H., *Irish Peasant Society* (London 1978)

Conlife, Denis and McKoy, Daniel, *Alcohol Use in Ireland: Some economic and social implications* (ESRI, Dublin 1993)

Connery, Donal, *The Irish* (London 1969)

Corish, Patrick J., *The Irish Catholic Experience: A historical survey* (Dublin 1985)

Cullen, James, *Temperance Cathecism* (Dublin 1892)

Curtin, Chris and Wilson, Thomas (eds.), *Ireland from Below: Social change and local communities* (Galway 1992)

Daly, Mary E., *A Social and Economic History of Ireland since 1800* (Dublin 1981)

———, Dublin, *the Deposed Capital: A social and economic history 1860–1914* (Cork 1984)

Dargan, Daniel, *Talks to Pioneers* (Dublin 1961)

De Burca, Marcus, *The GAA: a history* (Dublin 1980)

Doherty, Eddie, *Matt Talbot* (Milwaukee 1953)

Dudley Edwards, Ruth, *Patrick Pearse: The triumph of failure* (London 1979)

Drudy, P.J. (ed.), *The Irish in America: emigration, assimilation and impact* (Irish Studies 4, Cambridge 1985)

Dunne, John, *Headlines and Haloes* (Dublin 1988)

Dunne, John, *The Pioneers* (Dublin 1981)

Dunne, Tom, *The Writer as Witness: Literature as historical evidence: Historical Studies 16* (Cork 1983)

Edgar, John, *Scriptural Temperance: A discourse* (Belfast 1901)

Fallows, Marjorie, *Irish Americans, identity and assimilation* (New Jersey 1979)

Fanagan, John, *Belling the Cats: Selected speeches and articles of John Kelly* (Dublin 1992)

Farmer, Tony, *Ordinary lives: Three generations of Irish middle-class experience* (Dublin 1991)

Feeney, John, *John Charles McQuaid: The man and the mask* (Dublin 1974)

Fennell, Desmond, *The Changing face of Catholic Ireland* (New York 1981)

Fitzpatrick, Joyce, *The Young Drinkers: A cross-national study of social and cultural influence* (London 1978)

Foster R.F., *Paddy and Mr Punch: Connections in Irish and English history* (London 1993)

Ford, John C., *Man takes a Drink* (London 1956)

Gannon, P.J., *Fr James Cullen* (Dublin 1940)

Garvin, Tom, *Nationalist Revolutionaries in Ireland 1858–1928* (London 1987)

Glynn, Joseph, *Life of Matt Talbot* (Dublin 1928)

Gmelch, Sharon (ed.), *Irish Life* (Dublin 1979)

Griffin, John, *Neither Wine nor Strong Drink: a concise history of the temperance movement in Tralee* (Tralee 1977)

Hadfield, Andrew, *Strangers to that Land: British perceptions of Ireland from the reformation to the Famine* (Belfast 1994)

Halpin, J., *The Father Mathew reader on temperance and hygiene* (Dublin 1907)

Hallack, Cecily, *The Legion of Mary* (Dublin 1940)

Harkness, I.N., *A Vindication of Our Blessed Lord* (Belfast n.d.)

Harrison, Brian, *Drink and the Victorians: The temperance question in England 1815–1872* (London 1971)

Harvey, J., *Address of the Hibernian Temperance Society to their countrymen* (Dublin 1830)

Hey, Valerie, *Patriarchy and Pub Culture* (London 1986)

Hogan, Edmund, *The Irish Missionary Movement: A historical survey* (Dublin 1990)

Humphreys, Alexander, *New Dubliners: Urbanisation and the Irish family* (London, 1996)

Hunter, John A., *The Temperance Problem in Northern Ireland* (Belfast 1925)

Inglis, Tom, *Moral Monopoly: The Catholic Church in modern Irish society* (Dublin 1987)

Ireland, John, *A Message to Ireland* (Dublin 1899)

Kearns, Kevin, *Dublin Tenement Life: An oral history* (Dublin 1994)

———, *Dublin Pub Life and Lore: An oral history* (Dublin 1996)

Keenan, Desmond, *The Catholic Church in Nineteenth-Century Ireland: A sociological study* (Dublin 1983)

Kennedy, Kieran (ed.), *Ireland in Transition* (Cork 1985)

Keogh, Dermot, *Twentieth-Century Ireland: Nation and state* (Dublin 1994)

Kerrigan, Colm, *Father Mathew and the Irish Temperance Movement* (Cork 1992)

Lambert, W.R., *Drink and Society in Victorian Wales* (University of Wales Press 1983)

Larkin, Emmet: *James Larkin: Irish Labour Leader 1876–1947* (London 1965)

Levenson, Leah, *With Wooden Sword: A portrait of Frances Sheehy Skeffington, militant pacifist* (Dublin 1983)

Lee, Joe, *Ireland 1912–85: Politics and society* (London 1985)

Luddy, Maria, *Women and Philanthropy in Nineteenth-century Ireland* (London 1995)

Lyons, F.S.L., *Culture and Anarchy in Ireland* (London 1979)

McCarron, Sean, *Temperance Cathecism* (Dublin 1945)

———, *A Short Temperance Cathecism for Primary schools* (Dublin 1951)

McCarthy, Brian, *Alcohol and Drugs in Ireland Today* (Dublin 1971)

McGuckian, Bernard, *Pioneering for 80 years* (Dublin 1978)

McKenna, Lambert, *Life and Work of Rev James Aloysius Cullen* (London 1924)

McDonald, Walter, *Reminiscences of a Maynooth Professor* (London 1925)

MacErlain, J.C., *Wither Goest Thou? Or was Father Mathew right?* (Dublin 1910)

McRedmond, Louis, *To The Greater Glory: A history of the Irish Jesuits* (Dublin 1991)

Magee, Malachy, *One Thousand Years of Irish Whiskey* (Dublin 1980)

Maguire, John, *Father Mathew and His Times* (Dublin 1903)

Maher, Liam, *Temperance in Ireland* (Dublin 1959)

Mahon, Catherine, *Women and Total Abstinence* (Dublin 1920)

Malcolm, Elizabeth, *Ireland Sober, Ireland Free: Drink and temperance in nineteenth-century Ireland* (Dublin 1986)

Mooney, Leo, *A Guide to Dublin Pubs* (Dublin 1986)

Moran, D.P., *The Philosophy of Irish Ireland* (Dublin 1904)

O'Brien, John (ed.), *The Vanishing Irish* (New York 1957)

O'Brien, John and Travers, Pauric (ed.), *The Irish Emigrant Experience in Australia* (Dublin 1991)

O'Broin, Leon, *Frank Duff: A biography* (Dublin 1982)

O 'Doherty F and Mc Grath (eds.), *The Priest and Mental Health* (Dublin 1963)

O'Donavan, Donal, *Kevin Barry and His Time* (Dublin 1989)

O'Dwyer, Peter, *Towards a History of Irish Spirituality* (Dublin 1995)

O'Flaherty, Liam, *A Tourist's Guide to Ireland* (London 1929)

O'Grada, Cormac, *Ireland: A new economic history 1780–1939* (Oxford 1994)

O'Neill, Hugh, *The Temperance Question* (Belfast 1893)

O'Muiri, Reamonn, *Irish Church History Today* (Dublin 1990)

O'Rahilly, Alfred, *Fr William Doyle SJ* (London 1925)

O'Tuama, Sean, *The Gaelic League Idea* (Cork 1992)

Peillon, Michael, *Contemporary Irish Society: An introduction* (Dublin 1982)

Plaut, Thomas, *Alcohol Problems: A report to the nation by the Co-operative Commission on the study of alcoholism* (New York 1967)

Purcell, Mary, *Matt Talbot and His Times* (Dublin 1976)

———, *Remembering Matt Talbot* (Dublin 1954, 1990)

Pritchard, David, *Irish Pubs* (Wicklow 1985)

Rafferty, Oliver, *Catholicism in Ulster 1603–1983: An interpretative history* (Dublin 1994)

Reed, Andrew, *The Temperance Problem and the Liquor Licensing Laws of Ireland* (Dublin 1906)

Rothwell, Bill, *Alcohol: Ireland's beloved drug* (Dublin 1990)

Rynne, Stephen, *Father John Hayes* (Dublin 1960)

Scheper-Hughes, Nancy, *Saints, Scholars and Schizophrenics: Mental illness in rural Ireland* (University of California Press 1979)

Sheehy, Michael, *Is Ireland Dying? Culture and the church in modern Ireland* (London 1968)

Shiman, Lilian, *The Crusade against Drink in Victorian Britain* (New York 1985)

Stivers, Richard, *A Hair of the dog: Irish drinking and American stereotype* (New York 1976)

Sweeney, Hugh, *A Short Treatise on the Evils of Intemperance* (Dublin 1904)

Swift, Roger and Gilley, Sheridan, *The Irish in the Victorian City* (London 1985)

Swift, Roger and Gilley, Sheridan: *The Irish in Britain 1815–1939* (London, 1989)

Taylor, Lawrence, *Occasions of Faith: An anthology of Irish Catholics* (Dublin 1995)

Walsh, Robert, *The Effects of Intoxication* (Dublin 1903)

Williams, G.P. and Brake, G.T., *Drink in Great Britain 1900–79* (London 1980)

UNPUBLISHED THESES

Humphreys, Madeleine, 'Jansenists in high places: A study of the relationship between the liquor trade and manufacturing industry and the Cumann na nGaedheal government 1922–32' (University College Dublin, MA 1991)

McCarthy, Grace: 'Moral and political attitudes of the Catholic Hierarchy: An analysis of Lenten Pastorals 1932–45' (University College Dublin, MA 1989)

Sheppard, Andrew: 'The Irish parliamentary party, the Irish licensed trade and the politics of the 1909 budget' (University College Dublin, MA 1983)

Index